MODERN HUMANITIES RESEARCH ASSOCIATION
TEXTS AND DISSERTATIONS
VOLUME 81

INSTITUTE OF GERMANIC AND ROMANCE STUDIES
(UNIVERSITY OF LONDON)
BITHELL SERIES OF DISSERTATIONS
VOLUME 37


PRIVATE LIVES AND COLLECTIVE DESTINIES
CLASS, NATION AND THE FOLK IN THE
WORKS OF GUSTAV FREYTAG (1816-1895)

INSTITUTE OF GERMANIC AND ROMANCE STUDIES
# BITHELL SERIES OF DISSERTATIONS

Launched in 1978, this series publishes outstanding recent doctoral theses, accepted by universities in the United Kingdom and Ireland, across all fields of Germanic studies. Since 1989 the series has been published in collaboration with the Modern Humanities Research Association.

Recommendations for theses which might be considered for possible inclusion in the series should be made by the supervisor and/or examiner(s), and sent to Professor Ritchie Robertson, Convenor of the Bithell Editorial Board, St John's College, Oxford OX1 3JP. Proposals must be accompanied by a copy of the Examiners' Report and Abstract.

*Editorial Board*
Dr Judith Beniston, University College London
Professor Sarah Colvin, University of Birmingham
Professor Pól O Dochartaigh, University of Ulster
Professor Ritchie Robertson (*Convenor*), St John's College, Oxford
Professor Bill Marshall,
Institute of Germanic and Romance Studies, University of London
Dr John Walker, Birkbeck College London
Dr Godela Weiss-Sussex,
Institute of Germanic and Romance Studies, University of London
Professor David Wells, Birkbeck College London

MODERN HUMANITIES RESEARCH ASSOCIATION
# TEXTS AND DISSERTATIONS

Established in 1970, the series promotes important work by younger scholars by making the most accomplished doctoral research available to a wider readership. Titles are selected and edited by a Board of distinguished experts from across the modern Humanities.

*Editorial Board*
English: Professor Catherine Maxwell, Queen Mary, University of London
French: Professor William Brooks, University of Bath
Germanic: Professor Ritchie Robertson, University of Oxford
Hispanic: Professor Derek Flitter, University of Exeter
Italian: Professor Brian Richardson, University of Leeds
Portuguese: Professor Thomas Earle, University of Oxford
Slavonic: Professor David Gillespie, University of Bath

*Managing Editor*: Dr Graham Nelson

# Private Lives and Collective Destinies

Class, Nation and the Folk in the Works of Gustav Freytag (1816–1895)

*by*
Benedict Schofield

Modern Humanities Research Association
2012

*Published by*

*The Modern Humanities Research Association
1 Carlton House Terrace
London SW1Y 5AF
United Kingdom*

*© Modern Humanities Research Association and the
Institute of Germanic and Romance Studies, University of London, 2012*

*Benedict Schofield has asserted his right under the Copyright, Designs and Patents Act 1988 to be identified as the author of this work. Parts of this work may be reproduced as permitted under legal provisions for fair dealing (or fair use) for the purposes of research, private study, criticism, or review, or when a relevant collective licensing agreement is in place. All other reproduction requires the written permission of the copyright holder who may be contacted at rights@mhra.org.uk.*

*Copy-Editor: Nigel Hope*

*First published 2012*

*ISBN 978-1-907322-22-8 (hardback)
ISBN 978-1-907322-99-0 (paperback)
ISSN (Bithell Series of Dissertations) 0266–7932
ISSN (MHRA Texts and Dissertations) 0957–0322*

# CONTENTS

| | | |
|---|---|---|
| | Acknowledgements | vii |
| | Introduction | 1 |
| 1. | Towards a National Community: The *Vormärz* Poetry | 15 |
| 2. | Defining Class Identities: The *Vormärz* Dramas | 40 |
| 3. | Revolution and Reaction: Literary Practice and the Bourgeois Cause in the *Nachmärz* | 78 |
| 4. | Present Pasts: History, *Bildung*, and the *Volkskraft* | 125 |
| 5. | Writing Unification: Love as an Exercise in Nation-Building | 169 |
| | Conclusion | 193 |
| | *Bibliography* | 199 |
| | *Index* | 214 |

*This monograph is dedicated to all those in the Department of Germanic Studies at the University of Sheffield — both staff and students — who helped make work on it so enjoyable*

# ACKNOWLEDGEMENTS

This monograph originated as a PhD thesis in the Department of Germanic Studies at the University of Sheffield. Above all, my thanks must go to Professor Michael Perraudin, whose constant guidance, commitment, and critical insight were pivotal to its success, and to Dr Katy Heady, for her perpetual enthusiasm and input throughout its gestation. I am also very grateful for the comments made by Dr Caroline Bland, Professor Dirk Goettsche, Professor Ritchie Robertson, and Professor Gert Vonhoff on this manuscript, and for the advice provided by the team at the MHRA, in particular Nigel Hope and Dr Graham Nelson.

Many others have also been exceptionally generous with their ideas and time during this project, and I would like to thank all the staff in the Department of Germanic Studies at the University of Sheffield, particularly Professor Henk de Berg and Dr Henriette Louwerse, as well as my colleagues in the Department of German and Dutch at the University of Cambridge; at the Institute of Germanic and Romance Studies, London; and in the Department of German at King's College London. I am also thankful for the passion and knowledge of the staff of the Deutsches Literaturarchiv, Marbach; the Goethe und Schiller Archiv, Weimar; the Staatsbibliothek zu Berlin, Preußischer Kulturbestiz; the Bayerische Staatsbibliothek, Munich; the Universitätsbibliothek, Frankfurt; and the Gustav Freytag Archiv, Wangen im Allgäu. I would also like to acknowledge the significant financial assistance I received from the Arts and Humanities Research Council; the Association of German Studies; and the University of Sheffield. Part of Chapter 2 of this monograph appeared in a different form in my contribution 'Evolution or Revolution? The Literary Exchange of Karl Gutzkow and Gustav Freytag Across the *Vor- und Nachmärz*', in *Karl Gutzkow und seine Zeitgenossen*, ed. by Gert Vonhoff (Bielefeld: Aisthesis, 2011), pp. 169–82, and part of Chapter 3 in my contribution 'Gustav Freytag's *Soll und Haben*: Politics, Aesthetics and the Bestseller' in *The Nineteenth-Century German Bestseller*, ed. by Benedict Schofield and Charlotte Woodford (Rochester NY: Camden House, 2012) and I thank the editors of those volumes for their advice in producing my contribution.

Finally, this monograph would not have been possible without the unconditional support of my family and friends: Hilary, John, and Magdalen Schofield, Axel Bangert, Johannes Bäumel, Eleanor Burke, May Glover Gunn, Amy and Simon Green, Anna Linthe, Susannah Nightingale-Raabe, Joanne Richardson, Andrew Sills, Alyson Tapp, Owain Thomas, Alexander von der Goltz, Duncan Walsh, Laura Williams, and Andrew Wormald.

B. S., September 2011

# INTRODUCTION

It is a commonplace of German nineteenth-century studies to regard the 1848 revolutions as a turning point in the development of a politically engaged literature in Germany.[1] The *Vormärz*, it is argued, witnessed the rise of a politically and socially committed form of literature, exemplified by Heinrich Heine's conceptualization of the engaged poet as 'zu gleicher Zeit Künstler, Tribune und Apostel'.[2] But the failure of the 1848 revolutions to bring about major social change had marked the beginning of a retreat from overt political engagement in German literature. In some cases, such withdrawal had involved deliberate acts of de-politicization, most famously in the case of Adalbert Stifter, whose reworking in the early *Nachmärz* of the stories which he published in 1853 as *Bunte Steine* had been marked by his rejection of social unrest and a new emphasis on conservative values of 'Ordnung und Gestalt'.[3] Others, such as Heine, had reformulated their political radicalism into increasingly spiritual questions, while yet others — including Berthold Auerbach, Gustav Freytag, Heinrich Laube, and Theodor Mundt — had developed new modes of literary expression which focused on the private and individual, rather than the public and political.[4] By the early *Nachmärz* — so such reasoning goes — the era of *Tendenzliteratur* in Germany had come to a close.

In this monograph, I question the extent to which political tendentiousness ceased to find expression in literary production after 1848. Specifically, I consider the works of Gustav Freytag, an author frequently held up as a representative figure of a new bourgeois fiction in the post-revolutionary period, and analyse the degree to which his writings attempted to present a political agenda which actively promoted ideas of social and national change.[5] In particular, I examine the formation and transformation of his class and national agenda against the rapidly changing historical backdrop of the *Vormärz*, *Nachmärz*, and *Gründerzeit*. By considering all of Freytag's writings — from the early poetry and dramas, through to the final historical novels — I attempt to present for the first time a comprehensive analysis of this author's shifting but always highly constructed socio-political attitudes and their literary reflection. I argue that Freytag's writings were profoundly political, and that he developed a more coherent and far-reaching vision of social and political relations in Germany than thus far has been demonstrated by studies of his works. *Tendenzliteratur* might have lost its revolutionary zeal after 1848, but a politically engaged literary public sphere was very much alive.

Gustav Freytag was one of the most widely read German authors of the second half of the nineteenth century, producing a large and diverse oeuvre which included poetry (*In Breslau*), drama (*Die Brautfahrt, Der Gelehrte, Die Valentine, Graf Waldemar, Die Journalisten, Die Fabier*), the novel (*Soll und Haben, Die verlorene Handschrift, Die Ahnen*), works of cultural history (*Bilder aus der deutschen Vergangenheit*), dramatic theory (*Die Technik des Dramas*), biography (*Karl Mathy*), and journalism (for *Die Grenzboten* and *Im neuen Reich*). The series of obituaries, memorial articles, and biographies that followed his death in 1895 repeatedly stressed his significance as a major German author who had championed the bourgeois cause. Freytag was '[d]er Herold des deutschen Bürgertums', a 'repräsentive[r] Mann [der] Bourgeoisie'.[6] Freytag himself was keen to promote the idea that his life was representative, and his memoirs stress how his experiences were, for the most part, those common to his generation: 'was hier erzählt wird, [sieht] in der Hauptsache dem Leben und Bildungsgang von vielen Tausenden meiner Zeitgenossen sehr ähnlich'.[7]

Freytag was born in 1816, the son of the mayor of Kreuzberg, Silesia (now Kluczbork, Poland). According to the highly subjective account of his childhood in his memoirs, this early upbringing 'als Preuße, als Protestant und als Schlesier unweit der polnischen Grenze' (I, 4) was central to the development of his sense of regional and national identity — identities he saw as fundamentally intertwined and which are repeatedly touched upon in his writings. In 1835, Freytag began his studies in German philology at the University of Breslau (now Wrocław, Poland) under August Heinrich Hoffmann von Fallersleben, before moving to Berlin in 1836 to complete his doctoral dissertation on the roots of German national drama, and then his *Habilitation* thesis on the works of the tenth-century German canoness Hrosvith of Gandersheim. In 1839, he began work as a *Privatdozent* at Breslau University — an academic career which ended in unclear circumstances in 1844 — as well as undertaking military service, which was also cut short, because of ill health. During this period, Freytag became heavily involved in the activities of the Breslauer Künstlerverein and began to write and publish poetry, which culminated in his collection *In Breslau* (1845).

Throughout the 1840s, Freytag also worked on a series of plays: *Die Brautfahrt, oder Kunz von der Rosen* (written 1841; published 1844), *Der Gelehrte* (written 1844; published 1848), *Die Valentine* (written 1846; published 1847), and *Graf Waldemar* (1846–47), with varying levels of success. In 1847, he moved to Dresden, and in 1848 to Leipzig, where he became involved in associational life and met Julian Schmidt, together with whom he took over the editorship of *Die Grenzboten*, which would become one of the most influential national-liberal magazines of the post-revolutionary era. In his memoirs, Freytag presents the revolutionary events of 1848 as a turning point in his literary and political life, and it is true that the early *Nachmärz* saw the publication of two of his most successful works: the comedy *Die Journalisten* (written 1852; published 1854) and his social novel of business, *Soll und Haben* (1855). He ended the decade with a return to drama with the tragedy *Die Fabier* (1859), although this time with limited success.

The 1860s saw Freytag engage in an ever-diversifying range of projects. He published the first volume of his highly successful cultural history of Germany, the *Bilder aus der deutschen Vergangenheit*, in 1859, with additional volumes in 1862, 1866, and 1867. In 1863, he published a theory and history of drama, *Die Technik des Dramas*, and in 1864, his second novel, *Die verlorene Handschrift*. In 1866, he stood successfully for election to the inaugural 1867 session of the Reichstag des Norddeutschen Bundes, although he stepped down to return to writing after only one session of parliament. His engagement with national and class issues nevertheless intensified throughout the decade, and he was heavily involved through his journalism for *Die Grenzboten* in the fight for a liberalization of the Prussian constitution and German unification on a Prussocentric *kleindeutsch* model. The decade closed with his biography of *Karl Mathy* (1869), a major figure of the national liberal movement and close friend and mentor of Freytag.

From 1870 to 1871, Freytag was engaged by the Crown Prince of Prussia to act as a war correspondent on the Franco-Prussian conflict. His reports were published in *Die Grenzboten*. In 1871, Freytag parted from the *Grenzboten* and published briefly in *Im neuen Reich*, but was primarily occupied for the majority of the decade that followed with his last major work, the novel cycle *Die Ahnen*. Published in six volumes in 1872, 1873, 1874, 1876, 1878, and 1880, the novel told the story of a single German family from the early Middle Ages through to the mid-nineteenth century and was a literary sensation on its first publication. *Die Ahnen* effectively marked the close of Freytag's literary career. However, between 1886 and 1888 he worked on his *Gesammelte Werke*, for which he specially wrote the *Erinnerungen aus meinem Leben* (1887). Freytag died in 1895.

Most early critical writing on Freytag was biographical in nature. During his lifetime, several biographies were published, including Constantin Rössler's wholly affirmative *Gustav Freytag und die deutsche Dichtung der Gegenwart* (1860) and Conrad Alberti's similarly positive *Gustav Freytag* (1885). Freytag's death prompted a new wave of memorial articles, culminating in Hans Lindau's slightly more analytically conceived biography, *Gustav Freytag* (1907).[8] These works are of little interest for their interpretations of Freytag's literary writing (which rarely move beyond description and praise), but all three provide information about Freytag's life, for which the only other sources are his memoirs and his letters. These biographies must be read critically, for they were not conceived as dispassionate or critical accounts of Freytag's life, and are often highly anecdotal in approach. It should be noted that almost all biographical information about Freytag in both recent and past research stems from Rössler, Alberti, Lindau, and the *Erinnerungen*. A number of publications specifically on Freytag's literary writings did appear in the late nineteenth century, but these interpretations, like those in the biographies, primarily consist of affirmative description of the works, rather than critical analysis of them.[9]

The early twentieth century saw increasing research into Freytag's writings, and a number of doctoral dissertations of varying quality were published, including Georg Droescher's 1919 study of Freytag's comedies, *Gustav Freytag in seinen Lustspielen*, and numerous works on Freytag's political views.[10] Droescher's work is one of the very few to concentrate on Freytag's dramas, although it primarily consists of a detailed summary of the play's sources and reception.[11] The politically orientated interpretations from this period tend to focus closely on Freytag's national liberalism, exploring the topic through extensive quotation from his political journalism and placing this within a biographical framework entirely reliant on his memoirs. Of these works, Kurt Classe's *Gustav Freytag als politischer Dichter* (1914) is of the greatest interest, since it also considers Freytag's early literary writings within their political context. However, Classe's approach too is primarily descriptive rather than analytical.

Scholarly interest in Freytag entered a decline during the 1920s and 1930s, despite the continued popularity of his writing, and only a handful of dissertations were produced during these decades.[12] Whereas August Thiele's catalogue of Freytag's *Grenzboten* articles remains significant, Eduard Rothfuchs's biographical study is speculative and of minimal relevance. Erwin Laath's dissertation, meanwhile, is of greater interest for the illustration it provides into political changes in German culture during the rise of National Socialism than for its insights into Freytag.

The start of modern critical engagement with Freytag begins with T. E. Carter's 1967 essay on *Soll und Haben* and Jeffrey Sammons's response from 1968.[13] These two studies were of considerable influence on subsequent research into *Soll und Haben*, identifying five key areas of interest: (1) the novel's status as bestseller; (2) its significance as a work of realism; (3) its poetic presentation of the world of business; (4) its treatment of the aristocracy and the bourgeoisie; and (5) its depiction of the Jewish traders. Several studies followed, including works by Dieter Kafitz, Herbert Kaiser, Nancy Kaiser, Claus Richter, Michael Schneider, and Hartmut Steinecke, all of which considered the novel within debates on German realism, and by Gabriele Büchler-Hauschild, Renate Hermann, Peter Heinz Hubrich, Michael Kienzle, and Edward McInnes, which focused on the presentation of commerce and German-bourgeois ideologies in the text.[14]

Another topic which has prompted extensive academic interest is the question of Freytag's anti-Semitism in *Soll und Haben*. Critics such as Hubrich, Mark Gelber, and Martin Gubser have directly labelled Freytag an anti-Semite — a rather simplistic interpretation of both his private attitudes and the depiction of Jewish figures in his writings, and one which has rightly been countered by more nuanced readings from Hans Otto Horch, Klaus Christian Köhnke, and Michael Schneider, among others.[15] Both topics, the realistic and the anti-Semitic, continue to attract attention, despite the weight of research each has already generated, and *Soll und Haben* remains the central concern of almost all studies into Freytag. Recent investigations into the question of realism include Sabine Becker's wide-ranging *Bürgerlicher Realismus* (2003), while the Jewish question is re-explored (together with an original consideration of gender roles in *Soll und Haben*) in Christine Achinger's *Gespaltene Moderne* (2007).[16] Both topics also feature strongly in Florian Krobb's *150 Jahre Soll und Haben* (2005). Diverse in subject matter, this edited volume is perhaps most notable for drawing attention to the anti-Slavic tendencies in the novel, in contributions by Kristin Kopp and Hans J. Hahn — an issue which is explored further in Izabela Surynt's dissertation *Das 'ferne', 'unheimliche' Land: Gustav Freytags Polen* (2004).[17]

In recent years, a trend has developed towards exploring the less well-researched areas of Freytag's writing. Daniel Fulda, Elystan Griffiths, Claus Holz, Michael Limlei, Claus-Michael Ort, Lynne Tatlock, and Charlotte Woodford have all produced much-needed work on *Die Ahnen*.[18] Holz's dissertation is a comprehensive study of the novel, yet one which incorrectly denies it any political agency in the present. Griffiths, on the contrary, correctly notes a political agenda in *Die Ahnen*, but dismisses the romantic storylines of inter-class marriage as a distraction from these core political aims. Yet, as will be seen throughout this study, it is precisely through recourse to the world of romance and marriage that Freytag encodes his class agenda in accessible and popular ways for his target audience. Fulda, Ort, Limlei, and Woodford are all less concerned with the expressly political stance of the work than with its reactions to unification and its status as a historical novel, in studies that primarily consider the typicality — or not — of Freytag's approach to that genre.

Another beneficiary of this recent renewal of interest in the lesser-known Freytag has been the *Bilder aus der deutschen Vergangenheit*, a text often ignored in its entirety by literary studies.[19] Lynne Tatlock's study explores the relationship between regional and national history in the *Bilder* — an approach echoed in Celia Applegate's work on Freytag's history in her important study *A Nation of Provincials*. Both authors raise significant points, but underestimate the extent to which Freytag is intent on maintaining regional and national identities simultaneously in his writings.[20] These studies are complemented by two recent dissertations by Alyssa A. Lonner and Larry L. Ping.[21] Ping's work is primarily a work of historiography, and contains a number of useful insights into Freytag's position as a historian of the so-called Prussian School after 1848. Lonner's dissertation explores the depiction of history and folklore in Freytag's texts — a useful enterprise, although some important examples are not considered. Both Ping's and Lonner's work is notable, however, for considering Freytag's second novel, *Die verlorene Handschrift*, about which very little has otherwise been written.[22] Neither work considers *Die Ahnen*, however — a peculiar omission in both cases, since it is in *Die Ahnen* that the historical and folk agenda of the *Bilder* is revisited in the light of the *Reichsgründung* of 1871. Without the inclusion of *Die Ahnen*, neither dissertation can fully come to terms with the character of Freytag's national-historical project.

Despite the recent resurgence of interest in both the *Bilder* and *Die Ahnen*, *Soll und Haben* remains at the centre of research into Freytag. Curiously, his writings prior to the 1850s have attracted almost no critical interest at all, despite the fact that he enjoyed a varied and successful career as a dramatist and a poet in this period.[23] There is thus little understanding of Freytag's literary and political development over the full course of his lifetime — the extent, for instance, to which his politics and writings altered in response to events such as the revolutions of 1848 and the *Reichsgründung* of 1871, or the relationship between his works of different genres and eras. I aim to generate such an understanding, and thereby to contribute to a fuller picture of his writings and their socio-political agenda.

A few words should be said regarding the terminology used in this monograph. I consider Freytag's texts firmly within their social and political context: as reflections and expressions of socio-historical circumstance and change. I thus make frequent reference to German class relations and use the expressions middle classes/bourgeoisie, and upper classes/aristocracy, as class designators, following the general usage in historical and literary-critical writing about nineteenth-century Germany.[24] Although these terms can never be considered as value free, it is the values Freytag projects on to them that are of primary interest to the project. Wherever more specific class designation is required, I provide this in the text.

I also frequently refer to a social grouping Freytag called the *Volk*. Although often translated as the 'public', the 'people', or the 'nation', none of these terms fully capture Freytag's concept. In this study, *Volk* has thus been rendered directly as 'folk', since, as will be seen in Chapter 4, Freytag's notion resides in a historical, pre-modern concept of a folk identity which has supposedly remained in the German spirit throughout history. His related idea of the *Volkskraft*, however, remains in German, partly because an English translation cannot reflect the ambiguous nature of the term, but also to ensure that its indebtedness to the philosophical writings of Herder and Hegel remains clear, as discussed further in Chapter 4.

One further terminological issue also needs to be considered briefly: the question of how to speak of the German nation prior to the *Reichsgründung* of 1871. When I refer to Germany or the German nation, I generally mean the collection of individual states which, despite the sovereignty of each, were seen by many as part of a larger unit based on a cultural, linguistic, or more directly political community.[25] In many respects, I look at Freytag's literary invention of the nation: his attempt to create an 'imagined political community' (to borrow a term from the influential work of Benedict Anderson) prior to the foundation of this state in 1871.[26] Due consideration is given, too, to the role of the regions in this process, and the complex interplay that can occur between regional and national identity. As such, I also examine Freytag's attempts to create imagined regional communities, alongside and within a unified German state.

A final note should also be made regarding the various editions and sources used throughout this monograph. In the 1880s, Freytag began to work on a collected edition of his writings. The first edition of the *Gesammelte Werke* was published in twenty-two volumes by Hirzel in 1887, and a second one, also of twenty-two volumes, appeared in 1896. In subsequent decades, many further versions of the *Gesammelte Werke* were published, and the edition most frequently available today is that of Hirzel and Klemm, published in two series, each of eight volumes, and issued in 1915, though undated. There is no scholarly or critical edition of Freytag's writings. I use the second edition (1896) of the Hirzel *Gesammelte Werke* as the basis for citation (apart from when considering Freytag's poetry), since this is the last edition to have been personally supervised by Freytag and provides the most comprehensive collection of his writings. It is also the edition most frequently cited by existing German scholarship.[27]

Freytag's editorial practice frequently involved minor alteration to his works, which in some cases has led to differences between the first edition of his texts (available in microfiche form in the *Bibliothek der deutschen Literatur*) and their final form in the *Gesammelte Werke*.[28] In a limited number of cases, these changes are significant. Some of Freytag's early poems are excluded or altered, and his collected journalism tones down several politically polemical or personally libellous passages. The vast majority of changes, however, are minor and linguistic. Critical studies of Freytag have in general ignored these discrepancies, and yet they reveal the *Gesammelte Werke* in an interesting light — as Freytag's attempt to expunge from his writings those elements he saw as aesthetically weak or politically radical, in order to control his literary legacy.

Written for the 1887 edition of the *Gesammelte Werke*, Freytag's memoirs remain the single most important source of information about his life and works, and existing research has almost universally accepted their autobiographical narrative at face value. I also make frequent use of the memoirs, in order to help contextualize Freytag's literary production and explore his reactions to key social and political questions. However, I also view their content as inherently biased: as a non-neutral account whose perspectives on events such as 1848, or the composition of *Soll und Haben*, are written not just from a retrospective, but also from a visibly revisionist position.[29] Wherever possible, corroborating evidence for the events and attitudes described in the memoirs has been sought — in particular, evidence in Freytag's letters. Although these letters are in many respects equally partial, they have the advantage of having been written contemporaneously with the events they describe. By contrasting Freytag's letters with his memoirs, I aim to present a more nuanced account of Freytag's literary production and its relation to his life than has generally been achieved.

The vast majority of Freytag's letters are held in the archives of the Staatsbibliothek zu Berlin, Preußischer Kulturbesitz.[30] Many exchanges have been preserved, alongside thousands more letters written to Freytag, but to which his replies have been lost. A number of the letters have been published, including Freytag's exchanges with the historian Heinrich von Treitschke, the theatre director Emil Devrient, the Prussian minister and head of the German admiralty Albrecht von Stosch, and most significantly, Freytag's friend and quasi-patron, Duke Ernst of Coburg Gotha.[31] However, none of these publications was edited critically (the majority date from the early 1900s) and it is important to note that it is likely that some transcription error and bowdlerization has taken place.[32] Further letters are held by various university and state libraries in Germany, with the most extensive collections to be found at the Goethe und Schiller Archiv in Weimar, the Bayerische Staatsbibliothek in Munich, the Deutsches Literaturarchiv in Marbach, and the Gustav Freytag Archiv in Wangen im Allgäu — the last of these holding an important collection of Freytag's correspondence with his publisher.[33] These archives also hold manuscripts of Freytag's texts, with the majority of the major works housed in Weimar. Finally, Freytag's own extensive collection of books and pamphlets, many dating from the late Middle Ages and used as the basis for his work on the *Bilder aus der deutschen Vergangenheit* and *Die Ahnen*, can be found at the University Library in Frankfurt. Sources from across these institutions have been consulted in an attempt to provide as accurate an overview as possible in this study of the genesis and context of Freytag's literary writings.

Each of the main chapters of this monograph corresponds to a specific phase of Freytag's literary production, presented in chronological order — from the early poetry of the 1840s (Chapter 1) to the final historical fiction of the 1870s (Chapter 5). This approach is central to my overall argument, which, as set out above, analyses the development of Freytag's concepts of class and nation across his oeuvre and in relation to historical events. A helpful by-product of this chronological structure is that the study, although not conceived along such lines, also functions as an intellectual and literary biography of Freytag — the first of its kind in contemporary research. Each chapter opens with a discussion of the socio-historical and biographical context of the period under consideration, followed by detailed analyses of the developing political and class agenda in and across Freytag's works from that time. The discussion of each work is prefaced with its compositional history, based on a critical reading of the memoirs, letters, and manuscripts, and an analysis of its cultural and critical reception.

In Chapter 1, I consider the earliest stages of Freytag's literary production, specifically his attempt to develop a clear political voice in his *Vormärz* poetry. In particular, I examine a number of competing trends in Freytag's poetic output: his interest in folk traditions and narrative epics; his poetry celebrating bourgeois concepts of hearth and home; and an increasingly critical and socially reactive political poetry. I assess various influences on Freytag's early poetic output, including his involvement with the Breslauer Künstlerverein, and question the extent to which Freytag conceived of himself as a political writer in the earliest stages of his career. This forms the first-ever attempt to assess critically his poetry and its position within his wider oeuvre.

Freytag's career as a *Vormärz* dramatist is likewise an area that has barely been considered by modern research. Yet, as I demonstrate in Chapter 2, his dramas, which were often targeted by the censor, mark the arrival of a systematic class and national agenda in his writings, which reappears in his later, more famous works. The chapter analyses the patterns of class interaction in Freytag's plays, and reveals a strong anti-aristocratic tendency, which depicts the aristocracy as morally and politically bankrupt and unfit to rule Germany. I argue that Freytag's use of this anti-aristocratic agenda is representative of his increasing belief in the need for bourgeois leadership and the creation of a non-particularist, unified German state. Finally, I consider the assertion that Freytag was sympathetic to the cause of the writers known collectively as *Junges Deutschland*, and assess the actual extent of his *Vormärz* radicalism in the years leading up to the revolutions of 1848.

Freytag's reaction to 1848, which his memoirs present as a political and aesthetic watershed, is the core consideration of Chapter 3. Assessing the validity of the memoirs, I consider the nature of Freytag's literary and political projects in the *Nachmärz* and examine the extent to which his aesthetic, class, and national agendas developed or changed in response to the revolution. I pay particular attention to his presentation of class and racial interaction in *Soll und Haben*. I also look at the increasingly politically orientated *Nachmärz* plays, *Die Journalisten* and *Die Fabier*, exploring the degree to which they can be read as literary-political manifestos for the unification of Germany under bourgeois control. Contextualizing *Soll und Haben* among Freytag's other writings of the *Nachmärz*, I argue for a re-evaluation of current thinking about the political and aesthetic aims of his most famous work.

Chapter 4 considers Freytag's literary practice in the 1860s. As debates on the future shape of Germany began to increase in intensity and bourgeois demands for power and a more liberal constitution met with initial success, Freytag undertook two projects which, in different ways, considered the importance of history for class and national identity in Germany. I explore why Freytag chose to turn to the German past just as the hopes of the national-liberal political project appeared to be on the brink of realization in the present. I read *Die verlorene Handschrift* and the *Bilder aus der deutschen Vergangenheit* — two texts that have only recently become the subject of research of any kind — as attempts by Freytag to fuse his earlier concepts of class and nation into a wider myth of Germanness, embodied in a historical vision of the German folk.

In the final chapter of the monograph, I examine developments in Freytag's literary career in the aftermath of the *Reichsgründung* of 1871. I assess how, with Freytag's aim of German unification seemingly realized, his writing treated and reflected the topic of German nationhood in the 1870s. The core focus of the chapter is his novel cycle *Die Ahnen*, another relatively under-researched text, and I trace how the work reflects the central concerns of Freytag's earlier writing — not least his thematic interest in love stories and inter-class marriage. I argue that the novel cycle creates a historical myth of German national and class identity, but not through a nationalistic exploration of the triumphant progress of German history, but rather through an investigation of private lives in the face of historical processes. In the monograph as a whole I thus consider the extent to which Freytag's concepts of class and nation remained constant across his writings, despite the diverse, prolific, and in so many ways reactive nature of his works.

### Notes to the Introduction

1. On 1848 as a turning point, see *Vormärz–Nachmärz: Bruch oder Kontinuität?*, ed. by Norbert Otto Eke and Renate Werner (Bielefeld: Aisthesis, 2000), pp. 11–32; Peter Uwe Hohendahl, *Building a National Literature: The Case of Germany, 1830–1870* (Ithaca: Cornell University Press, 1989), pp. 209–17; Todd Kontje, *The German Bildungsroman: History of a National Genre* (Rochester, NY: Camden House, 1993), pp. 23–43.
2. Heinrich Heine, *Historisch-kritische Gesamtausgabe der Werke, Düsseldorfer Heine-Ausgabe*, ed. by Manfred Windfuhr, VIII.I: *Die Romantische Schule* (Hamburg: Hoffmann & Campe, 1979), p. 218.
3. Adalbert Stifter, *Werke und Briefe, Historisch-kritische Gesamtausgabe*, ed. by Alfred Doppler and Wolfgang Frühwald, II.II: *Bunte Steine* (Stuttgart: Kohlhammer, 1995), p. 13.

4. See Michael Minden, *The German Bildungsroman: Incest and Inheritance* (Cambridge: Cambridge University Press, 1997), pp. 175–204; Todd Kontje, *Private Lives in the Public Sphere: The German Bildungsroman as Metafiction* (University Park, PA: Pennsylvania State University Press, 1994), pp. 6–11.
5. On the representative nature of Freytag's writings, see, for example, Peter Heinz Hubrich, *Gustav Freytags 'Deutsche Ideologie' in 'Soll und Haben'* (Kronberg: Scriptor, 1974), pp. 32–40.
6. Conrad Alberti, 'Gustav Freytag', *Die Gartenlaube*, 29 (1886), 514–15 (p. 514); Franz Mehring, *Aufsätze zur deutschen Literatur von Hebbel bis Schweichel* (Berlin: Dietz, 1890), p. 63.
7. Gustav Freytag, *Gesammelte Werke*, I: *Erinnerungen aus meinem Leben* (Leipzig: Hirzel, 1896), p. 3. Further references to this edition are given after quotations in the text.
8. Conrad Alberti, *Gustav Freytag: Sein Leben und Schaffen* (Leipzig: Schloemp, 1885); Hans Lindau, *Gustav Freytag* (Leipzig: Hirzel, 1907); Constantin Rössler, *Gustav Freytag und die deutsche Dichtung der Gegenwart* (Berlin: Springer, 1860).
9. Including Ludwig Fulda, 'Gustav Freytag als Dramatiker', *Deutsche Revue*, 21 (1896), 69–79; Johannes Geffcken, 'Die Tendenz in Gustav Freytags *Soll und Haben*', *Zeitschrift für vergleichende Literaturgeschichte*, 13 (1899), 88–91; Adalbert H. Horawitz, *Gustav Freytag als Dichter und Historiker* (Vienna: Hölder, 1871); Paul Lindau, '*Die Ahnen*: Ein Roman von Gustav Freytag', *Nord und Süd*, 16 (1881), 218–84.
10. Kurt Classe, 'Gustav Freytag als politischer Dichter' (doctoral thesis, University of Münster, 1914); Oswald Dammann, 'Gustav Freytag und der Konstitutionalismus' (doctoral thesis, University of Freiburg, 1916); Georg Droescher, *Gustav Freytag in seinen Lustspielen: Inaugural-Dissertation* (Weida: Thomas & Hubert, 1919); Adolph Kohut, *Gustav Freytag als Patriot und Politiker* (Berlin: Schall, 1916); Otto Mayrhofer, *Gustav Freytag und das Junge Deutschland* (Marburg: Koch, 1907).
11. Others include Christa Barth, 'Gustav Freytags *Journalisten*: Versuch einer Monographie' (doctoral thesis, University of Munich, 1949); and Kenneth Bruce Beaton, 'Gustav Freytags *Die Journalisten*: Eine "politische" Komödie der Revolutionszeit', *Zeitschrift für Deutsche Philologie*, 105 (1986), 516–43.
12. Including Erwin Laaths, 'Der Nationalliberalismus im Werke Gustav Freytags' (doctoral thesis, University of Cologne, 1934); Paul Ostwald, *Gustav Freytag als Politiker* (Berlin: Staatspolitischer Verlag, 1927); Eduard Rothfuchs, 'Der Selbstbiographische Gehalt in Gustav Freytags Werken (bis 1855)' (doctoral thesis, University of Münster, 1929); Adolf Thiele, 'Gustav Freytag, der Grenzbotenjournalist' (doctoral thesis, University of Münster, 1924).
13. T. E. Carter, 'Freytag's *Soll und Haben*: A Liberal National Manifesto as a Best-seller', *German Life and Letters*, 21 (1967–68), 320–29; Jeffrey L. Sammons, 'The Evaluation of Freytag's *Soll und Haben*', *German Life and Letters*, 22 (1968–69), 315–24.
14. Gabriele Büchler-Hauschild, *Erzählte Arbeit: Gustav Freytag und die soziale Prosa des Vor- und Nachmärz* (Paderborn: Schöningh, 1987); Renate Herrmann, 'Gustav Freytag: Bürgerliches Selbstverständnis und preußisch-deutsches Nationalbewusstsein' (doctoral thesis, University of Würzburg, 1974); Hubrich, *Gustav Freytags 'Deutsche Ideologie'*; Dieter Kafitz, *Figurenkonstellation als Mittel der Wirklichkeitserfassung. Dargestellt an Romanen der zweiten Hälfte des 19. Jahrhunderts: Freytag, Spielhagen, Fontane, Raabe* (Kronberg: Athenäum, 1978); Herbert Kaiser, *Studien zum deutschen Roman nach 1848. Karl Gutzkow: 'Die Ritter vom Geiste', Gustav Freytag: 'Soll und Haben', Adalbert Stifter: 'Der Nachsommer'* (Duisburg: Braun, 1977); Nancy Kaiser, *Social Integration and Narrative Structure: Patterns of Realism in Auerbach, Freytag, Fontane and Raabe* (New York: Lang, 1986); Michael Kienzle, *Der Erfolgsroman: Zur*

*Kritik seiner poetischen Ökonomie bei Gustav Freytag und Eugenie Marlitt* (Stuttgart: Metzler, 1975); Edward McInnes, '"Die Poesie des Geschäfts": Social Analysis and Polemic in Freytag's *Soll und Haben*', in *Formen realistischer Erzählkunst*, ed. by Jörg Thunecke and Eda Sagarra (Nottingham: Sherwood Press, 1979), pp. 99-107; Michael Schneider, *Geschichte als Gestalt* (Stuttgart: Akademischer Verlag, 1980); Hartmut Steinecke, 'Gustav Freytag's *Soll und Haben* — ein realistischer Roman?', in *Formen realistischer Erzählkunst*, ed. by Thunecke and Sagarra, pp. 108-19; Hartmut Steinecke, 'Gustav Freytag: *Soll und Haben*', in *Romane und Erzählungen des bürgerlichen Realismus*, ed. by Horst Denkler (Stuttgart: Reclam, 1980), pp. 138-52.

15. Mark Gelber, 'Aspects of Literary Anti-Semitism, Charles Dickens' *Oliver Twist* and Gustav Freytag's *Soll und Haben*' (doctoral thesis, Yale, 1980); Hans Otto Horch, 'Judenbilder in der realistischen Erzählliteratur: Jüdische Figuren bei Gustav Freytag, Fritz Reuter, Berthold Auerbach und Wilhelm Raabe', in *Juden und Judentum in der Literatur*, ed. by Herbert A. Strauß and Christhard Hoffmann (Munich: dtv, 1985), pp. 140-71; Martin Gubser, *Literarischer Antisemitismus: Untersuchungen zu Gustav Freytag und anderen bürgerlichen Schriftstellern des 19. Jahrhunderts* (Göttingen: Wallstein, 1998); Klaus Christian Köhnke, 'Ein antisemitischer Autor wider Willen: Zu Gustav Freytags *Soll und Haben*', in *Conditio Judaica: Judentum, Antisemitismus und deutschsprachige Literatur vom 18. Jahrhundert bis zum Ersten Weltkrieg*, ed. by Hans Otto Horch and Horst Denkler (Tübingen: Niemeyer, 1989), pp. 130-47; Michael Schneider, 'Apologie des Bürgers: Zur Problematik von Rassismus und Antisemitismus in Gustav Freytags Roman *Soll und Haben*', *Jahrbuch der deutschen Schiller-Gesellschaft*, 25 (1981), 385-413.

16. Christine Achinger, *Gespaltene Moderne: Gustav Freytags 'Soll und Haben'. Nation, Geschlecht und Judenbild* (Würzburg: Königshausen & Neumann, 2007); Sabina Becker, *Bürgerlicher Realismus: Literatur und Kultur im bürgerlichen Zeitalter 1848-1900* (Tübingen: Francke, 2003).

17. Kristin Kopp, '"Ich stehe jetzt hier als einer von den Eroberern": *Soll und Haben* als Kolonialroman', in *150 Jahre 'Soll und Haben': Studien zu Gustav Freytags kontroversem Roman*, ed. by Florian Krobb (Würzburg: Königshausen & Neumann, 2005), pp. 225-37; Hans J. Hahn, 'Die "Polenwirtschaft" in Gustav Freytags Roman *Soll und Haben*', in *150 Jahre 'Soll und Haben'*, ed. by Krobb, pp. 239-54; Izabela Surynt, *Das 'ferne', 'unheimliche' Land: Gustav Freytags Polen* (Dresden: Thelem, 2004).

18. Daniel Fulda, 'Telling German History: Forms and Functions of the Historical Narrative against the Background of the National Unifications', in *1870/71-1989/90: German Unifications and the Change of Literary Discourse*, ed. by Walter Pape (Berlin: de Gruyter, 1993), pp. 195-207; Elystan Griffiths, 'A Nation of Provincials? German Identity in Gustav Freytag's Novel-Cycle *Die Ahnen* (1872-1880)', *Monatshefte*, 96 (2004), 220-33; Claus Holz, *Flucht aus der Wirklichkeit. 'Die Ahnen' von Gustav Freytag: Untersuchungen zum realistischen historischen Roman der Gründerzeit 1872-1880* (Frankfurt a.M.: Lang, 1983); Michael Limlei, *Geschichte als Ort der Bewährung: Menschenbild und Gesellschaftsverständnis in dem deutschen historischen Roman (1820-1890)* (Frankfurt a.M.: Lang, 1988); Claus-Michael Ort, 'Roman des "Nebeneinander" — Roman des "Nacheinander": Kohärenzprobleme im Geschichtsroman des 19. Jahrhunderts und ihr Funktionswandel', in *Zwischen Goethezeit und Realismus: Wandel und Spezifik in der Phase des Bürgerlichen Realismus*, ed. by Michael Titzmann (Tübingen: Niemeyer, 2002), pp. 347-75; Lynne Tatlock, '"In the Heart of the Heart of the Country": Regional Histories as National History in Gustav Freytag's *Die Ahnen* (1872-80)', in *A Companion to German Realism 1848-1900*, ed. by Todd Kontje (Rochester, NY: Camden House, 2002), pp. 85-108; Charlotte Woodford, 'Contrasting Discourses of Nationalism in Historical Novels by Freytag and Fontane',

in *German Literature, History and the Nation: Papers from the Conference 'The Fragile Tradition'*, ed. by Christian Emden and David Midgley, 2 vols (Berne: Lang, 2002), I, 253-76.
19. In her exposition of Freytag's life, Christine Achinger (pp. 13-15) — for example — mentions every work by Freytag (even the poetry and the journalism) except the *Bilder*.
20. See Celia Applegate, *A Nation of Provincials: The German Idea of Heimat* (Berkeley: University of California Press, 1990); Celia Applegate, 'The Mediated Nation: Regions, Readers and the German Past', in *Saxony in German History: Culture, Society and Politics, 1830-1833*, ed. by James Retallack (Ann Arbor: Michigan University Press, 2000), pp. 33-50; Lynne Tatlock, 'Realist Historiography and the Historiography of Realism in Gustav Freytag's *Bilder aus der deutschen Vergangenheit*', *German Quarterly*, 63 (1990), 59-74; Lynne Tatlock, 'Regional Histories as National History: Gustav Freytag's *Bilder aus der deutschen Vergangenheit* (1859-1867)', in *Searching for Common Ground: Diskurse zur deutschen Identität 1750-1871*, ed. by Nicholas Vazsonyi (Cologne: Böhlau, 2000), pp. 161-78.
21. Alyssa A. Lonner, *Mediating the Past: Gustav Freytag, Progress and German Historical Identity, 1848-1871* (Berne: Lang, 2005); Larry L. Ping, *Gustav Freytag and the Prussian Gospel: Novels, Liberalism, and History* (Berne: Lang, 2006).
22. The only other discussions of significance are Bernhard J. Dotzler, 'Litterarum secreta — fraus litteraria. Über Gustav Freytag: *Die verlorene Handschrift*', in *Literatur und Politik in der Heine-Zeit: Die 48er Revolution in Texten zwischen Vormärz und Nachmärz*, ed. by Hartmut Kircher and Maria Klanska (Cologne: Böhlau, 1998), pp. 235-50; Volker Dörr, 'Idealistische Wissenschaft: der (bürgerliche) Realismus und Gustav Freytags Roman *Die verlorene Handschrift*', *Zeitschrift für Deutsche Philologie*, 120 (2001), 3-33; Herbert Hahn, 'Die Bedeutung der Naturdarstellung in der Komposition von Gustav Freytags *Verlorene Handschrift*' (doctoral thesis, University of Greifswald, 1921); Alyssa A. Lonner, 'History's Attic: Artifacts, Museums, and Historical Rupture in Gustav Freytag's *Die verlorene Handschrift*', *The Germanic Review*, 82 (2007), 321-41; Richard Wicke, 'Gustav Freytags Romane *Soll und Haben* und *Die verlorene Handschrift*: Ein Beitrag zur Geschichte des Gesellschaftsromans im neunzehnten Jahrhundert' (doctoral thesis, University of Würzburg, 1949).
23. For instance, the only comments on Freytag's poetry to be found in anything other than a biographical account are by Erwin Lüer, 'Lyriktheoretische Betrachtungen zu den Gedichten Gustav Freytags', *Gustav Freytag Blätter*, 50 (1992-93), 8-22.
24. See Stefan Berger, *Germany: Inventing the Nation* (London: Arnold, 2004), pp. 66-75; Brent O. Peterson, *History, Fiction and Germany. Writing the Nineteenth-Century Nation* (Detroit: Wayne State University Press, 2005), pp. 199-266.
25. See Berger, p. 2.
26. Benedict Anderson, *Imagined Communities: Reflections on the Origin and Spread of Nationalism* (London: Verso, 1991), p. 6. For further explorations of the imagined nature of national identity, see Eric Hobsbawm, 'Introduction: Inventing Traditions', in *The Invention of Tradition*, ed. by Eric Hobsbawm and Terence Ranger (Cambridge: Cambridge University Press, 1983), pp. 1-14, and *Nation and Narration*, ed. by Homi Bhabha (London: Routledge, 1990).
27. All quotations from primary and secondary sources in this monograph are reproduced as printed in the original text, without any corrections or additions.
28. The *Bibliothek der Deutschen Literatur: Mikrofiche-Gesamtausgabe nach den Angaben des Taschengoedeke* (Munich: Saur, 1990) consists of 19,963 fiches covering first editions of German and translated works published between 1650 and 1900.
29. See the work on autobiography theory by Sidonie Smith and Julia Watson, *Reading*

*Autobiography: A Guide for Interpreting Life Narratives* (Minnesota: University of Minnesota Press, 2001).

30. The only index of the letters and other manuscripts held in Berlin was published in 1959 by Walther Gebhardt, 'Die Briefsammlung Gustav Freytags', *Jahrbuch der schlesischen Friedrich-Wilhelms-Universität zu Breslau*, 4 (1959), 152–75. The catalogue has recently been updated and digitized by the Staatsbibliothek, but is currently unavailable for use or dissemination in the public domain. Particular thanks must go to Hans-Jörg Lieder at the Staatsbibliothek for arranging my access to this digital catalogue.

31. *Gustav Freytag und Heinrich von Treitschke im Briefwechsel*, ed. by Alfred Dove (Leipzig: Hirzel, 1900); *Gustav Freytag's Briefwechsel mit Emil Devrient*, ed. by Alfred Dove (Brunswick: n.p., 1902); *Briefe an Albrecht von Stosch*, ed. by H. F. Helmholdt (Suttgart: Deutscher Verlag, 1913); *Gustav Freytag: Briefe an seine Gattin*, ed. by Hermance Strakosch-Freytag and Curt L. Walter-Van der Bleek (Berlin: Lehmann, 1913); *Gustav Freytag und Herzog Ernst von Coburg im Briefwechsel, 1853 bis 1893*, ed. by Eduard Tempeltey (Leipzig: Hirzel, 1904).

32. See Margret Galler and Jürgen Matoni, 'Einleitung', in *Gustav Freytags Briefe an die Verlegerfamilie Hirzel*, ed. by Margret Galler and Jürgen Matoni (Berlin: Mann, 1994).

33. Other editions of Freytag's letters include *Gustav Freytag an Theodor Molinari und die Seinen: Bislang unbekannte Briefe aus den Beständen der Universitätsbibliothek Wroclaw*, ed. by Edward Bialek (Frankfurt a.M.: Lang, 1987); *Gustav Freytag an Salomon Hirzel und die Seinen*, ed. by Alfred Dove (Leipzig: Breitkopf & Härtel, 1903); Georg Droescher, 'Gustav Freytags Schriftwechsel mit der Generalintendanz der königlichen Schauspiele zu Berlin', *Deutsche Rundschau*, 45 (1918), 129–46; Carl Hinrichs, 'Unveröffentliche Briefe Gustav Freytags an Heinrich Geffecken aus der Zeit der Reichsgründung', *Jahrbuch für die Geschichte Mittel- und Ostdeutschlands*, 3 (1954), 65–117, at pp. 70–80; J. Hofmann, *Gustav Freytag als Politiker, Journalist und Mensch: Mit unveröffentlichten Briefen von Freytag und Max Jordan* (Leipzig: J. Weber, 1922).

CHAPTER 1

# Towards a National Community: The *Vormärz* Poetry

It is a curiosity repeatedly noted in secondary literature on Gustav Freytag that, despite being one of the most commercially successful novelists of the nineteenth century, he does not hold a more prominent position in the German literary canon. Today best known for his 1855 social novel of business, *Soll und Haben*, Freytag remains something of a secondary figure in German literary history, dismissed respectively as a minor representative of German realism; as an author more concerned with bourgeois politics than literary aesthetics; and, in certain circles of criticism, as an anti-Semite. Literary surveys of the later nineteenth century tell how Freytag was quickly eclipsed by authors such as Theodor Fontane, Gottfried Keller, and, not least, Thomas Mann, who published that other great novel of German business, *Buddenbrooks: Verfall einer Familie*, in 1901, less than fifty years after Freytag's own work. By the mid-twentieth century, Freytag's popularity had all but vanished, both among the German readership and in the field of *Germanistik*.[1]

Given this context, it is hardly surprising that *Soll und Haben* remains the primary area of interest in literary studies of Freytag. Yet the novel by no means marked the beginning of his literary career. In fact, Freytag had been publishing for a decade before finding success with his first novel. In this chapter, I consider the earliest phase of Freytag's literary production, specifically his poetry of the *Vormärz* — that turbulent political and literary era which began arguably in the aftermath of the July Revolution of 1830, and which culminated in social revolution in Germany in 1848. Together with Chapter 2 on Freytag's *Vormärz* dramas, this chapter explores how his early literary production was both shaped by, and reflected, the political and aesthetic concerns of the time in which it was produced, as I seek to identify how formative these processes were for his subsequent writing in the post-revolutionary era.

## *In Breslau* (1845)

Freytag's earliest literary works were the poems brought together in 1845 in the collection *In Breslau*, published by the local Breslau publisher Johann Kern. The size of the initial print run is unknown, and there are no extant reviews of the volume. It was unsuccessful upon publication and has been almost entirely ignored by Freytag criticism. The collection is divided into three sections: *Bilder aus dem Volke, Ein Trinkgelage*, and *Feste in Breslau*.[2] The first of these consists predominantly of imaginative and historically orientated poems, many of which explore elements of folk myth and tradition. The second, as its title suggests, is a collection of drinking and festive songs, written to be performed at social occasions. The final section contains a series of celebratory poems written in honour of events from Freytag's own life, which also appear to have been produced with performance in mind. Interestingly, these divisions were removed from the reprint of *In Breslau* in the *Gesammelte Werke*, which also excludes seven of the original poems. In his memoirs, Freytag notes that he felt a number of his early poems had not stood the test of time, and it is possible that the alterations to the reprint of *In Breslau* were the result of his attempt to purge the *Gesammelte Werke* of elements he considered sub-standard.[3] Because of these later major alterations, in this chapter I use the original 1845 edition of the collection for citation, rather than the *Gesammelte Werke*, since the former provides the most comprehensive edition of Freytag's poetry.

Dating the poems of *In Breslau* is a challenge. The section *Bilder aus dem Volke* is dated '1839–41', but the majority of the individual poems in the collection are undated. Of those that have a date, the earliest is from 1838 ('Die Wellen'), and the latest from 1844 ('Scenen aus dem Maskenfest des guten König René'). If we accept these dates, then the poems stem from the same period of production as Freytag's first two dramas, *Die Brautfahrt, oder Kunz von der Rosen* (1841) and *Der Gelehrte* (1844). There are no references to the poems in the surviving letters of Freytag, and his biographers have in general dismissed the poetry as nothing more than youthful fancy. Consequently, the only source of information on the composition of Freytag's poems are his own memoirs, which provide a detailed — if highly subjective — account of their creation and context.

Freytag's assessment of his early poetry in his memoirs is self-confident in tone. Describing the development of his early poetic practice, he presents his talent as an inherent aspect of his regional identity and an inevitable consequence of his upbringing:

> Daß mir, einem Schlesier, das Versemachen nicht schwer wurde, ist fast vorauszusetzen, denn seit der Zeit der schlesischen Dichterschulen waren in meinem Heimatlande Gelegenheitsgedichte die unentbehrliche Beigabe

eines jeden Familienfestes, und wer dergleichen nicht selbst verfertigte, erhielt das Wünschenswerthe um ein Geringes von stets bereitwilligen Versifexen. (I, 101)

The memoirs paint a romantic image of Freytag's childhood as a time when communal and social forms of poetry were woven into the fabric of daily life. Continuing in this vein, Freytag notes how, as a *Gymnasium* student, he wrote countless poems based upon 'den gelegentlichen Hausbedarf der Familie und guter Freunde', and how he had many opportunities to practice his poetic skills, since, as the son of the local mayor of Kreuzburg, 'an Festen fehlte es nicht' (I, 101). For the most part, Freytag's statements on his early literary activity are part of a wider, idealized reminiscence of his childhood and should be treated with a degree of scepticism. However, what can be gained from a critical reading of the memoirs is a more general sense of how the young Freytag regarded poetry — not as a remote art form, distant from daily life, but as an integral part of existence through which concepts of family, home, and community could be confirmed and celebrated. Despite his idyllic account, Freytag does sound a note of caution in the memoirs about his early poetry:

> Dergleichen Gewöhnung an Schulmeisterverse und gereimte Prosa war innigem lyrischem Schaffen gar nicht günstig, weil die Seele sich an das vorschnelle und phrasenhafte Ausgeben gewöhnte. Auch in Breslau fand ich überreiche Gelegenheit zu solch anspruchslosem Machwerk. (I, 101)

Freytag suggests that the very upbringing that brought poetry to his attention could also become a form of aesthetic constraint, and underneath the self-aggrandizing tone of the memoirs he expresses unusual levels of self-doubt about the quality of his own poetic output. He notes, for instance, how 'aus früher und aus späterer Zeit [...] kaum etwas Singbares geblieben [ist]', and questions whether even those poems that have stood the test of time should be included in the *Gesammelte Werke* (I, 103–04):

> Da die Sammlung [*In Breslau*] doch einmal der Oeffentlichkeit übergeben [ist] [...], und da sie als Jugendwerk des Autors zuweilen erwähnt wird, so muß sie auch in einer Sammlung meiner Werke Aufnahme erbitten. Von den Reimen, welche einst fröhlicher Geselligkeit dienten, ist nur wenig aufgenommen [...]. (I, 105)

However, despite the superficially grudging tone, such a passage can also be read as a *captatio benevolentiae* to the reader, seeking their goodwill and preempting potential criticism of the youthful work. Interestingly, this gentle dismissal of the early poetry can also be found in a letter from Freytag to the Duke of Coburg-Gotha from 1853, accompanying a copy of *In Breslau*: 'Es ist viel Elfenkram und etwas Sentimentalität darin, und das ganze kaum würdig Ihre Zeit in Anspruch zu nehmen'.[4] Although Freytag made gestures that distanced himself from his early poetry, he was clearly pleased enough with his efforts to provide the Duke with a copy, and to include them in the *Gesammelte Werke*.

The memoirs state that Freytag began writing poetry in earnest during his recovery from his year of military service in 1839 (I, 98–99). Freytag embarked on military service at the relatively late age of 23, having chosen to prioritize the completion of his *Habilitation* thesis and his duties as a *Privatdozent* over his obligation to the state (for a more detailed account of Freytag's university career, see Chapter 2). Although he had originally obtained permission to serve for just one year, he was informed on arrival at the military academy that his relatively advanced age meant he would be required to undertake the full three-year period of service. According to the memoirs, he instantly fell ill, suffering in quick secession from gastroenteritis and influenza. Freytag's father appealed to the King for his son's one-year term to be reinstated, and Freytag returned to Breslau exhausted both physically and mentally. From the subjective account in the memoirs, it is hard to ascertain quite why Freytag's military service was so strenuous. Descriptions of the young author, however, portray him as a dandy, and thus perhaps he was uninterested in the army.[5] In later life, Freytag became an unqualified supporter of the Prussian army, but it is possible that the oddly negative depiction of conscription in his works *Die Ahnen* and the *Bilder aus der deutschen Vergangenheit* was influenced by his own experience of enforced military service.

The memoirs claim that it was during Freytag's recovery in Breslau that he rediscovered both 'die Spannkraft und den Uebermuth der Jugend' and his poetic abilities (I, 100–01). This suggests a connection between his physical and artistic recovery: the inverse, if you will, of Heinrich Heine's parallel between his physical collapse and his renunciation of poetic sensualism in 1848.[6] Characterizing Freytag's early poetry, the memoirs note: 'Ich hatte aber in dieser Zeit, wo ich viel allein war, noch eine kleine geheime Thätigkeit begonnen, ich machte Gedichte, nicht nur für Andere, sondern auch für mich' (I, 101). Freytag's memoirs could be read as suggesting that a form of aesthetic shift occurred during his period of illness and recuperation in 1839: one characterized by an increasing desire to move away from the socially determined poetry and *Gelegenheitsgedichte* of his childhood, and towards a poetry written for poetry's sake.

Certainly, it is clear that, while recuperating in Breslau, Freytag's engagement with poetry took on a more formal character. He became involved in the local Breslauer Künstlerverein, a small-scale literary association (small enough, indeed, not to be included in the virtually comprehensive *Handbuch literarisch-kultureller Vereine, Gruppen und Bünde*).[7] In his memoirs, Freytag repeatedly distances himself from the work of the *Verein*, which he recalls as 'ein[e] harmlose [...] Genossenschaft von Dichtern, Musikern und bildenden Künstlern

[...] [die] lebten fast sämmtlich in kleinen Verhältnissen mit mäßigem Talent, dessen Grenzen man leicht übersehen konnte' (I, 101-03). The condescension of these lines was no doubt the result of Freytag's desire when writing his memoirs to distance his own national success from such parochial roots. Nonetheless, although essentially biased, the commentary in the memoirs provides important details of the people with whom Freytag had contact at the association. These included numerous poets, not least Hoffmann von Fallersleben (hardly the marginal figure Freytag suggests in his description of the association). It was at this time that von Fallersleben published the first volume of his *Unpolitische Lieder* (1841), and Freytag himself had been a student of von Fallersleben while at university, defending him publicly when he was dismissed because of the political tendentiousness of his verse.

Also of importance was a lesser-known member of the association, August Geyder, who appears to have encouraged Freytag's interest in the collection and cataloguing of *Volkslieder*, a form to which Freytag claims to have felt particular affinity (I, 102): 'ich [war] kein lyrischer Dichter. Wenn mich etwas wirklich bewegte, so tönten in mir der Stimmung entsprechend stundenlang Worte und Noten irgend eines alten Volksliedes' (I, 103). That Freytag was interested in the tradition of the *Volkslied* and in collecting the poems is unsurprising. This popular activity — inspired by Herder, embodied by Arnim's and Brentano's influential *Des Knaben Wunderhorn* (1805-08), and continued by the Grimms and others — remained influential throughout the *Vormärz*, fuelled by a combination of aesthetic and political concerns (and clearly reflected, for instance, in Heine's poetry). Indeed, Freytag's memoirs state how the poems of *Des Knaben Wunderhorn* were often referred to and copied by the members of the Breslauer Künstlerverein (I, 103). Significantly, Freytag continued to collect folk songs and *Flugschriften* throughout his life, the resulting extensive collection eventually forming the source material for his historical articles in *Die Grenzboten* (1848-70), and his cultural history *Bilder aus der deutschen Vergangenheit* (1859-67), as well as his final two novels, *Die verlorene Handschrift* (1864) and *Die Ahnen* (1871-80). It is likely that Freytag's collection of *Volkslieder*, started while at the Breslauer Künstlerverein, marked the beginning of this wider *Flugschriftensammlung*.

Although the memoirs stress that Freytag was primarily interested in the *Volkslied*, he was not wholly disengaged from the world of political poetry either. The memoirs note how in the *Vormärz*: '[f]ür Deutschland war freilich die Zeit gekommen, wo die Unzufriedenheit mit dem Bestehenden überall in der Lyrik austönte' (I, 102-03). However, the older Freytag quickly moves to distance his own early poetry from such a politicized aesthetic:

> Was ich über die Persönlichkeit einiger Dichter erfuhr, trug nicht dazu bei, mich für diese Richtung der lyrischen Poesie zu erwärmen, welche von

dem Schaffenden eine ungewöhnliche Größe des Urtheils oder die Wucht heißer Leidenschaft fordern muß, wenn sie nicht unwahr und phrasenhaft werden soll. (I, 103)

The compliment Freytag pays to the political poet's ability to write with passion is undercut by his warning of the potential in such works for stylistic incompetence. One senses here a barely veiled critique of the politically engaged generation of poets writing around and after 1840. Instead of engaging with politics, Freytag's poetry, so his memoirs claim, was primarily interested in telling a story:

> Was mich zur Darstellung lockte, war fast immer eine Situation, in der ich eine andere Persönlichkeit empfand, die poetische Erzählung. Dieser Drang, kleine epische Stoffe lyrisch zu behandeln, pflegt auch bei großen Dichtern in einer gewissen Zeit ihres Lebens zu kommen und wieder zu vergehen [...]. Jetzt kam mir die Zeit, in der ich vorzugsweise gern gereimte Geschichten verfertigte [...]. (I, 104)

The suggestion here that Freytag wrote narrative poems in order to create alternative characters and personalities strikes one as a potentially distinctive trait of his poetry. Significantly, it is also a characteristic of his dramas from this period, not least *Die Brautfahrt oder Kunz von der Rosen*, in which the story of a dynastic marriage is told from the folk perspective of the poetic alter ego Kunz (see the further discussion of this play in Chapter 2). Nevertheless, as I will demonstrate in this chapter, many of the poems of *In Breslau* do contain political undertones — an aspect of Freytag's early poetic practice deliberately underplayed by the account of this period in his memoirs, and as yet unconsidered in studies of his life and works.

Despite Freytag's attempt in his memoirs to distance his early poetry from the social and political tendencies of *Vormärz* Germany, the importance of politics to the poems of *In Breslau* is made clear from the outset of the volume, not least in the collection's dedication, 'An Theodor Molinari'. This poem details the conversation of two friends — representations of Freytag and the local Breslau businessman Molinari — over some wine. The two men discuss life in *Vormärz* Germany — an era characterized by the Freytag figure as one of unfulfilled political potential:

> [...] Großes will die Zeit,
> Doch klein hat sie ein großes Volk gefunden,
> Den Wunsch lebendig, aber schwach die That. [...]
> Jetzt ist es Zeit, daß Mann zum Manne stehe,
> Und prüfend fördre des Genossen Werke,
> Selbst wo der Freund in andern Farben gehe,
> Noch am Contrast das eigne Sein verstärke.
> Denn wie verschieden auch die Saiten klingen,
> Wird jeder Ton nur einzeln voll und rein,

> So müssen sie unwiderstehlich sein,
> Wenn sie vereint das ganze Land durchdringen. (IB, i-ii)

Although the poem leaves unspecified the precise goal towards which Freytag desires the German folk to work, the sense of a burgeoning and potentially influential folk force in Germany is clearly expressed. This appears to be a precursor of Freytag's concept of the *Volkskraft*, developed in his historical writings of the late 1850s and early 1860s (and discussed throughout Chapter 4). The poem calls for social unity and the merging of political factions into one national voice capable of ringing across the country. Essentially, it seeks a form of German unification — emotional and political. This demand for nationhood is voiced more clearly in another poem from the collection, 'Unser Land':

> Schwerter und Waffen, hie deutsches Land!
> Die Träume werden Leben.
> Ja, irdisch wirst du in Kampf und Noth,
> Im deutschem Geist und im deutschen Tod.
> Das Vaterland soll leben! (IB, 97)

The tone of both these poems is reminiscent of much of the politically orientated poetry of the *Vormärz*, including the 'Bundeslied' of Freytag's friend and teacher, Hoffmann von Fallersleben — although the parallelism is too generic to allow a specific claim of literary influence:

> Trennt uns Glauben, Streben, Meinen,
> Eins soll, Eins soll uns vereinen —
> Brüder, reicht euch froh die Hand!
> Deutschlands Freiheit, Deutschlands Einheit,
> Und in ihrer schönsten Reinheit,
> Liebe für das Vaterland![8]

That Freytag chose to dedicate *In Breslau* to Molinari is in itself a political statement. In his memoirs, Freytag retrospectively paints Molinari as a form of sounding board for his own incipient political views:

> Er [Molinari] wurde mein Vertrauter, in dessen Gemüth ich Manches niederlegte, was mich innerlich bewegte [...]. Vor Allem war es die Politik, in der wir treu zusammen hielten. [...] Theodor war ein warmer Preuße und ein warmer Liberaler, er sah mit Schmerzen, wie die Regierung auf Irrwegen dahinschwankte, und zürnte der Haltlosigkeit, mit welcher das junge Freiheitsgefühl sich äußerte. (I, 119-20)

Although this account must be treated with caution, the memoirs make clear that it was through Molinari that Freytag met other young, liberally minded intellectuals during his time in Breslau: a collection of 'Gleichgesinnte' who shared his 'Sorge um die Zukunft des Vaterlandes' but rejected the volatility of the more radical social, political, and literary movements of the era (I, 120). That the two men had a considerable political influence on each other is corroborated by their extensive correspondence, which scrutinizes many of the significant developments in nineteenth-century German history, including the Schleswig-Holstein conflict, the German question, and, more abstractly, the need for a national idea to underpin German politics. Although no pre-1848 correspondence between the two men is extant, presumably because they only began to write to each other once Freytag had left Breslau for Dresden in 1848, it is reasonable to assume that their early friendship involved similarly liberally inclined political discussions. In this context, the dedication 'An Theodor Molinari' can be seen to mediate between the domains of friendship and politics, revealing how they can interact (something rarely seen in the more stridently political poetry of von Fallersleben or Georg Herwegh). This mediation between political and other domains recurs in a number of other poems in the collection, as will be seen below.

Alongside 'An Theodor Molinari', *In Breslau* contains a number of poems which reflect even more directly political concerns and events from the 1830s and the 1840s. These events include the removal of the Göttingen Seven from their university posts in 1838, the Rhine crisis of 1840 to 1841, the Weavers' Revolt in Silesia in 1844, and the Polish rebellion of the 1830s. In each of these cases, Freytag writes a poem which responds directly to the occurrence, producing in the process a form of political *Gelegenheitsdichtung*. Of these poems, it is 'Die Wellen' which Freytag specifically identifies in his memoirs as an example of his political verse. Composed in 1838, the poem appears to allegorize a conflict between monarchical rule and the rights of the folk. The waves of monarchical rule crash against the shore (representing the rights of the people), yet the shore remains strong against every assault:

> Sieh, großer Herr der Erde, die Wellenkönige an,
> Es stürzen ihrer tausend, viel Tausend Jahr heran,
> Sie heulen und zerschellen, wo blieb wohl ihre Wuth?
> Die Küste, Herr, die Küste steht fest in Gottes Hut.
> Das gute Recht des Volkes steht fester als Uferland,
> Es raget in die Höhe bis an des Himmels Rand,
> Es wurzelt in der Tiefe wohl tief in der Ewigkeit,
> Willst du das unterzwingen, du Well' im Meer der Zeit? (IB, 33)

Freytag's memoirs tell us that the above lines were written in response to the dismissal of the seven Göttingen professors in 1837 after they had protested against the annulment of the kingdom of Hanover's liberal constitution by the new king Ernst August I.[9] This could well be true, although it should be noted that there are no elements in the poem which directly reference the event. However, if we accept Freytag's word, then the arrest of the Göttingen Seven is represented in the poem as an attack by the state on the rights of the folk — another wave crashing on the shore. The tenor of the poem is not pessimistic, however, since, according to its allegory, these attacks on freedom are incapable of damaging the liberal cause in the long term, as the constitutional rights of the people are preserved 'tief in der Ewigkeit': enshrined in history and protected by God (IB, 33). In a neat inversion, Freytag ultimately presents the folk rather than the King as divinely ordained:

> So sagt doch, ihr Wasser der Tiefe, wo blieb die Königsgestalt,
> Die über Recht und Gesetze so dräuend erhob die Gewalt?
> So sagt doch, ihr Wasser der Tiefe, wo bleib die wilde Fluth?
> Die Küste, Herr, die Küste steht fest in Gottes Hut. (IB, 34)

'Die Wellen' suggests that the conflict between monarchical rule and the folk is not a recent phenomenon, but rather '[e]in altes Hadern und Hassen [...] zwischen Land und Meer' (IB, 34). Each of the waves can be seen to represent the many incursions of monarchical rule, of the Deutscher Bund and Federal Diet against liberal freedoms — incursions that had been occurring on a regular basis since the Congress of Vienna. However, the allegory as developed requires that such meanings be read into the text, rather than be derived from it — and thus the supposed political specificity of the poem diminishes: it becomes more abstract and less of a direct response to political events than Freytag suggests in his memoirs.

Elsewhere the parallel between Freytag's politics and poetry is more concretely expressed. 'Die Bauern und der Schulmeister', for instance — renamed 'Das tausendjährige Deutschland' in the *Gesammelte Werke* — marks Freytag's response to the Rhine crisis of 1840 to 1841. One of his *Gesellschaftslieder*, the poem is didactic and patriotic in tone:

> Wir hören von Deutschland und freier Zeit,
> Das wüßten wir gerne, wir Bauersleut'.
> Wir sitzen und trinken so fröhlich im Rund,
> Das ist zu Geschichten die glückliche Stund'.
>     Schulmeister, ach lieber Gevatter, erzählt,
>     Wie sich die Geschichte der Deutschen verhält.
>         Eure Lehren
>         Wir hören;
>         Ganz leise,
>         Wie Mäuse.
>         Seid still! (IB, 109)

The poem itself details a sequence of key events in German history, including the defeat of the Romans by Arminius, the rise of Charlemagne, the advent of Christianity, and the Wars of Liberation against the French. The tone is positive and the text as a whole conveys the kind of progressive understanding of history which, significantly, also underpins Freytag's later historical writings *Die Ahnen* and the *Bilder aus der deutschen Vergangenheit*. Importantly, too, the key moments of German history identified in the poem are precisely those examined in these later works. The core concerns of Freytag's work on German historical progress in the 1860s and 1870s can thus all be found in this single poem from 1841.

'Die Bauern und der Schulmeister' concludes its historical panorama with the most recent of patriotic moments from German history, the defence of the Rhine against the French:

> Und heute noch singt man aus Kreuzweg und Stein:
> Sie sollen nicht haben den deutschen Rhein!
> Dem Klugen die Sache ein Merkzeichen sei,
> Daß Deutschland noch heute gerettet und frei. (IB, 111)

Prompted by fears that France would renew her attempts to push her borders towards the frontier formed by the Rhine, a plethora of nationalistically orientated poems and songs had been produced in 1840 and 1841; and Freytag's work is clearly a part of this phenomenon. The similarities with Niklaus Becker's 'Der deutsche Rhein' (1840), with its refrain 'Sie sollen ihn nicht haben, den freien deutschen Rhein', are immediately apparent, and no doubt deliberate.[10] Stylistically, Freytag's poem also shares similarities to Herwegh, Ludwig Uhland, and von Fallersleben, embodying in its patriotic didacticism the 'Mischung von Volksmäßigem und Lehrhaftem' that Freytag's memoirs claim to have been the best feature of von Fallersleben's poetry (I, 102).

In 1844, the revolt of the Silesian weavers prompted Freytag to write politically again. The impoverishment of the weavers, and the bloody suppression of their rebellion, came for many liberal authors to symbolize both the socio-economic and the political crises that stood at the heart of *Vormärz* Germany. Freytag's memoirs record the events of 1844 in the following manner:

> Da drang in unser politisches und geselliges Treiben ein lauter Klageschrei von Noth der Spinner und Weber in den Gebirgskreisen. [...] Durch die neue Maschinenarbeit und durch das dürftige Leben mehrer Generationen war sie verkümmert und in sklavische Abhängigkeit von den Kaufherren, den regelmäßigen Abnehmern ihrer Waare, gerathen. Jetzt aber hatte Ungunst der Handelsverhältnisse ihr Leiden so hoch gesteigert, daß ein schnelles Eingreifen menschenfreundlicher Thätigkeit geboten war, um die Schrecken der Hungersnoth abzuwenden. Ueberall in Deutschland wurde für sie gesammelt [...], auch ich wurde dazu herangezogen. (I, 121)

Freytag's assessment of the situation in his memoirs is interesting, since he identifies the exploitation of the weavers as a key reason behind their uprising, and stresses the economic changes — specifically the effects of early industrialization in the form of machine-based automation — that lay at the root of the problem. He does not appear to see the Weavers' Revolt as a precursor of a greater revolution (as is the case in Heine's 'Weberlied', in which the weavers weave a threefold curse into the death shroud of 'Altdeutschland'), and seems more concerned with the humanitarian side of the crisis.[11] Admittedly, one must once again be cautious about such an interpretation: Heine's poem was contemporaneous with the crisis, whereas Freytag's memoirs were not, and it cannot be presumed that Freytag saw things the same way in 1844. Nevertheless, he did join the Breslau 'Central-Verein' in order to help raise funds for the weavers, and it was as part of this fundraising activity that he wrote a series of poems inspired by the crisis called the 'Lebende Bilder' (I, 121). Designed to be performed at a fundraising event, these poems were given the subtitle 'Soirée zum Besten der schlesischen Weber am 16. März 1844' (although the word *Soirée* was replaced with the less frivolous term *Vorstellung* in the *Gesammelte Werke* edition). The 'Lebende Bilder' open with a prologue, in which art comes on stage, dressed not in her usual regal attire, but as a beggar:

> Als Bettlermädchen steht sie an den Wegen
> Und bittend streckt sie euch die Hand entgegen,
> Und spricht: 'Ihr holden Freunde, gebt mir, gebt!
> Ich flehe heut im Namen vieler Armen;
> Denn wo das menschlich Schöne schafft und webt,
> Soll auch für Menschenleid das Herz erwarmen. (IB, 149)

A curiosity of the 'Lebende Bilder' is the fact that the prologue contains the only direct reference to the Weavers' Revolt in the entire sequence. The following seven poems are instead each based on a work of art — following in the tradition of the *Lebendes Bild* — and in only one can a potential reference to the revolt be noted, in 'Die heilige Elisabeth', about the patron saint of the poor: 'Dein größter Feind [war] das Elend, dein Segen ein Gruß des Armen' (IB, 151). The remainder of the poems range from a retelling of the story of the Pied Piper of Hamelin to an evocation of the beauty of the south, seemingly deliberately echoing Goethe's 'Kennst du das Land':

> In den Süden sollt ihr ziehen,
> Wo die Myrten festlich blühen,
> Wo das Leben kräftig lacht
> In der Farben voller Pracht. (IB, 152)

Of the pictures described, Vernet's *Judith und Holofernes* is perhaps the most famous, and had also attracted the attention of Heine in his *Französische Maler* (1833). With the technology of engraving and lithography firmly established by the 1840s, it is possible that Freytag came across Vernet's painting in either a book or a touring exhibition; equally possible is that Freytag had read Heine, especially given their common use of the relatively obscure historical figure Kunz von der Rosen at this same time (see the discussion in Chapter 2).

In focusing on works of art rather than on the plight of the weavers, Freytag's poem is quite distinct from the genre of *Weber-Lyrik* identified in studies by Christina von Hodenburg and Gert Sautermeister.[12] As was the case with Freytag's earlier poem 'Die Wellen', there is some disconnection between the events that inspired the work and the poetry produced. Yet while 'Die Wellen' can still be read as a political statement, if an abstract one, it is hard to see any political import in the 'Lebende Bilder', which juxtapose without any sense of irony the poverty of the weavers with escapist tales from classical and folk history and the sunny panoramas of Italy. If the poems are read as the product of a charitable event, then the emphasis was presumably on producing entertainment for the audience in order to raise funds, rather than in engaging poetically with the situation of the weavers.

Two further poems by Freytag were also directly inspired by political events in *Vormärz* Germany: 'Der polnische Bettler' and 'Die Granitschale'. The former was prompted by the Polish uprising of 1830–31 and is seemingly concerned with the plight of a Polish beggar, sitting on the steps of Breslau cathedral, yet ignored by all who pass:

> Hier steh' ich in fremden Landen, ein elender armer Wicht,
> Und wenn ich polnisch bitte, verstehn mich die Leute nicht,
> Und wenn ich polnisch bete, hier hören die Heiligen nicht,
> Du braune Mutter der Polen, hilf deinem armen Sohn,
> Du liebe heilige Mutter, ich zittre vor Hunger schon! (IB, 1)

The poem is peculiar since, in cataloguing the negative treatment of a Pole, it creates — at least to the modern reader — some sympathy for the Polish cause. Yet given Freytag's pro-Prussian sentiments and his negative depiction of the Poles elsewhere in his writings (see, for example, the discussion in Chapter 3), it would be surprising if this poem was intended to be read as a sympathetic portrait. In his memoirs, Freytag states that, although 'Der polnische Bettler' could be read as a compassionate response to Poland's demand for nationhood, this had never been his intention:

> Eines dieser Stücke, den 'polnischen Bettler', sandte ich dem Musenalmanach von Echtermayer und Ruge. [...] Ruge hatte angenommen, daß die Klage des Polen aus politischer Wärme für Polen eingegeben sei, die leider damals Modekrankheit des Liberalismus war. Er kannte mich nicht, sonst hätte er das Gegentheil herauslesen können. (I, 104)

However, the poem itself does little to support Freytag's own interpretation in his memoirs. There is neither any obvious irony which might lead one to read the text as a pastiche of the sympathy for Poles expressed by members of the *Polenvereine* that had formed across Germany in the early 1830s, nor does it read as a satire of the *Polenlieder* written by authors as diverse as Ludwig Uhland, Adelbert von Chamisso, August Graf von Platen, Nikolaus Lenau, and Franz Grillparzer. If we take Freytag's memoirs at their word, and see 'Der polnische Bettler' as expressing anti-Polish sentiments, then there is once again some disconnection between the historical background and the verse it prompted — in this case, a disconnection that almost entirely obfuscates Freytag's political point, even for a contemporary such as Ruge.

Freytag puts forward a more coherent political message in 'Die Granitschale'. The poem is a fantasy based around the giant granite bowl which had been intended to sit in the rotunda of the Altes Museum in Berlin, but which proved too large and thus became the centrepiece of the revived *Lustgarten*, where it now permanently rests, though again in a different position from that originally intended. The bowl was designed to demonstrate the technological prowess of Prussia, and all stages of the creation of the *Schale* — from the blasting of the stone to its lengthy journey across Germany — had captured the public imagination, with the bowl becoming a symbol of pride in the Prussian state.[13] In the poem, Freytag describes how three statues arranged around the bowl step down from their pedestals in the middle of the night to drink from it. The statues are of the field-marshals Blücher, Bülow, and Scharnhorst, heroes of the Wars of Liberation against France, and key Prussian reformers, who also appear in the final volume of *Die Ahnen*. Freytag manipulates the topography of Berlin for the purposes of his poem, since in the 1840s, these statues were not situated around the bowl but were further down Unter den Linden, on either side of the Neue Wache and between the Opera and the Kronprinzenpalais on what is now Bebelsplatz. (Today the statues can be found in the garden behind the Opera.) The poem reaches its climax as Blücher, who had been known colloquially as *Marschall Vorwärts*, proclaims:

> Vorwärts, ihr deutschen Männer,
> Zu Freiheit, Licht und Recht!
> Vorwärts mit deutschem Vertrauen,
> Mit alter Lieb' und Treu'! (1B, 100)

The tone here emulates that of Theodor Körner's poetry of the Wars of Liberation — no doubt deliberately so — and is rooted in a vision of history that views it as inherently progressive (as in 'Die Bauern und der Schulmeister'). However, Blücher's words have a peculiar effect on the *Granitschale*:

> Da sprang mit plötzlichem Krachen
> Der steinerne Becher entzwei. (1B, 100)

Although today the bowl is cracked — the result of an attempt to change its position in 1981 — it never suffered such damage in Freytag's lifetime, and it is thus initially unclear why he, as a Prussian patriot, should end his poem with the destruction of a symbol of Prussian pride. Yet when read within the context of Prussian politics in the 1840s, the destruction becomes a metaphor for a state that had prematurely forgotten her victory in the Wars of Liberation and her role as a potential force for German unification. Such a reading is strengthened by the fact that, in content, metre, and form, the poem echoes Goethe's 'Der König in Thule', which tells of the need to preserve loyalty and fidelity to the past. Unlike the king of Goethe's poem, who takes his loyalty to the grave and thus relinquishes the symbol of his sacred cup, the *Granitschale* has become a false symbol of Prussia, and has wrongfully replaced the memory of liberation and reform represented by the statues around it. With his imaginative invocation of *Marschall Vorwärts*, Freytag suggests that Prussia must move forward in the grand tradition of her past, rather than dally with superficial symbols of power. The poem is thus interestingly critical of Prussian political realities — while remaining staunchly supportive of the Prussian principle.

Although an analysis of Freytag's overtly political poetry in *In Breslau* does not reveal a systematic political agenda, each of the poems considered shares what is best termed a reactive quality. Responding to major national events, they reveal Freytag as both aware of the political developments of his day, and writing in response to them. As such, Freytag's poetic engagement with politics is far from unique, for in each of the events he writes about (the Göttingen Seven, the Rhine crisis, the Weavers' Revolt, the Polish question, the *Granitschale*) he joins a host of other authors who also poetically represented these key events in the political and social history of *Vormärz* Germany. Nevertheless, a number of central concerns can be traced across the poems, which in their continuation are distinctive: the significance of the German folk ('An Theodor Molinari', 'Die Wellen'), a strong Prussian identity ('Die Granitschale', 'Der polnische Bettler'), and calls for German unity ('Unser Land', 'Die Bauern und der Schulmeister'). Although at times there is a lack of connection between the poetry and its inspiration ('Die Wellen', 'Lebende Bilder', 'Der polnische Bettler') — perhaps the result of censorship concerns, although there is no evidence for this — these texts nevertheless provide us with a unique perspective on Freytag's early politics, as yet not integrated into existing criticism. They reveal a combination of attitudes — a national-liberal stance; a sense of continuous historical progress; a dismissal of revolution in favour of political and national unification — generally seen as characteristic of the *Nachmärz* and the *Gründerzeit*, rather than the *Vormärz*, and which in the post-revolutionary period would come to dominate fully Freytag's literary and political practice.

Although *In Breslau* contains several overtly political poems, much of the collection is formed of socially orientated and narrative verse, seemingly far removed from the political agendas of the *Vormärz*. Freytag himself called these works *Gelegenheitsgedichte*: a term he uses primarily to denote the semi-communal purpose of the poems, rather than a specific poetic form. In light of the account in Freytag's memoirs of his childhood and his involvement with the Breslauer Künstlerverein, the presence of such poetry in *In Breslau* is hardly surprising. These *Gelegenheitsgedichte* were written in response to a range of occasions, from anniversaries ('Dem Oheim, zum funfzigjährigen

Amtsjubiläum 1843'), to artistic events in Breslau ('Das Theater. Prolog zum 13. Novbr. 1842'). They are examples of what might be termed domestic poetry, although, as Todd Kontje has pointed out, the term domestic does not exclude a political reading, since it often entails 'reflections on private life and commentaries on public politics', upholding or subverting dominant social structures through domestic voices.[14]

Typical of Freytag's domestic poetry is 'Ein Geburtstag von Agnes Franz (März 1842)', a birthday toast formed of six interlinked poems. Agnes Franz was a local poet with whom Freytag had been lodging — along with Franz's four stepchildren — from 1842 to 1845. The work is clearly intended to be performed, with each of the poems being read aloud by the friends and family of Franz:

> Ein kleiner Zug der wohlbekannten Gäste
> Begrüßt die Dichterin an ihrem Wiegenfeste,
> Hör' gütig an, was sie dir schüchtern sagen,
> Die Laute sind's, die sie im Herzen tragen. (IB, 141)

The six poems explore various facets of Franz's character and life. In 'Die Hausfrau', she is praised for her qualities as head of the house and mother to her children:

> Im engen Raum des Hauses, da ist der Hausfrau Walten,
> Sie ebnet in emsigem Schaffen des Lebens Mühen und Falten,
> Sie denkt und sorgt für die Ihren, geräuschlos, still und fein,
> So daß ein Fremder meinet, es könnte nicht anders sein. (IB, 141)

At first glance, Freytag's poem appears to uphold the dominant understanding of the social function of women in the mid-nineteenth century, presenting an image of Franz as the domestic mother — what Kontje has termed the 'triple calling' of the nineteenth-century female as mother, wife, and manager of the household.[15] The poem depicts the home as a quiet retreat from the outside world — as a *Heimat* created by Franz for her children, for whom she constantly cares and provides (IB, 141). The emphasis on caring for children in the poem is significant, since it was an important trope of bourgeois domestic fiction in the nineteenth century, which tended no longer to view children 'as pawns to advance their parents' social status or financial situation', but rather as individuals whose 'personal happiness [...] was of central concern to their parents'.[16]

However, while seemingly upholding such bourgeois value systems, Freytag's poem also partially challenges these social norms. For Franz is also a poet, for whom the purely domestic realm of motherhood can become constraining:

> Doch wenn der Himmel gesenket ins Herz des Schaffens Lust,
> Und wem er mit Idealen gefüllt die sehnende Brust,
> Dem wird die enge Beschränkung der Frauen doppelt schwer,
> Dem wird der Raum des Hauses leicht drückend, kalt und leer. (IB, 141)

In pointing towards the potentially inhibiting effects of the *Hausfrauendasein*, and the tension between the prescribed role of motherhood and the desire to be a poet, there is an unexpected emancipatory element to Freytag's poem. Such an interpretation is supported by the following poem in the cycle, 'Die Poesie', which precisely celebrates Franz's status as a poet. Certainly, it is true that Freytag suggests that Franz's strength lies in fulfilling the roles of both mother and poet simultaneously:

> Du aber bist unser Vorbild nicht nur im Reich der Träume,
> Du hast mit den Strahlen der Gottheit geschmückt auch die engen Räume,
> Hast dir eine Heimat gegründet auch hier auf der kleinen Erde. (IB, 141)

But despite this, there appears to be an attempt — if somewhat strained — to reconcile these opposites and, in doing so, to push at the boundaries of prescribed gender roles. As a whole, the sequence of poems both upholds a bourgeois sensibility that stresses the significance of the home and family, and at the same time allows for a certain fluidity in female roles: mother and poet are no longer mutually exclusive categories. Such a move is significant, since in Freytag's plays and his later fiction (especially *Die Ahnen*), the German woman is a strong, dominant character, self-reliant and self-confident, and is able to move between domestic and political spheres, becoming in the process a form of German moral backbone. In this sense, aspects of Freytag's early domestic poetry can also be read politically: as reflections of social structures and (potentially) proposals for social change in the mid-nineteenth century.

Many others of the poems of *In Breslau* appear to have been written with performance in mind, including the majority of those contained in the second section of the collection, 'Ein Trinkgelage'. The title already identifies the social setting of these poems, which are either forms of *Trinklied* or deal with the theme of drinking itself. Characteristic of these works is 'Das Trinklied vom kleinen Teufel', which explains allegorically the highs of intoxication and the lows of the hangover, through the story of a small devil who comes to earth and, unaware that wine is under heaven's protection, becomes drunk and drowns in a wine vat:

> Dem Weine war dies Ruhm und Preis,
> Doch heimlich auch Verlust,
> Wir Zecher sind der beste Beweis,
> Noch zieht in unsre Brust
> Beim Trinken selbst der Himmel ein,
> Am nächsten Morgen — das Teufelein. (IB, 124)

As in many such songs, Freytag eulogizes the intoxication of wine, and the heavenly benefits it can produce. His memoirs recount how he was particularly impressed by Hoffmann von Fallersleben's drinking songs, which similarly glorify the godliness of drunkenness, and the similarities in the tone between the two men's *Trinklieder* (all probably produced at the Breslauer Künstlerverein) are striking, as the following lines from von Fallersleben's 'Der Wein zieht uns zum Himmel hin' demonstrate:

> Der Wein zieht uns zum Himmel hin,
> Die Sorge hin zur Erde.
> Drum laßt mich trinken immerhin,
> Auf das ich himmlisch werde.[17]

Freytag returns to the theme of the pleasures and pains of drinking in 'Die Blume des Weins'. The poem takes the form of an extended narrative detailing a monk's search for a miraculous rose that blossoms from a wine barrel every hundred years. The monk drinks his way along the Rhine in search of the mystical blossom, and meets a child who opens a huge wine-cellar hidden in the hillside. The overtones of folk myth, from the Pied Piper of Hamelin through to Friedrich Barbarossa and his sleeping army in the Kyffhäuser, are clear. This cave is the home of the flower, although the child issues a warning to the monk before he enters:

> Nur eine Viertelstunde vermagst du die Blume zu sehen,
> Versäumst du sie zu pflücken, so ist's um dich geschehen.
> Bis dahin bist du Herrscher, versuche jedes Faß. (1B, 119)

Midnight approaches and the flower blossoms in an eruption of flames. Intoxicated, the monk leaves it too late to pluck the flower and lunges at it, plunging head first into the flower's flames and passing out. Waking up next morning he discovers his nose and cheeks have been burnt a bright red by the heat of the flower. The mystical *Blume des Weins* is thus revealed as something far more prosaic — the flushed face caused by over-indulgence in alcohol. The poem is particularly interesting since its lengthy narrative form and fantastic imaginings set it apart from the shorter drinking songs of von Fallersleben and others, although thematically the poem is clearly still in this tradition.

'Die Blume des Weins' is one of several poems in which Freytag develops a narrative consisting of memorable characters and which explores his poetic imagination. The shorter of these poems, such as 'Das Schmugglermädchen' and 'Der Nachtjäger', seem directly influenced by the tropes, forms, and locations of the *Volkslied*. The influence of Ludwig Tieck (of whom Freytag was an admirer, dedicating his play *Die Brautfahrt* to the author), Joseph von Eichendorff, and, to an extent, Goethe, can be seen in their lines, such as:

> Der Sturm durchfährt den Föhrenwald,
> Die Sterne glänzen bleich und kalt,
> Großmutter lauscht mit starrem Blick,
> Die Bäume brechen, die Dohlen schrein,
> Und des Försters Kind

> Erzittert im Wind
> Und schaut in die schwarze Nacht hinein. (1B, 42)

The lengthier narrative poems are more complex, often in many parts and with multiple voices and characters. 'Junker Gotthelf Habenichts' is a moralistic allegory of national loyalty, based around the wordplay of the exclamation 'Gott helf'! ich habe nichts' (1B, 65). You might not always have earthly possessions, the poem argues, but loyalty to your nation will always be rewarded. In many respects, the poem is reminiscent of Johann Peter Hebel's equally moralistic, if more humorous poem 'Kannitverstan' (1808) — the tale of a German in Holland who realizes that his own life is just as valuable as the seemingly more extravagant existence of Mr Kannitverstan (a play on the Dutch phrase *Ik kan niet verstaan*, 'I don't understand').

Significantly, the majority of Freytag's longer narrative poems, such as 'Junker Gotthelf Habenichts', sound political notes. 'Des Burschen Ende' focuses on the mourning for a dead *Burschenschaftler* — a figure who symbolized liberal dissatisfaction with the particularist rule of *Vormärz* Germany, and who is here raised to the level of a national hero. Meanwhile 'Die Krone' — an exotic tale set in the Middle East — proposes, in a vein similar to 'Die Wellen', that the relationship between the ruler and the folk should not be exploitative, but reciprocal, and warns of a possible inversion in political power structures in favour of the folk:

> Denn wisse, gegenseitig ist die Pflicht:
> Des Königs Thräne für des Volkes Blut,
> Für Volkes Thräne zahlt des Königs [Blut]. (1B, 10)

The most complex of these poems is 'Ein Kindertraum', which combines *Volkslied* rhythms and elements of German fairy tale, as well as a political allegory of unjust leadership. Initially, the poem appears primarily concerned with German myth. As night falls on Midsummer's eve, a boy is lost in the forest. Frightened by the threatening trees and noises around him, he collapses, whereupon the once-threatening forest transforms into a positive landscape alive with mystical creatures, who conjure up a bed out of the plants around him:

> Und aus dem Kelche der Blumen und aus des Weihers Rohr
> Bewegten sich kleine Gestalten ins Sternenlicht hervor;
> Sie fuhren durcheinander und schwatzten und lachten laut,
> Und trugen nach emsiger Arbeit aus Moos und Haidekraut
> Ein weiches Lager zusammen. (1B, 52)

As the boy falls asleep, the poem follows his dreams, in which he joins forces with the creatures of the forest in order to foil a *coup d'état* in the elf monarchy, restoring power to where it rightfully belongs after it has been seized by a despotic leader:

> Schnell war der Kampf beendet, der Räuber und seine Macht
> Verschlossen in Mauselöchern und in des Mohnkopfs Schacht.
> Und Bäbi trat zum Knaben, mit seinem Lieb vereint,
> Und sprach sich tief verneigend: 'Erlaube, du holder Freund,
> Daß meine Unterthanen dich heut als Herrn bedienen.'
> Der Knabe saß und lachte: 'Ja, Prinz, ich erlaub' es ihnen.' (IB, 61)

The imaginative power of the poem is undeniable, and the dream sequence is particularly effective as the young boy is miniaturized and takes part in the world of the elves — perhaps echoing E. T. A. Hoffmann's *Meister Floh* (1822) or Carl Leberecht Immermann's *Tulifäntchen* (1830). The anthropomorphic qualities ascribed to nature are also reminiscent of Eichendorff, although, in contrast to Eichendorff's view of nature, the natural world in Freytag is only superficially dangerous and demonic. At heart, the forest is shown to be a place of sanctuary for the young boy.

As I have demonstrated in the above analysis, the variety of poetic forms in *In Breslau* is diverse, and ranges far beyond the expressly political works detailed in the opening stages of this chapter. Interestingly, virtually all of the poems revolve around acts of poetic imagination: Blücher stepping off the pedestal in 'Die Granitschale'; the Goddess of Poetry praising Agnes Franz in 'Ein Geburtstag'; the elf-coup in 'Ein Kindertraum'. To an extent, therefore, Freytag's poetry combines elements from different poetic discourses, frequently making no distinction between the imaginative, domestic, and political. However, political themes, in particular an underlying movement towards issues of political power, organization, and belief, are often present in the narrative and domestic poems, which express sentiments of national pride or folk identity — a clear indication of what is to follow as Freytag's literary career develops.

*In Breslau* also contains a number of poems in which Freytag directly tackles the question of the nature of the poet. Some depict the artist as concerned with acts of poetic imagination and inspiration, and describe the process of writing as an intoxicating, compulsive act. Others suggest that the poet who rejects political and social engagement in his poetry is ignoring his greater vocation. Often, however, Freytag attempts to reconcile these two positions. Freytag's *Gelegenheitsgedicht*, 'Das Theater (Prolog zum 13. November 1842)' — simply called 'Prolog zum 13. November 1842' in the *Gesammelte Werke* — makes a series of telling comments about the role of the artist. The poem opens by celebrating the opening night of a play, but soon digresses into a lengthy reflection on the nature of art, the artist, and the creative process. It describes how the artist, in this case an actor, only truly lives in the moment of artistic creation, a moment in which he experiences an almost overriding force against which he cannot fight:

> Der Künstler ist ein Kind der schnellen Stunde,
> Sein Leben ist ein Traum; nur Eine Stunde,
> Wenn die Gardine rauscht, die Lichter flammen,
> Dann kommt ihm das Erwachen, Glut und Leben,
> Dann schlägt Begeistrung über ihm zusammen,
> Was er im Herzen fühlt, will er euch geben,
> Die Seele zuckt, er kann nicht widerstreben. (IB, 127)

The idea of the captivating power of poetic inspiration in these lines is mirrored in Freytag's memoirs, where he speaks of the overwhelming impulse he felt as a young man to write verse: '[d]ieser Drang [...] Stoffe lyrisch zu behandeln' (I, 104). In fact, Freytag's memoirs frequently hint that there was a kind of poetic muse who provided him with the inspiration to write. In discussing the composition of *Soll und Haben*, for instance, Freytag notes how elements of the novel were presented to him by a muse as he slept (I, 180). Similarly, when talking about his dramas, he notes how he was repeatedly captured by an overarching 'poetische Idee' (I, 179) which dictated the action of the plays. A related sentiment is expressed in the dedicatory poem of the memoirs:

> Da zog's am Vorhang und das Fenster klirrte,
> Um Haupt und Herz ergoß sich helles Licht,
> Die Feder fühlt' ich in die Hand gedrückt,
> Und leise klang die Mahnung: 'schreib'. — Ich schrieb.[18]

Although such statements are undoubtedly part of Freytag's attempt in his memoirs to present himself as a form of literary genius, inspired by a poetic muse, this concept of the artist as responding to and enslaved by the call of poetic inspiration was clearly one he had developed early in his career, since it is also reflected in his poems. The theme is developed, for instance, in the poem 'Kunst und Wissenschaft' (renamed 'Winckelmann' in the *Gesammelte Werke*):

> Träume des Künstlers sie gleichen der Traube,
> Die in dem Dunkel schimmert und lacht;
> Tief in der Seele verschlungenem Laube
> Regt sich's lebendig in dämmernder Nacht,
> Bis von dem Safte die Trauben schwellen,
> Blitzend die heiligen Tropfen entquellen,
> Das Kunstwerk sich bildet als goldner Wein. (IB, 89)

Despite the allegorical mode of 'Kunst und Wissenschaft', the idea is similar to that of *Das Theater*: once again, the process of artistic creation begins with a dreamlike state out of which inspiration erupts from the soul, leading inexorably to a work of art. 'Kunst und Wissenschaft' also details the intoxicating qualities of the creative process, linking back to Freytag's *Trinklieder* and suggesting a connection between art, wine, and inspiration, similar to that found in Goethe's *West-östlicher Divan*:

> Und bei dem Mahle der Göttlichen fließet
> Hell in dem Becher der heilige Wein;
> Und der Mensch, der göttliche, gießet
> Selig die Kunst in das Leben hinein. (IB, 90)

Just like wine, art is intoxicating and can seemingly bring man closer to the divine.

A related perspective on the nature of the artist is developed in Freytag's short poem 'Die Beschwörung'. Deep in the forest, a young poet attempts to call up the spirits of the great German authors in order to improve his own literary skills. The authors are, however, damning of the young man's attempt to feed parasitically on their voices:

> Nur was in dir selbst erklungen, gibt reinen, vollen Ton,
> Und kannst du den nicht wecken, so schweige, Dichtersohn. (IB, 49)

That the artist is in possession of exceptional talents is also stressed in 'Albrecht Dürer', a poem based on the life of the medieval painter:

> Nicht sieht er mit Menschenaugen in unsere gute Welt,
> Es ist ein Strahl der Gottheit, der seinem Aug' entfällt. (IB, 27)

Together, these poems create an image of the poet as a unique creative force. Prey to the intoxicating qualities of artistic expression, poets are individual geniuses, to some degree separate from the mundane reality of everyday existence. However, Freytag also produced poems on the role of the artist which were not solely concerned with the act of poetic creation and imagination. 'Die Schöpfung des Künstlers' is an extended satire on the character of the artist, in which the poetic muse becomes an angel who, out of boredom, has fashioned the poet from random objects:

> Dann packt' er des lieben Herrgotts kostbarsten Trinkpokal [...]
> Und setzt' ihn schnell dem Leibe von Reben und Ranken vor;
> Der Griff war statt des Halses, der Henkel wurde Ohr, [...]
> Und holte Blüthen und Knopsen von allen Farben und Arten
> Und stopfte sie in die Rundung, das war des Bechers Hirn
> Und setzte den Becherdeckel darüber als Haar und Stirn. (IB, 91)

Since the poet's head is made of a chalice, the poem argues that he will be constantly drawn to wine: 'Sie können nicht verleugnen das goldne Becherlein' (IB, 93) — somewhat undermining the connection between wine and creativity set up elsewhere in *In Breslau*. In addition, since the angel has used flowers for the poet's brain, they are destined only ever to produce *Blumenpoesie*:

> Sie haben kein Gehirne, nur Blüthen in ihrem Kopf
> Und Knospen von allen Arten, mehr als ein Blumentopf, [...]
> Denn wenn Sie sprechen, fallen die Blumen aus dem Mund,
> Und wenn Sie schreiben, malen Sie Blumen auf den Grund, [...]

> Noch schlimmer aber wäre, was meine Mutter spricht:
> 'Sie haben auch Raupen im Kopfe!' — das wollte der Engel nicht. (IB, 93)

Underlying the satirical humour, these lines issue a form of critique of those poets who reside purely within an intoxicating world of wine and choose to focus solely on the aesthetic realm of flowers and beauty. Instead, Freytag suggests that poets can be more than this, and that their vocation lies in becoming a form of political tribune for the folk. This position is made clear in 'Der Sänger des Waldes'. The poem opens with 'die deutsche Muse' flying high above the German forests (IB, 29). Dressed for battle with helmet, shield, and sword, she appears to be part-Valkyrie, part-Germania:

> Vor zweimal Tausend Jahren flog über das deutsche Land
> Auf grauem Wolkenrenner ein Weib im Schlachtgewand,
> Die Locken unter dem Helme, den Schild am weißer Hand. [...]
> [Sie] streckte die Hände segnend hin über die Tiefe, die graue.
> Das war die deutsche Muse, sie weihte das Lied der Gaue. (IB, 29)

The muse's presence is felt immediately by a poet in the woods below, who begins to sing a rallying cry to his people:

> Er zählte die Stämme der Männer, des wilden Gottes Kinder,
> Und nannte die Heldenahnen, und stärker und geschwinder
> Erklangen die Schläge des Messers, erhob sich die Brust der Krieger. [...]
> Die Söhne des wilden Gottes begannen die Schlachtenlieder,
> Und schlugen mit ihrem Eisen den Tact in Römerglieder,
> Und sangen dieselbe Weise drei Tag' und Nächte lang. —
> Da hatte die deutsche Lyrik seltsamen, starken Klang. (IB, 30–31)

The poet in 'Der Sänger des Waldes' uses his skills to engage and inspire others: taking the inspiration of his muse, employing poetic imagination — but applying it to a cause. Poetry is not related to godliness or intoxication, but to battle — a national rally cry which would have reverberated politically in the *Vormärz*.

The sense of a different form of poetic engagement, to be found in 'Der Sänger des Waldes', is also explicitly expressed in 'An die Studenten'. The poem opens with a somewhat stereotypical image of the poet — one who sings of love, longing and loss:

> Ihr singt von Liebe ? — Ja, das Herz ist voll
> Und sehnt sich seine Fluthen auszugießen. (IB, 85)

The poem quickly changes tone, however, and argues that the poet's greater vocation is as a warrior, fighting for the future of Germany:

> Auch ihr seid Krieger, sollt zum Kampfe fahren,
> Ihr habt geschworen zu der Weisheit Fahnen. [...]
> Ihr sollt das Wissen härten bis zur That,

> Das Eisen des Gedankens bis zum Stahl. [...]
> Ihr sollt die Freiheit führen von den Bergen
> Des hellen Denkens in das dunkle Thal. (IB, 86)

The cry for action is similar to that in 'Der Sänger des Waldes', while the image of '[d]as Eisen des Gedankens' being forged into steel is reminiscent of Georg Herwegh's poem 'An Ferdinand Freiligrath', which also argues that the poetic pen could function as a sword of steel:

> Ihr müßt das Herz an eine Karte wagen,
> Die Ruhe über Wolken ziemt euch nicht;
> Ihr müßt euch mit in diesem Kampfe schlagen,
> Ein Schwert in eurer Hand ist das Gedicht.[19]

Ultimately, 'An die Studenten' proposes a form of engaged, politically orientated poetry which can coexist alongside tales of love, longing, and pain. For Freytag, it seems that the imaginative poet and the political poet were not mutually exclusive creatures, and that the intoxication and inspiration of the artistic process could be turned to many forms — including politics.

Gustav Freytag's poetic output in the 1840s is hard to characterize in either political or aesthetic terms. The collection *In Breslau* is home to a range of poems which reveal diverse interests: in folk traditions; in narrative; in private, domestic events; and in a politically aware and socially responsive verse. Given this variety, it is essential to keep in mind that Freytag's own terms for his works — *Gelegenheitsgedichte* and *Gesellschaftslieder* — are indications of his poetry's function, rather than their form. Indeed, if one element connects the poems of *In Breslau*, it is their performative purpose: the sense that these are social works produced for presentation in social settings — be that the home or the Breslauer Künstlerverein. *In Breslau* is thus a record of the bourgeois and social roots of Freytag's writing.

As noted throughout this chapter, Freytag's early poems are of considerable interest to scholarship, since they contain — in an incipient form — concerns and issues which became prominent in his later writing. The issue of German nationhood, for instance, has been seen to underlie many of the poems, while, on a more specific note, Freytag's Prussian identity was clearly evident in 'Die Granitschale'. Significantly, Freytag's interest in the German folk and the German past is also manifested in his poems — tendencies generally read as symptomatic of his writing in the 1860s, not the 1840s. In addition, the awareness of a German folk force, ready to come to power, which is present in poems such as 'An Theodor Molinari', 'Die Wellen', 'Die Krone', and 'Ein Kindertraum', is clearly a direct precursor of Freytag's later concept of the *Volkskraft*.

While one should remain cautious of reading Freytag's later impulses retrospectively into the poems of *In Breslau*, the trio of elements of interest in this study — class, nation, and folk — are all present in the collection. Certainly, they remain too disparate to be considered part of a coherent political agenda, but a sense of a German national community, rooted in middle-class and folk concerns, is nonetheless to be found in these imaginative works. And as I explain in the following chapter, it would be in Freytag's *Vormärz* dramas, written in the years immediately prior to the revolution of 1848, that these fragmented political positions began to take on both a clearer and a more strident form.

## Notes to Chapter 1

1. The often-reproduced statistics on readership, as well as a discussion of the novel's critical reception, can be found in T. E. Carter, 'Freytag's *Soll und Haben*: A Liberal National Manifesto as a Best-seller', *German Life and Letters*, 21 (1967–68), 320–29.
2. Gustav Freytag, *In Breslau* (Breslau: Johann Kern, 1845), pp. 3–4. Further references to this edition are given after quotations in the text together with the initials IB.
3. Gustav Freytag, *Gesammelte Werke*, I: *Erinnerungen aus meinem Leben* (Leipzig: Hirzel, 1896), p. 210. Further references to this edition are given after quotations in the text.
4. Gustav Freytag to Duke Ernst von Coburg-Gotha, 7 July 1853, in *Gustav Freytag und Herzog Ernst von Coburg im Briefwechsel, 1853 bis 1893*, ed. by Eduard Tempeltey (Leipzig: Hirzel, 1904), p. 3.
5. On Freytag's early appearance, see Conrad Alberti, *Gustav Freytag: Sein Leben und Schaffen* (Leipzig: Schloemp, 1885), pp. 34–35.
6. Heinrich Heine, *Historisch-kritische Gesamtausgabe der Werke, Düsseldorfer Heine-Ausgabe*, ed. by Manfred Windfuhr, III.1: *Romanzero; Gedichte. 1853 und 1854; Lyrischer Nachlaß. Text* (Hamburg: Hoffmann & Campe, 1992), p. 181.
7. *Handbuch literarisch-kultureller Vereine, Gruppen und Bünde, 1825–1933*, ed. by Karin Bruns, Rolf Parr, and Wulf Wülfing (Weimar: Metzler, 1997).
8. August Heinrich Hoffmann von Fallersleben, *Gedichte* (Berlin: Grote, 1874), p. 22.
9. See Karin Friedrich, 'Cultural and Intellectual Trends', in *19th Century Germany: Politics, Culture and Society, 1780–1918*, ed. by John Breuilly (London: Arnold, 2001), pp. 96–116 (p. 108).
10. Niklaus Becker, *Gedichte*, in *Bibliothek der deutschen Literatur: Mikrofiche-Gesamtausgabe* (Munich: Saur, 1999), B.1/F. 58.
11. Heinrich Heine, *Historisch-kritische Gesamtausgabe der Werke, Düsseldorfer Heine-Ausgabe*, ed. by Manfred Windfuhr, II: *Neue Gedichte. Text. Apparat* (Hamburg: Hoffmann & Campe, 1983), p. 150.
12. See G. Sautermeister, 'Religiöse und soziale Lyrik', in *Hansers Sozialgeschichte der deutschen Literatur vom 16. Jahrhundert bis zur Gegenwart*, ed. by G. Sautermeister and U. Schmid, V: *Zwischen Restauration und Revolution 1815–1848* (Munich: dtv, 1998), pp. 505–25; Christina von Hodenburg, *Aufstand der Weber: Die Revolte von 1844 und ihr Aufstieg zum Mythos* (Bonn: Dietz, 1997).
13. For full details of the *Granitschale*, see Sybille Einholz, 'Die Große Granitschale im Lustgarten: Zur Bedeutung eines Berliner Solitärs', *Der Bär von Berlin: Jahrbuch des Vereins Geschichte für Berlin*, 46 (1997), 41–59.
14. Todd Kontje, *Women, the Novel, and the German Nation, 1771–1871: Domestic Fiction in the Fatherland* (Cambridge: Cambridge University Press, 1998), p. 1.
15. Ibid., p. 5.
16. Ibid., p. 4.
17. Hoffmann von Fallersleben, p. 261.

18. The poem was removed from the memoirs in the second edition of the *Gesammelte Werke*. It can be found in the original 1887 edition: Gustav Freytag, *Erinnerungen aus meinem Leben* (Leipzig: Hirzel, 1887), no page.
19. Georg Herwegh, *Gedichte eines Lebendigen* (Leipzig: Max Helles, [n.d.]), p. 60.

CHAPTER 2

## Defining Class Identities: The *Vormärz* Dramas

Gustav Freytag was not solely preoccupied with his poetry collection *In Breslau* (1845) during the 1840s. Between 1839 and 1845, he was also intent on pursuing an academic career. Having completed his doctoral dissertation on the origins of German drama, and his *Habilitation* thesis on the writings of the nun Hrosvith of Gandersheim, in quick succession (in 1838 and 1839), he became a *Privatdozent* at the University of Breslau, where he lectured on medieval and contemporary German literature, as well as on poetry since Goethe and Schiller. The newly *habilitiert* Freytag was clearly ambitious and planned to write a definitive historical survey of German drama — a logical extension to his doctoral dissertation, which had sought to prove the independence of German theatrical forms from classical topoi. It appeared that Freytag's academic career would take precedence over his potential literary career, relegating his writing to a social activity to be pursued from within the Breslauer Künstlerverein.

However, five years into his activity as *Privatdozent*, Freytag's academic career came to a sudden and unexpected end. The precise reasons for his departure from the university are difficult to reconstruct securely, since our primary source of information about the event is Freytag's own account in his memoirs:

> Ich habe keinen Grund, zu bedauern, daß allmählich die Freude, selbst Dichterisches zu bilden, stärker ward, als der Drang, über dem zu verweilen, was Andere in alter und neuerer Zeit geschaffen haben [...]. Die Weigerung der Facultät, mir eine beabsichtigte Vorlesung über deutsche Culturgeschichte zu gestatten, gab die Veranlassung.[1]

In itself, the university's rejection of a series of lectures on the new discipline of *Kulturgeschichte* was hardly surprising — even the study of *Germanistik* was considered by many in the early 1840s as a dubious novelty. One suspects, however, that there were additional reasons for the premature end to Freytag's academic career. For one thing, Freytag was notoriously bad at public speaking, and had almost failed the oral exams for his *Habilitation* thesis (I, 94). In later life, while an *Abgeordneter* at the Reichstag des Norddeutschen Bundes, he was to face such severe difficulties in engaging in open parliamentary debate that he stepped down as a member of parliament after only one session (see Chapter 4 for a further discussion of this event). It seems unlikely that Freytag was a particularly effective university lecturer.

In addition, Freytag appears to have been embroiled in a number of personal and political disputes with his colleagues at Breslau University. In his biography of Freytag, Conrad Alberti notes how Freytag's seemingly innocuous habit of wearing pale gloves in the lecture theatre irritated his colleagues, who saw it as a dandyish affectation. Certainly more decisive, however, was the publication of a number of Freytag's political poems, and Alberti notes how 'Die Wellen' (1838), in particular, raised eyebrows among Freytag's colleagues.[2] One can imagine how this poem's liberal stance regarding the plight of the Göttingen Seven — forced from their university posts in 1837 after protesting at the removal of Hanover's liberal constitution — could have led the more conservative forces within the university to identify Freytag as politically suspect. Freytag can only have confirmed such suspicions when, in 1842, he openly supported Hoffmann von Fallersleben when the latter was forced to step down from his post at Breslau University after publishing the *Unpolitische Lieder* (1841). The memoirs may suggest that Freytag made a simple decision in 1845 to follow a literary rather than an academic path, but there appears to have been a more complex and politically driven motivation behind the events. It seems that Freytag had little choice in leaving — something which the memoirs are keen to underplay.

With his academic career faltering (though he continued to teach occasionally), Freytag — now aged twenty-eight — increasingly turned to drama. The theatre had preoccupied him throughout the *Vormärz*, and his interest had been more than just academic. In addition to his doctoral and *Habilitation* theses, Freytag had written two dramatic fragments in the late 1830s: *Der Hussit* (1837) and *Die Sühne der Falkensteiner* (1838). The early 1840s saw similar efforts, with a version of the fairy-tale *Dornröschen* and a libretto for an opera, *Russen und Tscherkessen*, also remaining incomplete. These incomplete dramas have never been published. The manuscripts are held at the Staatsbibliothek zu Berlin, Preußischer Kulturbesitz, but are in a highly fragmented state, with the majority of the sheets now lost. Because it is not currently possible to reconstruct them in any detail, they are not included in the following discussion of Freytag's *Vormärz* dramas. However, it is noteworthy in this context that these fragments are contemporaneous with the poems of *In Breslau*, which also often border on the dramatic, with several of the latter containing dialogue and stage directions. Clearly, the impetus towards dramatic performance was common to Freytag's writing during the *Vormärz*, irrespective of genre.

The four *Vormärz* dramas by Freytag under consideration here stem from a period of intense literary production. All four plays were written between 1841 and 1848, and superficially form a diverse corpus of work, ranging from comedy to tragedy and set in both historical and contemporary periods. Thematically, the plays touch on key facets of Freytag's socio-political ideology, by tentatively raising the question of German nationhood and developing a critical stance on the function of class structures within society. Critics, however, have rarely considered the importance of these early plays for Freytag's later oeuvre, and Dieter Kafitz has correctly classed Freytag as a 'vergessene[r] Dramatiker des 19. Jahrhunderts'.[3] Preferring to see Freytag as a social novelist, and thus as a product of the *Nachmärz*, critics forget that his aesthetic and political ideologies were forged in the tempestuous years of the *Vormärz*, and that his initial means of expression was not the novel, but the theatre.

### *Die Brautfahrt, oder Kunz von der Rosen* (1841)

*Die Brautfahrt, oder Kunz von der Rosen* was published in 1844, and written — if Freytag's memoirs are to be believed — in the summer of 1841 (I, 105). The earliest possible composition date of the play is indeterminable, although it was definitely completed by the end of 1841, since Freytag submitted it to a drama competition at the Berliner Hoftheater that year. The account of the competition in Freytag's memoirs is fully corroborated by his detailed correspondence between 1842 and 1847 with Graf Redern and Hofrat von Küstner, the two artistic directors of the Hoftheater.[4]

*Die Brautfahrt* is a historical play, set in Germany's medieval past — a setting it shares with the fragments *Der Hussit* and *Die Sühne der Falkensteiner*. Clearly, the medieval past held a particular fascination for Freytag — an apparent Romantic tendency in the young author. It was members of the Romantic movement — from poets to artists and architects — who first turned exclusively to the Middle Ages in their works, seeking in the past an era of supposed national unity with which to counter the sense of modern dissonance of the post-1789 period. This process was exemplified in the works of August Wilhelm Schlegel and Joseph Görres. Ludwig Tieck — one of Freytag's literary idols — was another of the many who heralded the supposedly medieval qualities of honesty, trust, order, and courtliness as core characteristics of a German national character. From traditionalists such as Joseph von Eichendorff to the radical *Burschenschaftler* in their *altdeutsche Tracht*, figures from diverse political backgrounds began to engage with the medieval and national past. In the words of Schlegel in his *Wiener Vorlesungen über neuere Geschichte* from 1810–11:

> Welche Gemälde bieten unsre Geschichte dar, von den urältesten Zeiten, den Kriegen mit den Römern an, bis zur festgesetzten Bildung des deutschen

Reichs! Dann der ritterlich glänzende Zeitraum des Hauses Hohenstaufen, endlich der politisch wichtigere und uns am nächsten liegende des Hauses Habsburg, das so viele große Fürsten und Helden erzeugt hat. Welch ein Feld für einen Dichter, der wie Shakespeare die poetische Seite großer Weltbegebenheiten zu fassen wüßte![5]

As if following Schlegel's command, an increasing number of dramatists — including Christian Dietrich Grabbe and Franz Grillparzer — produced historical dramas on the Houses of Hohenstaufen and Habsburg, detailing their inexorable rise to European dominance, and with it, the creation of a German Reich. In 1837, for instance, the popular dramatist Ernst Raupach concluded a cycle of sixteen plays entitled *Die Hohenstaufen* for the Hoftheater in Berlin. Almost a decade earlier, in 1829, Grabbe had similarly begun work on a projected cycle of six Hohenstaufen plays. Carl Leberecht Immermann also planned a Hohenstaufen cycle in the mid-1820s, of which only *Friedrich II* (1828) was ever completed, and in 1825 Grillparzer too turned to the national-historical and Habsburg past in his play *König Ottokars Glück und Ende* (1823–25).

Freytag's *Die Brautfahrt* also looks to the history of the House of Habsburg for inspiration, taking as its theme the marriage of Maximilian of Austria and Marie of Burgundy — the birth of the Habsburg Empire. The play follows Maximilian's journey across Burgundy to claim Marie's hand in marriage. We learn how the pair were betrothed to each other as infants, and how Maximilian and Marie have remained faithful in their love for one other, despite the breakdown of relations between the two states. As unrest sweeps across Burgundy, political pressures mount at Marie's court for her to marry. While her advisers urge her to submit to a politically desirous union with France, Marie remains firm in her love for Maximilian. Against this background, the bulk of the play relates Maximilian's adventures across Burgundy with his fool-companion Kunz. Surviving a series of skirmishes with the French, Maximilian arrives at Marie's court and the childhood betrothal is finally fulfilled.

Narratives dealing with the Hohenstaufen and Habsburg dynasties were of such popularity in the period from 1820 to 1840 that even the tale of Maximilian's *Brautfahrt* had been dramatized by other authors before Freytag began work on his play. Johann Ludwig Deinhardstein, the Viennese censor, co-director of the Burgtheater and popular playwright, had written a *dramatisches Gedicht* in five sections entitled *Erzherzog Maximilians Brautzug* (1832), while Heinrich Heine had used the figures of Maximilian I and Kunz in the *Schlusswort* to his *Englische Fragmente* (1830). Freytag's play thus stands in a literary tradition of historically themed projects which turn to a national past in order to talk, both directly and indirectly, of a national future — a political debate conducted by both conservatively minded authors supportive of the restoration, and more radical figures seeking social and political change for Germany.

Shortly after completing work on *Die Brautfahrt*, Freytag submitted the play to a drama competition run by the Prussian Hoftheater in Berlin. According to Freytag's memoirs: 'Das Stück war gerade fertig, als mir in der Zeitung eine Bekanntmachung der Hoftheater-Intendanz zu Berlin in die Hände fiel, worin diese einen Preis für ein Lustspiel höheren Stils aus der Gegenwart ausschrieb' (I, 105). Freytag immediately entered his play, encouraged by the potential remuneration of 50 *Taler* and the possibility of having it included in the repertoire of the Hoftheater. However, it seemed unlikely that *Die Brautfahrt* would win the prize, since the play's historical setting clearly ran counter to the competition's rubric. In addition, *Die Brautfahrt* was only intermittently humorous, which did not bode well for its success in a *Lustspiel* competition. Although *Lustspiel* is a slightly amorphous term, there is no evidence that anything other than a successful comic play was being solicited by the competition's organizers. Freytag's play oscillates between depictions of Maria's situation (generally serious and political in tone) and Maximilian's journey (mostly light-hearted and adventurous) — a division which prevents the development of a sustained comic narrative in the mould of Tieck, Brentano, or Grabbe.

The lack of sustained humour in the play does not, of course, necessarily mean that Freytag did not intend *Die Brautfahrt* to be comic. The play contains certain generic elements of a *Lustspiel*, such as a mix-up over the identity of Maximilian; the presence of buffoon-like figures with comedic names (like the Frenchman Monrepas); and weak attempts at witty repartee between Maximilian and his fool Kunz:

> KUNZ [...] Ich bitte dich, Max, hilf mir wenigstens die Thür verrammen.
> MAX Wozu? [...] Die Thür bleibt offen, der Max fürchtet keine Mörder. — Kunz, es ist ein frommer Glaube, daß jedes Menschenkind seinen Schutzengel habe; auch ich hab' einen Engel, und dem vertrau' ich mich.
> KUNZ Ich wollte lieber, du trautest einem hölzernen Balken.
> MAX Ei alle Thiere fürchten den Löwen, auch wenn er schläft [...].
> KUNZ Du ein Löwe? wärst du lieber ein Hase, dann könntest du wenigstens mit offenen Augen schlafen.[6]

Nevertheless, one suspects a more pragmatic reason for Freytag's choice of *Lustspiel* as his play's subtitle. This supposition is strengthened when one considers that Freytag's other *Vormärz* dramas, which contain similar comedic elements, are called *Schauspiele*. While there is no direct evidence to suggest that *Die Brautfahrt* began life as a historical *Schauspiel* which was then modified into a *Lustspiel* in response to the Hoftheater's competition, one should acknowledge the problematic status of *Die Brautfahrt* as a comedy. For it reveals a basic tension between Freytag's choice of subject matter and the demands of that genre — a tension which can be seen throughout the play.

Remarkably, although *Die Brautfahrt* fulfilled neither of the demands of the Hoftheater competition, Freytag was awarded joint first prize (the name of the other winner is lost). Writing to the *Theaterintendant*, Graf Redern, after hearing of his success, Freytag noted the apparent incongruity of his win:

> Aus den Zeitungen sehe ich mit herzlicher Freude, daß mein Lustspiel *Kunz von den Rosen* [...] einen der gesetzten Preise gewonnen hat. Es kam mir dies fast unerwartet, da das Stück den gestellten Anforderungen allerdings sehr widerspricht.[7]

A clue to the surprising success of *Die Brautfahrt* is perhaps to be found within the internal politics of the Hoftheater in the early 1840s. For in 1840, Prussian cultural institutions such as the Hoftheater found themselves with a new patron — Frederick William IV, the newly crowned King of Prussia. For many, the coronation of Frederick William IV represented a new beginning for Germany after forty-three years of increasingly stagnant and often reactionary rule by Frederick William III. Seemingly enlightened, nationally orientated and deeply romantic, Frederick William IV was known for his love of art and literature and his interest in the German past.[8] The hope invested in the new King soon proved groundless, prompting Heine to write of him:

> [Er] ward ein Zwitter, ein Mittelding,
> Das weder Fleisch noch Fisch ist,
> Das von den Extremen unserer Zeit
> Ein närrisches Gemisch ist.[9]

But in 1841, the year of the Hoftheater competition, expectations for Frederick William IV were still running high. Read within this context, one can understand why *Die Brautfahrt* attracted the attention of the Hoftheater. The play takes a Romantic look at the German past and details the birth of the House of Habsburg, the German Holy Roman Empire, and, by implication, the German nation — an ideal work with which to celebrate the coronation of the new patron and King. In his memoirs, Freytag notes his source of inspiration for *Die Brautfahrt*: 'Aus Fuggers *Ehrenspiegel des Hauses Oestreich* hatte ich die Werbung des Erzherzogs Maximilian um Maria von Burgund aufgenommen. Die bereits poetisch zugerichtete Erzählung gefiel mir so, daß ich ein Lustspiel daraus ersann' (I, 105). In fact, Freytag is known to have drawn on two sources for the play: Johann Fugger's *Ehrenspiegel des Hauses Oestreich* (1590–98), as mentioned in the memoirs, and also Maximilian's own autobiographical account in the *Weißkunig* (1516), as stated in a letter to Graf Redern in 1842.[10] The memoirs do not explain in detail why Freytag chose the story of Maximilian's *Brautfahrt* for his first play, and leave the reader with the impression that he simply stumbled across an appealing historical romance that was particularly well suited for a drama.

Yet the union of Burgundy and Austria in 1477 was an immensely symbolic moment in German history. In the late 1400s, Austria was in the process of building a kingdom, and Burgundy, too, was an established European power, renowned for its riches and with lands including present-day Belgium, the Netherlands, Luxembourg, Franche Comté and Burgundy itself. The dynastic marriage between the two houses enabled the House of Habsburg to inherit the Burgundian lands and wealth, which in turn powered the Habsburgs' rise to European dominance. Indeed, the tradition of dynastic marriage was of such significance for the Habsburgs that it became central to their mythology, as expressed in the dynasty's unofficial motto:

> Bella gerant fortes: tu, felix Austria, nube:
> Nam quae aliis, dat tibi regna Venus.[11]

Within Freytag's play, the marriage of Maximilian to Marie therefore not only represents the rise of the Habsburgs. It also invokes the image of France's subjugation to a Germanic power, and the expansion of the Austro-German borders to include the Netherlands and Belgium. Freytag's subject matter seems to have been chosen with a national reading in mind, its core event allegorically celebrating the birth of a German empire.

Given this national theme, it should be noted that Freytag describes Maximilian I, the Archduke of Austria, as a German. Take, for example, Marie's words of greeting to Maximilian at the climax of the play:

> MARIE [...] Sei mir willkommen, du treues deutsches Blut, ich hab' mich
> lange nach dir gesehnt. (II, 90)

Although this reassignment of German nationality to Maximilian is not entirely unusual for the period — in Grillparzer's *Ein Bruderzwist in Habsburg* (1848), Rudolf II is simultaneously 'wie Östreichs Haupt, wie Deutschlands Herr und Kaiser' — it nevertheless reinforces the German national sensibility of the play, presenting the House of Habsburg as the core of a German rather than an Austrian Empire.[12] Indeed, it is also noteworthy that the empire created by the marriage of Maximilian and Marie is *großdeutsch* in orientation, stretching from the Benelux countries in the north and west to Austria in the south and east. This vision of a *großdeutsch* Germany is distinct from Freytag's position in the *Nachmärz*, which is *kleindeutsch*. The national vision of *Die Brautfahrt* suggests that Freytag at one time subscribed to — or was at least not opposed to — a more open vision of Germany's borders than has been allowed for so far in Freytag criticism.

The subject matter of *Die Brautfahrt* thus provides a potentially rich basis for a national drama. The critic Kurt Classe — one of the few Freytag scholars to consider this early play — has taken this national reading one step further, suggesting that *Die Brautfahrt* is, in fact, an allegory of the Rhine crisis of 1840 — that dispute with the French over the western border of Germany to which

Niklaus Becker's 'Der deutsche Rhein' and Hoffmann von Fallersleben's 'Das Lied der Deutschen' bear testimony.[13] Classe does not develop his idea further, despite a number of similarities between *Die Brautfahrt* and the events of the Rhine crisis. The play is, for instance, concerned with a territorial redefinition of Germany, specifically of the western border, and also opens with a French invasion — reminders, if not direct parallels, of the concerns raised in Germany by the crisis. The play also criticizes the French, in terms which seem to echo their description in Becker's 'Der deutsche Rhein' as 'gierige Raben':[14]

> MAX [...] Der Franzos liebt das Niederland nicht, er freit um euch, wie ein hoffärtiger Junker um eine reiche Bürgerdirne, er ist lüstern nach eurem Gut und Gold [...]. (II, 36)

Freytag was clearly not immune to the potent patriotism dominant in Germany in 1840, echoing the 'Der deutsche Rhein' more directly in his poem 'Die Bauern und der Schulmeister' (1840):

> Und heute noch singt man aus Kreuzweg und Stein:
> Sie sollen nicht haben den deutschen Rhein![15]

Nevertheless, it is difficult to read *Die Brautfahrt* as a direct response to the Rhine crisis. The play is neither jingoistic nor essentially anti-French, and aside from the obvious thematic similarities outlined above, it does not develop a clear allegorical representation of the crisis within its narrative. The similarity is one of context, rather than of content. Instead, it appears as if Freytag was attracted to his historical source material by a more generalized recognition of a similarity connecting past and present, rather than by the desire to depict directly contemporary concerns in a historical scenario.

This is not to say that Freytag was always faithful to his source material, allowing the parallels between past and present to speak for themselves. On the contrary, when dramatizing the story of Maximilian and Marie, he diverged from the historical record in a number of ways. A key discrepancy is in his depiction of Maximilian's and Marie's marriage as the result of love:

> MARIE [...] Ich bin ein freies Weib, und ich will, ich kann nicht leben ohne Liebe. (II, 28)

> MARIE [...] Mein Herz und meine Hand hab' ich als Kind dem adeligsten Herrn der Christenheit verlobt und gedachte im Stillen ihm meinen Schwur zu halten, als ein ehrliches Weib. Lange trug ich meinen Eid allein, unsere Väter waren in Zwist gerathen und des alten Gelübdes wurde nicht mehr gedacht, aber es ist vor Gott und in meinem Herzen kräftig geblieben und die Zeit ist da, es einzulösen. (II, 66)

By emphasizing that the union was a love match, Freytag depicts the foundation of the Empire as more than simply fortuitous — as the chance union of two people and two states. Rather, it is stressed that it was the destiny of the two characters (and by extension, the two nations), to come together and unify.

Historically though, the marriage of Marie and Maximilian was born of political expediency, and the pair had never been betrothed as children. At the age of 14, Maximilian had briefly met Marie during initial marriage negotiations between their parents, Charles of Burgundy and Frederick of Austria, but the talks soon broke down and the engagement was never announced. Only later, after repeatedly suffering defeat at the hands of the French, did Charles give his blessing to the marriage and, even then, only as an means to gain support for his ailing empire. Freytag ignores this element of the historical narrative entirely, opening his play instead with the aftermath of Charles's death and the French invasion of Burgundy.

In these opening scenes, Freytag presents Burgundy as being in a state of civil unrest. Marie is faced with a possible uprising, and her citizens accuse her of treason for considering Maximilian's offer of marriage:

> HANNES    Es ist zu spät, sag' ich euch; wir sind verrathen durch die Herzogin Maria und ihre Räthe, sie wollen uns an das deutsche Reich verkuppeln, mit dem Maximilian verheiraten, dem Wildfang, der uns in die Tasche stecken wird und unsere Batzen dazu.
> EINZELNE    Das leiden wir nicht!
> HANNES    Recht so, und der König von Frankreich will es auch nicht leiden; er ist uns stets ein guter, gnädiger Nachbar gewesen, gar nicht stolz, immer freundlich, und hat auch einen Sohn, welcher für unsere Herzogin paßt; aber die Herzogin ist ein Kind und sträubt sich gegen ihr Glück, und hat dem französischen König auf seine Werbung grob geantwortet; darüber nun ist er zornig geworden und in unser Land gefallen. (II, 5-6)

However, historical accounts of the rise of the Habsburgs, such as that of Edward Crankshaw, relate a different picture from that proposed by Freytag. The majority of Marie's subjects were not in favour of a union with France, correctly fearing that a marriage with the Dauphin — actually only seven years old at the time, and thus hardly an appropriate match for Marie — would signify the utter subjugation of Burgundy to the French enemy.[16] By manipulating such details — by placing Marie in conflict with her people and by making the Dauphin a legitimate suitor — Freytag adds dramatic tension to Marie's choice. In addition, by revealing Marie to be utterly loyal in her love for Maximilian, despite the wishes of her people, Freytag again depicts their union as the result of a greater (romantic) destiny, rather than as a purely political alliance to prevent Burgundian subjugation to France. Throughout the play, Freytag thus manipulates his historical subject matter to fit both his dramatic needs and his ideological scheme — a tendency seen in his later works as well, most notably in his historical novel-cycle *Die Ahnen* (1872–80). In *Die Brautfahrt*, as elsewhere in Freytag, history is less a vehicle for pursuing the truth of events, and more the means with which to create a myth about the birth of the German nation.

Freytag's play differs in one other significant respect from the historical record — the presence of Kunz von der Rosen at Maximilian's side during the latter's *Brautfahrt*. Neither the *Ehrenspiegel des Hauses Oesterreich* nor the *Weißkunig* mention the presence of Kunz. In fact, according to these documents, the jester Kunz first became part of the royal entourage in 1488, over a decade after the events of the play.[17] It thus appears that Freytag anachronistically inserted Kunz into his version of Maximilian's time in Burgundy.

The inclusion of Kunz makes dramatic sense, since it creates a dynamic central pairing around which to build the play's narrative — the pairing of lord and fool which stands in a strong theatrical tradition stretching back to both Shakespeare and the Commedia dell'arte.[18] Yet Kunz's role in the play is clearly more significant than that of a theatrical sidekick or companion to Maximilian, as demonstrated by the play's title, which defies expectations by raising the fool Kunz, rather than the nobleman Maximilian I, to the status of dramatic hero. In his memoirs, Freytag claims that this foregrounding of Kunz was the greatest dramatic weakness of *Die Brautfahrt*, and was the result of his inexperience as a dramatist:

> Allmählich wurde mir der größte Fehler klar. Meine Lieblingsfigur war Kunz von der Rosen. Er war für mich der eigentliche Held, der mir den Stoff vertraulich gemacht hatte, und für ihn war in der Arbeit bei Weitem am meisten geschehen. Und doch war er seinem Wesen nach nur eine dramatische Gestalt zweiten Ranges, ein launiger Begleiter der Handlung, immer fertig, mehr der Autor selbst, als ein bewegter und handelnder Held. Das sollte für die Zukunft eine Lehre sein. (I, 112)

Freytag's late analysis of *Die Brautfahrt* is not only of interest because of its pertinent self-criticism. It also reveals how Kunz became central to the play's concept, acting as a figure of identification for the young author: a mediator between Freytag and the historical subject.

This is also Kunz's primary function for the audience of *Die Brautfahrt*. He explains the historical set-up of the play and often acts as a narrator during key moments, such as the climactic bridal procession. Intimately involved in the events, yet also excluded from them due to his social status as fool, Kunz becomes a form of *Volksstimme* within the aristocratic world of *Die Brautfahrt*. This folk status is emphasized at the end of the play when Kunz must decide whether to join Maximilian in the bridal procession or to watch it from among the people. Kunz symbolically chooses to join the folk, reinforcing the class distinction between himself and Maximilian and temporarily connecting with the play's audience, joining them in their role as spectator:

KUNZ   Nein, mir liegt heut etwas auf der Seele, das muß ich ausschrei'n;
       ich geh' unter das Volk Vivat rufen. (II, 85)

In such moments, Kunz moves beyond the traditional function of the theatrical fool and is temporarily recast as a mouthpiece of and for the people. Acting as a point of identification for the modern audience, he becomes an incipient form of Freytag's later concept of the *Volkskraft* — an ever-present bourgeois spirit which links past and present. When Freytag later described the function of the *Volkskraft* in the dedication to his *Bilder aus der deutschen Vergangenheit* (1859–67), he could well have been describing Kunz's role in *Die Brautfahrt*: 'Es rührt und es stimmt heiter, wenn wir in der Urzeit genau denselben Herzschlag erkennen, der noch uns die wechselnden Gedanken der Stunde regelt'.[19] In many respects, the folk function of Freytag's Kunz is also reminiscent of Heine's use of Kunz in the *Schlusswort* to his *Englische Fragmente* (1830). Heine's Kunz similarly sheds his function as the fool and becomes the spirit of the folk, symbolically represented by the loss of the bells from his fool's hat:

> Kunz von der Rosen, mein Narr, du hast ja die Schellen verloren von deiner rothen Mütze, und sie hat jetzt so ein seltsames Ansehen, die rothe Mütze.
> Ach, mein Kaiser, ich habe ob Eurer Noth so wüthend ernsthaft den Kopf geschüttelt, daß die närrischen Schellen abfielen von der Mütze; sie ist aber darum nicht schlechter geworden. [...] O, deutsches Vaterland! theures deutsches Volk! ich bin dein Kunz von der Rosen.[20]

Although Heine's depiction of Kunz is politically more radical than Freytag's — for Heine, he represents revolution — the similarity between the two figures, specifically in their function as figures of folk identification, certainly suggests that Freytag was aware of Heine's use of Kunz. We have no specific evidence that Freytag had read Heine, but given that Freytag lectured on contemporary German poetry since Goethe and Schiller, it seems extremely likely that he was, at the very least, aware of Heine's writings. Literary influence cannot be proved, but the similarities between the two passages remain significant.

Kunz not only functions as a means of identification with the folk within the play. He also acts as the mouthpiece for the more tendentious moments of *Die Brautfahrt*. Take, for instance, his remarks on the aristocracy:

> KUNZ   Ich hasse dies freche Junkerwesen wie den Tod. Trinken, lärmen, mit Zucht und feiner Sitte sich breit machen, ohne deren mehr zu haben, als nöthig ist, um einen Weinschenken zu betrügen, und ehrliche Leute verlachen, weil ihr Kleid nicht modisch zugeschnitten ist, das ist ihr Alles. Und dabei ließen sie Land und Volk erhenken, ohne daß ihnen der Daumen zuckte. Solch vornehme Müßiggänger sind die schlechtesten Pilze, welche der Sonnenschein aus der Erde zieht, und es ist mir eine wahre Freude, sie zu zertreten. (II, 44–45)

Such comments introduce a note of dissent into *Die Brautfahrt* which would otherwise be absent, and help balance the wholly positive depiction of the aristocrats Maximilian and Marie by invoking the spectre of a semi-debauched, exploitative, petty nobility. Admittedly, such moments are limited in number, and *Die Brautfahrt* cannot be read as a systematic anti-aristocratic critique. Nevertheless, Kunz's comments clearly contain incipient elements of the class critique which will recur with increasing frequency in Freytag's subsequent works, including the final three of his *Vormärz* dramas.

Kunz also voices criticism of a range of other targets, most frequently through a generalized lampooning of the French, although the folk too are not immune to his tongue:

> KUNZ   Gott des Himmels! Wie gleichst du diesem Buben, mein deutsches Volk! Du könntest ein Herr der Welt sein, wenn du nicht auch alle Tage Furcht hättest, dir die Hosen zu beschmutzen. (II, 35)

Although such comments are again intermittent, they also contain the basic elements of a message familiar to readers of Freytag's later works, namely that for Germany to reach its full potential, the folk must act together. It is also precisely the message of the opening poem of *In Breslau*, as noted in Chapter 1. Kunz's lines are a call to action for the German people, and as such speak as much to the generation of 1840 as to that of 1477. Kunz is the key figure of *Die Brautfahrt*: a form of connection to the historical past for both Freytag and his audience. Through Kunz, Freytag can add elements to his drama that would be absent from the historical narrative, articulating criticism — albeit unsystematically — against the aristocracy. By noting what Kunz condemns (the aristocracy, the French) and what he represents (a folk voice and a sense of Germany's national potential) we can identify not only the core concerns of *Die Brautfahrt*, but also Freytag's developing political ideology in the *Vormärz*.

One should not overplay a national reading of *Die Brautfahrt*. The play's pursuit of a national agenda remains fragmented and unsystematic, and the text suffers from a basic tension between its historical subject matter, the demands of the comedic genre, and the still incipient nature of Freytag's political ideologies. Consequently, the play frequently fails on all three fronts, satisfying neither as historical drama, nor as *Lustspiel*, nor as national project. It is hardly surprising that *Die Brautfahrt* struggled to gain an audience whenever it was staged. Ironically, the play was even refused performance at the Hoftheater in Berlin, despite its having won the theatre's competition: the *Theaterintendant* ultimately chose to pay Freytag compensation rather than stage the work — a fact known from Freytag's correspondence with the *Intendant*. This rejection can be seen as a negative assessment of the play's functionality as a practical piece of theatre and was undoubtedly a major blow for Freytag.

However, despite *Die Brautfahrt*'s structural problems, it is difficult not to read the play as at heart a political fable on Germany's rise to power. The marriage of Maximilian and Marie in 1477 and the subsequent revitalization of the House of Habsburg is a powerful moment from German national history. Take this moment and place it within the context of the political situation of 1840 — namely the renewed enthusiasm for monarchy surrounding Frederick William IV and the patriotic fervour resulting from the Rhine crisis — and the national tenor of Freytag's drama becomes inescapable. Freytag manipulates his historical material, stressing the role of destiny in the foundation of the German Reich through the love story, and introducing the figure of Kunz von der Rosen in order to provide a suitable folk voice in the play. The links to the *Englische Fragmente* raise the possibility that Freytag's Kunz could be an intentional de-revolutionization of Heine's figure, mirroring his own sense of foreboding at a forthcoming revolution (discussed in detail in Chapter 3). Freytag might not yet have found the correct balance between genre, content, and ideology, but the elements of class, nation, and folk so central to his later work are already recognizably present in the drama of *Die Brautfahrt*.

### *Der Gelehrte* (1844)

Freytag's follow-up to *Die Brautfahrt* could not have been more different in tone. From the historical comedy of Kunz and Max, Freytag's focus switched to a contemporary tragedy of the aristocracy and the folk: *Der Gelehrte*. Initially, dating the play appears simple. The edition in the *Gesammelte Werke* (1896) is dated 1844, and this is corroborated by the description of the play's composition in Freytag's memoirs. These mutually reinforcing claims are, however, difficult to verify. Freytag's memoirs do not record whether *Der Gelehrte* was ever published prior to its inclusion in the collected works, nor are there any known performances of the play which help locate its composition. One is seemingly left to rely on the unsubstantiated account in the *Gesammelte Werke*.

However, by working through the first editions of Freytag's works we can date *Der Gelehrte* with more accuracy. The play first appears in the 1854 edition of the *Dramatische Werke*, where it is dated 1844. A further clue can be found in a letter from Freytag to his publisher, Salomon Hirzel, from October 1847. In this letter — one of the few extant from the 1840s — Freytag talks about his *Vormärz* dramas:

> Aus dem mir übersandten Verzeichniß der Vorstellungen sehe ich, daß die letzte dritte doch 300 Thlr. gebracht hat, als ist sie doch wohl nicht abgespielt. [...] Ein kleines Stück von mir werden Sie in dem poetischen Taschenbuch für 48, Verlagsbureau finden. [...] Mein Winterstück ist leider noch nicht fertig.[21]

Three plays are under discussion in the letter. Alfred Dove, the editor of

Freytag's correspondence with Hirzel, has identified them as *Die Brautfahrt*, *Der Gelehrte*, and *Graf Waldemar* respectively. Dove's editorial handling of Freytag's letters has been criticized in recent research, and his identification of the texts under discussion in the letter appears similarly flawed.[22] It is unlikely, for instance, that the 300 *Taler* revenue refers to *Die Brautfahrt*, given the failure of that play during its early performances in 1842. A more likely candidate is Freytag's play *Die Valentine* (1846), which was in performance in 1847 and would have been generating revenue at the time of the letter's composition.

However, despite such inaccuracies, Dove's suggestion that the 'kleines Stück [...] in dem poetischen Taschenbuch für 48' refers to *Der Gelehrte* appears well founded.[23] It is corroborated by the critic Constantin Rössler, who notes in his 1860 study of Freytag that *Der Gelehrte* was first published 'in Ruge's *Poetischen Bildern*'.[24] The similarity between 'poetischen Taschenbuch' and *Poetischen Bildern* is striking, while the name Ruge undoubtedly refers to Arnold Ruge, an acquaintance from Freytag's Breslau days who was responsible for a series of anthological volumes in the mid-1840s with titles such as *Politische Bilder aus der Zeit* and *Die politischen Lyriker unserer Zeit*, and with whom Freytag had published one of his early poems, 'Der polnische Bettler' (see the discussion in Chapter 1). Working through such publications from the years 1847 to 1848, one can locate the first place of publication of *Der Gelehrte*: in Ruge's *Poetische Bilder aus der Zeit*, published in Leizpig in 1847. Given that Freytag was working on *Die Brautfahrt* for the *Hoftheater* competition in 1841, it seems likely that *Der Gelehrte* was primarily composed some time between 1841 and 1847, thus allowing for a composition date of 1844, as set out in Freytag's memoirs. If one compares all three published editions (1847, 1854, and 1896) it becomes clear that the 1847 text underwent a number of small revisions before being republished in 1854, while the 1896 edition is a reprint of the 1854 text with only minor typographic corrections.

*Der Gelehrte* itself remains a fragment: the first act of a proposed three-act tragedy. The setting is an estate close to an unnamed court, some time in the early 1840s, and is reminiscent of settings in both Joseph von Eichendorff's and Ludwig Tieck's works. Tieck's later novellas, such as *Des Lebens Überfluß* (1839), frequently detail life near the regional court and share Freytag's interest in the interactions between the aristocracy and the bourgeoisie. Freytag is known to have admired Tieck, as revealed in a letter from 1847 to Hirzel:

> Haben Sie die Güte, die Beilage [an edition of *Die Valentine*] an Tieck abzugeben [...]. Wir müssen recht hübsch mit ihm thun, denn er ist der letzte von den Großen, 'die ihr Titanenhaupt vor uns gewaltig schütteln'; wenn wir den Kopf schütteln, so will das nicht mehr viel sagen.[25]

Freytag's memoirs display a similar reverence towards Tieck, describing him as a 'Vertreter einer glorreichen Zeit deutscher Dichtkunst' (I, 142). Freytag even dedicated his 1847 play *Graf Waldemar* to the older author. It is easy to understand why the Romantic Tieck, with his interest in the medieval past and his morally inclined stance on social issues, would have appealed to Freytag. Both *Der Gelehrte* and *Des Lebens Überfluß* are, for instance, concerned with issues of social predetermination and the role of the individual within society. Although it is too great a step to suggest that Freytag's play was directly influenced by Tieck's late work — their common themes are too broad and are reflected in other writing of the period — the similarities remain intriguing and are strengthened by Freytag's enthusiasm for the older author.

*Der Gelehrte* opens with the academic Walter, who is working as an archivist on the estate owned by Leontine. Walter is in love with Leontine, and is excited at the prospect of her return from travels abroad. The names here strike one as having been borrowed from Eichendorff: Walter the bourgeois figure who *waltet*; Leontine the sensual and erotic female — identities that echo Eichendorff's novel *Dichter und ihre Gesellen* (1834). Romberg, a liberal journalist and Walter's friend, arrives, determined to persuade Walter to leave the academic profession and edit a new liberally inclined newspaper. Walter refuses and a heated exchange develops between the two friends on the nature of political engagement. Leontine returns home, breaking the news that, in order to settle an old family argument about the ownership of her estate, she is to marry the aristocrat Reginald. Reginald, who also appears, soon grows jealous of Walter's relationship with Leontine and connives to have Walter reassigned to a government position away from Leontine. Walter rejects the post, arguing idealistically that his abilities need to be used to serve the many, rather than the few. As Reginald announces his engagement to Leontine, Walter breaks down and, possessed by madness, leaves the estate with the intention of seeking an authentic existence among the folk.

Although the setting of *Der Gelehrte* is contemporary, Freytag chose to write the work in iambic pentameters. In his memoirs, the author explains how he 'fand eine Befriedigung darin, daß ich mich an einem modernen Stoff mit unserm dramatischen Jambus versucht und die Sprache gefunden hatte, in der nach meiner Meinung ein Schauspiel in Versen zu behandeln war' (I, 131). One senses that Freytag's choice of the iambic pentameter was not merely aesthetic. By choosing this metre, he could prove that contemporary concerns and political debates were appropriate subjects for a serious, high drama. His choice of tragedy as a genre can also be read in this light. Freytag's memoirs suggest he was pleased with the result, but, as will be seen in the following discussion, achieving a synthesis of modern content and classical form proved to be a greater challenge than the memoirs suggest, and *Der Gelehrte* would remain an experimental fragment.

The shift from the historical setting of *Die Brautfahrt* to the contemporary setting of *Der Gelehrte* was accompanied by a shift in genre: from comedy to tragedy. The young Freytag clearly enjoyed experimenting with different dramatic genres during the 1840s — years in which he also composed the fairy-tale fragment *Dornröschen* and the incomplete opera-libretto *Russen und Tschekerssen*. It is difficult, however, to view *Der Gelehrte* as a (for lack of another word) successful tragedy. On the most basic level, the incomplete nature of the text hinders any such assessment: the first act describes a series of events which could form the basis for a tragedy, yet we never witness the tragic outcome. In addition, Freytag's plans for the remaining two acts of *Der Gelehrte* propose a rather peculiar vision of a tragedy with a happy ending. Freytag explains the proposed ending to his play retrospectively in his memoirs:

> [D]ie zweite [Abteilung]: Gegensätze und Kämpfe, in welche Walter als Werkführer in dem Geschäft eines großen Steinmetzen mit den Arbeitern geräth [...]. Nachdem er verschwunden, erscheint Leontine als Verlobte des Fürsten auf Reisen, sie ist nach jener Trennung von Walter in Tiefsinn versunken [...]. Dritte Abtheilung: der Familienstreit ist auf's Neue entbrannt, die Güter der Leontine sind dem Fürsten zugesprochen, der Freund Walters ist sein Geschäftsführer geworden [...]. Conflicte, Erklärungen, Vereinigung der Liebenden. (I, 130)

Such comments lead one to question Freytag's understanding of tragedy as a genre. As an academic specializing in classical and German drama, Freytag could be expected to be aware of the core elements of classical tragedy and Aristotelian concepts such as *hamartia*, *peripeteia*, and *anagnorisis*. Yet his clearest statement on tragedy (in *Die Technik des Dramas* from 1859) rejects 'die wohltönenden Worte Schuld und Reinigung, Läuterung und Erhebung'.[26] Instead, Freytag develops his own idiosyncratic concept of 'das tragische Moment', which shares some elements with *peripeteia* but is far broader in its focus and does not have to end in sorrow:

> Das tragische Moment muß [...] folgende drei Eigenschaften haben: 1) es muß wichtig und folgenschwer für den Helden sein, 2) es muß unerwartet aufspringen, 3) es muß durch eine dem Zuschauer sichtbare Kette von Nebenvorstellungen in vernünftigem Zusammenhang mit früheren Theilen der Handlung stehen. (XIV, 85)

*Der Gelehrte* was written fifteen years before Freytag developed this definition in *Die Technik des Dramas*, yet strikingly, the first act of the play conforms to the later specifications for the tragic moment. For instance, it hints on several occasions at a tragic outcome, particularly in the love scenes between Walter and Leontine. These scenes are scattered with references to the lovers' dark and difficult future:

> WALTER [...] was ich fühl', ist Schwäche,
> Vielleicht ein Nervenreiz [...]

>     Er muß hinweg aus meines Lebens Bau,
>     Oder das Leben selbst in Trümmer gehn. (II, 116)
>
> WALTER  Mit finstrer Sorge seh' ich, daß ein Sturm
>     Ihr reines Dasein zu bewölken droht [...] (II, 119)

Such allusions are a form of dramatic shorthand between author and audience, playing on the audience's knowledge of tragic topoi and alerting them to the tragic potential of the relationship. Walter's sudden (if subtly prefigured) descent into mental turmoil at the end of the play is also an unexpected climax — 'es muß unerwartet aufspringen' — which has grave consequences for the protagonist — 'es muß wichtig und folgenschwer für den Helden sein' (XIV, 85). *Der Gelehrte* thus conforms to all the elements of Freytag's later concept of the tragic moment. Nevertheless, tragic love stories do not generally end in the successful union of lovers, and the tension between the tragic moment and the proposed outcome of the text remains somewhat glaring. Why propose a happy ending to a tragedy?

A closer reading of *Die Technik des Dramas* provides one potential answer. For this work of dramatic theory is primarily concerned with recasting the dramatic theories of Aristotle in order to allow a bourgeois tragedy to end with a positive, didactic message. Death, Freytag argues in his theory, often negates the edifying function of a tragedy, providing characters with easy absolution. Far better, he claims, would be a tragedy which demonstrates the need for absolution through life — through learning from the error of one's ways:

> In einer Zeit, in welcher man sogar über Abschaffung der Todesstrafe verhandelt hat, sind die Toten am Endes eines Stückes, so scheint es, leichter zu entbehren; wir trauen in der Wirklichkeit einer starken Menschenkraft zu, daß sie die Pflicht des Lebens sehr hoch halte, auch schwere Missethat nicht durch den Tod, sondern durch ein reineres Leben büße. (XIV, 99–100)

The precise mechanisms of this relatively complex, and to modern eyes peculiar, effort to produce a tragedy with a happy and moralistic end, are analysed in detail in Chapter 4. For current purposes, however, it is important to note how closely *Der Gelehrte* appears to fit the theoretical understanding of drama that Freytag later sets out — suggesting, potentially, that he had already been developing this theoretical model in his own dramatic practice of the *Vormärz*.

Another reason why Freytag might have chosen to give his tragedy a happy end lies in his concept of marriage as a tool of social structuring. While the incomplete nature of *Der Gelehrte* hampers a detailed analysis of this process in the play, the text nevertheless contains a number of elements which suggest that the inter-class relationship between the bourgeois Walter and the aristocrat Leontine was intended to function as part of an anti-aristocratic polemic. For instance, the aristocratic counter-lover Reginald is depicted negatively, as a scheming demagogue more interested in his own needs than those of others. In addition, the play emphasizes how the strong bourgeois figure Walter is able to rescue the relatively weak aristocrat Leontine:

> LEONTINE  [...] Denn immer fand
> Ich Sie mit meinem bessern Sein verbunden,
> So oft ich wankte. — Freund, ich wanke jetzt,
> Ich fühle mich getheilt, uneinig, schwach. [...]
> WALTER  [...] Sie haben mich gerufen, und ich will
> Ein Wächter sein für Sie [...] (II: 118–19)

Such elements conform to Freytag's pattern of the salvation of aristocratic figures through their interaction with the bourgeoisie, seen in his later works *Die Fabier* (1859) and *Die Ahnen*, and his following two plays, *Die Valentine* and *Graf Waldemar*. In order to function as a political statement, Walter and Leontine must marry, to form a socially symbolic inter-class union — even if this happy ending runs counter to the tragic love story already initiated. That Freytag's next two plays focus precisely on the symbolic value of inter-class relationships and contain vigorous anti-aristocratic commentary strengthens the supposition that this was also his original intention for *Der Gelehrte*.

A similar tension between the conflicting demands of genre and ideology can be seen in the depiction of Walter. At the climax of Act One, Walter decides to pursue an authentic life from among the folk. As noted in the discussion of Freytag's poetry, Freytag saw the folk as central to the future of Germany, and Walter's decision to join them is an important ideological statement of the play. Yet Walter's symbolic act of becoming one with the people is somewhat undermined by his simultaneous state of madness after losing Leontine to Reginald:

> ROMBERG  Du bist in Wahnsinn und ich lass' dich nicht!
> Dies starre Antlitz, dein verstörter Blick — (II, 131)

Walter's generic role as a deranged lover and his proposed role as spokesperson for the folk are hard-to-reconcile elements, which Freytag forces into an uncomfortable union. *Der Gelehrte* thus finds itself in a rhetorical bind, attempting to be a tragic love story with a happy ending, with a folk-hero suffering from insanity. It is a conflict that threatens to undermine the entire text.

The first act of *Der Gelehrte* is inherently political in tone. Early critics such as Hans Lindau, Kurt Classe, and Eduard Rothfuchs have argued that (to quote Classe) the play presents 'vollkommen ein Abbild der politischen Strömungen jener bewegten Epoche, die der Revolution des Jahres 1848 vorausging'.[27] These critics read the play as a direct expression of Freytag's political experiences of the 1840s: '[Freytag führt] als Grund zu seinem Drama an, daß er sich, obgleich er ein fester Liberaler war, oft im Gegensatz zu dem geräuschvollen und flachen Gebaren des Jungen Geschlechtes fühlte'.[28] However, as is often the case in early Freytag criticism, such interpretations are not based on a close analysis of the text, but rather — in the last example word for word — on Freytag's memoirs, which similarly state: 'Ich fühlte mich, obgleich ich ein fester Liberaler war, oft im Gegensatz zu dem geräuschvollen und flachen Gebahren des jungen Geschlechts' (I, 129–30). Despite such issues, Classe and Rothfuchs are nevertheless correct to argue for a political reading of *Der Gelehrte*. After the historical comedy of *Die Brautfahrt*, the play marks a more overtly political tone in Freytag's writing, and it attempts to engage with the present in a manner otherwise found only in a number of Freytag's early political poems. This tone is most frequently expressed through the character of Walter, especially during his lengthy debate with Romberg which opens Act One. Romberg has arrived to persuade Walter to take part in a new newspaper, intended to be the mouthpiece of liberal ideology among the folk:

> ROMBERG [...] Nie trat noch ein Unternehmen
> So glänzend, sicher, hoffnungsvoll an's Licht,
> Die Edelsten sind im Verein, das Volk
> Für freie Lebensformen zu erziehen. (II, 96)

Walter, however, is convinced that Romberg's liberal programme of education is nothing less than tyranny in a different form:

> WALTER [...] Ihr liebt das Volk, weil ihr's zu leiten hofft [...]
> Und hättet ihr die Herrschaft, die ihr sucht,
> Ihr wär't Tyrannen [...]. (II, 100–01)

Such discussions touch briefly yet significantly on the debates on the role of education within society prevalent in nineteenth-century Germany. In the first two decades of the century, Germany had developed an advanced and liberal education system under the leadership of Wilhelm von Humboldt. Humboldt believed in the educational ideal of individual development, and actively sought to exclude the state from educational policy and regulation.[29] However, by the 1840s, conservative forces increasingly sought to alter policy so that education would directly serve the needs of the state. Schools and universities were seen as institutions which could prepare citizens of all classes for an appropriate and productive role within the state.[30] This move was also prompted by a reactionary desire to curb potential forms of political radicalism within the education system — radicalism no longer solely located in the universities and the *Burschenschaften*. Debate frequently focused on the function of the *Volksschule* and the *Realschule* as institutions capable of both furthering and controlling the position of the folk within society.[31]

Such educational debates also found reflection in literature, with authors such as Jeremias Gotthelf producing morally inclined, popular, and educative works during the *Vor-* and *Nachmärz*, although one senses a clear distinction between the conservative, essentially controlling, educational schemes of Gotthelf and Romberg's desire to encourage 'freie Lebensformen' among the folk (II, 96). Nevertheless, the debate on education in the play and the connection Walter draws between freedom and control can be seen as reflecting the concerns of educational thinking in mid-nineteenth-century Germany. These questions were, indeed, symptomatic of an even larger issue of the era: that of the function of the state, the individual, and the class system within society.

Similar themes are also raised in *Der Gelehrte*. Walter's stance in the play is anti-hegemonistic, anti-particularist, and anti-tyrannical. He sees no difference between Romberg's concept of freedom for the folk and the despotism of the particularist state:

> WALTER [...] Ein Diamant
> Ist eure Freiheit, die ihr unsrem Volk
> Verehren wollt [...].
> [...] Ich aber bin
> Gewöhnt zu denken, daß der Diamant
> Und euer Feind, die Kohle, nach Natur,
> Art und Bestandtheil sehr genau verwandt,
> Fast eines und dasselbe sind. (II, 98)

Rejecting Romberg's concepts, Walter argues that the folk must come to self-awareness on their own terms, rather than through the imposition of education and ideals from above. He essentially becomes the mouthpiece for an incipient formulation of Freytag's concept of the *Volkskraft*. Like Kunz in *Die Brautfahrt*, Walter stresses the potential power of the German folk:

> WALTER Beschränke dich im Kreis des kleinsten Mannes,
> [...] Laß jeden Einzelnen zum Mann erst werden
> In seinem Kreise, wo er sicher schafft, —
> Dann reift das Volk von selbst für Mannesthat! (II, 99–100)

This positive vision of a folk force ready to rise to power stands in stark contrast to many conservatively inclined authors of the 1840s, such as Eichendorff and Gotthelf, and even differs from that of the liberally inclined Heine, whose feelings towards the folk fluctuated between identification ('Ich selber bin Volk') and fear ('Ich berichtete oft und bestimmt über die Dämonen, welche in den untern Schichten der Gesellschaft lauerten').[32] As a whole, Freytag's concept of folk is distinct from that of these authors, since it is essentially bourgeois in character, and rarely includes the working classes, the proletariat or the truly poor (an aspect discussed in detail in Chapter 4). Walter's function as the mouthpiece for the folk comes particularly strongly to the fore at the end of Act One, in a debate with a government minister. Walter argues that society is falling ill as a consequence of the division between government and folk — a tension that can only be overcome by joining the folk and using one's skills for the greater good:

> WALTER   Hier liegt der Weg, die Spannung zu vernichten,
> An der wir kranken, uns heraufzuziehen
> Den Tag, wo sich Regierung und das Volk,
> Der Gegensatz, zu schöner Einheit bindet [...].
> Ich blieb' ein Mann auf meine eigne Hand,
> Und säße nieder an dem Herd des Volkes,
> Zu schaffen und zu fühlen wie das Volk,
> In kleinem Kreise tüchtig stark zu sein,
> Damit ich stark sei für das große Ganze. (II, 123)

Essentially, Walter is proposing an inversion of the power hierarchies of 1840s Germany, where the folk takes power and the exploitative grip of particularism is overthrown. When questioned by the Minister as to who exactly would have power in this scenario, Walter's answer is unequivocal: 'Das Volk' (II, 123). If one combines this inversion of political hierarchies with the breakdown of class structures represented in the inter-class relationship of Walter and Leontine, then *Der Gelehrte* becomes a radical re-imagining of German society.

Walter acts on his words when, at the end of the play, he gives up his life as an academic and chooses to join the folk. However, in Walter's scheme it is not enough simply to join the masses; one must work with them too, using one's talents for the greater good. In stressing the significance of work as a moral and social responsibility, the ending of *Der Gelehrte* seems to point towards a key thematic thread of Freytag's later novel *Soll und Haben* (1855), prefiguring that text's motto: 'Der Roman soll das deutsche Volk da suchen, wo es in seiner Tüchtigkeit zu finden ist, nämlich bei seiner Arbeit'.[33] The conflict between academic life and practical work expressed by Walter in *Der Gelehrte* is also a central issue in Freytag's 1864 novel *Die verlorene Handschrift*, which details in part the clash between academic pursuits and the world of farming. Thus in many respects, *Der Gelehrte* is a repository for themes which repeatedly return in Freytag's later writings of the *Nachmärz* (detailed in Chapters 3 and 4).

Two distinct visions of German society are put forward in the play: Walter's belief in the power of the folk, and Romberg's political agenda of education. Although attention here has focused primarily on the statements of Walter, which prefigure many of the later issues raised in Freytag's writings, Romberg's counterarguments also deserve brief mention. In the play, Romberg voices an important plea for engagement with 'die Riesenfluth | Der Gegenwart' (II, 97), repeatedly criticizing Walter for his political apathy (reminiscent of Kunz's attack on the apathy of the bourgeoisie in *Die Brautfahrt*). It is important to note that it is Romberg's words which ultimately prompt Walter to join the folk and act upon his otherwise somewhat abstract vision of a German folk society — something Walter himself acknowledges:

WALTER  Ja, es ist jammervoll, wie schwach wir sind.
's ist eine Stunde kaum, da trieb ich höhnend
Den Freund [Romberg] vom Herzen, der mein Selbstgefühl,
Die sichre Ruh' des Denkers, warnend strafte.
Kaum eine Stunde, und ich bin zerbrochen [...]. (II, 115)

Romberg is thus an important catalyst in the play, his ideal of political engagement (if not the actual content of his ideology) finding affirmation in the text. Critics have failed to note that, within four years of completing *Der Gelehrte*, Freytag himself became the editor of the liberal magazine *Die Grenzboten* — a publication the aim of which was to promote the social, political, and artistic programme of the liberal bourgeoisie. Freytag, it would appear, would ultimately become Romberg, and thus Romberg's political views in the play cannot be dismissed outright, even if greater emphasis in the play is given to those of Walter.

Although the content of *Der Gelehrte* is clearly political, the text, by presenting political positions in the form of an argument between two friends, can be seen as stepping back from overt political engagement, privatizing the political discourse. This withdrawal from the public sphere is significant, since it is a process repeated in Freytag's later works. Freytag's novels *Soll und Haben*, *Die verlorene Handschrift*, and *Die Ahnen* all deal with political issues, but indirectly, through the private worlds of home, friendship, and love. Such a tendency — often seen as a reaction of *Nachmärz* fiction against the *Tendenzdichtung* of the *Vormärz* — is thus already present in Freytag's writings of the 1840s, an interesting and significant aspect to these early works.

The figures of Walter and Romberg are personifications of two sides in a political debate which is essentially concerned with Germany's future, indirectly raising issues of nationhood. Walter stresses how the folk will rise to power, but argues against the imposition of political ideals from above to achieve this goal. Although *Der Gelehrte* does raise the spectre of fundamental social change — the breakdown of political and class hegemonies — Freytag is not revealed to be a supporter of political revolution. Instead, the text stresses how a social evolution within the folk is the means to achieve a new social model.

However, like its predecessor *Die Brautfahrt*, *Der Gelehrte* ultimately succumbs to a conflict between the demands of genre and the ideological content it wishes to promote. Freytag's desire to present a class reconciliation through the marriage of Walter and Leontine runs counter to the demands of a tragic love story. Similarly, a positive tale on the future power of the folk would not normally end in tragedy, nor have for its main advocate a madman. For instance, although Georg Büchner's *Woyzeck* (1836–37) does have an apparently insane figure as its hero, and ends in tragedy, it does not attempt to combine this with an overtly didactic lesson about positive bourgeois values. One can understand why Freytag abandoned *Der Gelehrte* after its first act. There is simply no outcome that could satisfy these competing elements of ideology and genre.

### *Die Valentine* (1846) and *Graf Waldemar* (1846–47)

Given Freytag's difficulties in following the genre conventions of comedy and tragedy in his plays *Die Brautfahrt* and *Der Gelehrte*, it strikes one as significant that his final two theatrical projects of the *Vormärz* should be labelled merely *Schauspiele*. The *Schauspiel*, although generally serious in tone, does not adhere to tragic conventions, and moments of comedy can sit alongside more earnest themes.[34] Freytag appeared finally to find a form in which he could pursue both his theatrical and his political aims without compromising either.

Freytag wrote two *Schauspiele* in quick succession in the late 1840s — *Die Valentine* (1846) and *Graf Waldemar* (1846–47). In his memoirs, Freytag describes these two plays as 'Gegenstück[e]' (I, 141). Such a description seems appropriate: both plays share the same contemporary setting of 1840s Germany, and both revolve around inter-class relationships — in each, bourgeois figures present the upper classes with an alternative to a negatively depicted aristocratic value system.

Structurally, the melodramatic plots of the two plays are also similar. *Die Valentine* opens with the return to Germany of its hero, Georg, after fifteen years of exile. Georg had fled Germany while a student, fearing arrest for his *Burschenschaft* activities. Arriving at the court with a message for Valentine, the lady-in-waiting to Princess Marie, he stumbles on a world of political and marital intrigue. Marie must marry the Prince in order to secure the future of her lands and people, but Valentine also wishes to marry the Prince so as to increase her own political power. Georg attempts to persuade Valentine to give up her plans, and in the process, falls in love with her. Meeting secretly in Valentine's rooms, he convinces her that it is ambition, rather than love, that draws her to the Prince. Valentine admits as much, and she agrees to relinquish her scheme. However, before Georg is able to leave, he is discovered with Valentine and, to prevent a scandal, he poses as a thief and is arrested. After much soul-searching, Valentine chooses to sacrifice her own good name rather than see an innocent man wrongly imprisoned. Georg is released and the two confess their love for each other. The play ends by raising the prospect of Georg and Valentine using their combined talents to spearhead the rejuvenation of Germany and the folk.

The plot of *Graf Waldemar* similarly focuses on an inter-class relationship, set against the backdrop of a complex and increasingly melodramatic love story. The play opens with the aristocrat Waldemar learning that he has an illegitimate child. Gertrud, a market gardener's daughter, has been taking care of this child after it had been abandoned by its mother, Luise. In the meantime, Waldemar has become involved with a wealthy widow, Georgine. In turn, Georgine is facing the advances of her former brother-in-law, Fedor Jwanowitsch. Jealous of Waldemar's relationship with Georgine, Fedor plots to have Waldemar killed, but the attempt fails and a wounded Waldemar seeks refuge at Gertrud's house. During his recuperation, he falls in love with Gertrud. Georgine comes in a jealous rage to see Gertrud and, in a plot twist of great implausibility, reveals herself to be none other than Luise, the mother of Waldemar's child. Faced with her child, however, Georgine/Luise flees. Gertrud and Waldemar confess their mutual love, and the play ends with an image of the future greatness of Germany under the auspices of a strong bourgeoisie. Theodor Fontane has argued that the characters in *Graf Waldemar* are essentially copies of those to be found in Friedrich Schiller's *Kabale und Liebe* (1784).[35] But while it is true that the two plays share certain similarities in their depiction of the demagogy of the aristocracy and court life, it should be noted that such resemblances also stretch to *Die Valentine* and *Der Gelehrte* — indeed, it was surely difficult for a nineteenth-century German dramatist reflecting on aristocratic-bourgeois relations to avoid the model of *Kabale und Liebe*.

Dating *Die Valentine* is relatively straightforward. According to Freytag's memoirs, *Die Valentine* was written '[i]m Frühjahr 1846' (I, 134). Freytag's correspondence confirms this: he sent a copy of the play to the actor Emil Devrient on 13 July 1846, and the play went on to be performed in Leipzig during the winter season of 1846 (I, 136).[36] *Graf Waldemar* is slightly more intricate to date. Freytag's memoirs claim that the play was written '[i]m Herbst 1847' (I, 141). However, a letter from Arnold Ruge to Freytag from 19 April 1847 reveals that the work was composed considerably earlier: 'Endlich zu der Hauptsache Ihren Grafen Waldemar, den ich gleich zum Sylvester von meiner Frau mir habe vorlesen lassen'.[37] If Ruge's wife had read him *Graf Waldemar* over the New Year of 1846 to 1847, then the play must have been written in 1846, presumably directly after the completion of *Die Valentine*. Both plays were thus the product of a highly intensive period of writing by Freytag in 1846, which helps explain their similarity in form and theme.

*Graf Waldemar* was first performed in Berlin in June 1848. It was hardly a fortuitous time to open a new play in a country preoccupied with the aftermath of the 1848 revolution, and Freytag expressed exactly such concerns in a letter to the *Generalintendant* on 17 May 1848: 'Ihr Wunsch den *Waldemar* im Juni herauszubringen, macht mich betroffen. Ist denn wirklich bei der politischen und Sommerzerstreuung des Publikums Hoffnung, daß das Stück in dieser Zeit etwas machen werde?'[38] Freytag's fear that the combination of revolutionary turmoil and a holiday mood would wreck the chances of the theatrical success of *Graf Waldemar* was well founded. His memoirs lament: 'Es war ein leeres Haus mitten im Straßenlärm des Juni 1848 und der Verfasser saß im Parket fast allein' (I, 143). The play would never be a critical success, and, after an ill-fated revival in 1886, Theodor Fontane caustically noted that 'ein Wiederbelebungsversuch mit diesem seit beinah vierzig Jahren eingesargten Stücke' was hardly warranted.[39]

*Vormärz* Germany was home to an extensive system of press, literary, and theatrical censorship, and both *Die Valentine* and *Graf Waldemar* also fell under the scrutiny of the censor. The core elements of *Vormärz* censorship policy had been introduced in 1819 with the Karlsbad Decrees. The decrees instituted both *Vor-* and *Nachzensur* for all newspapers and for books of up to 20 *Bogen* (normally 320 pages) and strengthened the ability of individual states to issue their own supplementary controls. The decrees also established the right of the Bundesversammlung to intervene in the censorship mechanisms of any state.[40] In German theatres, *Vorzensur* became obligatory and was carried out by the *Intendanten* of the large city, state, and court theatres, and by the police in the regional theatres. In Austria, the system of theatre censorship was at its most rigorous, with a centralized Theaterzensurbehörde, itself a directorate of the centralized police, responsible for the censorship of theatrical texts.[41]

The events of the revolution of 1830 provided the states and Bundesversammlung with a further reason to strengthen censorship mechanisms. In 1835, the Bundesversammlung issued its infamous decree against the writers of *Junges Deutschland*, and several authors were forced into exile. The decree railed against writing which was sexually immoral, attacked religion, or criticized the socio-political climate in Germany, and it ordered that any author, publisher, or distributor of such material be held legally liable for its content. The decree was the most important of many issued in the 1830s which together demonstrate the tightening of controls around 1835.[42] In his summary of *Vormärz* censorship controls, Dieter Breuer notes:

> In diesen drei Vorwürfen: religiöse, politisch-soziale, moralische Normverletzung, begegnen wir wieder einmal den altvertrauten Zensurkriterien. Nur ein Kriterium hat sich verschoben: Herabwürdigung der 'bestehenden socialen Verhältnisse' [...]. Es verweist auf das Wunschdenken der hochadeligen Machthaber und ihrer konservativen Partei hinsichtlich der wachsenden Spannungen zwischen Adel und Bürgern einerseits, Bürgern und abhängigen proletarisierten Arbeitern andererseits.[43]

This additional social element to censorship controls helped make explicit an already implicit function of censorship as a means with which to curb expressions of social discontent. It is of particular significance when considering Freytag's plays, since it is precisely because of their depiction of tensions between the aristocracy and the bourgeoisie that these plays attracted the interest of the censor.

*Die Valentine* was particularly severely affected by censorship concerns. Although the play had been performed in Leipzig and Berlin during 1846 without problems, it faced difficulties with the censor when Freytag attempted to get it performed at the Hoftheater in Dresden. According to the account in Heinrich Houben's *Verbotene Literatur von der klassischen Zeit bis zur Gegenwart*, Freytag sent the play to Emil Devrient, who in turn passed it on to Graf Wolf Adolf von Lüttichau, *Intendant* to the Hoftheater. At the Hoftheater, however, the text was intercepted and read by Karl Gutzkow, the newly appointed *Dramaturg*. Houben argues that Gutzkow undertook the *Vorzensur* of Freytag's play:

> Aus seinem [Gutzkow's] eigenen langjährigen Kampf mit der Theaterzensur, vor allem der Hoftheater und der Dresdner Bühne im besondern, kannte dieser zur Genüge all die kleinlichen Rücksichten, die bei der Darstellung eines modernen Dramas in der vormärzlichen Zeit genommen wurden, und in seiner Stellung als Dramaturg mußte er wohl oder übel selbst den Zensor spielen.[44]

It is initially difficult to accept Houben's depiction of Gutzkow as a censor, given that — as Houben himself notes — Gutzkow had repeatedly fallen victim to the *Vormärz* censorship regime. Gutzkow had been named in the 1835 Bundesversammlung decree against *Junges Deutschland*, and had also served a prison term for the religious and moral offensiveness of his novel *Wally: Die Zweiflerin* (1835). Indeed, one questions how a radical such as Gutzkow had been able to rehabilitate himself with the authorities between 1835 and 1845 to the extent that they would appoint him to the position of *Dramaturg* at the Hoftheater.

Gutzkow's account of his time at the Hoftheater in his memoirs attempts to play down his role as *Vorzensor* of *Die Valentine*. Claiming that he had wanted to pass the play for performance, he notes that his concerns were limited to one scene, in which the Prince climbs into Valentine's bedroom window with less than noble intentions. According to Gutzkow, he suggested one alteration: 'für den jungen Fürsten lieber den Erbprinzen zu wählen'.[45] However, a letter from Gutzkow to Freytag on 23 January 1847 indicates that Gutzkow actually sought a series of more extensive changes to the text:

> Aus dem Fürsten muß ich einen jungen Erbprinzen, aus der Prinzessin eine Reichsgräfin (natürlich mit 'Durchlaucht') machen: das fühl' ich schon; aber auch Georg [...] muß etwas anders introduziert werden; denn so als Bürgerlicher spielt er am Hofe eine traurige Rolle. Ich schlage vor, ihn scheinbar als einen Engländer Sealsfield einzuführen; denn Engländern wissen Sie wohl stehen die kleinen Höfe von Weimar usw. sehr leicht offen.[46]

Although such changes might appear negligible, they were highly significant for the political message of Freytag's play. By turning the *Fürst* into an *Erbprinz*, for instance, the Prince's night-time seduction of Valentine can be excused as the forgivable error of an immature and over-excited juvenile. The aristocracy are no longer morally bankrupt, they are merely young. The demotion of the Princess to a *Reichsgräfin* further reveals Gutzkow's desire to situate the play amongst the upper nobility, rather than directly at the royal court. Most significant of all is Gutzkow's suggestion that Georg should become an Englishman. By the transformation of the radical *Burschenschaftler* into an English gentleman, the political heart of the play is effectively removed. Given Gutzkow's past, one suspects that these suggestions were made in order to help Freytag circumnavigate the censorship mechanisms of *Vormärz* Germany. Nevertheless, they effectively downgrade a politically tendentious text into mere melodrama. A highhandedness is detectable here, too, which would not be uncharacteristic of Gutzkow's attitude towards his peers.

Whatever Gutzkow's intentions, the future of *Die Valentine* was taken out of his hands through the personal intervention of the *Intendant*, Count von Lüttichau. In a letter to Gutzkow, von Lüttichau launched a savage and sustained attack on Freytag's play. *Die Valentine*, he claimed, was:

> ganz schlecht, nicht nur schlüpfrig, sondern anstößig im höchsten Grade [...]. Hof und seine Umgebung ist darin so prostituiert, was in jetziger Zeit ganz mit Unrecht, da dergleichen mindestens in Deutschland, wo es spielt, nicht mehr existiert, wie vielleicht vor 50 Jahren; [...] dazu ein Erbprinz künftiger Regent, der des Nachts durch Hülfe seines Helfershelfers auf der Strickleiter bey einer anständigen Dame einsteigt, mit den entschiedensten Absichten, wo wir hier den Prinzlichen Hof mit jungen Prinzen haben, die das Theater besuchen, und sich ein schlechtes Beispiel nehmen könnten [...]. Die Sitte der Frauen ist mit Füßen getreten; der Mensch, der es geschrieben, könnte mir bis in sein innerstes Mark verächtlich seyn, da ich diese Tendenz anstößiger finde, wie alle politischen und religiösen Beziehungen auf der Bühne, und kann ich diese Aufführung in keinem Fall gestatten [...].[47]

It is interesting that von Lüttichau's anger is not directed against the figure of Georg, the political radical who criticizes the lack of freedoms in Germany. Rather, there is a form of moral outrage in von Lüttichau's response, heavily coloured by his disquiet at the depiction of the aristocracy. His letter echoes criticisms frequently levelled against the licentious and politically tendentious works of *Junges Deutschland*, for instance during the censorship proceedings against Gutzkow's own *Wally*. Freytag felt unfairly treated and would forever blame Gutzkow for the debacle, launching a series of scathing attacks against him from the pages of *Die Grenzboten*: 'Ein schwaches, aber rastlos fleissiges Talent, zu beifallslustig, um Lob entbehren zu können, zu eitel, um Tadel zu ertragen, zu schwach, um ehrlich und wahr gegen sich selbst zu sein'.[48] Gutzkow, for his part, would always feel that he had been made a scapegoat for von Lüttichau's rejection of the play: 'Nun sah es aus, als sei meine Person das bisherige Hindernis der Zulassung gewesen! Die maßlose gehässige Sprache über mich, die in dem von Freytag angekauften Organ: *Die Grenzboten* in vieljährigen Gebrauch kam, schien darauf mir und Andern erklärt'.[49] The events surrounding *Die Valentine* would permanently sour the relationship between the two men.

The 'Gegenstück' (I, 141) to *Die Valentine, Graf Waldemar*, was less heavily affected by censorship issues. This was not so much because Freytag had successfully developed a form of *Selbstzensur* with which to voice his political and social viewpoints without arousing the suspicion of the authorities, but rather because of developments in the German political sphere. In 1848, the revolutionary uprisings across Germany led to a temporary lifting of theatre censorship; this began in Hessen-Darmstadt, before spreading to Frankfurt, Bavaria, Nassau, Gotha, Weimar, Kurhessen, Hannover, Prussia and ending in Saxony.[50] Houben notes how, faced with these prevailing circumstances, 'Lüttichau hatte plötzlich rasende Eile, mit der Zeit und ihren stürmischen Bewegungen gleichen Schritt zu machen'.[51] With the lifting of censorship controls, both *Die Valentine* and *Graf Waldemar* could be performed at the Dresden Hoftheater, *Die Valentine* on 13 April 1848 and *Graf Waldemar* on 29 October 1849.

*Graf Waldemar* had not, however, entirely escaped the strictures of the censor. In 1853, the board of the Burgtheater in Vienna refused to perform the play, objecting to the inter-class relationship between Gertrud and Waldemar. Heinrich Laube, who was *Intendant* in Vienna at the time (and, like Gutzkow, a former radical of *Junges Deutschland*), noted in his memoirs: 'Ich hatte mir auch die größte Mühe gegeben, den 'Grafen Waldemar' möglich zu machen. Die Zensur meiner Behörde aber sagte hartnäckig nein. Ein Graf soll eine Gärtnerstochter heiraten? In der Wirklichkeit mag's leider vorkommen, auf dem Burgtheater nie!'[52] It was only through Laube's direct intervention that the play was eventually performed in 1854. Laube hired an actress to play Gertrud who looked as if she were an aristocrat, thus placating the board of the theatre: 'Sie [the actress Marie Boßler] ist einfach, aber im Hintergrund merkt man den Adel; man glaubt, daß sie eine verkleidete Komtesse sein könnte'.[53] Even six years after the revolution, in a supposedly less repressive climate (although Wolfram Siemann has argued, not entirely convincingly, that the controls were actually more repressive after 1848), *Graf Waldemar* thus continued to face censorship problems because of its depiction of class: casting a critical eye at the aristocracy, revealing the particularist interests of the ruling classes, while stressing the moral and social superiority of the bourgeoisie.[54]

In the play, Freytag's negative depiction of the aristocracy is personified in the figure of Graf Waldemar. Waldemar, we learn, has given his life over to the pursuit of private pleasures, neglecting the responsibilities that come with his ruling position in society. So severe is his dereliction of duty that it has even been noted by the court:

HUGO   Gestern war ich zum kleinen Zirkel des Palais befohlen. Seine
       Hoheit frug, warum du niemals zu sehen seist [...]. Du bist in
       Gefahr, von dem Hofe aufgegeben zu werden [...]. Was man in
       den einzelnen Gruppen über dich flüsterte, Vieles mag unwahr
       oder entstellt sein, aber es blieb doch genug [...]. Waldemar, ein
       so reicher Geist, ein so adliger Sinn [...] und ein so verwüstetes,
       zerfahrenes Leben! (II, 228)

Waldemar's existence is consistently referred to as superfluous and pointless. When his horse dies at the opening of the play, for instance, we are left in no doubt about which of the two led the more valuable life:

GORDON   O es ist schändlich; wenn Zwei zusammen einen dummen
         Streich machen, der bessere von beiden muß immer die Zeche
         bezahlen. (II, 225–26)

Worse still, it is suggested that Waldemar's superficially positive relationship with the peasants on his estate is merely the cover for a morally dubious and exploitative one:

WALDEMAR   [...] Frage doch bei meinen Bauern nach, ob ich ihnen nicht ein
           liebevoller Herr bin, ich habe Nachsicht mit Steuerresten, und
           wenn ich ja ihre Frauen und Töchter küsse, sieh mich an, Hugo,
           die kommende Generation wird deshalb nicht schlechter werden.
           (II, 229)

Conducting liaisons and ignoring the needs of the state: Waldemar's life is depicted as devoid of productive work and dedicated to the pursuit of pleasure. Throughout *Die Valentine* and *Graf Waldemar*, the aristocracy are also criticized in more general terms:

GEORG   [...] Und doch sind es mannhafte, kräftige Jungen, schade um sie! —
        Welche Masse jugendlicher Kraft verdorrt unter euch ohne Nutzen
        für die Welt! In Zerstreuungen und nichtigen Erbärmlichkeiten
        welkt das frische Grün ihrer Seelen und zuletzt bleibt nichts übrig
        als der wunderliche Potpourri, den man Cavalierehre nennt. (II, 144)

Freytag's criticism repeatedly points to the missed potential of the aristocracy, returning indirectly to the theme of *Tatlosigkeit* first raised in *Der Gelehrte*. The superficial existence of the aristocracy is often the object of Freytag's satire. When the nobleman Udaschkin purchases a Sphinx to decorate his dog kennels, for instance, the act is lampooned as that of a man who cares more about what is fashionable than the inherent value of objects:

WALDEMAR   [...] wozu haben Sie eine Sphinx gekauft, mein Fürst, man
           kann sie nicht essen, man kann sie nicht trinken, man kann auch
           nicht auf ihr ausreiten.
UDSACHKIN  Ich baue einen Stall für meine Jagdhunde, da lasse ich das
           Ding vorsetzen. Es ist jetzt in der Mode, das wunderliche Zeug.

WALDEMAR   Nun, beim Zeus, eine äygyptische Sphinx endet damit, nach
zweitausend Jahren einen asiatischen Hundestall zu bewachen.
Das ist eine seltsame Carriere. [...] (II, 234)

*Die Valentine* likewise contains a strong anti-aristocratic polemic, as Freytag's attention turns to the machinations of court life and the self-serving nature of particularist rulers. It is Valentine's quest for power that is most directly criticized in the play, as she prioritizes her own self-interest above that of the people, the folk:

VALENTINE   [...] Ich sehne mich zu herrschen, ich strebe nach Einfluß.
Welcher Weg, seine Kraft geltend zu machen, bleibt dem Weibe, als die Liebe eines Mächtigen?
GEORG   Ich habe gesehen, daß Frauen mäßig waren, weise und besser die Fäden der Regierung zu halten wußten, als ein Mann. Auch Ihr Blick ist frei, Ihr Geist ist stark. Sie würden auf den Fürsten einen Theil Ihrer großen Seele übertragen, und manches Gute könnte daraus kommen — aber dennoch würde dieser Verbindung das Volk fluchen, und das Volk hätte Recht; denn für dieses Land giebt es kein anderes Heil, als die Vermählung des Fürsten mit der Prinzeß Marie. (II, 168)

The love triangle between Marie, the Fürst, and Valentine is more than a source of melodrama. It allows Freytag to reveal the 'Katzentritte' (II, 157) of the court officials as they attempt to control the forces of fate and love. Each political faction at the court seeks a romantic pairing that will further their own political needs, rather than the needs of the individuals involved, or, for that matter, the folk. The self-serving nature of the aristocracy is a motif which underlies Freytag's social critique.

However, despite its strength, Freytag's criticism of the aristocracy is not all-encompassing. Rather, it specifically targets the corruptive trappings of the aristocratic lifestyle. Essentially, Freytag appears to argue that Waldemar and Valentine are capable of a socially productive and morally sound way of life, but have become blinded to this possibility through their current existence. Upbringing, rather than blood, determines aristocratic behaviour:

GERTRUD   [...] Sie [sind] ungeduldig geworden und haben sich gewöhnt zu befehlen, und nehmen keine Rücksicht auf Andere. [...] Sie [haben] tolle Streiche gemacht und haben so viel Vergnügen genossen, daß Ihnen nichts mehr ein rechtes Vergnügen macht. (II, 266-67)

The social metamorphosis of Georgine in *Graf Waldemar* is a prime example of this process: a bourgeois woman is seduced both by the aristocrat Waldemar and by the aristocratic lifestyle of Udaschkin's brother, and is subsequently unwilling — or even unable — to return to her bourgeois roots. Waldemar, too, is frequently described in terms which reveal how his inherent value has been corrupted by a combination of riches and class status:

> HILLER  Ich habe dir immer gesagt, er [Waldemar] ist nicht böse, er ist gewiß ein so braver Mann wie Andere, er ist nur reich und vornehm, und deshalb müssen wir einige Nachsicht mit ihm haben [...], denn genau genommen, sind alle die vornehmen und reichen Leute nur unsertwegen da. — Wer würde uns die Kamelien abkaufen, oder unsern feinen Savoyerkohl, oder die Früchtschoten, wenn es keine Reichen gäbe? Wir haben den Vortheil davon, ein gesundes, kräftiges Leben, sie leiden darunter, denn sie essen sich Leib und Seele krank. (II, 261)

This potential for goodness in figures such as Waldemar and Valentine is significant, since Freytag's ideological aim rests on the ability of the aristocracy to reject the corrupting elements of the upper-class lifestyle in favour of bourgeois values. Critics have universally neglected the fact that Freytag's class warfare involves the synthesis of the aristocracy into the bourgeoisie, rather than its mere discrediting and disempowerment.

The possibility of the moral and social redemption of aristocratic figures through their interaction with the bourgeoisie is thus central to Freytag's class polemic. At the heart of Freytag's depiction of this process are images of illness, healing, and recovery. In both *Die Valentine* and *Graf Waldemar*, Freytag consistently describes the aristocracy as ill and the bourgeoisie as the cure. Take, for instance, Valentine's lines to Georg at the climax of *Die Valentine*:

> VALENTINE  Das ist deine Art, Kranke gesund zu machen, du guter Arzt. (II, 214)

> VALENTINE  [...] Ich sage nicht, daß das ein Unrecht von Ihnen war; denn Sie waren mein Arzt [...]. Sie heilten mich. (II, 220)

Such images of healing are also echoed in *Graf Waldemar*. Waldemar questions whether the moral virtues represented by Gertrud can lead him to take up a healthy lifestyle:

> WALDEMAR  [...] Thor, selbstsüchtiger Thor! Deine Nähe vergiftet, dein Gruß bringt ihr Verderben! Und kann selbst sie mich gesund machen? (II, 298)

Gertrud, meanwhile, describes herself as a form of medication for the sick upper classes:

> GERTUD  [...] Sie wollen mich nehmen, wie der Kranke eine Medicin nimmt, um gesund zu werden [...] (II, 304)

This process of healing is accompanied by a romantic tale in which the doctor (the bourgeoisie) and the patient (the aristocracy) fall in love. Some critics have argued that Freytag's depiction of these inter-class relationships does not allow for the difficulties that such a pairing would have faced in reality.[55] Yet such comments show a fundamental misunderstanding of Freytag's intent, which was not primarily realistic plausibility, but rather the ideological pursuit of the breakdown of class structures and the creation of a nation under folk rule. These relationships are symbolic, and their socio-political motivation is explicitly stated in the text:

> VALENTINE [W]ir beide, Sie der Mann aus dem Volke und ich die Aristokratin, [gehören] zu dem großen, stillen Bunde, welcher die nach Freiheit und Selbstgefühl ringenden Geister unserer Zeit vereinigt. (II, 208)
>
> VALENTINE [...] Wohin du gehst, dahin gehe ich auch, dein Gott ist mein Gott, dein Volk soll mein Volk sein! (II, 221)

This purpose was also recognized by Freytag's contemporaries, as revealed in the following enthusiastic reception of the play in a letter of 1847 by Arnold Ruge: 'Sie haben wieder einen Sünder [Waldemar] gebessert und wenn Sie so fortfahren, retten Sie uns noch vor der Revolution die ganze Aristocratie aus'.[56] Essentially, the two plays present a form of inverted rendering of George Bernard Shaw's later *Pygmalion* story, in which the aristocracy are educated and absorbed into the ways of the bourgeoisie, rather than the working classes. For Freytag, love and marriage are tools with which to restructure the hierarchies of German society.

Early academic studies of Freytag's *Vormärz* dramas have tended to read the plays within the context of *Junges Deutschland*. Eduard Rothfuchs, for instance, argued that *Die Valentine* reveals how Freytag's literary and political focus during the *Vormärz* 'liegt ganz und gar in den Fesseln des jungdeutschen Liberalismus'.[57] Robert Prutz's comments on *Graf Waldemar* also stressed the influence of *jungdeutsch* writing on Freytag, and are indicative of the anti-*Junges Deutschland* attitudes which permeate much of early Freytag criticism:

> Grade *Graf Waldemar* deckt die jungdeutsche Herkunft des Dichters am allernackesten auf, während das Publikum doch zu der Zeit, da das Stück vor die Lampen trat, die jungdeutsche Nervenkrankheit schon so ziemlich überstanden hatte und sich bereits von andern und inhaltsvolleren Interessen ergriffen fühlte.[58]

*Jungdeutsch* refers to the rather loose grouping of authors from the earlier *Vormärz*, including Heine, Laube, Weinbarg, Gutzkow, and Mundt, who were seen by the state regimes as politically and morally subversive and who rose to notoriety after being collectively banned by the German Bundesversammlung in 1835.[59] A case can certainly be made for the potential literary impact of *Junges Deutschland* on the young Freytag. During the 1840s, Freytag associated with authors linked to *Junges Deutschland*, and was especially close to Heinrich Laube. In his memoirs, Freytag stresses the strength of their friendship:

> Oft war ich im Hause von Heinrich Laube. [...] Er, der ältere, galt immer noch für einen Führer der jungdeutschen Richtung [und] ich folgte der Strömung, welche die deutsche Art in der Poesie zu Ehren bringen wollte. Den Gegensatz fühlten wir Beide, etwas davon hat auch in späteren Jahren bestanden, aber wir haben immer vermieden, das gute persönliche Einvernehmen dadurch zu stören. In Wahrheit war der gesammte jungdeutsche Trödel nicht seiner Natur gemäß [...]. (I, 136)

Freytag's memoirs may emphasize their ideological differences, but his friendship with Laube nevertheless opens up the distinct possibility of literary and political influence. Freytag's dealings with Gutzkow, though tense and in many ways inflicted rather than chosen, provide another example of his willingness to interact with supposed figures of *Junges Deutschland*.

In addition, aspects of both *Die Valentine* and *Graf Waldemar* mirror thematic tendencies frequently perceived as typically *jungdeutsch*. In *Die Valentine*, for instance, the *Burschenschaft* activities of Georg act as a constant reminder of his previous political radicalism, while his travels — to the United States (like Fink in *Soll und Haben*), South America, England, and Italy — also lend the play a cosmopolitan, international tone similar to the writings of *Junges Deutschland*.[60] Kurt Classe has argued that it is precisely this cosmopolitan air which identifies Freytag as a *Junges Deutschland* author.[61]

Certainly, Freytag's depiction of Georg's emigration to America is one of the most direct references to contemporary German society in *Die Valentine*. The lure of America for Germans was particularly strong in the 1840s: between 1840 and 1844, 110,000 Germans emigrated, with 90.9 per cent choosing America as their destination. Between 1845 and 1849, over 308,000 opted for emigration, with 92.4 per cent heading for America.[62] The majority of these cases of emigration were motivated by economic factors — a result of the 'hungry forties'.[63] The decade before the revolutions of 1848 had witnessed a gradual decline in production and demand for manufactured goods, along with significant structural changes resulting from proto-industrialization. Germany was afflicted by mass unemployment and social dislocation was an increasing problem, as people moved from the country to towns in search of work. Famine was also a danger for Germans during the *Vormärz*. The potato blight occurred in 1845 to 1846, and was followed by droughts in 1847 which destroyed the country's grain crops.[64] Although Germany did not suffer from the mass famine that afflicted Ireland in the mid-1840s, starvation nevertheless remained a very real danger for many of the poorest Germans. The crisis not only affected the truly poor: the working and even the middle classes began to suffer, and pauperization — which had predominantly been seen as a localized, seasonal phenomenon — was in danger of engulfing groups traditionally seen as safe from such conditions.[65] Thomas Nipperdey has argued persuasively that politically motivated emigration, although scarce, also had a significant impact on German national consciousness.⁶⁶ By choosing a hero who has emigrated on moral grounds, Freytag is thus making a clear political statement.

Nevertheless, on closer inspection, neither this cosmopolitan streak nor Georg's radical past can be construed as typical of *Junges Deutschland* writing. Georg's vocal opposition to the lack of political freedom in Germany is not based directly on the radicalism of *Junges Deutschland*, or on the positions of the even more radical authors of the 1840s, but rather on a bourgeois sense of national pride. His opinions are described as expressing 'Haltung und Biederkeit' (II, 191) — concepts alien to *Junges Deutschland*. Similarly, his cosmopolitanism is undercut by his *Heimweh* for Germany:

> GEORG   Ich habe keine große Pflicht, die mich an die Ferne fesselt, und meine Seele hat sich sehr nach deutscher Rede und Sitte gesehnt.
> (II, 136)

Equally unsustainable are attempts to identify a *jungdeutsch* immorality at the heart of *Die Valentine* and *Graf Waldemar*. Critics have frequently read the character of Waldemar as a typical example of the morally (that is to say, sexually) liberal *jungdeutsch* hero: '[Waldemar] ist wieder eine Spielart jenes beliebten jungdeutschen Heldentypus, [...] so wirft er denn seine ganze gärende Kraft auf das erotische Gebiet, er wird zum Don Juan'.⁶⁷ Certainly, *Graf Waldemar* does contain a number of mild sexual allusions. But the point of Freytag's drama — as revealed in the preceding discussion — is that Waldemar gives up his pursuit of pleasure in favour of a faithful existence with Gertrud. In fact, Freytag's plays are clearly ethically opposed to the sensualism that can be found in the Heine of the 1830s or in Büchner's *Dantons Tod* (1835). *Die Valentine* and *Graf Waldemar* cannot thus be considered as examples of *Junges Deutschland* writing. Ethically, the plays uphold, rather than dismantle, bourgeois values, in stark contrast to much writing of *Junges Deutschland*. Similarly, the cosmopolitan reach of the plays is undermined by their strongly national tone. The plays may be politically radical, but this radicalism is that of a bourgeois national liberalism and not that of *Junges Deutschland*. If anything, Freytag was intentionally amending *jungdeutsch* patterns in service of his own political cause in these plays.

In general, one senses that early critics were keen to present Freytag's *Vormärz* dramas as dallying with *jungdeutsch* tendencies in order to contrast his radical youth with the supposedly superior bourgeois morality presented in his *Nachmärz* novels *Soll und Haben* and *Die Ahnen*. However, such an interpretation of Freytag — essentially based around a caesura in 1848 — ignores the continuities in his political ideology across the *Vor-* and *Nachmärz*. As seen in this discussion, the bourgeois spirit was never far from the surface in Freytag's writings, and *Die Valentine* and *Graf Waldemar* both depict sustained attacks against the aristocracy by Freytag. The plays depict the ruling elites of Germany as self-interested, and Valentine and Waldemar are shown as pursuing their own personal pleasures to the detriment of the folk. However, the plays do not argue that the aristocracy are inherently corrupt. Rather, they are revealed as having been seduced by the trappings of their lifestyle. The aristocracy is repeatedly shown as finding salvation through interaction with the bourgeoisie, and the breakdown of class structures and subsequent destruction of the aristocracy represented in the inter-class love stories are presented as prerequisites for the foundation of a bourgeois German nation. Indeed, the politically symbolic inter-class relationships set out in these plays will become central to Freytag's subsequent writings, and form the premises of his three major novels of the *Nachmärz*: *Soll und Haben*, *Die verlorene Handschrift*, and *Die Ahnen*.

In a letter of 1846 to the *Generalintendant* of the Hoftheater in Berlin, Gustav Freytag details his motivations for becoming a dramatist: 'Ich fühle den Drang und die Kraft, der deutschen Bühne etwas zu werden und einer von den Brückenpfeilern zu werden, welche aus dem Misere gegenwärtiger Zustände zu einer kräftigeren und nationalen Entwicklung der Kunst zu führen haben'.[68] Freytag's ambitions as a dramatist would never be realized. His *Vormärz* dramas neither spearheaded a nationally themed revival in German drama, nor did they become the *Brückenpfeiler* for future generations of dramatists. Instead, Freytag's plays would be relegated to a footnote in literary history: those of a 'vergessene[r] Dramatiker des 19. Jahrhunderts'.[69] Freytag's exaggerated assessment of his dramatic abilities in his memoirs can only be read as an example of his revisionist attempt to secure a permanent position in the German literary canon:

> Durch die erwähnten Schauspiele hatte ich festen Fuß auf der deutschen Bühne gefaßt, ich war ein genannter Autor geworden, der von den Theatern mit Achtung betrachtet wurde. [...]. [I]ch durfte mir ohne Selbstüberhebung sagen, daß es zur Zeit in Deutschland Niemanden gab, der die technische Arbeit des Bühnenschriftstellers besser verstand als ich. (I, 143–44)

Although Freytag's *Vormärz* dramas did not achieve this desired longevity, they are nevertheless a fascinating documentation of a bourgeois liberal response to the social, political, and aesthetic radicalization of the *Vormärz*. In particular, the marked difference between Freytag's bourgeois radicalism and the radicalism of *Junges Deutschland* reveals how political tendentiousness was not the sole preserve of supposedly revolutionary authors, and that comparatively conservative-minded figures such as Freytag could equally engage in political and politicized writing.

Indeed, all the plays under consideration in this chapter are inherently political works. *Die Brautfahrt* is a fable of German unity. A romantic, national, and mythologizing look back to the medieval roots of the Habsburg Empire, it simultaneously casts a glance forwards to a German national unification in the form of a German Reich. *Der Gelehrte* stresses the role of work and the folk in the creation of a German nation — a foreshadowing of Freytag's *Nachmärz* novel *Soll und Haben* and a direct expression of what he would later term the *Volkskraft*. Finally, both *Graf Waldemar* and *Die Valentine* develop a fundamental dialectic between the values of the bourgeoisie and those of the aristocracy, proposing that the breakdown of class structures and the subsumption of the aristocracy are prerequisites for the foundation of a healthy, bourgeois German nation. The trio of elements central to Freytag's *Nachmärz* writings — class, nation, and the folk — are thus also firmly present in Freytag's *Vormärz* dramas.

## Notes to Chapter 2

1. Gustav Freytag, *Gesammelte Werke*, I: *Erinnerungen aus meinem Leben* (Leipzig: Hirzel, 1896), p. 131. Further references to this edition are given after quotations in the text.
2. See Conrad Alberti, *Gustav Freytag: Sein Leben und Schaffen* (Leipzig: Schloemp, 1885), pp. 34–35.
3. Dieter Kafitz, *Gründzüge einer Geschichte des deutschen Dramas von Lessing bis zum Naturalismus*, 2 vols (Königstein: Athenäum, 1982), II, 235.
4. See Georg Droescher, 'Gustav Freytags Schriftwechsel mit der Generalintendanz der königlichen Schauspiele zu Berlin', *Deutsche Rundschau*, 45 (1918), 129–46.
5. August Wilhelm Schlegel, in *August Wilhelm Schlegels Vorlesungen über dramatische Kunst und Literatur*, ed. by Giovanni Vittorio Amoretti, 2 vols (Bonn: [n.pub.], 1923), II, 309.
6. Gustav Freytag, *Gesammelte Werke*, II: *Dramatische Werke. Erster Band* (Leipzig: Hirzel, 1896), p. 18. Further references to this edition are given after quotations in the text.
7. Freytag, letter to Graf Redern, 9 April 1842, in Droescher, 'Gustav Freytags Schriftwechsel', p. 130.
8. See William Carr, *A History of Germany 1815–1990* (London: Arnold, 1991), p. 25.
9. Heinrich Heine, *Historisch-kritische Gesamtausgabe der Werke, Düsseldorfer Heine-Ausgabe*, ed. by Manfred Windfuhr, II: *Neue Gedichte. Text. Apparat* (Hamburg: Hoffmann & Campe, 1983), p. 148.
10. See Droescher, 'Gustav Freytags Schriftwechsel', p. 132.
11. 'The strong make war; thou, happy Austria, marry: | What Mars grants others, Venus gives to thee'. See Edward Crankshaw, *The Habsburgs* (London: Weidenfeld & Nicolson, 1971), p. 40.
12. Franz Grillparzer, *Sämtliche Werke, Historisch-kritische Gesamtausgabe Wien*, VI: *Ein Bruderzwist in Habsburg* (Vienna: Anton Schroll, 1927), p. 189.
13. Kurt Classe, 'Gustav Freytag als politischer Dichter' (doctoral thesis, University of Münster, 1914), p. 25.
14. Niklaus Becker, *Gedichte*, in *Bibliothek der deutschen Literatur: Mikrofiche-Gesamtausgabe* (Munich: Sauer, 1999), B.1/F. 58.
15. Gustav Freytag, *In Breslau* (Breslau: Johann Kern, 1845), p. 109.
16. Crankshaw, p. 40.
17. For a commentary on the sources of Freytag's play, see Georg Droescher, *Gustav Freytag in seinen Lustspielen: Inaugural-Dissertation* (Weida: Thomas & Hubert, 1919), pp. 9–10.

18. See Peter Haida, *Kritik und Satire im Lustspiel* (Stuttgart: Klett, 1989), p. 33.
19. Gustav Freytag, *Gesammelte Werke*, XVII: *Bilder aus der deutschen Vergangenheit I. Aus dem Mittelalter* (Leipzig: Hirzel, 1896), p. x.
20. Heinrich Heine, *Historisch-kritische Gesamtausgabe der Werke, Düsseldorfer Heine-Ausgabe*, ed. by Manfred Windfuhr, VII.I: *Reisebilder III/IV. Text. Apparat* (Hamburg: Hoffmann & Campe, 1986), p. 272.
21. Freytag, letter to Salomon Hirzel, 29 October 1847, in *Gustav Freytag an Salomon Hirzel und die Seinen*, ed. by Alfred Dove (Leipzig: Breitkopf & Härtel, 1903), p. 1.
22. See the comments by Jürgen Matoni in his introduction to volume one of *Gustav Freytags Briefe an die Verlegerfamilie Hirzel 1853–1864*, ed. by Jürgen Matoni and Margret Galler, 2 vols (Berlin: Mann, 1994).
23. Freytag, letter to Hirzel, 29 October 1847, in Dove (ed.), *Gustav Freytag an Salomon Hirzel*, p. 1.
24. Constantin Rössler, *Gustav Freytag und die deutsche Dichtung der Gegenwart* (Berlin: Julius Springer, 1860), p. 15.
25. Freytag, letter to Hirzel, 29 October 1847, in Dove (ed.), *Gustav Freytag an Salomon Hirzel*, p. 1.
26. Gustav Freytag, *Gesammelte Werke*, XIV: *Die Technik des Dramas* (Leipzig: Hirzel, 1896), p. 77. Further references to this edition are given after quotations in the text.
27. Classe, p. 31.
28. Eduard Rothfuchs, 'Der selbstbiographische Gehalt in Gustav Freytags Werken (bis 1855)' (doctoral thesis, University of Münster, 1929), pp. 18–19.
29. See Peter Uwe Hohendahl, *Building a National Literature: The Case of Germany, 1830–1870* (Ithaca: Cornell University Press, 1989), p. 255.
30. See Thomas Nipperdey, *Deutsche Geschichte 1800–1866* (Munich: Beck, 1998), pp. 451–53.
31. See Hohendahl, p. 262.
32. Heinrich Heine, *Historisch-kritische Gesamtausgabe der Werke, Düsseldorfer Heine-Ausgabe*, ed. by Manfred Windfuhr, VIII.I: *Zur Geschichte der Religion und Philosophie in Deutschland; Die romantische Schule. Text* (Hamburg: Hoffmann & Campe, 1981), pp. 13, 18.
33. Gustav Freytag, *Gesammelte Werke*, IV: *Soll und Haben. Erster Band* (Leipzig: Hirzel, 1896), p. 1.
34. See, for example, Henry Garland and Mary Garland, *The Oxford Companion to German Literature* (Oxford: Oxford University Press, 1976), p. 753.
35. Theodor Fontane, *Sämtliche Werke*, XXII.II: *Causerien über Theater* (Munich: Nymphenburger, 1964), p. 431.
36. See H. Houben, *Verbotene Literatur von der klassischen Zeit bis zur Gegenwart* (Hildesheim: Georg Olm, 1965), p. 199.
37. Arnold Ruge, letter to Freytag, 19 April 1847, in Günter Schulz, 'Briefe Arnold Ruges an Gustav Freytag', *Jahrbuch der Schlesischen Friedrich-Wilhelms-Universität zu Breslau*, 11 (1966), 240–52 (p. 248).
38. Freytag, letter to the *Generalintendant* of the *Hoftheater* zu Berlin, 17 May 1848, in Droescher, 'Gustav Freytags Schriftwechsel', p. 140.
39. Fontane, *Sämtliche Werke*, XXII.II, 433.
40. See Dieter Breuer, *Geschichte der literarischen Zensur in Deutschalnd* (Heidelberg: Quelle, 1982), p. 153.
41. See Breuer, p. 162. For a discussion of the differences in theatre censorship between Germany and Austria, see Katy Heady, *Literature and Censorship in Restoration Germany: Repression and Rhetoric* (Rochester, NY: Camden House, 2009).

42. For a full discussion and the texts of the decrees, see Ernst Robert Huber, *Dokumente zur deutschen Verfassungsgeschichte* (Stuttgart: Kohlhammer, 1978).
43. See Breuer, p. 157.
44. Houben, p. 199.
45. Karl Gutzkow, *Gutzkows Werke und Briefe: Autobiographische Schriften*, II: *Rückblicke auf mein Leben*, ed. by Peter Hasubek (Münster: Oktober, 2006), p. 359.
46. Karl Gutzkow, quoted in Houben, p. 199. Though Houben is the only source we have for the text of this letter, there is no reason to doubt its authenticity.
47. Quoted in Houben, p. 200.
48. Gustav Freytag, 'Fuer Herrn Dr Gutzkow und Herrn Heinrich Brockhaus 2', *Die Grenzboten*, 11 (1852), 437–40 (p. 439). Further attacks on Gutzkow can be found in Volumes 11 and 13 from the same year.
49. Gutzkow, *Gutzkows Werke und Briefe: Autobiographische Schriften*, II, 360.
50. See Breuer, p. 180.
51. Houben, p. 201.
52. Heinrich Laube, *Heinrich Laubes Gesammelte Werke*, ed. by H. Houben, XXIX.II: *Das Burgtheater* (Leipzig: Max Helles, 1909), p. 45.
53. Ibid., p. 67.
54. See Wolfram Siemann, 'Zensur im Übergang zur Moderne: Die Bedeutung des "langen 19. Jahrhunderts"', in *Zensur im Jahrhundert der Aufklärung: Geschichte — Theorie — Praxis*, ed. by Wilhelm Haefs and York-Gothart Mix (Göttingen: Wallstein, 2007), pp. 357–88.
55. See Hans Lindau, *Gustav Freytag* (Leipzig: Hirzel, 1907), p. 110.
56. Arnold Ruge, letter to Freytag, 19 April 1847, in Schulz, 'Briefe Arnold Ruges an Gustav Freytag', p. 248.
57. Rothfuchs, p. 34.
58. Robert Prutz, *Die deutsche Literatur der Gegenwart, 1848–1858,* 2 vols (Leipzig: Voigt & Günther, 1860), II, 96.
59. See Helmut Koopmann, *Das Junge Deutschland: Eine Einführung* (Darmstadt: Wissenschaftliche Buchgesellschaft, 1993), pp. 98–99.
60. On the typical features of the writing of *Junges Deutschland*, see Helmut Koopmann, *Das Junge Deutschland: Analyse seines Selbstverständnisses* (Stuttgart: Metzler, 1970), pp. 27–29.
61. See Classe, p. 37.
62. See Robert Lee, '"Relative Backwardness" and Long-Run Development: Economic, Demographic and Social Changes', in *19th Century Germany: Politics, Culture and Society, 1780–1918*, ed. by John Breuilly (London: Arnold, 2001), pp. 66–95 (p. 75).
63. Theodore Hamerow, *Restoration, Revolution and Reaction: Economics and Politics in Germany, 1815–1871* (Princeton: Princeton University Press, 1958), p. 75.
64. Ibid., pp. 75–77; Carr, p. 34.
65. See Christopher Clark, 'Germany 1815-1848: Restoration or Pre-March?', in *19th Century Germany: Politics, Culture and Society, 1780–1918*, ed. by John Breuilly (London: Arnold, 2001), 40–65 (pp. 56–58).
66. See Nipperdey, p. 114.
67. Otto Mayrhofer, *Freytag und das Junge Deutschland* (Marburg: Koch, 1907), p. 41.
68. Freytag, letter to von Küstner, 14 July 1846, in Droescher, 'Gustav Freytags Schriftwechsel', p. 134.
69. Kafitz, p. 235.

CHAPTER 3

## Revolution and Reaction: Literary Practice and the Bourgeois Cause in the *Nachmärz*

Gustav Freytag's memoirs provide the only substantial account of his reaction to the revolutions of 1848. Written in 1887, they are broadly critical of the social disorder engendered by the revolution, and present 1848 as a crucial turning point in Freytag's literary and political development, marking the beginning of his 'Arbeiten der Mannesjahre'.[1] The stance of the memoirs on 1848 has been largely accepted in secondary literature: both biographers and critics concur that 1848 was 'das entscheidende Jahr' in Freytag's intellectual development.[2] However, the extent to which 1848 marked a moment of real significance for Freytag, as well as the precise nature of his response to the revolution and its aftermath, have never been fully explored.

'Behind every revolt', wrote the historian William Carr, 'there lies a story of social discontent', and the socio-economic crisis of the 1840s — the era characterized as 'the hungry forties' — was a key factor in the outbreak of revolution in 1848.[3] The social question of the 1840s was most famously symbolized in the revolt of the Silesian weavers in June 1844, an event which prompted Heinrich Heine to write his 'Weberlied' and Freytag to produce his (far less polemical) 'Lebende Bilder' (as discussed in Chapter 1). Of importance, too, were the increasing levels of political discontent in late *Vormärz* Germany, expressed in the demands of the 1848 revolutionaries for constitutional liberalization and a free press. In the words of Eric Hobsbawm: 'The European economic cataclysm [had] coincided with the visible corrosion of the old regimes', creating the perfect conditions for an uprising.[4] Dissent first flared in Polish Galicia, part of the Austrian Empire, in 1846, and large-scale hunger riots soon followed throughout Germany in 1847. The revolution itself began in France, the uprisings in Paris in 1848 acting, as in 1789 and 1830, as a signal for European revolt. As Heinrich Heine had written in his *Einleitung* to Moltke's

*Kahldorf über den Adel* (1831): 'Der gallische Hahn hat jetzt [...] gekräht, und auch in Deutschland wird es Tag'.[5]

Freytag's memoirs display little enthusiasm for the revolution. The social and political upheavals of the late *Vormärz* are described as destructive earth tremors, in an image reminiscent of Heinrich von Kleist's novella *Das Erdbeben in Chili* (1805), in which an earthquake symbolizes the political and emotional force of the French revolution of 1789: 'Der Ausbruch kam plötzlich, doch nicht unerwartet. Seit einem Jahre hatten wir dahin gelebt wie Leute, welche unter ihren Füßen Getöse und Schwanken des Erdbodens empfinden' (I, 145). In the memoirs, Freytag claims that he recognized the need for change — 'Alles in den deutschen Verhältnissen erschien haltlos und locker, und Jeder rief, daß es nicht so bleiben könnte' — but states that he hoped for 'eine friedliche Entwickelung' to events (I, 145). This hope was shattered by 'die Schrecken des Straßentumults' in 1848 (I, 159). Although this account was written from a much later perspective, its negative appraisal of the reality of revolution is echoed elsewhere in Freytag's works. The final volume of his novel cycle *Die Ahnen* (1872–80) similarly describes 1848 as a 'widerwärtige[r] Carneval der Gasse', while *Soll und Haben* (1855) stresses the destructive impact of revolution on Poland after the insurrection of 1846:[6] 'Wenn Revolution so aussieht, sieht sie häßlich genug aus. [...] Sie verwüstet immer und schafft selten Neues'.[7] The historian Larry Ping has argued that Freytag 'regarded the very concept of revolution with horror', and on the basis of Freytag's memoirs and novels it seems clear that he found the act of revolution objectional.[8]

However, an important counter to the negative depiction of revolution in Freytag's memoirs is to be found in his literary writings of the *Vormärz*, which, as the discussion in previous chapters has shown, reveal him to have been a socially engaged author fighting for bourgeois rights in the face of aristocratic dominance — a supporter of major social change, if not a revolutionary. When we consider Freytag's relationship to 1848, therefore, a balance must be struck between his wish for social and political reform and his equal desire for the maintenance of social order. Interestingly, the coexistence of these two impulses appears to have been reasonably typical of politically interested yet non-radical authors writing on either side of 1848, Franz Grillparzer, Adalbert Stifter, and even Heine displaying similar ambivalence towards the act of revolution: greeting change, yet fearful of disorder.[9] Freytag may have been repelled by the physical act of revolution, but this should not be taken as an indication that he was against the process of social change. His memoirs also claim that 1848 was a turning point in his literary career:

> Da kam das Jahr 1848 und stellte Aufgaben, die größer waren als alle Eroberungen auf der deutschen Bühne. Als die erste Nachricht von den Berliner Barrikaden in Dresden eintraf, legte ich meinen Theaterkram bei

Seite, ich dachte mir, daß der Staat Kraft und Leben jedes Einzelnen für sich fordere [...]. (I, 145)

The memoirs argue that drama was unable to encompass or reflect the 'Strömung des Lebens' (I, 176) of the revolution, and that this new political era — in which the future form of the German nation would be fiercely debated — required a new mode of expression: '[D]ie großen geschichtlichen Verhältnisse, in denen ich als Schriftsteller mich tummelte [...], wollte[n] sich in den Rahmen eines Theaterabends, in die knappe Form des Dialogs, und in die kurzen Scenenwirkungen nicht einpassen' (I, 176). Instead of drama, Freytag was to devote himself to journalism, taking on the editorship of *Die Grenzboten* in 1848 and engaging fully in the political debates of *Nachmärz* Germany. However, it should be noted that Freytag's rejection of drama in 1848 was not as final as the biased and revisionist account in his memoirs suggest. In fact, his first literary work of the *Nachmärz* was the comedy *Die Journalisten* (1852), and he remained preoccupied with drama into the 1860s, publishing a tragedy, *Die Fabier*, in 1859, and his theoretical study *Die Technik des Dramas* in 1864. Freytag's aesthetic shift in 1848 is thus far from clear cut and it is important to question the extent to which the revolution and post-revolutionary period marked a significant move away from his literary and political concerns of the *Vormärz*.

### *Die Grenzboten* (1848–70)

*Die Grenzboten* was founded in Brussels in 1841 by the Austrian author Ignaz Kuranda and with the support of the Belgian novelist Hendrik Conscience, a figurehead of the Flemish Movement. The periodical originally focused on German–Flemish relations, but when the Flemish articles proved unpopular, its attention shifted to *Vormärz* Germany, and it quickly developed a reputation as a politically tendentious mouthpiece for authors previously associated with the *Junges Deutschland* movement.[10] Kuranda was a close friend of Heinrich Laube, Ludwig Uhland, and Heinrich Heine, exchanging an extensive correspondence with the last of these:

> Liebster Kuranda! Ich [Heine] danke Ihnen für die freundschaftliche Gesinnung, die sich in Ihrem Briefe ausspricht und freue mich, daß Ihr Unternehmen [*Die Grenzboten*] so bald ins Leben tritt; dieses kann für mich freylich von großem Nutzen seyn, in der Zukunft wie in der Gegenwart, und auf meine besten Wünsche, wo möglich auch auf thätigere Theilnahme, können Sie rechnen.[11]

Critical of the Deutscher Bund and *großdeutsch* in orientation, *Die Grenzboten* attracted the attention of the censor, was repeatedly targeted by the authorities in Saxony (where it was based), and was banned outright by the Wiener Zensurbehörde für das Habsburgerreich in 1842.[12]

The radical *Grenzboten* was not the most obvious of periodicals for a moderate liberal such as Gustav Freytag to become involved with. Nevertheless, when Kuranda returned to Austria in 1848 to found the *Ostdeutsche Post*, Freytag was persuaded by his friend Julian Schmidt to assume the editorship. Together they set about systematically redefining the political orientation of the periodical — in particular, by replacing its earlier *großdeutsch* orientation with a *kleindeutsch* one. In his memoirs, Freytag writes:

> Die neuen Inhaber beschlossen, die Zeitschrift zu dem Organ zu machen, in welchem das Ausscheiden Oestreichs aus Deutschland und die preußische Führung leitende Idee des politischen Theils sein sollte, dazu von liberalem Standpunkt ein Kampf gegen die Auswüchse der Demokratie und den Schwindel des Jahres. (I, 155)

This summary of the political agenda of *Die Grenzboten* is corroborated by many of Freytag's own articles for the periodical during the early *Nachmärz*. Freytag openly supported the unification of Germany under Prussian leadership ('Preußen [...] wird und muß [...] die Führerschaft Deutschlands übernehmen'), railed against the spread of universal suffrage, and repeatedly stressed the need for a *kleindeutsch* solution to the German question, using a range of rhetorical strategies, such as taking on the persona of an Austrian citizen coming to terms with exclusion from a greater Germany:[13] 'Hinweg mit der dreifarbigen Kokarde, sie ist eine Lüge geworden, denn sie bringt uns nicht mehr Vereinigung mit Deutschland, sondern Vernichtung für uns und Deutschland' (xv, 108). Freytag's *Grenzboten* articles provide significant insights into his political opinions and allegiances in the early *Nachmärz*. However, articles for *Die Grenzboten* were written anonymously, or, very occasionally, under a pseudonym — Freytag is known to have sometimes identified his articles with his initials, or with the symbol ♀. It is thus often difficult to establish exactly which were written by Freytag. The most extensive attempt to identify Freytag's *Grenzboten* articles is Adolf Thiele's 1924 thesis,[14] and the lack of understanding of Freytag's journalism remains a significant gap in Freytag-related research. In addition, the selection of Freytag's *Grenzboten* articles published in the *Gesammelte Werke* themselves require careful and critical reading, as many underwent significant re-editing prior to their inclusion — with Freytag removing 'ungeschickte und persönlich verletzende Stellen' (xv, v). Thus the articles, while of considerable interest, must be read critically and should not be seen as providing wholly reliable insights into Freytag's contemporary political ideas.

Although Freytag's articles for *Die Grenzboten* were primarily political, the periodical remains best known in German literary history for its development of the literary aesthetic of programmatic realism. Programmatic realism rejected the tendentiousness of *Vormärz* literature and stressed the importance of the English novel for the renewal of German literature after the failure of 1848. Unlike the French novel, which was nothing more than 'die bloße Copie der sogenannten Natur', the English novel (in Freytag's account) understood the need to seek the positive in everyday life — an optimistic social attitude that Freytag and Schmidt felt to be indispensable in the post-revolutionary era:[15]

> Der Realismus der Poesie wird dann zu erfreulichen Kunstwerken führen, wenn er [the author] in der Wirklichkeit zugleich die positive Seite aufsucht, wenn er mit Freude am Leben verknüpft ist, wie früher bei Fielding, Goldsmith, später bei Walter Scott und theilweise auch noch bei Dickens.[16]

Programmatic realism was not purely an aesthetic theory and was equally influenced by political concerns: that is, the need to establish an optimistic (and bourgeois) vision of society to overcome 'die Muthlosigkeit und müde Abspannung der Nation' after the revolutions of 1848 (IV, 3). The concept of realism developed by Freytag and Schmidt thus did not embrace an accurate portrayal of reality, but rather an ideologically enhanced vision of the inherent potential of reality: 'Der *Zweck* der Kunst, namentlich der Dichtkunst, ist, Ideale aufzustellen, d.h. Gestalten und Geschichten, deren Realität man wünschen muß, weil sie uns erheben, begeistern, ergötzen, belustigen u.s.w.; das *Mittel* der Kunst ist der Realismus'.[17] Schmidt, in particular, placed significant emphasis on the need for programmatic realism to seek its heroes in: 'unserer Arbeitsstube, in unserem Comptoir [...]. Der Deutsche ist am größten und schönsten, wenn er arbeitet. Die deutschen Romanschriftsteller sollen sich deshalb um die Arbeit der Deutschen kümmern'.[18] This emphasis on work, as well as on a positive vision of society, would be reflected in Freytag's 1855 novel *Soll und Haben* — rightly identified as a key text of programmatic realism and a founding work of the late nineteenth-century literary aesthetic of *Bürgerlicher Realismus*.[19] For Freytag and Schmidt, the post-1848 era not only required a new form of political engagement, but a new vision of literature — and both programmes were pursued from within the pages of *Die Grenzboten*.

During the early *Nachmärz*, Gustav Freytag also became involved in the work of two associations: the Dresdner Handwerkerverein (founded in 1848) and the Literarisch-politischer Verein (founded in 1852). Freytag's lifetime witnessed an explosion in the popularity of such associations, with groups existing for almost every interest: literary, musical, business, and professional, as well as more politically orientated organizations such as the Nationalverein. The historian David Blackbourn has argued that such organizations were central to bourgeois pride and self-perception after 1848, and should be regarded as part of a 'silent bourgeois revolution' of the nineteenth century.[20]

Freytag's involvement in associational life in Germany is, in itself, unsurprising. As seen in Chapter 1, he had already been centrally involved in the Breslauer Künstlerverein and the humanitarian Central-Verein. In many respects, his involvement in the Dresdner Handwerkerverein was an extension of this charitable work, with the 'Arbeiter, Gesellen und Gehülfen' (I, 149) of Dresden replacing the Silesian weavers as the recipient of his charity. According to his memoirs, Freytag first met these working men at the Fremdenverein — an organization for non-Saxons living in Dresden. After listening to their stories of poverty and exploitation, Freytag claims that he suggested that they could alleviate their suffering by joining forces and founding an association along the lines of those enjoyed by the middle and upper classes:

> [I]ch rechnete ihnen vor, wenn jeder der Anwesenden von seinem Verdienste monatlich nur wenige Groschen abgebe, so könnten sie sich auch einen Saal miethen mit Kronleuchter und Tapeten, mit einem erwählten Kastellan, der ihnen zu billigem Preis Speise und Getränk verkaufe, mit Zeitungen zum Lesen, vielleicht später mit einer kleinen Bibliothek, einem Gesangverein, u.s.w. (I, 149)

If we are to trust the rather romantic account of the memoirs, it was thus that the Fremdenverein was transformed, apparently under Freytag's leadership, into the Handwerkerverein — an association, as the above list of activities indicates, which sought to introduce the working classes to the *Bildung* of the middle classes through literature, newspapers, music, and debating. Interestingly, Freytag's memoirs also suggest that he was worried from the outset that the association might become a breeding ground for non-bourgeois political ideologies:

> Der Verein hatte in seinen Statuten erklärt, daß er keiner politischen Partei angehöre, doch war natürlich die Politik von den Erörterungen nicht fern zu halten, und es galt hier zunächst den Unsinn abzuwehren und zu verhindern [...]. Dies war keine bequeme Aufgabe [...]. (I, 150–51)

In fact, Freytag's memoirs stress how the members of the association required the constant supervision of figures such as himself — that is, the educated bourgeoisie — in order to prevent infighting or their becoming radicalized. The attitude of the memoirs towards the workers is clearly disparaging. Indeed, they are often presented as simple souls, as children subordinate to a bourgeois parent:

> Im Ganzen muß ich wahrlich sagen, daß mich der Verkehr gelehrt hat, wie gutherzig und anhänglich die Seelen in diesen Kreisen des Volkes sind. Aber auch, daß sie in der Empfindung eigener Schwäche zu Werkzeugen ihrer Führer werden, und daß ein Vereinsleben, wie das geschilderte, nur gedeihlich wirken kann, wenn es von gebildeten Männern unablässig behütet wird. (I, 152)

Underlying such prejudice there seems to be an element of caution or fear in Freytag at the potential power of the working classes, and one could view the Dresdner Handwerkerverein as a means with which the bourgeoisie were able to curb the potential radicalism of the *Handwerker* through directed *Bildung*. Indeed, the extent to which the working classes — from proletariat to *Handwerker* — could be controlled via education was often discussed in liberal educational debates in the 1840s and 1850s.[21] It should, however, also be noted that the memoirs were written in 1887, and that Freytag's later understanding or sense of an increasing proletarian threat in the 1880s may have coloured his description of life at the association in the late 1840s.

In 1852 — by which time the Dresdner Handwerkerverein had folded (for unkown reasons) — Freytag became attached to the Literarisch-politischer Verein. Financed by Duke Ernst von Coburg Gotha, this secret society was dedicated to the promotion of German unification under Prussian leadership — essentially, the same programme Freytag and Schmidt were pursuing in *Die Grenzboten*. Freytag's memoirs remain silent about the existence of the association, and Klaus Christian Köhnke has claimed that its work was first revealed in the Duke's memoirs in 1888.[22] This is, however, incorrect, since Freytag's biography of Karl Mathy from 1869 mentions the work of the *Verein* (see the later discussion in Chapter 4). Taken together with Freytag's letters to the Duke from the 1850s, the precise workings of the association can be revealed. The primary aim appears to have been to circumvent the censorship controls of the *Nachmärz* by distributing fortnightly anonymous brochures, the *Autographische Korrespondenz*, detailing the political situation in Prussia: '[D]ie Aufgabe [war] die öffentliche Meinung in Preußen zu revolutionieren'.[23] Freytag's letters present an interesting perspective on the difficulties faced by such an operation: we learn, for instance, that the brochures were regularly confiscated by the authorities, and that Hirzel, the publisher of one of the brochures, was targeted by a police investigation in an attempt to identify the members of the group.[24] The letters show the reaction to be in full force by the early to mid-1850s and press freedom to be severely limited:

> Aber durch die Tagespresse ist vorläufig nicht viel mehr zu erreichen. Die Zeitungen sind fast alle auf dem Punkt angekommen, wo ihre Existenz in Frage gestellt ist. Sie sind zur äußersten Vorsicht gezwungen und jede Redaction schreibt mit einem Knebel vor dem Mund. [...] Die *Kölnische*, die *Weser-*, die *Nationalzeitung*, selbst die kleinen *Grenzboten* stehen so, daß bei jedem mißliebigen Artikel Schließung ihrer Pressen oder ein Einfuhrverbot zu erwarten steht. Ueber die meisten Oppositionsblättern schweben Preßprozesse. Diese Gesetze und ihre Handhabung sind abscheulich. Solche Zustände machen jede Redaction vorsichtig und bedenklich auch da, wo ein Bedenken nicht nöthig wäre. Eine Besserung unserer Zeitungssprache hängt jetzt ab von einer größern Erregtheit der öffentlichen Meinung und von dem Grade des Einflusses, den die allgemeine Stimmung auf die Executivbeamten ausübt. Die Presse hat zum Volk gesprochen, jetzt muß das Volk sie stützen und ihr Muth machen, mehr zu wagen.[25]

Freytag himself would eventually come into conflict with the authorities because of his work for the association, facing arrest for the illegal distribution of privileged information about Prusso-Russian political relations through the brochures.[26] Because of the warrant, Freytag was forced to leave Prussia in 1854, and had to ask the Duke for protection until the threat of arrest was finally lifted a year later. Freytag's work for the Literarisch-politischer Verein is thus of twofold significance, shedding light on the nature of press censorship in the *Nachmärz* and revealing the true extent of his political agenda, which is shown to be not merely an establishment one, but something more directly oppositional. This radical tendency in his early politics has hitherto been underestimated in research into Freytag.

### *Die Journalisten* (1852)

After a number of years working on *Die Grenzboten*, Freytag returned to the theatre with *Die Journalisten*, by far the most successful of his dramas. The play became a standard repertory work in the late nineteenth and early twentieth centuries, and Christa Barth has collected statistics which reveal that it repeatedly outperformed both Gotthold Ephraim Lessing's *Minna von Barnhelm* (1767) and Heinrich von Kleist's *Der zerbrochene Krug* (1806).[27] The play has generally been read as a literary response to Freytag's experiences at *Die Grenzboten*, providing comic insights into the world of journalism and celebrating the short-lived period of press freedom between the 1848 revolution and the onset of the reaction, which set in almost immediately after the failure of the revolution, and gained momentum from 1849 to 1850.[28] From the outset, however, *Die Journalisten* was criticized for its ill-defined portrayal of party politics, with even those close to Freytag, such as Julian Schmidt, noting the vagueness of Freytag's political vision in the play.[29] Nevertheless, the play clearly reveals Freytag's reaction to the political realities of the early *Nachmärz*, registering the position of the bourgeois national-liberal project after the failure of 1848.

The compositional history of *Die Journalisten* is convoluted. According to Freytag's memoirs, the play was written in the summer of 1852, in response to a recent election:

> Ich schrieb das Lustspiel *Die Journalisten* in den drei Sommermonaten nieder. Nie ist mir ein Plan so schnell fertig geworden als dieser [...]. Die Vorbilder für die kleinen Typen der Charaktere fand ich überall in meiner Umgebung, auch die Handlung: Wahl eines Abgeordneten [...] lag sehr nahe. (I, 172)

However, as has been noted in criticism, this description of an exceptionally fast and easy composition is contradicted by a letter from Freytag to the actor

Eduard Devrient in November 1852:[30]

> Was Sie für das Stück sagen, ist freundschaftlich [...]. [W]as Sie dagegen bemerken, will ich präcisieren, es ist etwas schlotterig gearbeitet. Ich weiß das. Ich kann es nicht entschuldigen, aber erklären. Das Stück ist nicht in einem Sommer gemacht. Schon vor 3 Jahren schrieb ich die meisten Scenen und ließ sie unlustig liegen. Diesen Sommer habe ich's überfahren und zusammengebaut und da wollte es hier und da nicht passen. Bei dem nächsten Stück soll dieser Theil der Technik besser sein.[31]

From this letter, it appears that *Die Journalisten* was written primarily in 1849, before being reworked in 1852, and that Freytag remained dissatisfied with the result. It also suggests that Freytag still saw himself predominantly as a dramatist as late as 1852, planning to do better 'bei dem nächsten Stück' — further evidence that his supposed aesthetic shift away from drama in 1848 was far from clear cut.

Critics have been quick to excuse the discrepancy between Freytag's memoirs and his letter. Christa Barth has argued that 'die Einzelheiten waren natürlich dem Gedächtnis des greisen Dichters entrückt', while Hans Lindau claims that the memoirs simply refer to the revision of the play in 1852.[32] Neither argument convinces, and one senses that the memoirs are deliberately obfuscating the circumstances of the composition of *Die Journalisten*. Possibly, Freytag simply wished to present himself as an author for whom writing was an easy, natural process — indeed, the memoirs open with an image of the literary muse granting Freytag inspiration. One suspects, however, that he was equally keen to avoid the suggestion of a tendentious connection between the play and the revolution of 1848 — consistent with the habit of the memoirs, seen in earlier chapters, to downplay the radicalism of Freytag's works and stress instead the consistency of his artistic vision.

Barth has argued that Freytag actually began work on *Die Journalisten* in 1848, although her evidence — a reference by Freytag to an unnamed work in a letter to Ludwig Tieck from 1848 — is inconclusive.[33] Of greater significance is Barth's suggestion that the election in *Die Journalisten* was inspired by that of Freytag's acquaintance, Arnold Ruge, to the Frankfurt Parliament in May 1848:

> Bei den Breslauer Wahlen in der Revolutionszeit ereignete sich tatsächlich ein Fall, der an die äußere Handlung in den *Journalisten* stark erinnert: ein um die Stadt altverdienter Wahlkandidat wird im Wahlkampf durch einen weit jüngeren, aber politisch erfahreneren besiegt. Dies war Arnold Ruges Erfolg über den Stadtgerichtsrat Heinrich Simon im Mai 1848, als die Bürger Breslaus ihre Abgeordneten für das Frankfurter Parlament wählten.[34]

The election of Ruge bears a striking similarity to the plot of *Die Journalisten*, and although there is no conclusive evidence that Freytag directly reproduced

Ruge's victory, he did habitually write from experience (as seen in his poems, in *Soll und Haben*, and in the scenes at the *Union* newspaper in *Die Journalisten*). *Die Journalisten* was thus potentially inspired by events in 1848 and primarily written in 1849, before being revised in 1852.

*Die Journalisten* was first performed in October 1852 and was published in 1852 in a five-act *Bühnenausgabe*; this was then republished in 1853 in four acts (the version subsequently used as the basis for the *Gesammelte Werke* edition). Although the play was immediately accepted for performance in Leipzig, Dresden, and Breslau, it was initially rejected by the *Intendant* of the Hoftheater in Berlin, Botho von Hülsen. Ironically, this was precisely the fate that had befallen *Die Brautfahrt* (1841) at the Berlin Hoftheater under the previous *Intendant*, Hofrat von Küstner (see the discussion in Chapter 2). In a letter from December 1852, Freytag wrote of his confusion over the rejection of *Die Journalisten*:

> [Ich] erhalte von Hülsen die Exp. der *Journalisten* mit der kurzen geschäftlichen Anzeige zurück, daß das Stück zur Aufführung an seinem Theater nicht geeignet sei. Ich hatte an ihn so freundlich geschrieben, wie man an einen Gentleman schreibt und enthalte mich aller Reflexionen über diese Antwort, die vorläufig zu nichts führen würden. Dagegen möchte ich doch sehr gern wissen, bevor ich weitere Schritte tue, was für Gründe die Intendanz zu so unbedingter Ablehnung gehabt hat. Das Stück wird in Dresden, es soll sogar in Wien einstudiert werden, es ist also fast unmöglich, dass irgend ein politisches Bedenken die Annahme gestört hat.[35]

In fact, it was indeed 'ein politisches Bedenken' which had prevented Hülsen from accepting Freytag's play. Hülsen would later write to Freytag, explaining that he had rejected *Die Journalisten* because 'die Wahl und parlamentarische Angelegenheiten und die Besprechung darüber [waren] ein Spiegel der Zustände' and thus, he felt, unsuitable material for the Hoftheater.[36] Hülsen's explanation — specifically his concerns over Freytag's depiction of free elections — reveals quite clearly the impact of the reaction in the early 1850s.

It was not only in Berlin that *Die Journalisten* faced problems. In Vienna, too, Heinrich Laube, the *Intendant* of the Burgtheater, came into conflict with the theatre's management over his production of the play. Freytag appears to have been unaware of this when he claimed in his letter that a Viennese production was in preparation.[37] The concerns in Vienna were not, as in Berlin, over the play's depiction of free elections, but rather the positive depiction of press freedom. Laube was required to demonstrate to the authorities that 'der Journalistenstand [...] nicht geschont wird' in the play before a licence for performance was granted, which it eventually was.[38] In fact, Laube was doing battle on two fronts, also attempting to gain sanction for Freytag's 1846–47 play *Graf Waldemar*, which the Burgtheater had rejected because of its depiction of inter-class marriage (see the discussion in Chapter 2).

The problems that *Die Journalisten* faced in Berlin and in Vienna shed a fascinating light on the state of affairs in German and Austrian theatre in the mid-1850s, as the supposed liberalization of censorship after 1848 came into increasing conflict with the reaction. Freytag appears to have avoided direct contact with state and police censors both before and after 1848, yet, as the above discussion reveals, he still faced the threat of censorship — but indirectly, through the decisions of individual *Theaterintendanten* and their superiors. The path to performance was long and difficult, even for a politically relatively moderate author such as Freytag.

*Die Journalisten* itself details a local election in an unnamed provincial town. Oldendorf, a bourgeois academic and editor of the liberal newspaper *Die Union*, is standing for the liberal party. His conservative opponent is his friend Oberst Berg, a correspondent for the conservative newspaper *Der Coriolan*. Oldendorf's campaign is managed by the bourgeois Bolz, while that of the Oberst is run by the aristocrat von Senden. The latter attempts to win the election by securing the support of the most important voters through a party held in their honour. Bolz, however, subverts this plan, and Oldendorf wins the election. The subsequent rift between the Oberst and Oldendorf means that Oldendorf is unable to marry the Oberst's daughter, Ida. Adelheid, a local aristocrat and former childhood sweetheart of Bolz, reveals how von Senden tricked the Oberst into standing against Oldendorf and, as a result, the friends and lovers are reconciled. In revenge for electoral failure, von Senden conspires to buy the *Union*, turning the liberal newspaper into a conservative mouthpiece, but Adelheid intervenes, purchasing the *Union* herself and passing the editorship on to Bolz. The play ends with the engagement of Adelheid and Bolz, the victory of the liberals in the election, and the salvation of the liberal newspaper. *Die Journalisten* thus presents in hopeful terms the victory of the liberal party over the conservatives (and indirectly the success of the bourgeoisie over the aristocracy), extolling the virtues of political and press freedom in the post-revolutionary era.

Although *Die Journalisten* revolves around the electoral battle between the liberal Oldendorf and the conservative Oberst Berg, the democratic process described in the play is very much in its infancy. The election is an indirect one, and the candidates are not fighting for the votes of the general public — there is no universal suffrage — but for those of 100 *Wahlmänner* who are charged with deciding the outcome of the election:

> KÄMPE [...] Von den 100 Wahlmännern unserer Stadt gehören 40 mit Sicherheit zu uns [the liberals], ungefähr ebenso viel stehen auf den Listen der Gegenpartei [the conservatives], der Rest von etwa 20 Stimmen ist unsicher. Es ist klar, daß die Wahl nur mit sehr kleiner Majorität vor sich gehen wird.[39]

Freytag's description of an indirect election accurately mirrors the nature of democracy in mid-nineteenth-century Germany, where, despite rising demands for universal suffrage, the majority of elections were decided by *Wahlmänner*.[40] The elections in 1848 to the Frankfurt Parliament are a case in point. The Frankfurt Vorparlament decreed that the elections to the Frankfurt Parliament should be based upon universal male suffrage, with (in the words of Carr) 'every independent citizen who had attained his majority' allowed to vote.[41] In reality, however, 'it was left to the various states to define the conditions of "independence"', and many states disenfranchised large sections of the population, the majority implementing indirect elections.[42]

Freytag takes a critical stance towards indirect elections in *Die Journalisten*, illuminating clearly the ways in which the system was open to abuse. A central set-piece of the comedy is, for instance, von Senden's attempt to win over the *Wahlmänner* by laying on a party:

BOLZ      [...] [E]s ist eine politische Gesellschaft, bei welcher Senden Director ist. Sie hält einen großen Fischzug nach Wahlmännern. (III, 29)

BLUMBERG      [...] Es kann nicht fehlen, die Leute müssen Herzen von Stein haben, wenn sie ihre Stimmen nicht geben zum Dank für ein solches Fest. (III, 45)

BOLZ      [...] Aber wenn ich mir denke, diese Leute sind nicht zusammengebeten, damit sie recht von Herzen vergnügt sind, sondern damit sie nächstens ihre Stimmen dem oder jenem Herrn geben, so werde ich kalt. (III, 58–59)

The conservatives believe that by bribing the key *Wahlmann* — the bourgeois wine merchant Piepenbrink — they can secure victory, but their plan backfires after Bolz infiltrates the celebration and persuades Piepenbrink to support the liberal cause instead. However, Piepenbrink joins the liberals not because of their policies or ideological convictions ('Seine politischen Ansichten kümmern mich hier nicht', III, 60), but merely because of the flattery of Bolz, who wins him over by praising the quality of his wine:

PIEPENBRINK      Wissen Sie was, Herr Doctor [Bolz], da Sie den gelbgesiegelten aus meinem Keller doch schon kennen und ein sehr verständiges Urtheil abgegeben haben, wie wär's, wenn Sie ihn hier noch einmal versuchten? Die Sorte wird Ihnen besser schmecken. Setzen Sie sich zu uns, wenn Sie nichts Anderes vorhaben, wir schwatzen dann eins zusammen. (III, 56–57)

It is hard to escape Freytag's somewhat disillusioned suggestion in these scenes that the election is ultimately dictated by the contents of Piepenbrink's wine-cellar rather than by the justness of the liberal cause — a bitter note also identified by Classe: 'Der Rotwein des Herrn Piepenbrink gewinnt infolge des indirekten Wahlverfahrens namhaften Einfluß auf die innere Politik Preußens'.[43]

Freytag's critique of indirect elections can also be seen in his *Grenzboten* articles from 1848 and 1849 (written during the same period as most of *Die Journalisten*). In them, he rails against the process, directing his ire at the (fictional) figure of Michael Mroß:

> Michael Mroß! Ihr werdet diesen Brief nicht lesen. Lest ihr doch, wie ich höre, niemals; am wenigsten deutsch, von dessen Kenntniß und Einwirkungen ihr euch möglichst rein erhalten habt. [...] Michael Mroß! Ihr seid [...] ein ungelehrter, einfältiger Mann [...]. Wie steht's mit eurem politischen Glaubensbekenntniß, Michael Mroß? [...] Der Hauptgrund, [...] der mich trieb, eure unbehilfliche Person an das Tageslicht zu ziehen, ist der Kampf für ein großes Princip. Ich behaupte nämlich und will beweisen, daß eure Wahl und die zahlreichen Wahlen von euresgleichen, welche ein sehr unrühmliches Fakt und für alle Parteien höchst beklagenswerth sind, nur möglich wurden durch das falsche Princip indirecter Wahl. (xv, 3–9)

Freytag scornfully rejects the indirect elections which have allowed Mroß — a farmer from Polish lands who scarcely speaks German — to have a seat in the Frankfurt Parliament. Essentially, if indirect elections can result in the election of a working-class and Polish-speaking representative, then he feels the process has failed. Freytag also disapproved of universal male suffrage, as imposed by Bismarck during the 1867 elections to the Reichstag des Norddeutschen Bundes:

> Mit den Wahlen wird es Ernst. Und doch ist dies allgemeine Wahlrecht das leichtsinnigste aller Experimente, welche Graf B[ismarck] jemals gewagt hat. Niemand weiß, ob er gewählt wird. Und das wird in den nächsten Jahren noch schlimmer sein. Denn die Wahl liegt in den Städten in der Hand der Arbeiter, auf dem Land in der der kleinen Leute, Tagelöhner und Knechten.[44]

Rather, Freytag seems to favour a direct but restricted franchise — presumably because it is less corruptible than indirect elections (the process revealed in *Die Journalisten*), while also not letting the uneducated masses, the workers and the poor, partake in the political process (as universal male suffrage would allow).

Freytag is, essentially, only interested in democracy in so far as it provides the educated middle classes with a voice in the political process, and he is content to disenfranchise all those he does not wish to hear. He does not subscribe to the view that it is the choice of the majority that holds moral legitimacy. His dislike of any uncertainty in the electoral process underlies his critique of the indirect elections in *Die Journalisten* (the fact that Piepenbrink could just have easily voted for the conservatives had they praised his wine first), and is reflected in his treatment of the theme in his *Grenzboten* articles. In the aftermath of 1848, *Die Journalisten*, together with the *Grenzboten* articles, reveals Freytag as excited at the prospect of a new, bourgeois era, yet fearful of the consequences certain electoral models could have for his vision of a bourgeois-dominated German nation-state.

The political battle between liberals and conservatives at the heart of *Die Journalisten* is explored through the friendship of the liberal Oldendorf and the conservative Oberst Berg. This dramatization of the political within a private friendship is very much reminiscent of Freytag's *Vormärz* dramas, discussed in Chapter 2, in which personal relationships were used as a vehicle with which to explore wider political and social themes. *Die Journalisten* has been criticized for its lack of political clarity, and it is true that the play contains little political detail. Nevertheless, Freytag maintains a clear division between the liberal and conservative parties in the play, which is not only revealed in the divided friendship of Oldendorf and the Oberst, but also in the two politically opposed newspapers at the heart of *Die Journalisten* — the liberal *Union*, and the conservative *Coriolan*:

> OBERST Es war schon arg genug, daß er [Oldendorf] die Zeitung [*Union*] übernahm; daß er sich aber jetzt von seiner Partei hat verleiten lassen, als Wahlcandidat für die Kammern aufzutreten, das kann ich ihm gar nicht verzeihen. (III, 5–6)
>
> OBERST Seit Sie [Oldendorf] Journalist geworden sind, Ihre Union redigiren und dem Staat alle Tage vorhalten, wie mangelhaft er eingerichtet ist, seit der Zeit sind Sie nicht mehr der Alte. (III, 6)

It is significant that journalism is almost exclusively considered to be a political activity in the play. Although we do gain occasional insights into the everyday workings of a newspaper (especially in Act One, Scene Two), these ultimately are secondary to journalism's function as a political mouthpiece — in the case of the *Union*, one which criticizes the state and seeks social change. Indeed, the climax of the comedy revolves around the link between politics and journalism, as von Senden attempts to purchase the *Union* solely in order to shift its political affiliation to the conservative cause:

> OLDENDORF [...] Erlauben Sie mir auf den Kern der Sache zu gehen. Soll mit diesem Wechsel des Eigenthümers auch eine Aenderung in der politischen Haltung des Blattes verbunden sein?
> SENDEN (*vortretend*) Allerdings, Herr Professor, das war bei dem Kaufe die Meinung. (III, 108)

The groupings of Oldendorf–Bolz–*Union* and Oberst-von Senden-*Coriolan* thus present a clear liberal-conservative divide, and also a class distinction between a bourgeois-orientated liberalism on the one hand, and a petty-aristocratic conservatism on the other.

Throughout *Die Journalisten*, characters are also shown negotiating between public careers (in politics or journalism) and private lives (friendship and love). It is not only the friendship between Oldendorf and the Oberst that is threatened by political difference; so is Oldendorf's love for Ida, the daughter of the Oberst:

> OLDENDORF Du kannst dir denken, wie peinlich meine Stellung im Hause des Obersten geworden ist. Der würdige alte Herr entweder kalt oder heftig, die Unterhaltung mit beißenden Anspielungen gewürzt, Ida leidend, ich sehe oft, daß sie geweint hat. Siegt unsere Partei [the liberals], werde ich Abgeordneter der Stadt, so fürchte ich, ist mir jede Hoffnung auf eine Verbindung mit Ida genommen. (III, 23–24)

Similarly, the aristocrat Adelheid finds that Bolz, her childhood sweetheart, is unwilling to give up either politics or journalism in favour of love, and that they have unwittingly become opponents in the political battle:

> ADELHEID [...] Sie sehen, Herr Konrad, auch wir sind Gegner geworden.
> BOLZ [...] Ich fürchte Ihren Unwillen, ich zittre bei dem Gedanken, daß diese Wahl Ihnen unlieb sein könnte.
> ADELHEID So suchen Sie die Wahl zu verhindern!
> BOLZ Das kann ich nicht [...]. (III, 51–52)

The political tensions of the play are thus fully embedded in private relationships — an aspect to Freytag's writings which will become increasingly important in his *Nachmärz* novels. Critics who note the lack of overt politics in *Die Journalisten* tend to underestimate the inherently symbolic and political nature of the romances and friendships in the play. *Die Journalisten* eschews detailed political arguments, perhaps assuming that the contemporary audience of a political comedy would already be aware of the political stakes. Nevertheless, it maintains a clear political division at its core, which, through its very abstraction, allows one to project one's own understanding of liberal and conservative on to the text — no doubt one reason why *Die Journalisten* continued to enjoy success into the twentieth century.

It is also significant that the two romances in *Die Journalisten* continue to embody the pro-bourgeois class polemic central to Freytag's *Vormärz* dramas. The marriage of Adelheid and Bolz is, for instance, an inter-class pairing in the vein of the *Vormärz* dramas discussed in Chapter 2: Adelheid is a landed aristocrat with an estate (III, 13), workers (III, 18), and considerable income (III, 14), whereas Bolz is merely the pastor's son:

> BOLZ [...] Ja, allerdings kenne ich sie [Adelheid]. Wir sind aus demselben Dorf, sie vom Schlosse, ich aus dem Pfarrhaus [...]. (III, 26)

Childhood sweethearts, the pair were separated — so we learn — by Adelheid's father, who saw the relationship as unsuitable: 'Der Held [Bolz] wurde aus seiner Familie, aus seiner Heimat entfernt und die Heldin [Adelheid] saß einsam in ihrem Burgsöller und weinte um den Verlorenen' (III, 43).

The inter-class relationship between Bolz and Adelheid is, however, slightly different from those in Freytag's *Vormärz* dramas. For Adelheid is a positive figure, in many respects the heroine of the play, and thus her relationship with Bolz does not represent her cure or rescue from an aristocratic lifestyle, as was the case for the aristocratic figures in *Graf Waldemar* and *Die Valentine* (1846). Nevertheless, Adelheid is brought into the bourgeois fold through marriage: *verbürgerlicht* into the liberal political cause through her love for Bolz and her purchase of the newspaper the *Union*. The inter-class relationship in *Die Journalisten* is thus still symbolic of wider processes of bourgeoisification, but refrains from the expressly anti-aristocratic polemic of the *Vormärz* dramas.

The relationship between Oldendorf and Ida Berg is harder to read in terms of inter-class marriage, since the class status of Ida is unclear. Her father, Oberst Berg, is never directly described as aristocratic, though it is likely that, as a monarchist, conservative, and ex-military officer, he is a member of the petty aristocracy. The aristocracy dominated the commissioned ranks of the military well into the *Nachmärz*, and in 1860, 86 per cent of *Obersten* — Berg's rank — were still from aristocratic backgrounds.[45] Given that the *Landwehr* — the bourgeois-dominated militia — was liberal in attitude, it is unlikely that Oberst Berg served in this section of the army.[46] Even if not inter-class, the marriage between a general's daughter and a bourgeois newspaper editor was, in itself, socially transgressive, and thus can be read as part of a wider social critique in Freytag's play.[47]

*Die Journalisten* both continues and develops Freytag's aesthetic and political schemes of the *Vormärz*. As in his pre-1848 dramas, Freytag stresses the significance of the bourgeoisie for Germany's future, conveying this message through politically divided friendships (Oldendorf and the Oberst) and socially divided love stories (Adelheid and Bolz, Oldendorf and Ida). *Die Journalisten* presents the electoral victory of the liberal bourgeoisie over conservative forces, criticizing the indirect elections, but welcoming the political freedoms the new era offers the bourgeoisie. The combination of Oldendorf and Bolz — of the liberal party and the free press — is presented as central to the future of Germany, and the political ideologies of the play are clearly and systematically depicted. *Die Journalisten* is, however, also distinct from Freytag's *Vormärz* dramas. Freytag's standard opposition of the *Vormärz* — that between the bourgeoisie and the aristocracy — is partially reformulated as an opposition between liberals and conservatives. Class issues are not entirely excluded from the play — there is, as noted, an inter-class marriage between Adelheid and Bolz — but in the post-1848 era, Freytag appears to be partially replacing straight class-antagonism with party-political antagonism — something for which the Frankfurt Parliament would have provided a model.

## Soll und Haben (1855)

In 1855, after seven years dedicated primarily to journalism, Freytag produced his first novel — the major social novel of business, *Soll und Haben*, which embodied the literary-political notion of programmatic realism developed in *Die Grenzboten*. Immediately feted, then gradually forgotten: *Soll und Haben* and its fate in many respects foreshadowed Freytag's own rise and fall in the German literary canon. Nevertheless, *Soll und Haben* is one of the few works by Freytag to continue to attract critical attention and it is a contentious work, chiefly because of its anti-Semitic and anti-Slavic tendencies (as noted in the Introduction). Yet the novel is rarely contextualized within Freytag's wider writings — despite the fact that this '"Bibel" des Bürgertums'[48] manifestly both perpetuates and deviates from the socio-political position of Freytag's *Vormärz* dramas, and is the basis on which all his subsequent writing stands.

Despite the comparatively large number of studies on Gustav Freytag's *Soll und Haben*, the compositional history of the novel has rarely attracted critical attention. This disregard for the precise circumstances of the novel's production is remarkable, given the frequency with which it is read as a product of its time: as representative of a specific set of beliefs held by the German bourgeoisie in the post-revolutionary era.[49] The majority of accounts of the genesis of *Soll und Haben* simply reiterate the few details in Freytag's memoirs — that the novel was published 'zu Ostern 1855' and 'in drei hübschen Bänden' (I, 178), and that it was begun in Summer 1853 (I, 176). Instead of a detailed account, Freytag's memoirs discuss the aesthetic and structural theories he followed when writing *Soll und Haben*. The novel was, the memoirs claim, based on the same dramatic principles Freytag had developed as a playwright during the *Vormärz*:

> [D]ie Theile der Handlung sind in der Hauptsache dieselben wie im Drama: Einleitung, Aufsteigen, Höhepunkt, Umkehr und Katastrophe. In *Soll und Haben* sind die gelungene Schurkerei Itzigs, der Ruin des Freiherrn und Ehrenthals, und die Trennung Antons aus dem Geschäft der Höhepunkt des Romans, und die Rückkehr Antons in das Geschäft mit Allem, was daraus erfolgt, die Katastrophe. (I, 179)

The critic Gabriele Büchler-Hauschild has read these lines as a direct expression of Freytag's 'Romantheorie', arguing that these five stages of drama are reflected in the novel's structure.[50] Certainly, Volumes One and Two of *Soll und Haben* could represent the elements *Einleitung* and *Aufsteigen*, while various events in Volumes Three to Five can be classed as *Höhepunkt* and *Umkehr*. Yet the novel ultimately evades such classifications: Fink's return from America in the penultimate volume could, for instance, function as a *Höhepunkt*, an *Umkehr*, or a *Katastrophe*, depending on one's perspective. It is also impossible to read Anton's return to Schröter's and his marriage to Sabine — the symbolic climax of the novel — as a *Katastrophe*, as Freytag's memoirs suggest. The five stages of drama are simply not reflected in the six volumes of the novel.

Significantly, the dramatic structure of *Einleitung, Aufsteigen, Höhepunkt, Umkehr,* and *Katastrophe* is also absent from Freytag's *Vormärz* dramas. In fact, this progression first appears in Freytag's 1859 play *Die Fabier* (discussed later in this chapter), and is a central theoretical point of his work of 1864, *Die Technik des Dramas* (discussed in Chapter 4). It would appear that Freytag's memoirs take a theoretical concept he first developed in the late 1850s and project it back on to the composition of *Soll und Haben*, suggesting a false continuity between the novel, *Die Technik des Dramas*, and, implicitly, the *Vormärz* dramas. This reveals much about the agenda of revision in the memoirs, but little about the composition of *Soll und Haben*.

Freytag's correspondence from the post-revolutionary period also sheds little light on the work's composition. In July 1854, Freytag noted in a letter to his publisher that *Soll und Haben* would be completed within six weeks (although in fact it took eight months, an anomaly discussed below).[51] The only other reference comes in November 1855, when Freytag writes to Duke Ernst von Coburg Gotha, asking for his opinion on the novel.[52] The letters and memoirs, taken together, appear to indicate that *Soll und Haben* was begun prior to July 1854, had been completed by Easter 1855, and was in circulation by November 1855.

However, further information can be found in a handwritten compositional history of the novel, purportedly written by Freytag and held at the Staatsbibliothek zu Berlin, Preußischer Kulturbesitz.[53] Entitled '*Soll und Haben. Geschichte des Romans*' and first examined in detail by Klaus Christian Köhnke, this manuscript describes how *Soll und Haben* was the product of two phases of work: an initial stage which lasted until July 1854, and a second stage from August 1854 until April 1855:

> Im Sommer 1854 ging ich von August ab mit Ernst an die Vollendung [...]. Von August bis zum Schluß des Decembers schrieb ich die 2te Hälfte des 3ten, die landwirtschaftlichen Scenen des 4ten, das 5te und den Anfang des 6ten Buches. Mitte Januar 55 kam ich in Leipzig an, nachdem ich Ende December mit Hirzel in Gotha abgeschlossen hatte und ihm den Anfang zum Druck übergeben. Der Druck began Anfang Januar. [...] [W]ährend des Drucks corrigierte ich noch das Manusc. und füllte die Lücken aus (Schluß des 3ten Buches, einiges aus dem vierten und sechsten). Mitte April war der Druck beendet, am 19ten wurden versandt.[54]

On the basis of this document, Köhnke argues that *Soll und Haben* was initially conceived as a three-volume work, focusing solely on Anton's adventures in Germany and his first, brief trip to Poland. Köhnke reasons that Freytag's letter to Hirzel from July 1854 supports his thesis, since Freytag's claim that the novel will be finished in six weeks must — in the light of the manuscript — refer to a version of the novel limited to three volumes.[55] The additional eight months

Freytag ultimately required were used to write Volumes Four, Five, and parts of Volumes Three and Six, expanding the original conception of *Soll und Haben* into a far grander scheme.

Köhnke's interesting thesis has not, as yet, been reflected in recent research into the novel. Certainly, elements of his argument remain difficult to confirm — the compositional history is dated only retrospectively to 1855, and since Freytag did not write his novels in longhand, but narrated them to scribes, the manuscripts of *Soll und Haben* at the Goethe und Schiller Archiv in Weimar do not immediately reveal two separate phases of work on the novel. Köhnke also does not attempt to explain why Freytag might have extended the three volumes into six. His thesis, then, while important and suggestive, has yet to be fully substantiated.

*Soll und Haben* is plotted as a combination of *Bildungsroman* and adventure story, centred on the maturation of the hero, Anton Wohlfart. Orphaned shortly after completing his *Abitur*, Wohlfart enters a traineeship at the trading house of T. O. Schröter, and the opening volumes of the novel trace his swift rise through the ranks of the business. Anton's success is paralleled by that of his former classmate, the Jewish figure Veitel Itzig, who has similarly taken on an apprenticeship at the Jewish trading house of Ehrenthal. At Schröter's, Anton strikes up a friendship with the aristocrat Fink, who eventually leaves to pursue his future in America. Through Fink, Anton is introduced to aristocratic society, and begins to fall in love with Lenore von Rothsattel. Itzig, meanwhile, has become involved in a complex plot to bankrupt Lenore's father, the Freiherr von Rothsattel. Anton learns of these plans while attempting to secure some of Schröter's goods caught up in a local insurrection in Poland. The Freiherr ignores Anton's warnings, and Itzig succeeds in ruining the aristocrat.

In the second half of the novel, the Freiherr and his family are forced to move to a rundown estate in Poland. Lenore begs Anton to accompany them and help them make a living; he agrees, and leaves Schröter's, much to the dismay of his colleagues. In Poland, Anton strives to impose order on the estate, but faces the constant danger of an uprising by Polish rebels. Fink returns from America, and takes over the running of the estate, successfully defending the Rothsattels against a Polish attack. Fink proposes to Lenore, and Anton leaves the estate and returns to Germany, where he meets Itzig again, now a successful trader. Itzig commits a murder and drowns in the town's river. Back at Schröter's, Sabine Schröter shows Anton the company's secret accounts — its *Soll und Haben* — and kisses him, simultaneously securing Anton both as a husband and as a partner in the business. Freytag's novel thus successfully embeds the social and political hopes of the bourgeoisie within an entertaining novel, creating what was to become supposedly the most popular German novel of the late nineteenth century.[56]

Critical studies of *Soll und Haben* have consistently noted the central position bourgeois values play in the novel. Anton's *Wilhelm Meister*-like education, his preference for work and stability over adventure and romance, and the novel's central juxtaposition of bourgeois values with those of the aristocracy, Poles, and Jews, have been detailed extensively (see the Introduction). Yet there are also tensions in the novel's depiction of bourgeois values — not least in the merging of business ethics and bourgeois ideologies at T. O. Schröter's, the central location of *Soll und Haben*.

T. O. Schröter's is both Anton's workplace and his home (unmarried employees receiving room and board within the company's building). From the outset, Schröter's is presented as a paragon and paradigm of order:

> Im Centrum der Bewegung, gleichsam als Sonne, um welche sich die Fässer und Arbeiter und Fuhrleute herum drehten, stand ein junger Herr aus dem Geschäft, ein Herr mit entschlossener Miene und kurzen Worten, welcher als Zeichen seiner Herrschaft einen großen schwarzen Pinsel in der Hand hielt, mit dem er bald riesige Hieroglyphen auf die Ballen malte, bald den Aufladern ihre Bewegungen vorschrieb. (IV, 40)

The mass of barrels, workers, and receipts at Schröter's obeys an all-powerful, if undetectable force — the gravity of business — and at the heart of the commotion stands Pix, deploying his paintbrush as a conductor might his baton. The passage both posits the existence of an inherent, natural order at Schröter's (the image of the solar system) and contains a more directly hierarchical vision of control (the image of conductor and orchestra). This second image of a hierarchy is repeatedly emphasized throughout the novel:

> Anton stand unter der gemeinsamen Oberhoheit der Herren Jordan und Pix und entdeckte bald, daß er die Ehre hatte, kleiner Vasall eines großen Staatskörpers zu sein. [...] In dem vordern Comtoir war Herr Jordan die erste Person, der Generalstatthalter seiner kaiserlichen Firma. (IV, 84–86)

The company is presented in pseudo-feudal terms, as an institution where Schröter (the lord) rules over employees (vassals) who 'gehörten seinem Haushalt an' (IV, 64). The 'fürstliches Ansehen' (IV, 58) of the company may seem outmoded, but the novel stresses how the order symbolized by Schröter's makes an essential contribution to the successful conduct of both business and life: 'es war ganz gemacht, bei seinen Theilhabern feste Gesinnung und ein sicheres Selbstgefühl zu schaffen' (IV, 58). Schröter's provides its employees not only with an education in business, but also a social education: a means of developing an ethos and a middle-class identity.

For Anton, Schröter's becomes more than simply a home, a *Zuhause*; it is a form of *Heimat* towards which he can feel pride as he might towards his regional or burgeoning national identity — indeed, Anton's pride in Schröter's is not dissimilar to patriotism. He develops a complex, symbiotic relationship with the business, its building and contents. The rooms and walls physically respond to his absence and presence — fantastical moments generally ignored by critics keen to focus on Freytag's realism:[57]

> Alles im Hause schläft, in allen Stuben und Kammern sind die Menschen zur Ruh gegangen, Alles schläft und Niemand denkt daran, daß Er [Anton] sich zur Heimkehr bereitet [...]. Aber das große Haus [Schröter's] weiß es, und in der Nacht rührt sich's in allen Winkeln, und es knistert im Holz, und es summt in den Galerien [...]. Wer heut Nacht die gelbe Katze [aus Porzellan] sehen könnte, der würde sich wohl wundern. Sie leckt sich und strählt sich [...]. Kein Mensch weiß, daß er zurückkommen wird, aber das Haus merkt es, und es schmückt sich und öffnet seine Thüren, den heimkehrenden Freund zu empfangen.[58]

It is the pull of this *Heimat* which prevents Anton from following Fink to America at the halfway point of the novel (IV, 358); it is the pull of this *Heimat* which calls him back from his colonial adventure in Poland at the text's climax (V, 306). Schröter's is where 'der beste Theil [seines] Herzens ist' (V, 295), a 'festes ehrenhaftes Ziel für sein Leben' (IV, 573). Ultimately, Anton's *Heimat* is not simply the physical surroundings of Schröter's, but also the values it represents — a moral anchor which calls him back however far he travels.

Critics generally have noted how the ideological function of Schröter's is thrown into relief by its juxtaposition with the Jewish trading house of Ehrenthal's. The bourgeois solidity of Schröter's, the 'ruhige[r] und solide[r] Glanz der Einrichtung' (IV, 64), contrasts with the garish and decrepit façade of Ehrenthal's premises: 'Es war kein guter Charakter in dem Hause, wie eine alte Zigeunerin sah es aus, die über ihr bettelhaftes Costüm ein neues buntes Tuch geworfen hat' (IV, 46). Sabine Schröter, the 'gute Fee' (IV, 65) of the Schröter household, is praised for her love of heirlooms, while Ehrenthal's wife is satirized for possessing a 'Geschmack für das Neueste und einen sehr energischen Willen in Theetrinken, Stutzuhren, Möbelstoffen und anderen Eigenschaften' (IV, 136).

Freytag uses this difference in appearance to symbolize a deeper division in the values embodied by the two businesses. Schröter's is home to a bourgeois work ethic, personified in the hero Anton:

> Wir alle, die wir hier sitzen und stehen, sind Arbeiter aus einem Geschäft, das nicht uns gehört. Und jeder unter uns verrichtet seine Arbeit in der deutschen Weise [...]. Keinem von uns fällt ein zu denken, so und so viel Thaler erhalte ich von der Firma, folglich ist mir die Firma so und so viel werth. Was etwa gewonnen wird durch die Arbeit, bei der wir geholfen, das freut auch uns und erfüllt uns mit Stolz. (IV, 309)

The employees of Schröter's work for work's sake: for pride and self-fulfilment, rather than for financial remuneration. This stands in stark contrast to the motivations of the Jewish traders, such as Veitel Itzig, who are repeatedly depicted as driven by greed and the belief in a magic recipe 'durch welche ein armer Handelsmann unfehlbar Glück, Gold und alle Güter der Erde erwerben kann' (IV, 125). Whereas Anton is inspired by 'ein poetischer Duft' (IV, 7) of business he experienced as a child (as his mother ground coffee beans), Itzig is motivated by a far more mercantile and eventually megalomaniacal vision of business. It is not that the bourgeois figures in the novel understand the value of hard work while the Jewish traders are inherently lazy. No one in *Soll und Haben* — not even the hero Anton — works as hard as Veitel Itzig:

> Dabei hatte er [Itzig] die Tugend, nie zu ermüden, er war den ganzen Tag auf den Beinen [...]. Er gönnte sich selbst keine Stunde des Genusses, seine einzige Erquickung war, an den Fingern die Geschäfte abzählen, welche er gerade im Gange hatte, und seinen Gewinn berechnen. (IV, 117)

Rather, it is the motivations for working which distinguish the two groups: Jewish traders who think 'an nichts Anderes [...] als an Erwerb' (IV, 539), and bourgeois figures for whom work is a question of pride and enjoyment, but never of monetary gain for its own sake. Schröter's success is, of course, measured by profit, but it is profit earned for the business and (in Freytag's conceptualization) for the greater good, rather than the benefit of the individuals involved.

The bourgeois work ethic of Schröter's is also contrasted with that of the aristocracy. Schröter explains to Anton that the aristocracy will always fail in business, 'weil ihm das fehlte, was dem Leben jedes Menschen erst Werth gibt, ein besonnenes Urtheil und eine stetige Arbeitskraft' (IV, 559). The aristocracy, we are told:

> sind gewöhnt wenig Arbeit zu haben und viel Vergnügen, Alles wird ihnen zu leicht gemacht im Leben von Klein auf. [...] Ist so Einer höchstens zwei Mal im Tage durch seine Wirthschaft gelaufen, so denkt er, er hat gearbeitet. (IV, 258)

The aristocracy may be work-shy, but they desire wealth, and like the Jewish figures, engage in aggressive forms of exploitative capitalism. As with Veitel Itzig, the Freiherr is not incapable of hard work (IV, 341), but '[w]as ihn lockte, fortwährend, unwiderstehlich, das war der schnelle Gewinn' (IV, 256). The motivations of the aristocracy and the Jewish figures are thus similar — a desire for money at any cost — and contrast strongly with the almost anti-materialist work ethic of Anton and his co-workers at Schröter's. Schröter's, Freytag argues, is a machine in which each employee functions as a cog. For the machine to run smoothly, each cog must give up individual gain and work for the whole: 'Sie sind jetzt als Rad eingefügt in die Machine, und es wird von Ihnen erwartet, daß Sie das ganze Jahr regelmäßig abschnurren' (IV, 67). This image of Schröter's as a machine — as a cooperative where all are equal — sits somewhat awkwardly next to the strongly hierarchical vision of the business which Freytag also develops in the novel. One senses that this slight inconsistency in the depiction is the result of an underlying tension in Freytag's own vision of business. Freytag clearly wanted *Soll und Haben* to show the triumphant success of the bourgeois business model in the 1840s, yet he is equally keen to present the work ethic of Schröter's as a corrective to the rampant, aggressive capitalism of the Jewish traders and the aristocracy. Consequently, Schröter's is depicted as a thriving commercial enterprise (with workers securing an upward flow of capital within a hierarchy) but with an anti-materialist work ethic (where employees are cogs who work for work's sake — a metaphor that Freytag clearly intends to be positive, rather than dehumanizing, in tone). The two images are not mutually exclusive, but neither are they fully compatible. This duality explains many of the peculiarities in the novel's depiction of business, not least the manner in which Schröter's is decapitalized — only rarely in the novel do we witness a financial transaction at Schröter's, compared to the many deals undertaken by Ehrenthal, Itzig, and the Freiherr. Schröter's is thus home to both bourgeois-capitalist and anti-materialist impulses, a tension never successfully resolved by Freytag.

Freytag's description of T. O. Schröter's has been criticized frequently in secondary literature as outmoded: a relic from a bygone age of business hardly suited to the demands of modern capitalism.[59] Freytag himself stresses the old-fashioned nature of the business in the novel: 'Das Gebäude, der Haushalt, das Geschäft waren so altertümlich, solid [...]. Das Geschäft war ein Waarengeschäft, wie sie jetzt immer seltener werden' (IV, 58). Few critics have considered, however, why Freytag should choose an outmoded institution as the main location of his novel. Christine Achinger has argued that the outdated trading house is required so that Freytag can stress the sense-filled poetry and exoticism of business.[60] Michael Kienzle comes closer to the truth when he suggests that Freytag uses Schröter's to represent 'eine [aus] vorindustrieller Vorrats- und Hausväterwirtschaft stammende Moral [...] in [der] Zeit des Industriekapitalismus'.[61]

Yet Schröter's is not merely the last bastion of an outmoded bourgeois morality in the face of amoral capitalism. Certainly, the anti-materialist work ethic and values it represents function as an effective counter to the self-serving capitalist urges of the Jewish traders and the aristocracy. But Schröter's also represents the economic success story of the bourgeoisie, and, through Anton's marriage to Sabine at the novel's conclusion, the company is shown as capable of continuing into the new economic era. Anton provides Schröter's with new energy, with 'Jugendkraft und einen geprüften Sinn' (V, 404). If Schröter's were not outmoded, Anton would be denied this role as its saviour, and his status as the novel's hero would be placed in jeopardy. It is precisely the outmoded nature of Schröter's that allows Anton to become a figure of rejuvenation for the company, preserving its bourgeois values into the next generation. Far from being a mistake by Freytag, the outmoded nature of Schröter's is thus central to the symbolic role of the company in the novel. The combination of Anton and Schröter's — of a hero and his *Heimat* — guarantees the survival of a bourgeois form of capitalism into the new economic era. Indeed, Anton and Schröter's form the ideological heart of *Soll und Haben*, the dual forces of 'Volk' and 'Arbeit' mentioned in Julian Schmidt's programmatic motto to the text: 'Der Roman soll das deutsche Volk da suchen, wo es in seiner Tüchtigkeit zu finden ist, nämlich bei seiner Arbeit' (IV, 1).

Intriguingly, however, although *Soll und Haben* is most frequently read as a novel of German business, over half of the text is set in Poland. Life at T. O. Schröter's — so central to the first three volumes — is gradually eclipsed by two adventure stories: Anton's rescue of Schröter's assets in Poland after the 1846 uprisings (in Volume Three) and his colonial adventures alongside the aristocratic Rothsattel (in Volumes Four, Five, and Six). There has been a tendency in Freytag criticism to view these two adventures as one single episode, which uses Poland 'als früher Wegweiser in der Konsolidierung und Verbreitung eines deutschen Kolonialdiskurses'.[62] However, while both Polish episodes must be read against the background of colonial discourses, they are clearly two individual events, which invoke colonial ideas for different ends.

Anton first travels to Poland in Volume Three of *Soll und Haben*, in order to retrieve, together with Schröter, a caravan of goods that has become stranded in the country after a local uprising. Freytag's memoirs claim that these scenes were partially inspired by his own experiences in Krakow in 1846, when the Austrian annexation of the city from Russian Congress Poland led to revolution: '[I]ch selbst bin mit meinem Freunde Theodor [Molinari] beim Ausbruch der polnischen Revolution in die Nähe von Krakau gereist' (I, 182). Theodor Molinari, as noted in Chapter 1, was a businessman in charge of a trading house in Breslau, which is generally accepted to have been the model for Schröter's, and the similarities between the actual and fictional trip are striking. Although Krakow is never named directly in *Soll und Haben*, we learn that the uprising has occurred in the 'Grenzländer im Osten' (IV, 371), more specifically in 'eine große polnische Stadt unweit der Grenze' (IV, 372) — geographic hints which support the supposition that Krakow provided the inspiration for these scenes.

The critic Kristin Kopp has noted how Anton's initial trip to Poland contains several elements common to colonial adventure stories.[63] Before leaving for Poland, Anton reads James Fenimore Cooper's *The Last of the Mohicans*, and begins to anticipate his forthcoming trip in Cooperesque images of adventure and battle:

> [Anton] ging nach seinem Zimmer, packte geräuschlos eine Reisetasche, holte die damascirten Pistolen heraus, [...] und warf sich halbentkleidet auf das Bett. [...] 'Gut,' dachte Anton. 'Wir reisen in Feindesland, wir schlagen uns mit den Sensenmännern und wir zwingen sie unsere Waaren herauszugeben. [...] [Anton] fühlte nach seinen geladenen Pistolen in der

> Rocktasche und stieg in den Wagen, selbst geladen mit den edelsten und
> seligsten Gefühlen, welche je ein junger Held gehabt hat. (IV, 380–81)

Kopp's analysis is largely convincing, especially given the prominence of the intertextual link to Cooper.[64] However, her interpretation overlooks the subtle irony with which Anton's dreams of colonial adventure are treated. The image of a gun-toting Anton stands, for example, in comical juxtaposition to his otherwise morally pedantic nature, and it is clear that Anton's destiny is not to become a colonial hero, but rather to be a symbol of the regularity and level-headedness of the bourgeoisie. Significantly, Anton's romantic notions of adventure and his projection of a 'Wild West-Semiotik' on to Poland are immediately undercut by his travelling companion Schröter, who coolly reminds his employee that they are on a business expedition:[65]

> [G]egen die Pistolen bewies Herr Schröter eine Kälte, welche den kriegerischen Muth Antons ein wenig dämpfte [...].
>     'Ich glaube nicht, daß Ihnen gelingen wird, durch die Puffer unsere Waaren wieder zu erobern. Sie sind geladen?'
>     Anton bejahte und erwiederte mit dem letzten Rest seines kriegerischen Selbstgefühls: 'Es sind gezogene Läufe.'
>     'So?' sagte der Prinzipal ernsthaft, nahm die Pistolen aus der Tasche, rief dem Postillion zu, die Pferde anzuhalten, und schoß kaltblütig beide Läufe ab. 'Es ist besser, wir beschränken uns auf die Waffen, die wir zu gebrauchen gewöhnt sind.' (IV, 381–82)

Anton's colonial dreams are thus quickly dispatched and, in place of the gun, Schröter and Anton are revealed as possessing the weapons of the bourgeoisie: order, discipline, hard work, education, and culture — values shown as lacking in Polish society:

> Es gibt keine Race, welche so wenig das Zeug hat, vorwärts zu kommen und sich durch ihre Capitalien Menschlichkeit und Bildung zu erwerben, als die slavische. [...] Als wenn Edelleute und leibeigene Bauern einen Staat bilden könnten! [...] Sie haben keinen Bürgerstand. [...] Das heißt, sie haben keine Cultur. [...] [E]s ist merkwürdig wie unfähig sie sind, den Stand, welcher Civilisation und Fortschritt darstellt und welcher einen Haufen zerstreuter Ackerbauer zu einem Staate erhebt, aus sich heraus zu schaffen. [...] [D]as Geheimnis [ist] offenbar geworden, daß die freie Arbeit allein das Leben der Völker groß und sicher und dauerhaft macht. (IV, 382–83)

Polish society, Freytag argues, lacks a middle class, and without this class, there is no culture (and without culture, no civilization). The strongly xenophobic, anti-Slavic commentary revealed in these lines is a clear counterpart to the anti-Semitic content of *Soll und Haben*, though it is the latter which continues to receive most attention in modern commentary.

This anti-Polish sentiment is also echoed in Anton's and Schröter's reactions to the revolution that has shaken Poland: 'Wenn Revolution so aussieht, sieht sie häßlich genug aus', comments Anton, to which Schröter replies: 'Sie verwüstet immer und schafft selten Neues' (IV, 402). Revolutionary Poland is socially disordered, without political or military hierarchy: a state of anarchy which is the precise opposite of Anton's ordered life at T. O. Schröter's. All aspects of society have been affected by the revolution, even that life-blood of the state, the economy: 'Das Land war wie ein gelähmter Körper, langsam rollte das Geld, dies Blut des Geschäftslebens, von einem Theile des großen Leibes zu dem andern' (IV, 371). The situation in Poland is so grave that Anton is forced to remain in the country in order to preserve what he can of Schröter's trade. The future appears hopeless, but, through Anton's diligent application of the lessons he has learnt during his apprenticeship at Schröter's, he eventually masters the chaos which surrounds him:

> Der Verkehr hatte Vieles, was in deutschen Augen als wild und unregelmäßig galt. Und doch übte die Gewohnheit, Verpflichtungen zu erfüllen, einen so großen Einfluß auch auf mutlose Naturen, daß Antons Beharrlichkeit mehr als einmal den Sieg errang. (IV, 432)

There is, undoubtedly, a colonial undertone to Anton's successful imposition of bourgeois business values on the unruly Poles — it is, ultimately, part of a project of civilization. (Kopp's otherwise persuasive analysis surprisingly does not note this point.) Yet in general, Poland is not depicted as a land ripe for colonization, but is rather instrumentalized as a practical example of how chaos can be overcome by order — of the significance of the values represented by Schröter's. Indeed, upon leaving Poland, Anton does not view his time in the country as a successful act of colonization, and national themes and the idea of German expansion into Poland are never mentioned. On the contrary, his experiences have strengthened his loyalty to Germany, his class, and his bourgeois existence:

> Ich habe gute Gesellen auch in der Fremde gefunden, und doch ist mir bei Vielem, was ich erlebte, die Ueberzeugung gekommen, daß es kein größeres Glück gibt, als sich in seiner Heimat mitten unter seinen Landsleuten tüchtig zu rühren. (IV, 508–09)

In spite of the colonial undertones, thus, it is issues of class, rather than of nation, which dominate Anton's first adventure in Poland.

A nationally orientated colonial theme is first expressed explicitly during Anton's second trip to Poland (in Volumes Three to Six). According to Freytag's memoirs, this second trip was partially based on events which occurred in Strelno in 1848 (I, 183). Strelno was in West Prussia, and existed in a state of territorial limbo, belonging to Prussia, but excluded from the Deutscher Bund. That events in *Soll und Haben* are based on Freytag's experiences in West Prussia seems likely, since the novel's description of well-established German enclaves side-by-side with Polish settlements accurately depicts the situation in the region, as well as forming a convincing background for the exploration of colonial themes. As in Anton's first visit to Poland, the spectre of Fenimore Cooper haunts the text: 'Wenn mir Jemand gesagt hätte, daß ich dich [Anton] als roth und schwarz bemalten Indianer, eine Streitaxt in der Hand und Skalplocken an der Hosennaht, wiederfinden würde, ich hätte den Mann für wahnsinnig erklärt' (v, 152). Anton and Fink are described as 'Colonisten auf neuem Grunde' (v, 298); as soldiers protecting 'den Grenzstein unserer Sprache und Sitte [...] gegen unsere Feinde' (v, 299). Florian Krobb has noted how such comments can be read within debates on the German question of the 1850s, specifically as a 'Legitimierung des deutschen Herrschaftsanspruches'.[66] Certainly, Freytag believed in Germany's right to rule over areas of Poland; yet one should be wary of seeing this as indicative of a *großdeutsch* attitude towards the German question, as Krobb's analysis suggests. For Freytag was ultimately in favour of a *kleindeutsch* solution (as shown clearly in his articles for *Die Grenzboten*). The proto-colonial attitudes of *Soll und Haben* should thus not be read as a direct expression of a wider expansionist nationalism, but as limited to specific debates on German–Slavic relations.[67]

Throughout the second Polish adventure, the country is once again described in terms of disorder. Indeed, when Anton finally strays across a well-maintained property, he is able to identify it instantly as that of a German colonist: 'Hurrah! hier ist eine Hausfrau, hier ist Vaterland, hier sind Deutsche' (v, 25). Significantly, the order and cleanliness of the German housewife is no longer simply a symbol of bourgeois efficiency (as was the case in the opening three volumes of *Soll und Haben*), but has become a symbol of national pride — of 'Vaterland'. Bourgeois values have been nationalized. Similarly, Poland is no longer criticized for its lack of a middle class (Anton's primary criticism during his first visit), but has become a foil against which German national identity is revealed:

> Erst im Auslande lernt man den Reiz des Heimatdialekts genießen, erst in der Fremde, erkennt man, was das Vaterland ist. (v, 20)
>
> In einer wilden Stunde habe ich [Anton] erkannt [...], wie sehr mein Herz an dem Lande hängt, dessen Bürger ich bin. (v, 155)

*Heimat*, once synonymous with bourgeois values and the Schröter house, is no longer part of a class ideology, but a national identity.

A parallel to this nationalization of middle-class principles can be found in the changing depiction of Anton. In the opening three volumes of *Soll und Haben*, Anton was primarily a figure of identification for the bourgeoisie. Yet in the second Polish adventure, he is transformed into a national folk figure, aware of his affinity with Germany and the people: 'er fühlte jetzt zuweilen mit Stolz, daß er [...] einer aus dem Volke war' (v, 59). This second set of colonial scenes is clearly an attempt by Freytag to place the bourgeoisie at the heart of a national agenda, a feature which distinguishes them from Anton's first outing in Poland.

It is clearly important to consider the two Polish episodes in *Soll und Haben* as separate entities. Both contribute to a colonial discourse, but to differing extents. The first Polish episode, although influenced by the works of Fenimore Cooper, ultimately views Poland not as a land for colonization, but as a foil against which key bourgeois values of discipline and order are revealed. Neither Anton nor Schröter display any wish to colonize the Poles. Rather, after securing their goods, they return to Germany, a safe haven of order after the disorder of Poland. The second Polish episode is distinctly more colonial in tone, directly supporting the German colonial cause and repositioning the bourgeois values of the first three volumes as national values, transforming Anton from a bourgeois hero into a national hero.

The differences between the two episodes are representative of a greater shift within the narrative of the novel, which moves from class-based to nationally based themes at its halfway point. This shift in emphasis was not without consequences for the internal logic of *Soll und Haben*, leading to tensions between the themes of class and nation — not least in the novel's depiction of the aristocracy. As seen in Chapter 2, the relationship between the middle classes and the aristocracy is central to Freytag's writing. Freytag's *Vormärz* dramas used inter-class marriages as a symbol for bourgeois victory over the aristocracy and the defeat of the social and political hegemonies of the upper classes. The opening volumes of *Soll und Haben* appear to follow this trend, repeatedly alluding to the downfall of the aristocracy, introducing inter-class relationships, and stressing the significance of bourgeois values for Germany's future. Even the first idyllic description of the Freiherr's estate — dominated by Freytag's deliberate mimicry of Eichendorffian imagery — is undercut by a sense of disquiet, as the Baronin expresses fear at a potential change of fortune:[68] 'Mir is manchmal, als könnte so viel Sonnenschein nicht ewig währen; ich möchte demütig entbehren und fasten, um den Neid des Schicksals zu versöhnen' (IV, 28). The Freiherr von Rothsattel is similarly concerned with the state of his current happiness, all too aware how quickly his current situation could unravel: '[E]in einziger ungeordneter Geist [...] hinreicht, das auseinander zu streuen, was emsige Vorfahren an Goldkörnern und Ehren für ihre Nachkommen gesammelt haben' (IV, 26). Freytag's foreshadowing of the Rothsattels' downfall peaks when the Freiherr decides to open a sugar beet factory on his estate. The reader is left in no doubt that this is the crucial point in the family's downfall, as Freytag conjures up a Gothic combination of pathetic fallacy and doom-laden symbols, which is reminiscent of the descriptions to be found in Eichendorff's and Kleist's prose:

> Im Getreide schwirrten die Grillen lauter als sonst, unaufhörlich tönte ihr warnender Ruf [...]. Die kleinen Vögel [...] riefen einander zu, daß etwas

> Furchtbares über ihre Felder hereinbreche [...]. Die wilden Blattpflanzen am Wege [...] waren mit graulichem Staub überzogen und sahen aus wie Gewächse einer untergegangenen Welt [...]. Und als der Schäfer [...] vorüberschritt, sah der Mann so grau und schattenhaft aus wie ein Gespenst aus dem Grabe [...]. In rothem Feuer stand das Schloß mit seinen Thürmen und Mauern vor dem Freiherrn, helle Flämmchen brannten auf den Spitzen der Thürme in die Wolken hinein [...]. [K]ein Zeichen des Lebens war in dem Hause zu erspähen, das Schloß war ausgestorben [...], und die Leute konnten sich erzählen, daß hier einst ein schönes Schloß war, in dem ein stolzer Baron lebte, das sei aber lange, lange her. — Ein gefallenes Haus, eine untergegangene Familie! (IV, 335–37)

Interestingly, amidst these images of destruction and downfall, the Freiherr's son arrives, a symbol of youth and regeneration. Faced with his child, the Freiherr dismisses his alarming visions of disaster and pursues his plans for the factory. This decision, it turns out, hides the bitterest of ironies, since it not only leads to the family's bankruptcy, but also to the death of the son during the family's exile in Poland. The Freiherr realizes too late that 'es war die Leichensäule seines Geschlechts, die er auf seinem Gut aufgebaut hatte' (IV, 545). Significantly, even during the factory's brief period of productivity, the Freiherr senses the calamitous nature of his decision:

> [Der Freiherr] schritt zu der Fabrik, wo die Leute noch auf die Ankunft des Herrn warteten, und erblickte seinen Namenszug, der aus bunten Lampen zusammengesetzt über der Thür brannte, darüber die siebenzinkige Krone seines Geschlechts; und er wandte die Augen ab, der Glanz der Lampen stach ihn in die Seele. (IV, 485)

When, at the end of Volume Three, the Freiherr is bankrupted and attempts suicide, the apocalyptic visions of the downfall of the aristocracy in the first three volumes of *Soll und Haben* appear to have been realized. Had *Soll und Haben* originally been intended to close with Volume Three, as Köhnke has suggested, then the novel would have been a straightforward tale of the aristocracy's destruction: a continuation of Freytag's anti-aristocratic polemic from the *Vormärz* in the most forceful of forms.[69]

However, *Soll und Haben* does not close with the death of the Freiherr. Instead, his suicide attempt fails, and the aristocratic family are able to secure a run-down estate in Poland. Correspondingly, the focus of the novel shifts away from Schröter's and Germany, and towards the life of the Rothsattels in colonial Poland — a seeming reprieve from their destruction so directly foreshadowed in the opening volumes of the novel. A number of critics have argued that the aristocracy undergo a process of bourgeoisification in Poland — that they are granted salvation, but only by taking on the values and characteristics of the bourgeoisie. Mark Gelber has noted that 'der Roman [präsentiert] Beispiele von aristokratischer Neuorienterung [...] und eine klare Vorstellung von den produktiven Möglichkeiten "rehabilitierter" Aristokraten', while T. E. Carter has seen the aristocracy's colonial adventures in Poland as 'a rejection of the old aristocracy, but an acceptance of the new aristocracy'.[70] However, an analysis of the colonial scenes in Poland fails to support such arguments. Certainly, Anton is shown to turn around the fortunes of the Polish estate through the application of his bourgeois qualities of hard work and order. But the novel never suggests the aristocracy themselves are *verbürgerlicht* through this process. On the contrary, the Rothsattels view Anton as an employee — as a servant even — and symbolically refuse to eat at the same table as him (v, 51). Neither the Freiherr nor the Baronin is physically able to work (v, 53, 195), and Lenore quickly loses interest in her attempt to take charge of the finances of the estate (v, 59-60). The aristocracy, far from becoming more bourgeois, actually retreat into their own class while in Poland, refusing to take communion with the German folk (IV, 56) and only socializing with a local Polish aristocratic family (IV, 60-62). Ironically, it is precisely these Polish aristocrats who are leading the Polish uprising against the German colonial presence in Poland, something only Anton — who is not blinded by aristocratic class prejudice — can see: 'Es schien ihm [Anton] nicht männlich und nicht würdig, daß die deutsche Familie sich so hingebend unter Gegnern bewegte, welche wahrscheinlich in diesem Augenblick Feindliches gegen sie und ihr Volk im Sinne hatten' (v, 67). The return of the aristocrat Fink to the estate and his quick accession to the position of estate manager — replacing the bourgeois Anton — further reveals the absence of the bourgeoisification of the aristocracy during these colonial scenes. Anton explicitly defers to Fink's superior skills — 'Von jetzt ab übernimm du [Fink] den Befehl' (v, 216) — while the workers on the estate immediately see Fink as their de facto leader, even while Anton is officially in charge: 'In das Leben jedes Einzelnen kam durch den Gast [Fink] ein neuer Zug, auch die Wirthschaft empfand seine Gegenwart, und der Förster war stolz, einem solchen Herrn die Honneurs des Waldes zu machen' (v, 193-94). The aristocracy are thus neither destroyed nor *verbürgerlicht* in the second half of Soll und Haben. Rather, a shift takes place as the novel progresses and they are granted salvation — albeit outside of Germany and within a socially and nationally useful colonial project, as founders of 'ein neues deutsches Geschlecht' (v, 398). This allows Freytag to inject a directly national note into the novel, but at the cost of the class polemic he had so carefully cultivated in the opening volumes. The themes of class and nation are thus — unexpectedly perhaps — ultimately revealed as uneasy bedfellows in Soll und Haben.

Similar tensions can be found in the romantic relationships of Soll und Haben. In the first three volumes, Freytag carefully develops a pair of inter-class love stories: between the bourgeois Anton and the aristocratic Lenore, and between the bourgeois Sabine and the aristocratic Fink — exactly the same process as in the *Vormärz* dramas. Fink's and Sabine's relationship is left unspoken for much of the novel, before Fink finally proposes to Sabine — a proposal that also incorporates a declaration of love for the bourgeoisie: '[I]ch habe hier das Glück und die Innigkeit eines deutschen Haushalts kennen gelernt. Sie, mein Fräulein, habe ich immer als den guten Geist dieses Hauses verehrt' (IV, 361). Anton's feelings for Lenore begin at their first meeting, when she offers him fruit, Eve-like in her temptation (IV, 18). Their interaction during the regular dance evenings strengthens his feelings (IV, 195–97) and Lenore tentatively reciprocates (IV, 228). Anton's attachment is strong enough that he is willing to sacrifice his *Heimat* — Schröter's — in order to help Lenore's family in Poland: 'Ein Paar Mädchenaugen ziehen ihn von uns ab, es erscheint ihm ein würdiges Ziel seines Ehrgeizes, Geschäftsführer der Rothsattel zu werden' (IV, 564). Strikingly, both of the proposed inter-class pairings in *Soll und Haben* mirror similar pairings in Freytag's *Vormärz* dramas. Fink's and Sabine's relationship is, for instance, a direct duplicate of that between Waldemar and Gertrud in *Graf Waldemar* — the wild aristocrat coming to respect the values of a bourgeois housewife. Similarly, Anton and Lenore mirror the pairing of Saalfeld and Valentine in *Die Valentine* — a headstrong aristocratic female, partnered with a bourgeois hero willing to sacrifice his life for her honour (see the discussion in Chapter 2). There is thus a strong element of continuity between Freytag's *Vormärz* dramas and *Soll und Haben*, not remarked upon in existing secondary literature.

However, these inter-class love stories never materialize in the novel. Instead, they are refashioned into two intra-class pairings. Consequently, the novel diverges from the model of inter-class relations developed in Freytag's *Vormärz* dramas and appears to promote the division of the classes, rather than their merging. Antje Anderson is alone among critics in analysing these intra-class marriages, providing an illuminating contrast with the English novel in the mid-nineteenth century:

> Diese scharfe und betonte Abgrenzung der sozialen Klassen voneinander ist dem englischen Roman fremd. Obwohl auch der englische Roman ähnlich wie *Soll und Haben* oft das Bürgertum in den Vordergrund stellt und als Verhaltensmaßstab nimmt, basiert die Vorrangstellung der *middle classes* oft auf der Vermischung und Verbindung mit dem Adel, nicht auf Abgrenzung.[71]

Anderson argues that 'der kulturhistorische Hintergrund für diesen Unterschied ist, daß das Verhältnis der sozialen Schichten in England und in Deutschland in der Mitte des neuzehnten Jahrhunderts grundverschieden war'.[72] Essentially, while inter-class marriages were possible in England, they were impossible in Germany, and 'es [war] für die zukünftige gesellschaftliche Entwicklung [Deutschlands] [...] notwendig [...], daß sich das Bürgertum vom Adel abgrenzt, wenn es politisch und kulturell die Vorreiterschaft übernehmen will'.[73]

Anderson's arguments would be convincing, were it not for the evidence of Freytag's other works. For as soon as one contextualizes *Soll und Haben*, it is clear that Freytag did believe in the social possibility of inter-class marriage in the mid-nineteenth century — a theme that is key to all his writings, from his first drama to his last novel. Why is it, then, that *Soll und Haben* chooses to emphasize the division of the classes over their merging?

Quite simply, had Freytag pursued the theme of inter-class relationships, he would have undermined his greater aim for *Soll und Haben* — the promotion of German business and bourgeois values. Consider the outcome, had the inter-class relationships been pursued fully. If Fink had married Sabine, he would have become a central figure at Schröter's: both part of the family and the heir to the business. The future of German capitalism would have been represented in the alliance of the bourgeoisie and the aristocracy, with the aristocracy in the ascendancy. Anton — the supposed hero of the novel — would have been pushed to the periphery, his *Bildung* rendered pointless. Similarly, had Anton married Lenore, he would have found himself lending his bourgeois energy to resurrecting the aristocratic estate in Poland — a renewal of aristocratic power in the form of a colonial project. Both endings would decentralize the bourgeoisie in favour of the aristocracy — clearly, an impossible outcome for a class crusader such as Freytag. Florian Krobb has argued that the love stories in *Soll und Haben* are of little critical interest.[74] Yet, as the above discussion has revealed, they in fact play a central role in the novel and Freytag's decision in the end to pursue a series of intra-class rather than inter-class relationships directly determined the ideological tenor of his novel. Far from being irrelevant, the private relationships in *Soll und Haben* should thus be seen as key bearers of Freytag's political and social message: an instrumentalization of a love story for ideological ends.

Gustav Freytag's letters and memoirs reveal the broad range of intentions behind *Soll und Haben*. Freytag variously claimed that the novel's aim lay in '[politische] Tendenz', that it detailed the 'Ruin eines adeligen Gutsbesitzers' and that it had 'das Verhältnis zweier Liebende [als] leitende Idee'.[75] In addition, the novel was supposed to reveal 'das [...] Volk [...], wo es in seiner Tüchtigkeit zu finden ist, nämlich bei seiner Arbeit' (IV, 1), hoped to overcome 'die Muthlosigkeit und müde Abspannung der Nation' (IV, 3), and had as its 'poetische Idee' (I, 179) the pragmatic doctrine that one's dreams should never become one's master. Given this surfeit of themes, it is clear why Hubrich has argued that Freytag 'wollte zu sehr und zu vieles' in *Soll und Haben*.[76]

Two overarching themes nevertheless dominate the novel: the promotion of a bourgeois class ideology and the development of a German national identity. The former is symbolically represented in the institution of Schröter's: an interface for bourgeois and business values and a *Heimat* for the novel's hero, Anton Wohlfart. Throughout the opening three volumes of *Soll und Haben*, bourgeois values are contrasted with a trio of non-bourgeois ideologies — those of the Jews, the aristocrats, and the Poles. The national theme reaches its apogee in the colonial adventures of the final three volumes, as Anton develops an increasing sense of his German and folk identity. Both themes are symbolically expressed in the intra-class relationships with which the novel concludes. Anton and Sabine are paragons of bourgeois virtue, securing the future economic dominance of the middle class, while Fink and Lenore found something approaching a new German dynasty as part of a colonial project in Poland.

Such conclusions offer a convincing account of Freytag's intentions for *Soll und Haben*. However, as revealed in the discussion above, they do not wholly account for a number of complexities and inconsistencies in the depiction. *Soll und Haben* opens by prophesying the downfall of the aristocracy, but closes with their salvation as colonists. Inter-class romances are developed along the lines of Freytag's *Vormärz* dramas, but are suddenly transformed into less precarious intra-class romances. The heart of *Soll und Haben* — the institution of Schröter's — is subordinated to a colonial story, and out of a *Bildungsroman* there develops a tale of foreign adventure. As it were, Goethe morphs into Fenimore Cooper.

A number of critics have argued that these shifting attitudes towards the aristocracy, along with the novel's move from a class-based polemic to a national one, expose the 'breakdown of Freytag's socio-ethical structure', revealing an uncertainty in the middle class after the failure of the 1848 revolution.[77] Steinecke has gone so far as to argue that *Soll und Haben* is a record of the 'Ängste und [...] Traumata' of the bourgeoisie after 1848.[78] However, *Soll und Haben* does not appear to be a text plagued by insecurity. On the contrary, it presents a wilful view of society where a confident bourgeoisie has survived the perils of industrialization and capitalism. By the mid-1850s, it should be remembered, the bourgeoisie were the economic core of German life and had already begun to rediscover their political voice through organizations such as the Nationalverein, of which Freytag was a founding member.[79] Freytag himself had fought repeatedly for bourgeois and national interests in *Die Grenzboten* and written the politically optimistic comedy *Die Journalisten*. It is oddly anachronistic to claim that in 1855 the bourgeoisie still felt the need to lick the wounds inflicted by 1848.

Freytag does not suffer from ideological insecurity, but rather from what could be termed a surfeit of ideology. *Soll und Haben* presents the downfall of the aristocracy and the economic victory of the bourgeoisie, but finds it expedient to grant the aristocracy a reprieve as colonists in Poland, introducing a national theme to the novel. As a consequence, attention in the later volumes drifts away from Schröter's and the business and class values it represents, a problem Freytag resolves by reversing a set of inter-class romances into intra-class pairings. By stressing the division of the classes rather than their merging, the novel must compromise its class polemic, but as a result is able to extol the importance of both bourgeois and national identities simultaneously. The emphasis placed on the division of the classes in *Soll und Haben* is thus primarily a pragmatic compromise, an expedient response to conflicts within the narrative. Vitally, it should not be seen as a precise expression of Freytag's vision of class relations. For, in favouring division over merging, *Soll und Haben* remains the exception rather than the rule in Freytag's oeuvre. That critics continue to argue that the core of Freytag's bourgeois ideology lies in the strict division of the classes mainly reflects a neglect of those other works of his for which he is now less famous — a myopic *Soll und Haben*-centricism.

## *Die Fabier* (1859)

Freytag's next significant literary text after *Soll und Haben* was the drama *Die Fabier*. Set in the early Roman Republic, and written in strict iambic pentameters, *Die Fabier* initially stands in stark contrast to the contemporary themes and predominantly realist aesthetic of the novel. Indeed, the majority of critics have treated *Die Fabier* as an anomaly in Freytag's oeuvre, a work of minimal critical interest, 'weil [es] stofflich von Allem, was der Dichter vor- und nachher geschrieben hat, so wesentlich verschieden [ist]'.[80] However, despite the specificity of its historical context, the play's depiction of the conflict between the patricians (the privileged class) and the plebeians (the citizens) of fifth-century Rome can be read as an allegorical representation of Freytag's contemporary class concerns. While remaining broadly faithful to historical accounts of early Roman society, *Die Fabier* reveals much about Freytag's vision of social and political life in the mid-nineteenth century, and the play is a less perplexing sequel to Freytag's novel than it at first appears.

According to Freytag's memoirs, he began work on *Die Fabier* in the summer of 1858 and completed the play in early 1859 (I, 192). However, the memoirs are contradicted by Freytag's correspondence with his friend Eduard Devrient (who was interested in staging the play), which reveals that *Die Fabier* was actually the result of a much lengthier, dispute-ridden, and remarkably collaborative process between the two men. The Freytag–Devrient letters first mention *Die Fabier* in June 1857, when Devrient writes to Freytag asking for a copy of the play — suggesting that *Die Fabier* was either complete, or nearing completion, a year before Freytag's memoirs state he began work on it.[81] No letters exist for the period from July 1857 to March 1858, but it is clear that Freytag did not send Devrient a copy of *Die Fabier* in the interim, since in April 1858 Freytag wrote: 'Mein Stück erhalten Sie zuerst, sobald ich mit der Vereinigung der Verse fertig bin, welche Arbeit zu der lästigsten der Erde gehört'.[82] Ultimately, Devrient would have to wait until March 1859 — practically another year — before receiving a copy of *Die Fabier*: 'Beifolgend send ich [Freytag] Ihnen [Devrient] das erste Exemplar des Trauerspiels, welches der Verleger mir zuschickt. Es hat lange gedauert [...] mit großen Unterbrechungen, Krankheit, Tod meines Bruders, zuletzt ein Brand in der Druckerei'.[83] Although the difficulties detailed in Freytag's letter no doubt played a role in the delay in the publication, the correspondence between Freytag and Devrient clearly reveals that the play was the result of at least two years' work, and not the single summer Freytag's memoirs claim.

The publication of *Die Fabier* in 1859 did not, however, mark the end of its compositional history. The Freytag–Devrient letters reveal how over the next two years and nine months — until December 1861 — the two friends engaged in an extensive, increasingly fractious debate about the content, form, and language of the play. From the outset, Freytag was aware of the dramatic weakness of *Die Fabier*, warning Devrient that the work was essentially unsuitable for performance:

> Wenn aber das Stück auch für die Bühne geschrieben ist, so würde es doch, so scheint mir, selbst bei kräftigerem Leben unserer Theater eine schwere Aufgabe sein, in gegenwärtigem Zustand mag es wohl aussehn wie ein Ungethüm, herb, lang, übermäßig schwer und zweifelhaft [...]. Das Alles empfand ich lebhaft während der Arbeit.[84]

These comments stand in direct contradiction to Freytag's memoirs, which explicitly state that he was unaware of the theatrical problems of *Die Fabier* until its first performance (I, 194). Devrient shared Freytag's concerns, noting the extreme length of the text and the density of its language:

> Das römische Kostüm der Rede, die Umwundenheit und Ungenauigkeit des Ausdrucks lähmt die große und schöne Energie der Gedanken. Ich fürchte sehr, die Schauspieler werden die Sprache nicht verständlich bringen, und selbst der beste Redner wird Mühe haben, daß ihm der Hörer sympathisch folgt.[85]

However, Devrient's greatest complaint concerned the outcome of the tragedy, which, he felt, undermined the work's key theme: the pursuit of inter-class marriage between the plebeians and patricians. Devrient's letters reveal that Freytag's 1859 version of *Die Fabier* did not conclude with the legalizing of inter-class marriage (which is the case in the *Gesammelte Werke* edition).[86] He urged Freytag to alter this aspect of the drama:

> Am besten aber ist es gewiß: das Ehegesetz in seiner ganzen staatlichen Wichtigkeit in dem Stücke fast dominieren zu lassen. [...] In Ihrer Tragödie bleiben die Junker Sieger, auch im Untergange, die Bauerntölpel haben sich für die gnädigen Herrn totschlagen lassen, nichts weiter [...]. Das ist wirklich nicht erbaulich, lieber Freund.[87]

Freytag was to follow Devrient's advice, centralizing the theme of inter-class marriage and concluding the play with the plebeians being granted the right to marry patricians: 'Ihre Striche und kleinen Bemerkungen habe ich wohl sämmtlich gehorsam adoptiert. Es war mir die detaillierte Mittheilung lehrreicher und förderlicher als irgend ein anderer Einfluß von Außen, den ich je erfahren'.[88] By altering the play's conclusion so that it ends with the sanctioning of inter-class marriage, Freytag fundamentally strengthens its anti-aristocratic and pro-bourgeois stance — a politically significant shift, albeit one which had been externally prompted. (Freytag's initial unwillingness to end *Die Fabier* with the authorization of inter-class marriage possibly stemmed from concerns over historical accuracy, as detailed in the following discussion.) A second edition of *Die Fabier*, incorporating Devrient's suggested alterations, was published in December 1861, and was dedicated to Devrient — an acknowledgement, surely, of the impact he had on the final form and content of the play.[89]

The performance history of *Die Fabier* is almost as complex as that of its composition. Freytag's memoirs claim that he sent the text in 1859 to 'Laube in Wien, Devrient in Karlsruhe, sonst nur nach Berlin, Dresden und zwei bis drei Theater' (I, 193), although this is contradicted by his letters to Devrient, in which he claims that the latter was the only *Intendant* to have received a copy and was Freytag's sole choice as director.[90] By February 1860, however, Freytag had also sent the play to Dresden, frustrated at the time it was taking to stage the play in Karlsruhe. He informed Devrient: 'Da es nicht möglich war, in Karlsruhe den Anfang zu machen, so ist mir Dresden doch noch lieber als ein anderes Theater'.[91] The first performance of *Die Fabier* took place in Dresden in April 1860, and the play was badly received (a point on which the letters and memoirs concur).[92] Devrient eventually directed his own production in the winter of 1860, with greater success — though performances of *Die Fabier* were limited in number and the play never became a repertory work.

Despite the relative failure of *Die Fabier* on stage, it was nevertheless considered for the prestigious Schiller Prize, awarded every three years to the best German drama. Devrient was a member of the commission charged with awarding the prize, and his diaries reveal the pivotal role he played in short-listing Freytag's tragedy: '[Ich] hatte alle scharfgespitzten Pfeile der ganzen Commission, die wahrhaft himmelverdunkelnd auf die *Fabier* abgeschossen wurden, mit meiner einzigen Brust aufzufangen und zu pariren'.[93] Freytag did not, however, view his nomination for the Schiller Prize as an honour. Early in the proceedings, the commission leaked the fact that they had struggled to find any dramas worthy of inclusion in the competition, and Freytag was embarrassed that his work was being publicly identified — even if indirectly — as mediocre. This feeling only deepened when the news broke that *Die Fabier* was not the outright winner but would share the prize with Gustav Heinrich Gans von Putlitz's tragedy *Das Testament des Großen Kurfürsten* (1858). In a letter to the Prussian Minister for Culture in October 1860, Freytag wrote:

> Ferner hat, wie verlautet, die Kommission als eventuelles Auskunftsmittel vorgeschlagen, dem Trauerspiel *Die Fabier* die verheißene Geldsumme, dem *Testament des Kurfürsten* die Denkmünze zu erteilen. Es ist im Interesse der Preisverteilung selbst zu wünschen, daß diese Teilung nicht vorgenommen werde. Welches soll hier der erste, welches der zweite Preis sein?[94]

In a move that appears selfless, but which was designed to disassociate himself from the whole debacle, Freytag suggested to the Minister 'daß der gesamte Preis statutengemäß auf Herrn zu Putlitz übertragen werde'.[95] The commission eventually decided not to award the prize to either party, and Freytag continued to view the incident 'mehr [als] Kränkung [denn] als Ehre' (I, 199).[96]

Freytag's tragedy is set in the early years of the Roman Republic and against the backdrop of the battle of Cremera in 477 BC. The primary historical source for the play was Livy's *Ab Urbe Condita*, which Freytag probably came across in the *Römische Geschichte* (1854–56) of his friend and *Grenzboten* collaborator Theodor Mommsen.[97] As the play opens, the Veientes have attacked Rome, pillaging the homes of the patricians, but sparing those of the plebeians, thereby increasing tensions between the two groups and raising the prospect of civil war. The gens Fabia, the most powerful of the patrician families, suspect Sicanius, the Tribune of the Plebs (the representative of the plebeians in the Senate), of supporting the Veientes. When Sicanius subsequently vetoes the plans of the gens Fabia to declare war on the Veientes, they kill him — a crime so serious that, if discovered, it could bring down Rome. Spurius, the new Tribune, discovers the truth behind Sicanius' death and tries to blackmail Consul Fabius into legalizing inter-class marriage between the plebeians and the patricians. In the meantime, Spurius' son Icilius has fallen in love with Fabia, the daughter of the Consul, though they cannot consummate their love since they belong to different classes. After a further attack by the Veientes, the gens Fabia again declare war, although their plans are once more vetoed by the Tribune of the Plebs. The Consul decides the gens Fabia shall fight alone and, although they are successful in battle, they are ambushed by the surviving Veientes on their way back to Rome. Spurius allows plebeian troops to go to the rescue of the gens Fabia, but on the condition that inter-class marriages be permitted — a condition granted by the Senate. Icilius also goes to the aid of the gens Fabia, but dies with them on the battlefield. The play ends with a double victory for the plebeians: the downfall of the gens Fabia and the authorization of inter-class marriage.

Although the Roman setting of *Die Fabier* is an exception among Freytag's

German-centred writings, even the briefest summary of the tragedy's plot reveals the relevance of the play's themes for German society in the mid-nineteenth century. *Die Fabier* revolves around the increasing conflict between the (aristocratic) patricians and the (bourgeois) plebeians of Rome. The patricians have lost their connection to the people of Rome, with whom they share a common ancestry, but whom they now lead as tyrants:

> SICANIUS [...] Jetzt dünkt der Mann von altem Landgeschlecht
> Sich wie ein König, zählt die Ahnenreih'
> Bis zu den Göttern, und den Göttern gleich,
> Theilt er mit seinem Volke nur die Luft,
> Nicht Ehe, nicht Gericht, die Würden nicht. (III, 116)

This process is exemplified in the gens Fabia. Once the founders of the city, they are now seen as wolves (the sign of their gens) threatening the plebeian lambs:

> SICANIUS [...] Jetzt zählt dreihundert Krieger das Geschlecht [the gens Fabia],
> Noch trägt das Wolfshaupt Jeder auf der Brust,
> Doch wir [the plebeians] sind jetzt die Lämmer ihrer Weide. (III, 117)

Sicanius, the Tribune of the Plebs, is plotting to bring about the downfall of the aristocracy and secure Rome for the plebeians. He arranges for the Veientes to attack Rome, but with the key proviso that 'Die Güter nur des Adels sucht der Feind' (III, 139). Essentially, Sicanius attempts to bring about a bourgeois revolution by exacerbating the division between the two classes, escalating discontent to the point of rebellion:

> NUMERIUS Den Adel und die Bürgerschaft entzwei'n,
> Unfrieden streuen zwischen Hof und Hof,
> Das Volk empören gegen den Senat,
> Das, Consul Roms, ist die Vejenterlist. (III, 140)

The opening of *Die Fabier* thus presents Rome as a city on the brink of revolt, divided along class lines and with the plebeians ready to rise up against the tyranny and particularist interests of the aristocracy — a situation which would have struck a chord for many Germans for whom the revolutions of 1848 and the political crises of the *Vormärz*, not least the demands for constitutional and social reform, were still a recent memory.

The play does not, however, endorse the revolutionary stance embodied by Tribune Sicanius, and presents an alternative solution to the class conflict threatening Rome. This is expressed by the plebeian Spurius, who stresses how social evolution, rather than political revolution, is the key to social change:

> SPURIUS [...] Unbillig eifert der Tribun [Sicanius] und eilt
> Zu brechen der Geschlechter Herrschermacht.
> Die Arbeit thut allein der Gott der Zeit,
> Der Alles bricht [...]. (III, 131)

Spurius identifies a folk force in Roman society, which, he claims, will rival and ultimately outstrip the power of the aristocracy, whom he criticizes for their decadent behaviour and for shirking their responsibilities:

> SPURIUS [...] Sie [patricians] sitzen hier auf schön geschnitzten Stühlen
> Von Elfenbein, weissagen uns und herrschen.
> Ihr junges Blut verschwendet Gold und Habe
> Auf reiche Waffen, Ruhm und Kriegerthat,
> Auf Sklavenmädchen aus Hellenenland,
> Und ihre Herden zählt ein schlauer Vogt.
> Derweile wachsen wir [the plebeians] durch harte Arbeit
> Auf unsrer Scholle, still und ungemerkt
> Mehrt sich der Landgenossen Hab' und Kraft.
> Jetzt brauchen sie uns gnädig Dienern gleich,
> Die Enkel werden ihnen Helfer und vielleicht
> Der Enkel Enkel einst ihr starker Herr. (III, 131)

Spurius paints a progressive image of a folk force ready to rise to power which will rightfully assume a ruling position through their diligent application of 'harte Arbeit' — the core value of Freytag's bourgeois ideology. Spurius' words are reminiscent of Freytag's 1844 tragedy *Der Gelehrte*, which similarly emphasized the key role of work in the maturation and self-realization of the bourgeoisie:

> WALTER [...] Laß jeden Einzelnen zum Mann erst werden,
> In seinem Kreise, wo er sicher schafft, —
> Dann reift das Volk von selbst für Mannesthat!⁹⁸

In turn, Spurius' criticism of the gens Fabia for neglecting their responsibilities and devoting their time and resources to private pleasures is identical to the criticism levelled against Graf Waldemar in Freytag's 1847 drama *Graf Waldemar*:

> HUGO    Waldemar, ein so reicher Geist, ein so adliger Sinn [...] und ein so
>         verwüstetes, zerfahrenes Leben! (II, 228)

One is also reminded of *Soll und Haben* and the criticism of the Freiherr von Rothsattel, who is 'gewöhnt wenig Arbeit zu haben und viel Vergnügen' (IV, 258), as well as of the emphasis placed on the work ethic of T. O. Schröter's in the novel. The criticism levelled at the patricians of Rome in *Die Fabier* and the thematic emphasis on work thus mirror elements of Freytag's social critique developed in his earlier works.

Rejecting revolution, the play embraces inter-class marriage as a means by which to promote the bourgeois cause. As in Freytag's other dramas (and, to an extent, in *Soll und Haben*), *Die Fabier* explores this theme through an inter-class love story. The patrician Fabia is in love with the plebeian Icilius, but Icilius rejects Fabia's romantic advances, citing the impossibilities of a cross-class relationship:

> ICILIUS  Nicht also, Jungfrau. In der Hügelstadt
> Neigt sich die Fürstentochter nicht dem Sohn
> Des Landmanns. [...]
> Ich bin kein Held, den so du ehren darfst. — (III, 134–35)

Freytag stresses how their relationship is not only socially impossible, but illegal — 'Der Geschlechter Brauch | Verbietet solch ein Bündnis' (III, 165) — and the final three acts of *Die Fabier* focus on Spurius' attempts to convince Consul Fabius and the Senate to legalize inter-class marriage.

Fascinatingly, the emphasis on class conflict and inter-class marriage in *Die Fabier* is not an anachronistic projection of nineteenth-century concerns on to the Roman past by Freytag. Between 509 and 287 BC, Rome was shaken by conflicts between the plebeians and patricians, and plebeian agitation led to the Senate's approval of inter-class marriage in 445 BC.[99] In addition, the issue of marriage rights features heavily in Livy's account of the foundation of Rome, which details the horror that many patricians felt at the prospect of a law sanctioning inter-class relationships:

> That he was introducing a confounding of family rank, a disturbance of the auspices both public and private, that nothing may remain pure, nothing uncontaminated; that, all distinction being abolished, no one might know either himself or those he belonged to. For what other tendency had those promiscuous intermarriages, except that intercourse between commons and patricians might be made common after the manner of wild beasts; so that of the offspring each may be ignorant of what blood he may be, of what form of religion he was; that he may belong half to the patricians, half to the commons, not being homogeneous even with himself?[100]

In *Die Fabier*, Spurius argues that inter-class marriages will quell the conflict between the plebeians and the patricians, echoing his historical counterpart, the Tribune of the Plebs Canuleius, who argued, according to Livy, that if the law was not passed, 'ye sever the bonds of civil society and split one state into two'.[101] Freytag thus follows classical sources in *Die Fabier*, accurately representing the desire of the plebeians to destroy the patrician monopoly in government and society, and revealing the destabilizing effects of class divisions for the Roman state.

However, *Die Fabier* does employ dramatic licence, truncating the recorded events and adding storylines which increase the intensity of the drama. Prime among these are the murder of Sicanius and Spurius' attempts to coerce Consul Fabius into sanctioning inter-class marriage by threatening to reveal the complicity of the gens Fabia in Sicanius' death:

> SPURIUS [...] Zwiespältig hadern Adel und Gemeine,
> Zwei Völker lagern sie auf einem Markt,

> Dieselben Götter und die gleichen Feinde,
> Und ewig doch geschieden Haus und Bett.
> Das stachelt die Tribunen, kränkt die Menge,
> Den Edeln treibt's zum Morde. [...]
> So lang' wir lebten, klang es: Rache, Rache!
> In Brautgesängen endet das Geschrei.
> Und darum fleh' ich jetzt von deiner Macht
> Das Recht der Ehe zwischen uns und euch. [...]
> Das Recht der Ehe wird der theure Preis,
> Um den ein Volk des Toten [Sicanius'] Blut verzieht. (III, 200–03)

These dramatic scenes have no counterpart in Livy, who merely states that the marriage laws were repealed in the hope that the plebeians would enlist in the Roman army — a rather more prosaic motivation: '[The patricians] agreed that the law regarding inter-marriage should be passed, judging that by these means [...] the commons, content with the inter-marriage law, would be ready to enlist'.[102] Indeed, Freytag diverges significantly from Livy's record in *Die Fabier* by proposing a link between the downfall of the gens Fabia and the repeal of the marriage laws. The play suggests that the law was changed so that plebeians would agree to rescue the gens Fabia in the battle of Cremera. In fact, the battle of Cremera took place in 477 BC, while the repeal of the marriage laws occurred in 445 BC. As stated above, one suspects that Freytag initially hesitated to conclude *Die Fabier* with the authorization of inter-class marriage becaue he wished to avoid the historical distortion it would introduce to the play. However, by following Devrient's suggestion and presenting the two events concurrently, Freytag achieves a dramatically powerful conclusion. The potent image of the downfall of the aristocracy and the ascendancy of the bourgeoisie may be historically imprecise, but it is a suggestive allegory which ultimately reflected more closely Freytag's hopes for the breakdown of class structures in *Nachmärz* Germany.

*Die Fabier*, therefore, is a broadly accurate rendering of the political clashes between the aristocracy and the bourgeoisie in the Roman Republic, but also a manipulated version of that history, using the past as a forum with which to reveal a political allegory of social change. While in his memoirs Freytag dismisses the play as 'ein kleiner gelehrter Zopf' (I, 194), it nevertheless marked the return of an explicitly anti-aristocratic tone to his writings after the relative calm of *Die Journalisten* and the complexities of *Soll und Haben*. The aristocracy are shown to have squandered their abilities, ignored the value of hard work, and become tyrants in the place of leaders. The play's climax — depicting the downfall of the aristocracy and the success of the bourgeoisie — closes with the demand for 'Versöhnung den Geschlechtern und dem Volk' (III, 276), stressing the need for the merging of the classes and echoing the political position of Freytag's *Vormärz* dramas. Focusing on inter-class marriage and revealing the dangers of class division for the future of a nation, *Die Fabier* should be read as an allegory of the political situation of Germany in the mid-nineteenth century — in its way almost as important a text for understanding Freytag's bourgeois ideology as *Soll und Haben*.

The 1850s were, in many respects, the most diverse years of Gustav Freytag's career. He experimented with different dramatic genres, from contemporary comedy to historical tragedy, and broke new ground with his social novel *Soll und Haben* and the aesthetic of programmatic realism. He dedicated himself to journalism, editing *Die Grenzboten*, and he joined the Literarisch-politischer Verein, promoting the bourgeois liberal cause and the ideal of a unified Germany under Prussian leadership. The decade also proved to be Freytag's most fruitful as an author, generating his two most successful and enduring literary works: *Die Journalisten* and *Soll und Haben*.

In many ways, it is correct to view 1848 as a moment of transition for Freytag. Rejecting drama in favour of journalism, Freytag clearly sought a greater level of political engagement in the issues of his day. The editorship of *Die Grenzboten* provided him with the opportunity to influence public opinion in a manner impossible in his *Vormärz* dramas, and his only literary work from the revolutionary period, the comedy *Die Journalisten*, similarly reveals his increased interest in politics. Rather than focusing on the class antagonisms central to Freytag's *Vormärz* dramas, this play explores the political antagonism between liberals and conservatives and reveals the exact nature of Freytag's democratic instinct. *Soll und Haben* marked another important shift in Freytag in the *Nachmärz*: away from drama and towards the novel. Following the life of Anton Wohlfart, *Soll und Haben* is in every sense a *Bildungsroman* — educating both its hero and its reader in the ways and values of the bourgeoisie. Contrasting bourgeois values with a trio of non-bourgeois ideologies (those of the aristocracy, the Jews, and the Poles), the novel both develops Freytag's anti-aristocratic polemic of the *Vormärz* and explores more explicitly national themes. The aristocracy face financial ruin and are recast as colonials, fighting for Germany's borders, while Anton marries into the trading house of T. O. Schröter's, securing the position of the bourgeoisie as the economic powerhouse of the German nation. The novel presents bourgeois ideologies as specifically national ideologies — a significant development in Freytag's writing.

The decade closed with *Die Fabier*, which returned to class issues and deployed many aspects of the anti-aristocratic arguments developed in Freytag's *Vormärz* dramas. Often seen as an exception within Freytag's oeuvre, the play in fact turned to the historical past in order to illuminate the needs of the present, and reflects Freytag's belief in the necessity of the breakdown of aristocratic hegemony for the foundation of a healthy nation-state — be that the Roman Republic or a unified Germany. *Die Fabier* also marked an important development in Freytag's literary practice, which in the 1860s would increasingly concern itself with historical subject matter. For Freytag, the 1850s were thus marked by both continuity and change. *Die Journalisten* and *Soll und Haben* were both specific responses to the post-revolutionary era — affirmations of bourgeois self-confidence in a new social and political age. Both represented a continuation of the bourgeois national-liberal project Freytag had begun during the *Vormärz* and with which he persisted in *Die Fabier*. Despite the diversity of his literary production in the 1850s, Freytag remained committed to the bourgeois cause — a cause which would finally bear fruit in the 1860s, though not wholly to his satisfaction.

## Notes to Chapter 3

1. Gustav Freytag, *Gesammelte Werke*, I: *Erinnerungen aus meinem Leben* (Leipzig: Hirzel, 1896), p. 171. Further references to this edition are given after quotations in the text.
2. Paul Ostwald, *Gustav Freytag als Politiker* (Berlin: Staatspolitischer Verlag, 1927), p. 18.
3. See William Carr, *A History of Germany 1815–1990* (London: Arnold, 1991), p. 33; Theodore Hamerow, *Restoration, Revolution, Reaction: Economics and Politics in Germany, 1815–1871* (Princeton: Princeton University Press, 1972), p. 75.
4. Eric Hobsbawm, *The Age of Revolution, 1789–1848* (London: Weidenfeld & Nicolson, 1995), p. 308.
5. Heinrich Heine, *Historisch-kritische Gesamtausgabe der Werke, Düsseldorfer Heine-Ausgabe*, ed. by Manfred Windfuhr, XI: *Ludwig Börne und kleinere politische Schriften. Text. Apparat* (Hamburg: Hoffmann & Campe, 1978), p. 134.
6. Gustav Freytag, *Gesammelte Werke*, XIII: *Die Ahnen: Sechste Abtheilung* (Leipzig: Hirzel, 1896), p. 305.
7. Gustav Freytag, *Gesammelte Werke*, IV: *Soll und Haben: Erster Band* (Leipzig: Hirzel, 1896), p. 402. Further references to this edition are given after quotations in the text.
8. Larry L. Ping, *Gustav Freytag and the Prussian Gospel: Novels, Liberalism, and History* (Oxford: Lang, 2006), p. 53.
9. See Michael Perraudin, 'Sinn und Sinnlichkeit im Deutschland des Vor- und Nachmärz', in *Formen der Wirklichkeiterfassung nach 1848: Deutsche Literatur und Kultur vom Nachmärz bis zur Gründerzeit in europäischer Perspektive I*, ed. by Helmut Koopmann and Michael Perraudin (Bielefeld: Aisthesis, 2003), pp. 13–42.
10. See Eberhard Naujoks, 'Die Grenzboten (1841–1922)', in *Deutsche Zeitschriften des 17. bis 20. Jahrhunderts*, ed. by Heinz-Dietrich Fischer (Munich: Dokumentation, 1973), pp. 155–57.
11. Heinrich Heine, letter to Ignaz Kurunda, 17 September 1841, in Heinrich Heine, *Werke. Briefwechsel. Lebenszeugnisse, Säkularausgabe*, ed. by Nationale Forschungs- und Gedenkstätten der klassischen deutschen Literatur, Weimar, and Centre National de la Recherche Scientifique, Paris, XXI: *Briefe 1831–1841* (Berlin: Akademie-Verlag, 1970), p. 424.
12. See Naujoks, p. 156.
13. Gustav Freytag, *Gesammelte Werke*, XV: *Politische Aufsätze* (Leipzig: Hirzel, 1896), p. 44. Further references to this edition are given after quotations in the text.
14. Adolf Thiele, 'Gustav Freytag, der Grenzbotenjournalist' (doctoral thesis, University of Münster, 1924), p. 219.

15. Julian Schmidt, review of *Der natürliche Sohn* (Alexandre Dumas), in *Die Grenzboten*, 1 (1858), 344–46 (p. 346).
16. Julian Schmidt, 'Der neueste englische Roman und das Princip des Realismus' (1854), quoted in *Realismus und Gründerzeit: Manifeste und Dokumente zur deutschen Literatur, 1848–1880*, ed. by M. Bucher and W. Hahl, 2 vols (Stuttgart: Metzler, 1975), II, 94.
17. Julian Schmidt, quoted in Hartmut Steinecke, *Romantheorie und Romankritik in Deutschland*, 2 vols (Stuttgart: Metzler, 1975), II, 304, footnote 18.
18. Julian Schmidt, quoted in Steinecke, *Romantheorie und Romankritik*, I, 207.
19. See Sabina Becker, *Bürgerlicher Realismus: Literatur und Kultur im bürgerlichen Zeitalter 1848–1900* (Tübingen: Francke, 2003), esp. pp. 96–98 and pp. 179–81.
20. David Blackbourn and Geoff Eley, *The Peculiarities of German History* (Oxford: Oxford University Press, 1984), p. 197.
21. See Peter Uwe Hohendahl, *Building a National Literature: The Case of Germany, 1830–1870* (Ithaca: Cornell University Press, 1989), p. 262.
22. See Klaus Christian Köhnke, 'Ein antisemitischer Autor wider Willen: Zu Gustav Freytags Roman *Soll und Haben*', in *Conditio Judaica: Judentum, Antisemitismus und deutschsprachige Literatur vom 18. Jahrhundert bis zum Ersten Weltkrieg*, ed. by Hans Otto Horch and Horst Denkler, 2 vols (Tübingen: Max Niemeyer, 1989), pp. 130–47 (p. 135).
23. Freytag, letter to Duke Ernst von Coburg Gotha, 18 May 1854, in *Gustav Freytag und Herzog Ernst von Coburg im Briefwechsel, 1853 bis 1893*, ed. by Eduard Tempeltey (Leipzig: Hirzel, 1904), p. 24.
24. Freytag, letter to Duke Ernst, 11 September 1855, in Tempeltey (ed.), pp. 45–46.
25. Freytag, letter to Duke Ernst, 18 May 1854, in Tempeltey (ed.), p. 23.
26. For a detailed account of the arrest warrant, see Johann Schultze, 'Gustav Freytag und die preußische Zensur', *Preußische Jahrbücher*, 183 (1921), 331–44.
27. See Christa Barth, 'Gustav Freytags *Journalisten*: Versuch einer Monographie' (doctoral thesis, University of Munich, 1949), pp. 119–20.
28. On the play, see Eduard Rothfuchs, 'Der selbstbiographische Gehalt in Gustav Freytags Werken (bis 1855): Ein Beitrag zur Frage der Wechselwirkungen von Erlebnis und Dichtung' (doctoral thesis, University of Münster, 1929), pp. 35–37; Kurt Classe, 'Gustav Freytag als politischer Dichter' (doctoral thesis, University of Münster, 1914), p. 47; Georg Droescher, *Gustav Freytag in seinen Lustspielen: Inaugural-Dissertation* (Weida: Thomas & Hubert, 1919), pp. 55–57. On the reaction, see Carr, pp. 64–65.
29. Julian Schmidt, *Geschichte der deutschen Literatur seit Lessings Tod*, III (Leipzig: [n.pub.], 1858), p. 100.
30. See Hans Lindau, *Gustav Freytag* (Leipzig: Hirzel, 1907), pp. 130–32, and Kenneth Bruce Beaton, 'Gustav Freytags *Die Journalisten*: Eine "politische" Komödie der Revolutionszeit', *Zeitschrift für deutsche Philologie*, 105 (1986), 516–43 (p. 517).
31. Freytag, letter to Eduard Devrient, 25 September 1852, in Emil Devrient, 'Briefwechsel zwischen Gustav Freytag und Eduard Devrient', *Westermanns illustrierte deutsche Monatshefte*, 91 (1901–02), 130–33 (pp. 131–32).
32. Barth, p. 50; Lindau, p. 130.
33. See Barth, p. 51.
34. Barth, p. 52.
35. Freytag, letter to Werner, 16 Decemeber 1852, quoted in Barth, p. 112.
36. Botho von Hülsen, letter to Freytag, 15 May 1857, in Georg Droescher, 'Gustav Freytags Schriftwechsel mit der Generalintendanz der königlichen Schauspiele zu Berlin', *Deutsche Rundschau*, 45 (1918), 129–46 (p. 144).

37. See Freytag's letter to Werner, 16 December 1852, quoted in Barth, p. 112.
38. See Heinrich Laube, *Heinrich Laubes Gesammelte Werke*, XXIX.II: *Das Burgtheater* (Leipzig: Max Helles, 1909), p. 255.
39. Gustav Freytag, *Gesammelte Werke*, III: *Dramatische Werke: Zweiter Band* (Leipzig: Hirzel, 1896), p. 21. Further references to this edition are given after quotations in the text.
40. See Hans J. Hahn, *The 1848 Revolutions in German-Speaking Europe* (London: Longman, 2001), pp. 124–26.
41. Carr, p. 41.
42. Ibid.
43. Classe, p. 50.
44. Freytag, letter to Duke Ernst, 21 January 1867, in Tempeltey (ed.), p. 213.
45. See H. W. Koch, *A History of Prussia* (London: Longman, 1978), p. 181; Emilio Willems, *Der preußisch-deutsche Militarismus: Ein Kulturkomplex im sozialen Wandel* (Cologne: Wissenschaft und Politik, 1984), pp. 60–62.
46. See Carr, p. 75.
47. See Beaton, p. 533.
48. Becker, p. 179.
49. See, for example, Renate Herrmann, 'Gustav Freytag: Bürgerliches Selbstverständnis und preußisch-deutsches Nationalbewußtsein: Ein Beitrag zur Geschichte des nationalen-liberalen Bürgertums der Reichgründungszeit' (doctoral thesis, University of Würzburg, 1974), and Peter Heinz Hubrich, *Gustav Freytags 'Deutsche Ideologie' in 'Soll und Haben'* (Kronberg: Scriptor, 1974).
50. Gabriele Büchler-Hauschild, *Erzählte Arbeit: Gustav Freytag und die soziale Prosa des Vor- und Nachmärz* (Paderborn: Schöningh, 1987), p. 72.
51. See Freytag's letter to Hirzel, 13 July 1854, in *Gustav Freytag an Salomon Hirzel und die Seinen*, ed. by A. Dove (Leipzig: [n.pub.], 1902), p. 9.
52. Freytag, letter to Duke Ernst, 11 September 1854, in Tempeltey (ed.), p. 31.
53. The document can be found in *Kapsel 1 (Varia)* of the *Briefsammlung Gustav Freytags* at the Staatsbibliothek zu Berlin, Preußischer Kulturbestiz.
54. Quoted in Köhnke, pp. 132–33.
55. See Freytag's letter to Hirzel, 13 July 1854, in Dove (ed.), p. 9.
56. See the statistics gathered in T. E. Carter, 'Freytag's *Soll und Haben*: A Liberal National Manifesto as a Best-seller', *German Life and Letters*, 21 (1967–68), 320–29.
57. Alyssa Ann Lonner's recent work has begun to redress this balance. See *Mediating the Past: Gustav Freytag, Progress, and German Historical Identity, 1848–1871* (Oxford: Lang, 2005).
58. Gustav Freytag, *Gesammelte Werke*, V: *Soll und Haben. Zweiter Band* (Leipzig: Hirzel, 1896), pp. 307–08. Further references to this edition are given after quotations in the text.
59. See Hubrich, p. 54; Büchler-Hauschild, pp. 83–84, and Michael Kienzle, *Der Erfolgsroman: Zur Kritik einer poetischen Ökonomie bei Gustav Freytag und Eugenie Marlitt* (Stuttgart: Metzler, 1965), p. 18.
60. Christine Achinger, '"Prosa der Verhältnisse" und Poesie der Ware: Versöhnte Moderne und Realismus in *Soll und Haben*', in *150 Jahre 'Soll und Haben': Studien zu Gustav Freytags kontroversem Roman*, ed. by Florian Krobb (Würzburg: Königshausen & Neumann, 2005), pp. 67–86 (p. 67).
61. Kienzle, p. 22.
62. Kristin Kopp, '"Ich stehe jetzt hier als einer von den Eroberern": *Soll und Haben* als Kolonialroman', in Krobb (ed.), pp. 225–37 (p. 237).

63. Ibid., p. 228.
64. Ibid., p. 229.
65. Ibid.
66. Florian Krobb, 'Einleitung: *Soll und Haben* nach 150 Jahren', in Krobb (ed.), pp. 9–28 (p. 18).
67. That the two were seen as distinct in contemporary debates is revealed in Brian Vick's illuminating work *Defining Germany: The 1848 Frankfurt Parliamentarians and National Identity* (Cambridge, MA: Harvard University Press, 2002), pp. 120–22.
68. See Achinger, pp. 68–69.
69. See Köhnke, p. 133.
70. Mark Gelber, 'Antisemitismus, literarischer Antisemitismus und die Konstellation der bösen Juden in Gustav Freytags *Soll und Haben*', in Krobb (ed.), pp. 285–300 (p. 297); Carter, p. 326.
71. Antje S. Anderson, 'Ein Kaufmann "von sehr englischem Aussehen": Die literarische und soziokulturelle Funktion Englands in *Soll und Haben*', in Krobb (ed.), pp. 209–23 (p. 221–22).
72. Anderson, p. 222.
73. Anderson, pp. 222–23.
74. See Krobb, 'Einleitung', p. 23.
75. Freytag, letter to Heinrich Geffecken, 23 July 1856, in Carl Hinrichs, 'Unveröffentliche Briefe Gustav Freytags an Heinrich Geffecken aus der Zeit der Reichsgründung', *Jahrbuch für die Geschichte Mittel- und Ostdeutschlands*, 3 (1954), 65–117 (pp. 75–76); Freytag, quoted in Hubrich, p. 57.
76. Hubrich, p. 57.
77. Jeffrey L. Sammons, 'The Evaluation of Freytag's *Soll und Haben*', *German Life and Letters*, 22 (1968–69), 315–24 (p. 321).
78. Hartmut Steinecke, 'Gustav Freytag: *Soll und Haben* (1855): Weltbild und Wirkung eines deutschen Bestsellers', in *Romane und Erzählungen des bürgerlichen Realismus*, ed. by Horst Denkler (Stuttgart: Reclam, 1980), pp. 138–52 (p. 149).
79. See Hamerow, ch. 13.
80. Droescher, *Gustav Freytag in seinen Lustspielen*, p. 103.
81. Eduard Devrient, letter to Freytag, 8 June 1857, in Devrient, p. 139.
82. Freytag, letter to Devrient, 27 April 1858, in Devrient, p. 201.
83. Freytag, letter to Devrient, 28 March 1859, in Devrient, p. 201.
84. Ibid.
85. Devrient, letter to Freytag, 22 September 1859, in Devrient, p. 206.
86. This first edition of *Die Fabier* can be found in: *Bibliothek der deutschen Literatur: Mikrofiche-Gesamtausgabe* (Munich: Sauer, 1999), B.9/F.3951–3952.
87. Devrient, letter to Freytag, 15 May 1859, in Devrient, p. 203.
88. Freytag, letter to Devrient, 12 October 1859, in Devrient, p. 204.
89. See Devrient's letter to Freytag, 30 October 1861, in Devrient, p. 350.
90. See Freytag's letter to Devrient, 28 March 1859, in Devrient, p. 201.
91. Freytag, letter to Devrient, 10 February 1860, in Devrient, p. 210.
92. See Freytag's letter to Devrient, 18 April 1860, in Devrient, p. 210, and compare with Freytag, I, 193.
93. Devrient's diary entry from the 14 September 1860 is quoted in the commentary to his *Briefwechsel* with Freytag. See Devrient, p. 346.
94. Freytag, letter to Minister von Bethmann-Hollweg, September 1860, in Ilka Horovitz-Darnay, 'Gustav Freytag über den deutschen Staatspreis und über *Die Fabier*', *Deutsche Revue*, 31 (1906), 40–52 (p. 49).

95. Freytag, letter to Minister von Bethmann-Hollweg, September 1860, in Horovitz-Barnay, p. 49.
96. See Freytag, letter to Minister von Bethmann-Hollweg, September 1860, in Horovitz-Barnay, p. 50.
97. See Lindau, p. 180.
98. Gustav Freytag, *Gesammelte Werke*, II: *Dramatische Werke: Erster Band* (Leipzig: Hirzel, 1896), p. 100. Further references to this edition are given after quotations in the text.
99. See P. A. Brunt, *Ancient Culture and Society: Social Conflicts in the Roman Republic* (London: Chatto & Windus, 1978), pp. 42–44.
100. Titus Livius, *The History of Rome: The First Eight Books*, trans. by D. Spillan (London: Bell, 1896), pp. 251–52.
101. Ibid., p. 255.
102. Ibid., p. 256.

CHAPTER 4

## Present Pasts: History, *Bildung*, and the *Volkskraft*

As noted in the previous chapter, a central tendency of Freytag's writing in the 1850s was the increasing conflation of class and national concerns in his work. *Die Journalisten*, *Die Fabier*, and, in particular, *Soll und Haben* all bear witness to Freytag's impulse to nationalize the class polemics of his *Vormärz* dramas. Despite the apparent diversity of Freytag's literary production between 1860 and 1870, which included a history of Germany, a biography, a theory of drama and a novel, a similar integration of class and national issues can be seen in his writings of the 1860s — the decade which saw the project of national unification advance to the point of realization.

The 1860s were also a period of increased political engagement for Freytag himself. His letters from the decade reveal the extent to which he felt that a new political era was dawning for the middle classes, and one which could potentially far exceed the limited successes of 1848: 'Die Wogen heben sich. Und wir sind erst im Anfang. Es sind die ersten Symptome einer starken Bewegung des Volkes, vor welchen wir stehen. Sie mag leicht tiefer und gewaltiger werden, als die von 48'.[1] Certainly, the decade was one of considerable political turmoil in Germany. Tensions escalated between Prussia and Austria, as the two powers fought for dominance over German-speaking Europe, both in the aftermath of the 1864 Schleswig-Holstein conflict and during the Austro-Prussian war of 1866. The German question continued to be debated with passion in both political circles and the press, until the Prussian victory over Austria in 1866 altered the balance of opinion in Germany towards a *kleindeutsch* solution and ultimately led to the foundation of the Norddeutscher Bund and Reichstag in 1867. These events not only directly influenced Freytag's writings of the era, but also led him to active political engagement, and, as I will reveal in this chapter, the 1860s in many ways marked the highpoint of Freytag's political engagement — both through his increasingly politicized poetry and through his venture into practical politics.

Throughout the 1860s, Freytag was active in several political associations. Central among these was the Kitzinger Kreis, a group which sought to influence the political future of Germany through the press, and consisted predominantly of contributors to *Die Grenzboten*. In its aims, the group can be seen as a form of successor to the Literarisch-politischer Verein of which Freytag had been a member in the early 1850s (as discussed in Chapter 3). Through the Kitzinger Kreis, Freytag came into contact with several significant figures. These included Moritz Busch, one of the chief historians of the Bismarck era, and Max Jordaan, the first director of the Nationalgalerie (and who also took over the editorship of *Die Grenzboten* in 1871). Of greater significance were Karl Mathy, Baden's minister of finance and a staunch supporter of Prussia, whose biography Freytag wrote in 1869, and the historian Heinrich von Treitschke, whose presentation of German history from a Prussian perspective is partially reflected in the final volumes of Freytag's own history, the *Bilder aus der deutschen Vergangenheit*.[2]

Little is known about the precise activities of the Kitzinger Kreis. It is rarely mentioned in Freytag's letters and not at all in his memoirs, though there is a passing reference to it in his biography of Karl Mathy. On the basis of these limited sources, it appears that the group started meeting in Leipzig in 1859, and took its name from the public house in which they assembled. Treitschke provides us with the most detailed description of the group, in a letter to his father from 1862:

> Ueberhaupt ist dieser Freytagsche Kreis jetzt mein angenehmster Umgang, obwohl ich weitaus der Jüngste und fast der einzige Unbeweibte darunter bin. Wir treffen uns dreimal in der Woche eine Stunde lang, und selten vergeht die Unterhaltung, ohne daß ein verständiges Wort gesprochen wird.[3]

Interestingly, Treitschke's letter makes the Kitzinger Kreis sound less like a political association and more like a politically orientated *Stammtisch* for Freytag's friends. Certainly, Freytag does seem to have been the central figure of the group, and its membership was solely dependent on who was resident in Leipzig at the time. Freytag's letters, for instance, note his disappointment when Mathy leaves Leipzig, and thus the group, in 1864, and his excitement when Treitschke moves to the city later that year.[4]

The Kitzinger Kreis should not, however, be dismissed as merely a circle for the politically like-minded. It appears that the group did have some form of political programme, since in 1867 it successfully put forward one of its members, Eduard Stephani, the deputy mayor of Leipzig, for election to the newly formed Reichstag des Norddeutschen Bundes. In this light, Friedrich Schulze's characterization of the group as existing somewhere 'zwischen "Salon" und "Partei"' seems fitting.[5] Although the political reach of the Kitzinger Kreis was undoubtedly narrower than that of the Literarisch-politischer Verein, it nevertheless provided Freytag with social and political connections which fed directly into his literary and journalistic work of the decade.

In 1867, Freytag himself became a candidate for the Reichstag des Norddeutschen Bundes, though not on behalf of the Kitzinger Kreis, but of the Nationalverein, an important organization which brought together moderate national liberals, and the primary aim of which was to achieve a *kleindeutsch* unification of Germany under the initial leadership of Prussia. The Nationalverein, founded in Frankfurt am Main in 1859, differed substantially from the Kitzinger Kreis, since it was, in many respects, a political party, with over 30,000 members, and in 1867 it became the basis for the national-liberal faction of the Reichstag. Freytag was one of the first members of the organization, together with his friend Theodor Molinari and his publisher Salomon Hirzel. In his memoirs, he retrospectively notes that:

> Dies Unternehmen, die Liberalen der einzelnen deutschen Staaten mit einander zu verbinden und durch den Zusammenhang auf gemeinsame Thätigkeit vorzubereiten, hielt ich für den größten Fortschritt, den das politische Leben im Volke [...] gemacht hatte [...]. [I]ch wurde mit Freuden Mitglied des Vereins und bin ihm, so lange er bestand, treu geblieben.[6]

Freytag's career as a member of parliament was not a success. He disliked the electoral process, and his letters from the period heavily criticize Bismarck's introduction of universal male suffrage (which was, in fact, restricted both by age and tax payments under the system of *Dreiklassenwahlrecht*). This continued a critique of electoral reform he had begun in articles in *Die Grenzboten* in 1848 as well as in his 1852 drama *Die Journalisten* (see the discussion in Chapter 3). From his letters, it is clear that Freytag's dissatisfaction with the electoral process stemmed mainly from the lack of control that universal suffrage had introduced to the system. He complains — amusingly, from a contemporary perspective — that the new system meant that he was denied any certainty of victory, despite the extreme effort he had to put in to gain popularity:

> Ach, dies allgemeine Wahlrecht ruiniert den Charakter, fünfzig Jahre habe ich mich um Popularität nicht gekümmert, und jetzt sende ich einen Blumenstrauß an eine Wochnerin, von der ich nicht weiß, ob sie einen Jungen order ein Mädel taufen läßt, und schüttle hundert guten Freunden die Hand, deren Namen ich nicht weiß und niemals wissen werden. Pfui, Bismarck, das war kein Meisterstreich. Und zuletzt wird doch noch irgend ein Anderer gewählt![7]

Though ultimately victorious in the election, Freytag was not an adept parliamentarian. Transcripts of the single session in which he spoke reveal that he was shouted down by his colleagues, and had, in addition, misunderstood parliamentary procedure in attempting to speak on a topic that had not been tabled for discussion.[8] His memoirs, perhaps unsurprisingly, choose to gloss over this fact, admitting that his 'Stimme war zu schwach' for a parliamentary career, but failing to mention that he resigned his position as soon as the first session of parliament had ended, a third of the way through his mandate (I, 225).

Freytag's letters to the Duke of Coburg Gotha provide an alternative account of his experiences at the Reichstag. Explaining his resignation, he stresses that his decision not to return was not the result of a lack of political or parliamentary ability: '[A]uch fühle ich mich für die politische Laufbahn nicht allzu ungünstig ausgestattet, ich habe mich vorsichtig zurückgehalten, aber mit dem Gefühl, daß ich bei einiger Uebung mit Reden und Rathen wohl bestehen würde'.[9] Rather, he reasons, he felt that his literary activities should take precedence over his political career. This is not, he assures the Duke, because he wishes to reject politics, but precisely because he feels literature is now the more effective medium for political expression:

> Doch kehre ich in meinen Federtopf zurück, wie Hans Dudeldee im Märchen. Denn ich habe für mein Volk eine andere Aufgabe zu erfüllen. Ich bin in einer Zeit, die in energischer, aber einseitiger Kraftentfaltung begriffen ist, einer der wenigen Bewahrer der idealen Habe unseres Volkes. [...] Ich bin 51 Jahr und habe noch etwa 10 Jahr rüstigen Schaffens. Und die Zeit beginnt mir zu rennen. In der Politik ist zweifelhaft, was ich leiste und nütze, in meinem Fach weiß ich's. Damit ist nicht gemeint, daß ich mir den Mund zubinden will. Im Gegentheil. Aber ich entsage der Parlamentscarriere, und werde nicht Politiker von Profession.[10]

Freytag's sense that his literary career provided him with the only way to continue to influence the German people directly is significant, though in many respects his letter to the Duke is as economical with the truth about his departure from Berlin as his later memoirs. Only at the end of the letter do we get a sense of his despondency at the failure of his parliamentary career: 'Es war ein harter Kampf. Aber ich bin fertig. Ich bleibe der bescheidene Hausfreund meines Volkes, ich bleibe bei der Poeterei, ich krieche in meinen Federtopf zurück'.[11] Crawling back into his inkwell, Freytag argues — in an attempt at self-justification — that it is political poetry which should take precedence over practical politics.

Such contemporary political concerns are not, however, immediately reflected in either of his two major literary projects of the 1860s. His novel of academia, *Die verlorene Handschrift* (1864), is set in the absolutist Germany of the late 1820s, and focuses on intellectual questions of philology and historical research, while the *Bilder aus der deutschen Vergangenheit* (1859–67) presents a historical panorama of the German past, beginning with the *Völkerwanderung* and ending just short of the present day, in 1848. It is perhaps the lack of obvious engagement with the present in these texts that accounts for the minimal level of critical interest they have generated. The handful of studies which have considered *Die verlorene Handschrift* and the *Bilder* all examine the works from a historical perspective, and fail to reflect on their wider significance within Freytag's aesthetic and political development. Yet, as I will show in the following discussion, the two texts are pivotal to that development, turning to the German past in response to the needs of the present, and fusing Freytag's class and national concerns into a wider, national-liberal critique of national life in Germany.

### *Bilder aus der deutschen Vergangenheit* (1859–67)

The nineteenth century witnessed a proliferation of historical writing in Germany. On the one hand, increasing national sentiment led historians such as Heinrich von Treitschke and Heinrich von Sybel to read the past from a deliberately contemporary Prussian perspective, founding what became known as the Prussian School of History. On the other hand, Leopold von Ranke and Theodor Mommsen supported a purportedly objective approach to history, based on the critical analysis of sources and unfettered by the politics of the present. This division between subjective and objective history itself concealed a further distinction, between those who saw the historical process as inherently progressive, and those who believed in its infinite diversity. Ranke, in particular, became embroiled in an increasingly public debate on the nature and purpose of historical enquiry, arguing against a Hegelian vision of history, the systematically progressive nature of which he saw as obscuring a multiplicity of potential historical outcomes.[12] It was in the midst of these debates that Gustav Freytag began publishing his *Bilder aus der deutschen Vergangenheit*. Based on witness testimony, yet emphasizing a progressive and politicized vision of history, the *Bilder* sit somewhat uneasily between a Rankean source-based approach to history and the explicitly politically tendentious writings of the Prussian School.

Freytag originally conceived of the *Bilder aus der deutschen Vergangenheit* as a single-volume collection of the articles on German history that he had first published in *Die Grenzboten* between 1855 and 1857. Published in 1859, the first volume detailed the sixteenth and seventeenth centuries, and adhered closely to the style and content of the original essays, each of which had consisted of a reproduction of a piece of oral testimony accompanied by an introduction and commentary by Freytag. In the third of the *Grenzboten* articles published under the series title *Bilder aus der deutschen Vergangenheit*, Freytag explained the aims of the essays:

> Diese Bilder, welche in Nr. 23 u. 24 d. Bl. begannen und weiter fortgesetzt werden sollen, haben den Zweck durch Berichte von Zeitgenossen solche

> Anschauung von dem Privatleben unsrer Vorfahren zu geben, welche dazu helfen, uns das Treiben der Vergangenheit verständlich zu machen.[13]

More often than not, the documents used were from Freytag's own extensive collection of letters and pamphlets from the sixteenth and seventeenth centuries (now housed in Frankfurt University Library).[14] Carefully catalogued and divided into a range of topics by Freytag himself, from *Gesetz, Sitte, Mode* to *Zeitungen und politische Neuigkeiten aus Deutschland*, this collection testifies to the depth of Freytag's interest in German history and philology. It is also characteristic of the passion for collecting and preserving items from the past which became prevalent in the early and mid-nineteenth century.[15] For the first volume of the *Bilder*, Freytag also drew on the resources of the Monumenta Germaniae Historica — one of many well-established historical associations in mid-nineteenth century Germany dedicated to medieval German studies.[16] The extent to which Freytag saw himself as the curator of these documents is shown by the fact that the 1859 edition of the *Bilder* names him as editor, rather than author. This claim of editorship suggests that Freytag — at least initially — believed that these pieces of testimony spoke for themselves and did not require the extensive analysis or commentary of an author or historian.

In 1862, Freytag published a second volume of the *Bilder*, entitled *Neue Bilder aus dem Leben des deutschen Volkes*, which expanded the historical reach of the cycle into the eighteenth and nineteenth centuries. Significantly, Freytag is no longer named as editor, but as author — a shift reflected in the content of the volume, which argues more directly for a personal and politicized view of history. Freytag's memoirs claim the *Neue Bilder* were written in response to popular demand (I, 190), though his correspondence with his publisher Hirzel does not corroborate this claim.[17] It is, however, not impossible that this was the case: Alyssa Lonner states that the *Bilder* were half as successful as *Soll und Haben* — if true, a considerable achievement for a work of cultural history.[18]

In 1867, Freytag wrote a further volume for the series, this time on the German Middle Ages, which completed the work. Unlike its predecessors, however, this volume was not based on articles from *Die Grenzboten*. This final volume was then added to a heavily abridged and reworked version of the 1859 and 1862 volumes, and these three were published together under the title *Bilder aus der deutschen Vergangenheit*. Reprinted essentially unaltered in the *Gesammelte Werke* of 1896, this combined edition is the one used in the present monograph. In his memoirs, Freytag claims that the final set of changes in 1867 was required in order to unify his history:

> Sehr bald erwies sich als nothwendig, auch das bereits Gedruckte neu zu ordnen und zu vertiefen, um die junge Arbeit mit der früheren zu einem einheitlichen Werk zu verbinden. Neu geschrieben wurde der erste Band *Aus dem Mittelalter* und fast ganz der zweite *Vom Mittelalter zur Neuzeit*,

nur an den Schluß konnten einige Abschnitte aus der früheren Arbeit gefügt werden. (I, 222–23)

Although it is likely that, after twelve years' work, the three volumes of the *Bilder* required reformulation in order to function as a cohesive whole, one also suspects that the new political climate in 1867 led Freytag to recast elements of his text. The Prussian constitutional conflict was reaching its peak, and a belief in a possible national unification was increasingly widespread — factors that no doubt affected the ultimate tone of Freytag's history, which in its final volume increasingly promotes unification under Prussian hegemony. Although a systematic comparison of the different versions of the *Bilder* is beyond the scope of this study, the indications are that successive revisions of the text saw an increasing Prussification of the content, the closer it approached to 1867. This assessment is partially corroborated by the fact that, in his memoirs of 1887, Freytag recast the *Bilder* as a wholly Prusso-national project, noting how the cycle was completed symbolically at the same time as the victory in the Austro-Prussian War of 1866 and the subsequent ratification of the Prussian constitution and foundation of the Reichstag: 'Mich aber erfüllte mit heimlichem Stolz, daß die Beendigung des Werkes mit dem Erfolge des Jahres 1866 zusammenfiel' (I, 223). That this emphasis in the memoirs on the Prussian element of German history is not an accurate picture of the cycle is revealed in the coming discussion.

Upon publication, the *Bilder* gathered considerable critical praise. Treitschke wrote that Freytag's work had 'einen unberechenbar großen Einfluß', while Wilhelm Scherer, a reviewer in the *Preußische Jahrbücher*, went so far to claim that 'es [ist] die beste deutsche Geschichte, die wir haben'.[19] However, these comments — regularly cited in secondary literature on the *Bilder* — must be read with caution. Treitschke, for instance, was a close friend of Freytag and, as seen, a member of the Kitzinger Kreis. He was also the editor of the *Preußische Jahrbücher*. This publication itself had received its start-up funds from the Literarisch-politischer Verein, of which Freytag was a core member. The impartiality of such reviews is therefore questionable.

They are, however, of interest in other ways. Both reviews suggest, for instance, that the main market for Freytag's history was not academia, but the middle classes. Scherer comments how '[d]ie gelehrte Arbeit, die dahinter steckt, wird gerade von den Gelehrten nicht gemerkt oder nicht beachtet',[20] while Treitschke is even more explicit, noting how the *Bilder* is 'eines der seltenen Geschichtswerke, welche von Frauen verstanden und mit Freude gelesen werden können'.[21] It appears that contemporaries saw the *Bilder* as packaging national history in a format suitable for consumption in the private sphere, rather than as a work of strictly scholarly intentions.

Recent studies of the *Bilder aus der deutschen Vergangenheit* have predominantly focused on Freytag's position as a historian of the Prussian School. Larry Ping has argued that the *Bilder* should be seen as the work par excellence of Prusso-centric historiography, positioning Freytag within a group of intellectuals loyal to a *kleindeutsch* vision of German national unity.[22] Celia Applegate has similarly stressed the dominance of a Prussian-orientated nationalism in the *Bilder*, claiming that Freytag's history 'effectively erased "region", "place", and all intermediate social groupings and phenomena' in favour of a master-narrative of Prussian dominance.[23] For these critics, the *Bilder* take on the appearance of national history in order to promote a more particularist vision of Prussian hegemony.

Lynne Tatlock and Alyssa Lonner take a different stance in their studies of the *Bilder*. Tatlock has argued that the *Bilder* deliberately emphasize regional identity, preserving the 'particular and fragmented' in order to create a 'utopian vision' of German nationhood.[24] Lonner, too, regards the use of regional and folk identity in the *Bilder* as an attempt to create an 'imagined community' (borrowing Benedict Anderson's useful concept).[25] For Tatlock and Lonner, Freytag's history legitimizes Germany's claim to nationhood through the production of a national historical myth which is not solely Prusso-centric in attitude. Freytag's stance on German unification in the *Bilder* is clearly of significance, yet the focus on the relative significance of Prussia in existing critical studies is somewhat misleading. Certainly, the final chapters of the *Bilder* argue polemically for Prussia to play a central role in the act of German unification, yet, as I will show, through the majority of the work it is not Prussian hegemony that acts as the constant in Freytag's national history, but the German folk.

Unsurprisingly for a national history, the issue of Germany's borders and the question of territorial expansion are central to the *Bilder aus der deutschen Vergangenheit*. From the outset, Freytag stresses how expansionism and settlement have been key to the shaping of Germany, starting with the *Völkerwanderung* of Germanic tribes during the third to fifth centuries: 'Die Geschichte der Völkerwanderung ist die Geschichte der Besiedlung Europa's durch die Germanen'.[26] In particular, Freytag directs attention towards the eastern borders of Germany, noting how the Germans' failure to settle the 'fruchtbare[s] Gebiet' of Eastern Europe during the *Völkerwanderung* remains 'ein Schade der deutschen Geschichte [...], den wir noch heute fühlen' — not least because the area was subsequently settled by 'slavische Stämme' (xvii, 36–37).

These initial comments on Germany's expansionist politics and her relationship to Eastern Europe become a pivotal feature of the history, as Freytag repeatedly focuses on life in disputed border regions. The history notes, for instance, how the German colonization of Eastern Europe and Silesia between 1250 and 1350 was 'die größte That des deutschen Volkes in jenem Zeitraum', and when describing the rise of the city at the turn of the fourteenth century, it is Silesian towns such as Breslau that are detailed.[27] By the mid-fourteenth century, according to Freytag's account, the very heart of Germany existed in the east: Prague is now the capital and home to the 'erste deutsche Universität' (XVIII, 317). This last point is of considerable significance, since the initial phases of German colonial expansion explored by Freytag in the *Bilder* are depicted as explicitly civilizing and educative in nature — a common topos of nineteenth- and twentieth-century colonial discourse — with Breslau and Prague functioning as beacons of German *Bildung* in the Slavic lands.[28] Throughout, the Slavic people are presented as being without history or culture: 'Und es ist kein Zufall, daß die [...] Slaven im Norden der Donau ganz ohne Heldensagen aus ihrer Wanderzeit sind, sie haben offenbar in jener Zeit das Selbstgefühl eines starken Volksthums nicht gehabt' (XVIII, 163). It is the Germans who arrive as bearers of culture and civilization: 'Die Weltsprache jener Zeit: das Latein, der Glaube des gekreuzigten Christus, alle Wissenschaft, Verkehrsrecht und Kriegführung, Kunst und Handwerk mußten aus deutschem Land zu den Slaven kommen' (XVIII, 160). The similarities here with the second of the Poland-set sections of *Soll und Haben* (discussed in the previous chapter) are clear. In the novel, Poland was described (in the words of Schröter) as devoid of culture: 'es ist merkwürdig, wie unfähig sie sind, den Stand, welcher Civilisation und Fortschritt darstellt und welcher einen Haufen zerstreuter Ackerbauer zu einem Staate erhebt, aus sich heraus zu schaffen'.[29] The Slavic people are contrasted negatively with Anton and Schröter, who arrive as representatives of knowledge and order.

Tatlock has argued that Freytag's vision of German identity in the *Bilder* is highly inclusive, and that the focus on the East reveals how he believed that 'the Germans [were] in no sense racially pure and, furthermore, that the cultures of various foreign peoples [...] have significantly shaped German intellectual life and cultural institutions'.[30] Tatlock is correct to note that Freytag allows for a certain level of cultural pluralism, though she fails to acknowledge fully the extent to which German identity is always the dominant partner in this pluralistic mix. Freytag does not suggest, as she argues, that 'Germans are able to benefit from and absorb foreign influence, indeed entire peoples, while maintaining an essential Germanness'.[31] Rather, he explicitly states that Germanness subsumes and colonizes the weaker, non-German characteristics:

> Aber unser Gemüthsleben, die Weise, wie wir die Welt in unsern Seelen aufnehmen und abspiegeln, unsere charakteristischen Neigungen und Schwächen, unser Idealismus, auch die Grundlagen unserer Sitten sind so gut wie der Goldschatz unserer Sprache ein Familienerbe der Germanen des Tacitus, ein Erbe, welches mit unwiderstehlicher Gewalt uns allen Gemüth, Gedanken, Erfindung im Zwange deutschen Lebens ausbildet. Dies ist ein unzerstörbarer Besitz, der trotz vielen Wandlungen in der Zeit

> und trotz unablässiger Einwirkung des Fremden uns eigenthümlich und ebenso ureigen geblieben ist, wie deutsches Wesen in der Urzeit war. Durch ihm wird alles fremde Blut, das in unsere Bevölkerung rinnt, in deutsche Art umgesetzt. (XVII, 35)

Freytag does not truly believe in cultural pluralism here, nor is his programme one of integration — it is one of colonial dominance.

It is difficult to read Freytag's analysis in the *Bilder* of Germany's relationship with Eastern Europe without drawing parallels with the issue of Germany's borders in the nineteenth century — the so-called German question. As a proponent of a *kleindeutsch* solution, Freytag believed that some areas to the east of Germany — most notably Posen and East Prussia — were German both in culture and in blood, a view shared by many *kleindeutsch* advocates.[32] In emphasizing the long-standing nature of German settlement of these lands, and in repeatedly focusing on Silesia as a source of evidence, the *Bilder* provide a form of historical justification for this belief. To an extent, this is also a personal issue for Freytag: Silesia was his birthplace and he considered himself to be a 'Kind der Grenze' (I, 4). Tatlock has argued that Freytag sees 'Silesia [as] a microcosm of the entire German nation, even as it represents the last outpost of German culture'.[33] Even more significantly, however, the border state of Silesia acts as a symbol for the success of the German colonial project and a means by which to display the civilizing nature of the German spirit — the same themes explored in the second Polish section of *Soll und Haben*.

The *Bilder* also consider the significance of work, trade, and business for German history. As in *Soll und Haben*, business is seen almost exclusively as the preserve of the bourgeoisie, and at the centre of all social processes. In a chapter entitled *Auf den Straßen einer Stadt (nach 1300)*, Freytag notes how the increase in trade and the growth of towns went hand in hand, with middle-class businessmen functioning 'vorzugsweise [als] Städtegründer' (XVIII, 237). Towns are shown to have caused a significant shift in power, away from the feudal courts and the aristocracy, and towards the middle classes — especially towards traders and businessmen. These traders not only embody the ever-increasing economic independence of a middle class from the financial stranglehold of the court; they also represent a new set of social values, including 'Treue und Rechtschaffenheit' (XVIII, 234). These values had once been those of knights and vassals, but now belong to a new urban middle class, and are contrasted with the outmoded 'Vasallenreiterei' of the courts: 'Bereits zweihundert, ja hundert Jahre nachdem die Städte des innern Deutschlands gegründet waren, rührten sie sich als starke politische Macht, sie bildeten ein neues Fußvolk, welches gegen die Vasallenreiterei der Edeln kämpfte' (XVII, 422). Significantly, Freytag draws a link between these values and German business, presenting German traders as exporting not only their goods, but also their culture:

[The trader] hat, wo er hinkam, überall höhere Cultur verbreitet [...]. [Er] hat blühende Städte geschaffen [...]. [Er] hat [...] die Bildung seiner Zeit mit den Bedürfnissen, die er aufregte und befriedigte, in ferne Länder getragen, er hat zuerst die Völker der Erde zu einer großen Einheit verbunden, und er [...] hat die Ehre seiner Nation, die Ueberlegenheit deutschen Wesens, ja sogar den Umfang und die Grenzen des Reichs bewacht und erweitert in einer Zeit, in welcher Kaiser, Fürsten und Ritterschaft nicht im Stande waren nach großer Politik zu handeln. (XVIII, 234)

Where court and Kaiser failed, the businessman succeeded, and became both defender of the German nation, and a civilizing expansionist force. Essentially, this is another expression of the colonial project detailed above, phrased in the language of commerce:

Nicht jeder Hof und nicht jede Stadt, die der deutsche Kaufmann gebaut, dauert bis zur Gegenwart als Contor unseres Volksthums unter den Fremden, aber viele hundert Quadratmeilen sind durch seine helfende Arbeit mit unserer Cultur und Sprache und mit unserer Eigenart erfüllt, zum großen Theil völlig deutsches Land geworden. (XVIII, 256)

Once again, the similarities with Freytag's earlier writings — specifically with *Soll und Haben* — are numerous. Both works ultimately present the businessman as a form of national warrior. On the home front he represents middle-class values which contrast with those of an outmoded ruling elite. Abroad, he acts as a promoter of German trade and, with that, German moral standards and civilization. Similarly, both the *Bilder* and *Soll und Haben* stress that work is the central bourgeois value. As noted in the *Bilder*:

Nicht in der Poesie und nicht in der Wissenschaft, ja vielleicht nicht in Geselligkeit und Familienleben jener Jahre gewannen die liebenswerthe Innigkeit des deutschen Gemüthes und die opfervolle Hingabe an frei erwählte Pflicht ihren höchsten Ausdruck. Sie gewannen ihn aber in der Werkstatt. [D]as war [...] eine echte Poesie. [...] An einfache Waren und schmuckloses Geräth gaben Millionen Arbeiter ihre beste Kraft hin, aber sie thaten es mit dem Gefühl eine Kunst zu besitzen [...]. (XVIII, 148)

Here one hears direct echoes of the description of the 'Poesie des Geschäfts' (IV, 377) from *Soll und Haben*, and again, one senses that Freytag's history is coloured by contemporary concerns, presenting the reader with an image of the past which legitimizes the bourgeoisie's claim to economic (and ultimately political) dominance in the nineteenth century. National history and contemporary class concerns merge in an act of bourgeois validation.

One of the most striking aspects of Freytag's *Bilder aus der deutschen Vergangenheit* is the minor role it assigns the aristocracy in German history. In *Soll und Haben*, the superiority of the middle classes was made clear through its contrast with the decadence and decay of the aristocracy, and in the *Vormärz* dramas, a morally bankrupt aristocracy was subsumed into an ethically superior bourgeoisie. This aristocratic Other against which the bourgeoisie is defined is less prominent in the *Bilder*. Most notably, only bourgeois figures are given a voice in the text. The documents and testimonials offered by Freytag in each chapter are those of average citizens (teachers, traders, doctors), and when Freytag is obliged to use the works of ancient historians or religious chroniclers, the selections always promote those values Freytag identified as middle class (trust, honesty, the home).

Nevertheless, the *Bilder* do not completely expunge the aristocracy from German history and a ruling elite is present in numerous guises throughout. In the early periods, this is in the form of courtly culture (as in Freytag's historical drama, *Die Brautfahrt*) or the powerful institutions of the church (which are also criticized in the early volumes of *Die Ahnen*). In the later periods, a more recognizable aristocracy is described, although only two chapters of the *Bilder* explore their history in any detail, most notably in Freytag's description of the Thirty Years War and its aftermath. This event holds a central position in the *Bilder*, which describe it as a 'Menschenalter von Blut, Mord und Brand, beinahe völlige Vernichtung der beweglichen Habe, Zerstörung der unbeweglichen, geistiges und materielles Verderben der gesammten Volkes' — a caesura in Germany's path to nationhood which set the country back 'um zweihundert Jahre'.[34]

The *Bilder* suggest that, prior to the outbreak of the Thirty Years War, the class battle between the bourgeoisie and the aristocracy was essentially over. In an anachronistic image, Germany's administration, its economy, and its educational system are shown to be in the secure hands of the middle classes:

> [D]ie Geschäfte der Fürsten und ihrer Gebiete, die Stellen am Kammergericht, die Spruchcollegien an den Universitäten, fast die gesammte Rechtspflege und Verwaltung waren nicht in den Händen des Adels; der größte Wohlstand, das beste Behagen war durch Handel und Handwerk in die Städte geleitet. So war bis zum Jahre 1618 die Nation auf gutem Wege, das selbstsüchtige Junkerthum des Mittelalters zu überwinden. (XX, 297)

This is a socially tendentious and ahistorical picture, which would surely strike any modern historian of German history as bizarre. Yet Freytag clearly presents the early seventeenth century as a form of middle-class idyll roughly foreshadowing the bourgeois nation state he was fighting for in the 1860s. After the Thirty Years War, however, Freytag describes how '[d]ie Kraft des Burgerthums war [...] vollständig gebrochen, [und] die Schwächen des Adels entwickelten sich [...] zum Nachtheil des Ganzen'. The aristocracy's rise to dominance in the post-war years leads him to call the period 1650–1750 'der allerschlechteste Abschnitt der ganzen neuern Geschichte Deutschlands' (XX, 297–98). The primary reason for this was the inability of the aristocracy to modify and reduce their extravagant spending — a failure to administer their estates correctly, combined with a lack of a bourgeois work ethic: 'Aber was das Hauptleiden war, eine große Menge hatte nicht den mäßigen Sinn, sich dauernd um die Wirthschaft zu kümmern und die Ausgaben nach den sicheren Einnahmen des Gutes zu beschränken' (xx, 316). These are, of course, precisely the weaknesses seen in Freytag's earlier aristocratic figures, in particular the Freiherr von Rothsattel in *Soll und Haben*. In an intertextual link with his earlier novel, Freytag describes 'die Erwerbung [eines] verpfändeten Gutes' (xx, 315), which mirrors the fate of von Rothsattel, who similarly mortgaged his estate into bankruptcy. In addition, just as the Rothsattels are revealed to be outmoded, so Freytag notes how in the seventeenth century the middle classes came to see 'die Vorrechte des Adels, welche ihm eine Sonderstellung im Volke gaben, für veraltet' (xx, 346). In particular, he criticizes the granting of aristocratic titles through *Adelsbriefe* as a dangerous remnant of the past. This was a major concern of Freytag's in the 1860s, and is a theme picked up again in *Die verlorene Handschrift*.

According to the historical narrative of the *Bilder*, the ruin into which the aristocracy had led Germany during the Thirty Years War and the post-war years could only be resolved through the renewed intervention of the bourgeoisie, their values and work ethic. Central to this were their 'uralte[s] Bedürfnis von Ordnung und Zucht, altheimische[r] Fleiß und [ein] liebebedürftiges Gemüth, endlich auch [ein] untilgbares Pflichtgefühl' (xx, 352). Industry, duty, order: these are also the values of Anton and his colleagues at T. O. Schröter's, and of the bourgeois heroes of Freytag's *Vormärz* dramas. Yet again, Freytag's analysis of the past appears to be heavily indebted to his contemporary views. Indeed, he leaves us in no doubt about this, as — unusually for the *Bilder* — Freytag breaks with the timeline of his history and deliberately points out the similarities between the post-Thirty Years War period and events in the nineteenth century:

> Das Bürgerthum ist nicht mehr wie im Mittelalter ein Stand, der andern Ständen gegenübersteht, es ist die Nation selbst geworden. [...] Alle Privilegien, durch welche der Adel sich bis zur Gegenwart eine Sonderstellung in dem Volke zu bewahren sucht, sind ein Unglück und Verhängniß für ihn selbst geworden. [...] Aber stärker als vor zweihundert Jahren erhebt sich gerade jetzt gegen solche der Haß und die Verachtung des Volkes. (xx, 346–47)

Using the German past as a mirror to the German present, the *Bilder aus der deutschen Vergangenheit* are, above all else, a tale of bourgeois success — excluding aristocratic testimony, focusing on the promotion of middle-class values through colonial expansion and trade, and criticizing directly the privileges of the aristocracy.

In the dedication and introduction to the *Bilder aus der deutschen*

*Vergangenheit*, Freytag sets out the theoretical understanding of history on which his work is based. He argues that German history is determined by the interaction of two elements. On the one hand, there stands the autonomous individual, free in judgement and action: 'Für sich und seine Zwecke lebt der Mensch, frei erwählend, was ihm schade oder nütze; verständig formt er sein Leben, vernünftig beurteilt er die Bilder, welche aus der großen Welt in seine Seele fallen' (XVII, 23–24). On the other hand, there stands the *Volkskraft* — a supra-individual force, not unlike a collective folk unconscious, which binds a population together and determines many of an individual's actions:

> Aber nicht mehr bewußt, nicht so zweckvoll und verständig wie die Willens-kraft des Mannes, arbeitet das Leben des Volks. Das Freie, Verständige in der Geschichte vertritt der Mann, die Volkskraft wirkt unablässig mit dem dunkeln Zwange einer Urgewalt [...]. (XVII, 24)

The dialectic between the individual and the *Volkskraft* set out in the introduction to the *Bilder* echoes philosophical and historical debates from the nineteenth century on the relationship between determinism and individual freedom, and which found their most famous expression in the first volume of Schopenhauer's *Die Welt als Wille und Vorstellung* (1818–19). Indeed, Freytag's concept of the *Volkskraft* initially appears to contain an undercurrent of what is commonly termed Schopenhauerean pessimism, as he describes mankind striving to reach certain goals, unaware that a greater force is determining its actions.

This initial impression of a Büchner-like 'Fatalismus der Geschichte' is, however, quickly dispelled, as Freytag sets out what he sees as the outcome of the interaction between the individual and the *Volkskraft*.[35] The dialectic, he argues, is a progressive one, which will lead to the 'Wachsthum und [...] Befreiung des deutschen Bürgers'.[36] This image of bourgeois liberation is instantly recognizable to those familiar with Freytag's earlier writings, and it comes as little surprise to discover that Freytag's concept of history is also coloured by the national sentiment found elsewhere in his work:

> Das Leben einer Nation [verläuft] in einer unaufhörlichen Wechselwirkung des Ganzen auf den Einzelnen und des Mannes auf das Ganze. [...] Wie der Mann, entwickelt auch das Volk seinen geistigen Gehalt im Laufe der Zeit, gefördert und gehemmt, eigenthümlich, charakteristisch, originell, aber mächtiger und großartiger. (XVII, 22–24)

The dialectical relationship proposed here is clearly rooted in Hegelian philosophy, while the explicit link Freytag draws between the state, the individual, and progress is also reminiscent of Herder's philosophy of history in *Auch eine Philosophie der Geschichte zur Bildung der Menschheit* (1774). Indeed, Herder's concept of the *Geist des Volkes* and Hegel's reworking of this as the *Volksgeist* are surely intellectual precursors of Freytag's own concept of the

*Volkskraft* — a form of collective folk identity both formed by and forming the individual, and which acts as the motor of historical change.[37]

The introduction to the *Bilder* (and in contrast to Hegel) also rejects the notion that there are great individuals who create historical change, and emphasizes instead the significance of the folk, the common citizen, as the true witness and voice of history: 'Nur wie das Leben Einzelner, zumeist der Kleinen, unter den großen politischen Ereignissen verlief und durch den Zug der deutschen Natur gestaltet wurde, wird in einer Reihe von Bildern gezeigt' (XVII, 21). Interestingly, Freytag appears to break with this concept when he praises Martin Luther in an extended biographical portrait of the reformer in the chapter 'Doktor Luther' (later republished with great success as a separate pamphlet):

> Jetzt kommen die Jahre, wo sich der Mann [Luther] über der Arbeit von Millionen erhebt, um einem ganzen Jahrhundert das Gepräge seines Geistes aufzudrücken. Solche Zeiten im Leben eines Volkes gelten immer für die großen Momente seiner Geschichte. (XVIII, 467)

It is initially hard to see how such statements can be reconciled with the dialectical nature of the *Volkskraft* set out in the introduction to the *Bilder*, and critics such as Ping have noted how Freytag's discussion of the Reformation follows a '"great man" approach' to historiography.[38] However, on closer inspection it is clear that Luther, like every citizen, is ultimately also enmeshed in the historical dialectic between the individual and the *Volkskraft*. Freytag describes Luther as having risen '[a]us dem großen Quell aller Volkskraft', and notes that, despite his significance, 'der Geist der Nation [erträgt] solche Herrschaft einer einzelnen geschlossenen Persönlichkeit [...] nicht lange'.[39] A close reading of the description of Luther reveals that the main area of interest is not Luther the man, but the legacy of his teachings — teachings which fed back into the *Volkskraft*, thus continuing the dialectic. Freytag explains:

> Je kräftiger, vielseitiger und eigenartiger die Individuen ihre Menschenkraft entwickeln, desto mehr vermögen sie zum Besten des Ganzen abzugeben, und je mächtiger der Einfluß ist, welchen das Leben des Volkes auf die Individuen ausübt, desto sicherer wird die Grundlage für die freie Bildung des Mannes. (XXI, 1)

Interestingly, however, the *Volkskraft* is not solely a force of change and progress. It also represents a form of historical continuity. Borders may shift and political ideologies fluctuate, Freytag argues, but the German spirit and German character remain remarkably consistent: 'Es ist ein langer Weg [...] und doch haben zweitausend Jahre unserer Geschichte in Tugenden und Schwächen, in Anlage und Charakter der Deutschen weit weniger geändert, als man wohl meint' (XVII, x). For Freytag, it is a comfort to realize that the German of the present is connected to the German of the past through the *Volkskraft*: 'Es rührt und es stimmt heiter, wenn wir in der Urzeit genau denselben Herzschlag erkennen, der noch uns die wechselnden Gedanken der Stunde regelt' (XVII, x). This desire to stress both continuity and change has been widely seen as a weakness of Freytag's historical model, with critics such as Lynne Tatlock arguing that it renders the *Bilder* 'a muddle of essentialism and constructivism [as Freytag] both argues that [...] superior German habits of mind and heart always existed and that they evolved over the centuries as a product of history'.[40] Tatlock expresses the tension well, yet it is questionable whether the two elements of continuity and change are mutually exclusive to the extent she suggests. Certainly, the combination — however peculiar — serves Freytag's aims well. By presenting the German character as fundamentally stable, he is able to create a sense of German historical belonging and a common past, and by stressing the evolution of German society through the ages, he reveals his own era as the pinnacle of historical progress. There is a clear logic underlying the system, expressed in the (typically activist) final lines of the entire work: 'Möge auch dieses Buch ein wenig dazu helfen, daß uns Kampf und Verlust unserer Ahnen verständlich werde, Kampf und Sieg der Gegenwart aber groß und glückverheißend' (XXI, 493). This process of looking both backwards and forwards is, in fact, characteristic of all Freytag's writings — not least of *Soll und Haben*, which also stressed the need for continuity (of bourgeois values in the era of capitalism) and change (the rise to social and economic dominance of the bourgeoisie in the face of aristocratic political hegemony). The *Volkskraft* is the ultimate expression of this dual perspective, linking past and present in a constant dialectic. The *Bilder* are significant as they mark Freytag's first direct use of the term *Volkskraft*, which had been left unnamed and implicit in his earlier works, but was to become a central thematic concern of both *Die verlorene Handschrift* and *Die Ahnen*.

In many respects, it is possible to view the *Bilder aus der deutschen Vergangenheit* as a form of programmatic history — a politically and ideologically conditioned presentation of the past, similar to the agenda of programmatic realism that Freytag had pursued in *Soll und Haben*. Looking back at the past from a contemporary perspective, Freytag sees the history of Germany as intimately connected to the history of bourgeois liberation, a perspective founded on a Hegelian sense of the progressive nature of history. Thematically, the aristocracy are criticized as an outmoded hegemonic system, and Freytag's decision to exclude their testimony from his set of historical sources denies them a voice in history. Instead, German identity is shown to rest on a series of eternal middle class values — trust, honour, house, and home — exported by businessmen along with their goods and imposed in the East in the name of colonialism. The history reveals how inextricably linked concepts of class and nation were for Freytag in the 1860s, to the extent that the middle classes almost become synonymous with the German nation-state in the work. In addition, as

I will demonstrate later in this chapter, the *Bilder* have much in common with Freytag's contemporary fiction, forming a complex set of references linking his historical and literary works in ways hitherto unexplored in critical studies of his writing.

### Karl Mathy (1869)

Freytag's history of bourgeois liberation in the *Bilder aus der deutschen Vergangenheit* ends with the 1848 revolution, although — understandably perhaps — little attention is given to the failure of the political programme of the revolutionaries. However, two years after completing work on the final volume of his history, Freytag published a biography of his recently deceased friend Karl Mathy, a member of the national liberal movement during the 1850s and 1860s. Exploring recent historical developments, in particular the Prussian constitutional conflict, the biography can be seen, as Freytag himself noted in his memoirs, 'in gewissem Sinne [als] eine Fortsetzung der *Bilder*' (I, 234).

According to Freytag's memoirs, *Karl Mathy* was written 'zu Siebleben [...], im Sommer und Herbst des Jahres 1869' (I, 234) — dates corroborated by a letter from Freytag to the Duke of Coburg Gotha from December 1869.[41] The memoirs portray Freytag's motivations for writing the biography as being primarily personal, suggesting it was written out of friendship ('Es sollte der Dank sein, den ich dem geschiedenen Freunde für zehnjährige brüderliche Treue abstattete') and at the request of Mathy's widow: 'Seine Gattin sprach in der Stunde des Wiedersehens den Wunsch aus, daß ich den Nachlaß des Geschiedenen durchsehen und sein Leben beschreiben möge' (I, 234). There is little reason to doubt these initial motivations behind the biography, especially given the close friendship that had developed between Freytag and Mathy in the Kitzinger Kreis. However, the memoirs' assertion that the book could be read as a continuation of the *Bilder* also suggests that Freytag saw a political purpose to the project. In fact, Freytag's letters from the period of the text's composition reveal how he began to view it as an opportunity to chart recent German history: to explore the significance of the victory of Prussia over Austria in the war of 1866 and the subsequent granting of a Prussian constitution. Once again, history and politics are fused in a deliberately didactic project: 'Die Biographie Mathy's [...] habe ich dazu benutzt, um den Deutschen etwas aus der nächsten Vergangenheit in das Gedächtnis zurückzuwerfen, was Viele über den Ereignissen von 1866 vergessen zu haben scheinen'.[42] In addition, the structure of *Karl Mathy* parallels that of the *Bilder*. Just as the *Bilder* used eyewitness testimony as the basis for each chapter, so *Karl Mathy* is organized around extracts from Mathy's letters, diaries, and works. As Freytag noted in his memoirs: 'Für die letzten fünfzehn Jahre seines Lebens fand ich reichliches

Material in seinen Tagebüchern, für die frühere Zeit, die in Vielem noch lehrreicher war, [gab es] nur zufällig erhaltene Briefe und Berichte seiner alten Freunde' (I, 234). The two texts are further linked by the fact that the final volume of the *Bilder* closed with a lengthy quotation from Mathy's account of his time as a schoolteacher in Switzerland. The biography also incorporates several references to the *Bilder*.

Few critical studies of Freytag mention *Karl Mathy*, and the recently renewed interest in the *Bilder* has, as yet, failed to translate into similar interest in the biography, despite the connections between the two. Ping briefly notes that 'Freytag chose Tacitus's *Agricola* as his literary model for the work', but does not reference this claim, which would otherwise be of considerable interest, given the prominence of Tacitus' writings in Freytag's later novel *Die verlorene Handschrift*.[43] There are certainly superficial similarities between the two texts. Like *Karl Mathy*, the *Agricola* is a biography (of Gnaeus Julius Agricola, Tacitus's father-in-law), which uses Agricola's life as the background for a survey of political life in Roman Britain. Aside from this, however, there is little in *Karl Mathy* to indicate that Freytag 'abandoned his popular style for a classical model', as Ping claims.[44] On the contrary, the combination of the personal and the political in the work is typical of Freytag's biographical portraits published in *Die Grenzboten* throughout the 1850s and 1860s, and collected in the *Gesammelte Werke* under the title *Lebensschilderungen*. Equally little is known about the sales of *Karl Mathy*, although, given the success of *Soll und Haben*, and the (according to Freytag) strong sales of the *Bilder* and *Die verlorene Handschrift*, a new work by Freytag would undoubtedly have attracted attention in the 1860s. It is questionable, however, whether Mathy's biography generated much interest — he was not a major national figure — and the general lack of attention generated by the text in secondary literature (both contemporaneous with Freytag and more recent) suggests that it was not seen as a major addition to Freytag's oeuvre.

Karl Mathy was born in 1807 and died in 1868, and his life encompassed all the major political and social events of nineteenth-century Germany, preceding the unification in 1871. Mathy was a passionate national liberal and the story of his life is, in Freytag's telling, also that of liberalism's response to the revolutions of 1830 and 1848, to the development of German business and industry, to the impact of the post-1848 reaction on the middle classes, and to the debates about the unification of Germany under Prussian leadership. His lifetime was a period of progress and development for the liberal cause, as Freytag himself noted in the opening chapter of the biography: 'Die sechzig Jahre seiner [Mathys] Erdenlebens umschließen das Aufsteigen der deutschen Volkskraft aus Verarmung und politischem Elend zu verhältnismäßigem Wohlstand und zu einer Großmacht'.[45] As in the *Bilder*, Mathy's life provides the testimony which Freytag uses to illuminate wider social and political themes. When Freytag describes Mathy's early career as a journalist in the *Vormärz*, for instance, this biographical detail is used as the basis for Freytag's own commentary on press freedom, *Vormärz* censorship controls, and individual liberty under particularist rule. Similarly, when Mathy is elected to the Badische Ständeversammlung in 1846 to 1848, Freytag uses segments of Mathy's speeches not only to reveal how Mathy favoured reform over revolution — a political stance common to both men — but also to launch his own critique of the revolutionary action of 1848.

This pattern is repeated throughout the biography, and, as a result, it often becomes difficult to distinguish where Mathy's life ends and Freytag's opinions begin. Politically, the two men were clearly altogether similarly inclined. Both were members of the Nationalverein, the Kitzinger Kreis, and collaborated on *Die Grenzboten*. It is thus unsurprising that, at times, their political voices should merge and overlap in the biography. Affinities between the two men can be seen, for instance, in Mathy's stance on universal male suffrage. Freytag quotes from Mathy's speeches on voting reform in the Frankfurt Parliament, in which Mathy argued that universal suffrage would lead to a 'Massenherrschaft, die durchaus nicht der Ausdruck des Volkswillens ist und die auch durchaus nicht die Freiheit sichert, sondern zum Despotismus führt' (XXII, 300–01). This is precisely the position of Freytag in his articles for *Die Grenzboten* in 1848 and his 1852 play *Die Journalisten* (as discussed in Chapter 3). Freytag's and Mathy's voices also merge in Freytag's depiction of Mathy's career as a banker. Freytag describes (although this time without corroborating statements by Mathy himself) Mathy's distrust of the economic changes underway in Germany in the 1850s, especially the shift away from a nationally orientated system of trading goods and towards an internationally directed shares market:

> Und Mathy merkte wie Menschennatur in diesem heftigen Kampf um das Geld geformt wurde, und das Massenhafte der moralischen Verbildungen wurde ihm widerverwärtig. [...] [F]ür den [...] Geschäftsmann [fing] der wärmste Antheil an den Unternehmungen da [an], wo der gemeine Nutzen zum eigenen Vortheil wurde, für Mathy aber da, wo der Vortheil des Einzelnen allgemeinen Nutzen schuf. (XXII, 370–73)

The moral distaste at greed contained in these lines, and the sense that trade should benefit the greater good, rather than the individual, is strikingly similar to Freytag's own position in *Soll und Haben*. That novel also stressed the fundamental connection between business and bourgeois values and proposed a curiously decapitalized vision of trade, in which individual gain was presented as a form of moral corruption, symbolized by Jewish and aristocratic figures (see the discussion in Chapter 3). When Freytag describes the 'lichtvolle Gegenfarbe' which Mathy sees in an 'alte ehrenfeste Firma, welche ruhig auf alten Verbindungen stand' (XXII, 371), it is as if he is describing the firm of T. O.

Schröter from *Soll und Haben*. The many connections to Freytag's literary work seen in the *Bilder* can also be found in *Karl Mathy*.

Two further themes link *Karl Mathy* to Freytag's wider literary practice. First, although much of the text is concerned with political developments, it is also rich in detail about Mathy's private life, and repeatedly emphasizes 'das deutsche Glück eines eigenen Haushalts, die hingebende Liebe einer guten Frau und das sorglose Lachen der Kinder' (XXII, 14). Mathy is essentially described as a paragon of bourgeois virtue, as loyal to his family as he is to his political ideals. Secondly, he is presented as a Prussian patriot, one of the:

> Auserwählten, in denen die große Idee des preußischen Bundesstaates zuerst heraufwuchs zu fester maßvoller Forderung [...]. [E]r war der einzige Nichtpreuße, der den Kampf für diese Idee in verantwortlicher Stellung von den ersten Anfängen bis zu seinem Lebensende treu durchgeführt hat. (XXII, 419)

Mathy is, in fact, presented in the biography as having a double identity: both regional and national. On the one hand, he is a loyal servant of the state of Baden, pursuing a career in the civil service and in the local press, despite many setbacks and an antagonistic relationship with the state authorities. On the other hand, he is a supporter of national unification under the leadership of Prussia — an unexpected stance, given the rivalry between Baden and Prussia since Baden's withdrawal from the Heiliges Römisches Reich Deutscher Nation in 1806 and her military alliance with France through the Rheinbund. Yet it is precisely the fact that Mathy encompasses both a Baden and a Prussian identity that is of significance. Through Mathy, Freytag can stress how loyalty to a regional identity and trust in Prussian leadership are — despite historical, military, and geographic differences between the states — mutually compatible. Like the final volumes of the *Bilder*, *Karl Mathy* stresses the need for national unification and the primacy of Prussia in that process, but allows the political dominance of Prussia to coexist with a regional identity, presenting Germany as a land unified in its diversity. Although *Karl Mathy* was initially the result of Freytag's friendship with Mathy, Freytag thus ultimately instrumentalized the biography for political ends, seeing the project as an opportunity to re-educate his reader about recent German history — not least the importance of the middle classes and of Prussia to German unification. Mathy's life provided the ideal subject matter. His political faith in Prussia showed the possibility of synthesizing regional and national identities, his home life was apparently that of a model middle class citizen, and his journalistic and political work reflected the key historical events of the era. In its educative and historical aims, *Karl Mathy* can truly be seen as an extension of the *Bilder aus der deutschen Vergangenheit*, providing that cycle with a suitably triumphant conclusion — the granting of the Prussian constitution in 1867.

## Die Technik des Dramas (1863)

While working on the *Bilder aus der deutschen Vergangenheit*, Freytag also began to gather material for a practically orientated theory of drama and tragedy, published in 1863 as *Die Technik des Dramas*. At first glance, this theoretical work appears to have little in common with the explicitly social and national tendencies that are present in Freytag's other writings from the 1860s. Yet, as I will show in the following discussion, this literary theory does reflect Freytag's class concerns, as he attempts to update the classical, Aristotelian model of drama for a new political age, and in the process seeks to educate a new generation of German dramatists.

Little is known about the composition of *Die Technik des Dramas*. Unusually, Freytag does not discuss the work in his memoirs, and it is mentioned only fleetingly in his extant correspondence. It is possible, however, to date the text's publication with relative precision, with the help of two letters Freytag wrote to the Duke of Coburg Gotha. On 5 December 1862, Freytag briefly notes that *Die Technik des Dramas* has been completed, and a subsequent letter from 5 January 1863 reveals that it has been published.[46] Hans Lindau has noted that *Die Technik des Dramas* is partially based on articles that Freytag first published in *Die Grenzboten* — the result, therefore, of a process of amalgamation and adaptation similar to that behind the book edition of the *Bilder aus der deutschen Vergangenheit* discussed earlier in this chapter.[47] The primary basis for the text was a series of articles on dramatic theory entitled *Das Schaffen des dramatischen Dichters*, which Freytag wrote in 1861. Lindau has, in addition, identified essays by Freytag from 1849 (*Vergangenheit und Zukunft unserer dramatischen Kunst*) and 1853 (*Die deutschen Theater und der Bühnendichter*) which were reworked and included in the later work.[48] For Freytag, the 1860s thus opened with a period of intense literary consolidation, as he took elements from his journalism and developed them into substantial works of aesthetic theory and cultural history.

*Die Technik des Dramas* itself was designed to act as a combination of dramatic theory and practical handbook for playwrights, as Freytag notes in its dedication:

> Was ich Ihnen darbiete, soll kein ästhetisches Handbuch sein, ja es soll vermeiden das zu behandeln, was man Philosophie der Kunst nennt. [...] Denn unsere Lehrbücher der Aesthetik sind sehr umfangreiche Werke und reich an geistvoller Erklärung, aber man empfindet zuweilen als Uebelstand, daß ihre Lehren gerade da aufhören, wo die Unsicherheit des Schaffenden anfängt.[49]

Like the *Bilder*, *Die Technik des Dramas* is didactic in intention. In it, Freytag sets out a number of rules for writing a successful drama, interspersed with an analysis of the roots of drama in classical theatre. As in the *Bilder*, Freytag uses extensive examples, in this case from the classical canon, to elucidate his educational points, referring frequently to the works of Sophocles, Euripides, and Aeschylus. He also provides examples from what he terms a Germanic theatrical tradition, represented primarily by Shakespeare and supported by Goethe, Schiller, Kleist, and Lessing (to whose *Hamburgische Dramaturgie*, of 1767, Freytag's own text is clearly indebted).

Central to *Die Technik des Dramas* is an analysis of dramatic structure. Freytag rigidly presents a play as consisting of five acts — the *Einleitung, Steigerung, Höhepunkt, Umkehr*, and *Katastrophe* — which are then joined by a further three parts: the *erregendes Moment*, the *tragisches Moment*, and the *Moment der letzten Spannung* (XIV, 102–22). According to Freytag, this eight-part structure should also be present microcosmically in each scene, and all elements of the drama — including characterization — should develop logically out of its demands. Freytag famously presented this structure pictorially in what became known as the Freytag Pyramid (see Figure 4.1).[50]

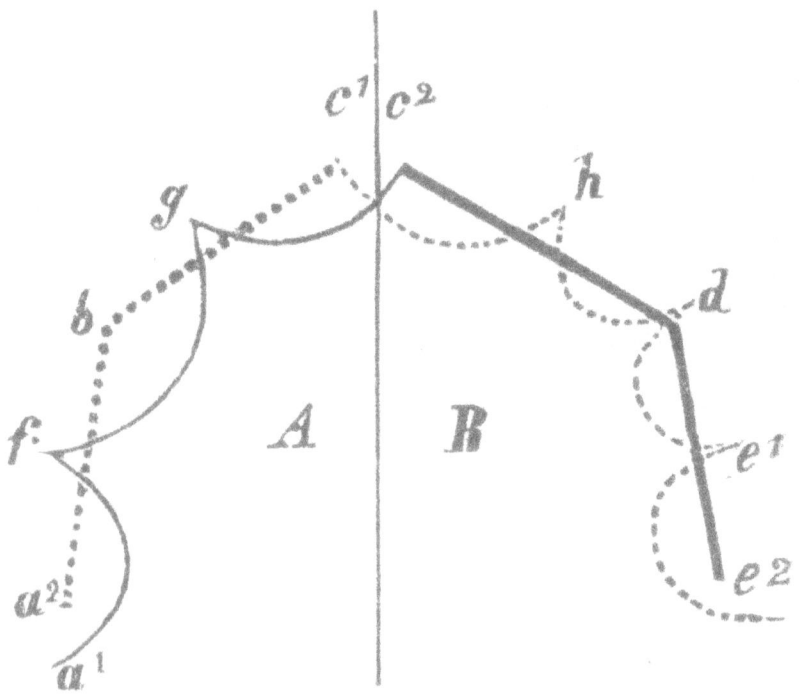

FIG. 4.1. *The Freytag Pyramid* (XIV, 183)

Freytag's interest in the dramatic form and its roots in classical drama is no doubt a result of his work as a young academic on the origins of drama — a project he pursued in both his doctorate and his *Habilitation* thesis, and which he intended to expand into a history of the German theatre, but never completed owing to his unexpected departure from Breslau University in 1845 (as discussed in Chapter 2). To an extent, *Die Technik des Dramas* could be read as the late, and somewhat truncated, realization of this plan.[51]

On publication, Freytag's work attracted considerable critical attention — most notably from Wilhelm Dilthey, the German philosopher and historian, who published a lengthy four-part review in the *Berliner Allgemeine Zeitung* between 26 March and 9 April 1863. In it, Dilthey praised Freytag for producing 'ein auf dem griechischen Philosophen ruhendes System der dramatischen Technik [...], welches uns für die Reform des Dramas von durchgreifender Bedeutung zu sein scheint'.[52] The interest generated by *Die Technik des Dramas* was great enough for Freytag to be invited to become a member of the prestigious Schiller Commission, charged with awarding the Schiller Prize for the best new German drama of 1863: 'Freilich hat es auch eine unangenehme Folge gehabt [...]. Der preußische Minister Mühler hat mich eingeladen, in die Commission zu treten, welchen den dramatischen Schillerpreis für dieses Jahr zu vertheilen hat'.[53] Freytag's lack of enthusiasm for the role is, perhaps, understandable — this was precisely the prize which he himself had won with *Die Fabier* some four years earlier but had ultimately rejected after the public debacle surrounding its award (see the discussion in Chapter 3). Freytag did, however, take up the post, recasting it as an honour in his memoirs, where he also claims that the position provided him with character studies for his 1864 novel *Die verlorene Handschrift* (I, 200). *Die Technik des Dramas* is also one of the few texts of Freytag which is in print nowadays, in a heavily abridged and updated version intended for use by German students.[54] The Freytag Pyramid, in particular, remains popular in both Germany and the United States, although it is now so divorced from its original context as to be hardly recognizable as the analytical tool Freytag describes.

*Die Technik des Dramas* was in many respects a surprising project for Freytag to undertake in the early 1860s. His 1859 tragedy, *Die Fabier*, had been poorly received, and it was well over a decade since the success of his comedy *Die Journalisten* (see the discussions in Chapter 3). In the interim, he had achieved considerable fame with *Soll und Haben* and the *Bilder aus der deutschen Vergangenheit*. Why return to drama? Freytag's correspondence with the Duke of Coburg Gotha provides some insight into this question. In a letter which reveals the extent to which Freytag believed his writings had gained influence among the German public, he explains how he plans to exploit his recent literary success to write *Die Technik des Dramas*, allowing him to make a direct contribution to German cultural debates:

> Es geschah nicht ohne sehr bestimmte Zeittendenz, daß ich das Buch schrieb. Da die Deutschen meinen Worten einigen Antheil gönnen, so schien mir grade jetzt der Moment zu sein, wo wieder ein kleines Gewicht auf die ästhetische Wagschale des deutschen Lebens geworfen werden mußte.[55]

A letter from December 1862 provides further detail about Freytag's specific aims for *Die Technik des Dramas*, describing the text as a form of corrective to what he saw as an increasing debasement of dramatic values and forms in the German theatre: 'Es ist ein Versuch, der Formlosigkeit und dilettantischen Verwilderung, welche in dem schwierigsten Genre der Poesie einreißt, entgegenzutreten'.[56] Freytag's concern about the corruption and decadence of contemporary drama was a common theme of critical and theoretical writing about the theatre in the post-1848 period. Julian Schmidt, for instance, Freytag's friend and collaborator on *Die Grenzboten*, had expressed similar concerns in his literary-critical articles for the journal (which later formed the basis for his highly influential *Geschichte der deutschen Literatur seit Lessing's Tod* of 1858). Theodor Mundt, Hermann Hettner, Rudolf Gottschall, Friedrich Vischer, Otto Ludwig, and Robert Prutz similarly wrote works of dramatic theory in the 1850s and 1860s motivated by a sense that the German theatrical tradition was under threat from an upsurge of mediocrity. Common to all their works was a return to and reaffirmation of Aristotelian traditions of drama. As Edward McInnes noted in his survey of theories of drama in the post-1848 era:

> '[Die] dramentheoretischen Bemühungen [...] wiesen fast alle eine stark bestätigend-erhaltende Tendenz auf — einen Willen, die Formkonzeption des Dramas im Sinne der klassizistischen Gattungspoetik zu bewahren'.[57]

McInnes places Freytag's theory of drama firmly within this tradition, and the work does contain several of the common features of dramatic theory he has identified. For instance, *Die Technik des Dramas* argues that German drama is suffering 'an übergroßer Zuchtlosigkeit und Formlosigkeit' (xiv, 5), and demands a return to the 'dramatische Werkstätte des Alterthums' (xiv, 6). The work also stresses the superior aesthetic status of drama as compared with the novel (xiv, 296), and it reaffirms Lessing's understanding of Aristotle in the *Hamburgische Dramaturgie*, favouring unity of action above the other unities (xiv, 18–20). Similarly, the positive assessment of the future of German drama in *Die Technik des Dramas* mirrors what McInnes sees as a general tendency in these works to promote 'eine zu erwartende ideale Zukunft der Kunst'.[58]

> Vielleicht scheint auch Ihnen eine Zeit nicht mehr in unerreichbarer Ferne zu liegen, in welcher der Deutsche mit Selbstgefuhl und stolzem Behagen das eigene Leben mustert. Dann mag der Frühling für ein reichliches Blühen des Dramas gekommen sein. (xiv, x)

However, in other respects, *Die Technik des Dramas* differs from similar works of theory written by Freytag's contemporaries. For instance, although Freytag stresses the significance of dramatic rules, he also argues that a 'Technik des Dramas nichts Feststehendes, Unveränderliches [ist]' (XIV, 3). McInnes has noted how although critics were calling for a renewal of drama at this time, '[d]as führte aber keineswegs zu grundlegenden Zweifeln an den noch als unantastbar angesehenen Gattungsgesetzen'.[59] Freytag, on the contrary, argued that the rules of drama must constantly be renewed, in order to allow for 'eine Wandlung und Fortbildung nach den Bedürfnissen der Zeit' (XIV, 6). Central to this attempt to invigorate German drama was Freytag's desire to see bourgeois themes and narratives take a central position in a new dramatic tradition:

> Das Drama der Neuzeit hat in den Kreis seiner Stoffe ein weites Gebiet aufgenommen, welches der ältern Tragödie der Griechen, ja in der Hauptsache noch der Kunst Shakespeare's fremd war: das bürgerliche Leben der Gegenwart, die Conflikte unserer Gesellschaft. Kein Zweifel, daß die Kämpfe und Leiden moderner Menschen eine tragische Behandlung möglich machen [...]. (XIV, 100)

Freytag's aim of promoting a bourgeois tragedy appears at first somewhat outmoded, given that works by Lessing and others from the 1750s onwards had already been characterized as a form of *bürgerliches Trauerspiel*, in which the act of catharsis took on a strongly morally enlightening function. However, Freytag clearly felt that Lessing had not gone far enough in his adaptation of Aristotle. In *Die Technik des Dramas* he notes, for instance, his dissatisfaction with the conclusion of *Emilia Galotti* (1772), arguing that Emilia's murder does not provide the cathartic ending a contemporary audience requires:

> So ist die Katastrophe in *Emilia Galotti* für unsere Zeit bereits nicht mehr im höchsten Sinne tragisch, weil wir von Emilia und ihrem Vater männlicheren Muth fordern. Daß die Tochter sich fürchtet verführt zu werden, und der Vater darum verzweifelt, weil doch der Ruf der Tochter durch die Entführung geschädigt ist, statt mit dem Dolch in der Hand sich und seinem Kinde den Ausweg aus dem Schlosse zu suchen, das verletzt uns die Empfindung [...]. Dann bleibt freilich immer noch der größere Uebelstand, daß dem Odoardo in der That weit näher lag, den schurkischen Prinzen als seine unschuldige Tochter zu töten. (XIV, 265–66)

In Freytag's view, the bourgeois audience is no longer willing to accept death as both highpoint and solution to a drama. The tragic climax should not take the form of absolution through death, but absolution through life and the process of learning from the error of one's ways. In essence, Freytag is attempting to redefine the Aristotelian concept of catharsis in *Die Technik des Dramas* (as Lessing had done previously in the *Hamburgische Dramaturgie*), arguing that the process of purging and renewal in Aristotle must now be accompanied by a more explicitly didactic process. In addition, he is rejecting the private conclusion to *Emilia Galotti* and suggesting instead the need for a more public resolution (in the form of the politically tendentious assassination of the Prince). It is not, one should note, that Freytag is against death as an ending in itself. It must simply be accompanied by the appropriate moral lesson. This can be seen at the end of his own self-termed tragedy *Die Fabier*, in which the moral virtue of the bourgeoisie is upheld through the death of its plebeian protagonist (see the discussion in Chapter 3).

It is difficult not to read Freytag's concept of tragedy and drama against the background of his own bourgeois ideologies. His proposal for the bourgeoisification of tragedy — which at times appears nonsensical to modern eyes — is simply yet another reflection of his social and political beliefs. His reformulation of catharsis is typical in this respect: it is an attempt to place his progressive world-view (detailed above with reference to the *Bilder* and the *Volkskraft*) into an Aristotelian model of drama. That Hegelian dialectics and Aristotle do not merge comfortably is no barrier for him, and *Die Technik des Dramas* should be read as a serious attempt by Freytag to fuse his positive bourgeois ideology with what he believed to be the highest form of art.

In his survey of dramatic theory in the post-1848 period, Edward McInnes also notes how it was often concerned with divorcing drama from politics — a tendency he also sees in *Die Technik des Dramas*:

> Man verlangte darüber hinaus, daß das Drama sich von jeder entscheidenden Berührung mit den politisch-sozialen Verhältnissen der Zeit fernhielt. [...] In der *Technik des Dramas* führt Freytag eine ebenso scharfe Absonderung der Dramenform von der sozialen Wirklichkeit durch.[60]

Certainly, Freytag's theory of drama conforms to many of the features McInnes discerns as typical — the sense of the superiority of drama, the fear of its decay, and the hopes for its regeneration through a reaffirmation of classical forms. However, in arguing that the rules of drama can be updated to fit the needs of the time, *Die Technik des Dramas* engages more closely with socio-political realities than McInnes's analysis allows. The argument put forward in *Die Technik des Dramas* that tragedy is capable of encompassing contemporary bourgeois themes is clearly an attempt to prove that tragedy is not merely the preserve of royalty and aristocrats, and that bourgeois heroes are also worthy of treatment in the highest form of art. But implicit in this are Freytag's political concerns, and an attempt to reclaim not only the artistic but also the political spheres of society for the bourgeoisie. In addition, in reimagining Aristotle in order to allow a bourgeois tragedy to end with a positive, didactic message, Freytag develops a theory of drama which fundamentally reflects the pedagogical, progressive, and pro-bourgeois sentiments expressed so vividly in his other writings. Freytag's concept of tragedy as set out in *Die Technik des*

*Dramas* is clearly an ideologically determined version of tragedy — a form of programmatic tragedy, akin to the programmatic realism of *Soll und Haben* and the programmatic history of the *Bilder*. Far from maintaining a strict division between politics and the theatre, Freytag's *Die Technik des Dramas* is formed by his very understanding of society, in particular his wish to promote the values of the middle classes.

### Die verlorene Handschrift (1864)

For his second novel, *Die verlorene Handschrift*, Freytag returned to the subject of German history first raised in the *Bilder aus der deutschen Vergangenheit*, although the novel is equally concerned with issues of historiography and the functions — both positive and negative — of historical enquiry. Set in the recent past of particularist Germany, the novel is thematically concerned with a more ancient history, and follows the increasing obsession of a historian in his quest for a lost book of Tacitus' *Historiae*. Highly didactic in tone, the novel considers at length the contemporary importance of the *Volkskraft* for German society, alongside a thoroughly critical examination of the aristocracy and its privileges. As such, it echoes concerns raised in both the *Bilder* and *Soll und Haben*.

According to Freytag's memoirs, *Die verlorene Handschrift* was published 'im Herbst 1864 in drei Bänden' (I, 202). Freytag suggests that the central event of the novel — the quest for a lost manuscript — was based on an actual search he had considered undertaking with his friend, the philologist Moritz Haupt, after hearing a rumour about an unknown work by Livy hidden in a local country house:

> [Haupt] offenbarte [...] mir im höchsten Vertrauen, daß in irgend einer westfälischen kleinen Stadt auf dem Boden eines alten Hauses die Reste einer Klosterbibliothek lägen. Es sei wohl möglich, daß darunter noch eine Handschrift verlorener Dekaden des Livius stecke. Der Herr dieser Schätze aber sei, wie er in Erfahrung gebracht, ein knurriger, ganz unzugänglicher Mann. Darauf machte ich ihm den Vorschlag, daß wir zusammen nach dem geheimnißvollen Hause reisen und den alten Herrn rühren, verführen, im Nothfall unter den Tisch trinken wollten, um den Schatz zu heben. (I, 201)

The passage is intriguing. Given that Freytag had drawn extensively on Livy when writing *Die Fabier* (as noted in Chapter 3), it is likely that he would have been excited at the possibility of discovering a lost work by the historian, and in general the parallels with the narrative set-up of *Die verlorene Handschrift* are striking. However, the parallel is almost too neat, and, given the inaccuracies in the compositional accounts of Freytag's other works in his memoirs, it is important to view this story as solely anecdotal — if true, entertaining; if not, a fiction deriving from the novel itself. It is certainly not definitive evidence, as Lonner has argued, that 'the novel's events are based on an actual episode from Freytag's life'.⁶¹

Both Ping and Lonner fully accept the account of the novel's composition as set out in the memoirs.⁶² Freytag's letters, however, reveal in far greater detail the lengthy process behind the writing of *Die verlorene Handschrift*. One of the earliest references is from January 1863, in which Freytag notes to Molinari: 'ich sitze viel über meinen Büchern und brüte über den neuen Roman'.⁶³ A year later, in February 1864, progress on the novel had stalled entirely: 'Wenn nur der verfluchte Roman nicht durch Schleswig Holstein so arg gestört würde, ich habe 2 Monate verloren und ich bin noch jetzt nicht so drin, wie ich sollte'.⁶⁴ The loss of two months' work on the novel were the result of Freytag's duties writing for and editing *Die Grenzboten*, and his need to report on the Schleswig-Holstein conflict. Overwork was clearly an issue for Freytag at this time, and by August 1864 he was forced to cut back on his duties for the journal in order to meet the deadlines for the novel: 'Leider wird meine eigene Schreiberei [for the *Grenzboten*] schwach sein, da ich jetzt unter einer andern Verpflichtung [*Die verlorene Handschrift*] arbeite'.⁶⁵ By September 1864, the first two volumes of *Die verlorene Handschrift* were complete, though the final volume was still in preparation. The memoirs claim this final volume was delayed by illness (I, 202), though no mention is made of this in the letters, which simply note Freytag's struggle to complete the work:

> Unterdeß habe ich an dem Unglücksroman drucken lassen, jetzt sind c. 45 Bogen gesetzt und gedruckt, 30 noch zurück, und ich habe noch viel daran zu thun. Doch bin ich verbissen darauf wie ein Hamster, und gehe nicht eher von hier fort, bis die Geschichte zu Ende ist.⁶⁶

Taken as a whole, the letters suggest that the writing of *Die verlorene Handschrift* was a trying period for Freytag. Work began some time in late 1862, and was completed by Christmas 1865. However, Kurt Classe has argued for a much earlier start date for the novel, in 1856.⁶⁷ Classe bases this assertion on a comment by Eduard Tempeltey in his edition of Freytag's correspondence with the Duke of Coburg Gotha. In a letter to the Duke from June 1856, Freytag apologizes for presenting him with yet another example of *Soll und Haben*, comically suggesting 'daß seine Bände [of *Soll und Haben*] zur Parkettierung eines mäßigen Zimmers ausreichen würden'.⁶⁸ Freytag then continues: 'Ich aber wollte, ich koennte Ew. Hoheit den neuen Roman fertig uebersenden. Es ist ein spröder Stoff und macht mir nachdenkliche Stunden'.⁶⁹ In a footnote, Tempeltey notes: 'Also schon damals hat Freytag den Plan zur *Verlorenen Handschrift* gefaßt'.⁷⁰ Tempeltey has not misdated the letter, and the reference to a new novel is plainly stated. Clearly, an accurate date for the start of work on *Die verlorene Handschrift* is of importance to a reading of the novel, given the marked difference between the political climate of the reaction and the more hopeful situation for liberal opinion in the 1860s. However, if Freytag was speaking of *Die verlorene Handschrift* in his letter from 1856, then it is most likely that he was referring to an initial plan or idea and not a complete text. According to his memoirs, Freytag generally narrated his novels to scribes, having only planned a rough outline beforehand (I, 180–81). Significantly, the first reference to *Die verlorene Handschrift* in Freytag's extant correspondence with his publisher's family, the Hirzels, comes in 1863, when he notes that 'der bereits oft erwähnte Roman Ihres Verlags fühlt das dringende Bedürfnis eine Thatsache zu werden'.[71] Although planning may well have begun earlier, it is clear that most of the work on the novel took place in the early 1860s.

Freytag's difficulties in writing *Die verlorene Handschrift* not only stemmed from overwork, but also from his choice of material. As he noted in a letter to Treitschke from December 1864: 'Die Schwierigkeit der Arbeit lag wohl darin, daß die Grundlage der Erzählung nur ein kleiner Novellenstoff war'.[72] Although the initial idea for the novel was indeed limited in scope, Freytag eventually expanded it into a complex work which oscillates between two substantial main narratives. The first of these details the search for a lost manuscript of Tacitus by the philologist-historians Felix Werner and Fritz Hahn. Instead of finding Tacitus, Werner finds love, in the figure of Ilse, the daughter of the owner of the farming estate believed to house the manuscript. Ilse and Werner marry and Ilse is forced to adapt, not without difficulties, to the intellectual world of academia after many years of practical work in the country. Werner is invited to catalogue the estate of the local absolutist Prince, which provides him with the opportunity to continue his quest for the lost manuscript of Tacitus. This search induces a state of near-obsession in Werner, who becomes blind both to Ilse's unhappiness, and to the moral danger she is in as she becomes the object of the Prince's romantic advances. It takes the outside intervention of friends from the town, combined with the Prince's mental breakdown, to awaken Werner to the danger his marriage has been in. The novel closes with the dramatic reconciliation of the pair on the farming estate where they had first met, as flood waters reveal the former hiding place of the lost manuscript — which turns out to have been destroyed centuries earlier. Werner realizes that it is love, rather than knowledge, that is the most important factor in life.

This melodramatic story is accompanied by a bourgeois social comedy surrounding the two hat-makers Hummel and Hahn. The two families live opposite each other and their business rivalry spills over into their home lives. This rivalry is threatened, however, by the burgeoning love between Fritz Hahn and Laura Hummel (essentially, a recasting of Romeo and Juliet, but with a happy ending). After much confusion, including the near-bankruptcy of one of the firms, Fritz and Laura marry and the two families are reconciled. From these two narratives Freytag develops a rather unwieldy novel, with chapters switching between the quest narrative and the social comedy, between esoteric discussions on the nature of learning and critical accounts of bourgeois-aristocratic relations. The novel certainly failed to replicate the aesthetic and critical success of *Soll und Haben* — Freytag himself notes the unenthusiastic response of critics in his memoirs. Precise sales figures are unknown, although Freytag's memoirs state that *Die verlorene Handschrift* sold approximately half as many copies as *Soll und Haben* (I, 204). Given the success of *Soll und Haben*, this would be — if correct — a rather respectable figure.

There are few critical studies of the novel. Larry Ping's perspective on the text is primarily that of a historian. He contextualizes the novel within dominant strands of historical thought in the 1860s, and argues that 'Freytag intended *Die verlorene Handschrift* to be a monument to the German historical profession in much the same way that *Soll und Haben* celebrated the honour and productivity of the German merchant'.[73] This concept of *Die verlorene Handschrift* as a reworking of *Soll und Haben*, but with the historian, rather than the businessman, as hero, is raised in almost every study that mentions the text.[74] Ping's analysis is rich in historical detail, but he fails to consider the novel from a literary-critical perspective, often reading the text solely as a historical source and seemingly accepting the positions taken by the novel uncritically. Alyssa Lonner is generally more successful in her consideration of the novel, especially in her depiction of the rural economy in the text, although her treatment of Freytag's attack on the aristocracy — which she sees as marking 'the death of absolutism' — fails to account for the full complexity of Freytag's social view.[75] As will be seen in the following discussion, *Die verlorene Handschrift* is more sophisticated in its political agenda than either Ping or Lonner allow, and pushes Freytag's concepts of class and nation into new and unexpected areas.

*Die verlorene Handschrift* is the most overtly didactic of Freytag's novels. The narrative is regularly broken up by lengthy passages on topics ranging from Tacitus to *Tannhäuser*, most often in the form of monologues by its historian-hero, Werner. Given this tendency, it is easy to understand why the text has a reputation as being a novel of *Bildung* in which, to quote Ping, Freytag presents 'the history profession as the high priesthood of the nation's cultural heritage'.[76] However, the presentation of history in the text does not only involve the 'canonization of the history profession'.[77] The seductive side of academic research and the dangers inherent in living solely for the past are also key themes of the novel — a fact overlooked in Ping's analysis. I will explore both aspects of the text — the historian as educator, and history as a site of potentially negative fixation — in the remainder of this chapter.

Throughout the opening volumes of the novel, Werner is the mouthpiece for Freytag's own highly specific historical concept of the *Volkskraft*, first introduced in the *Bilder*. Critics have noted that Freytag's final novel, *Die Ahnen*, can be seen as a literary reworking of the *Bilder*, but it is equally important to recognize that *Die verlorene Handschrift* is also an intellectual successor to his cultural history. Werner is provided with multiple opportunities to speak about the nature of history and the historian's task. The majority of these scenes involve Ilse, the local farmer's daughter with whom he has fallen in love. This is a significant pairing, since it allows for a directly didactic dialogue between the erudite townsman Werner, and the intelligent but uneducated country girl Ilse. The reader is placed together with Ilse as a passive recipient of the educational facts presented by Werner. Early in the novel, for instance, when Ilse admits to Werner that she has always been frightened of history, since in her experience it never ends well, Freytag has Werner respond with a lengthy defence of the discipline, which directly echoes his own vision of the positive historical dialectic presented in the introduction to the *Bilder*, and detailed earlier in this chapter. In the words of Werner:

> [W]ir errathen, daß in den Menschen, welche zerbrechen, und in den Völkern, welche zerrinnen, noch ein höheres geheimes Leben waltet, welches nach ewigen Gesetzen schaffend und zerstörend dauert. Und einige Gesetze dieses höhern Lebens zu erkennen und den Segen zu empfinden, welchen dies Schaffen und Zerstören in unser Dasein gebracht hat, das ist Aufgabe und Stolz des Geschichtsforschers. Von diesem Standpunkt verwandelt sich Auflösung und Verderben in neues Leben. Und wer sich gewöhnt, die Vergangenheit so zu betrachten, dem vermehrt sie die Sicherheit, und sie erhebt ihm das Herz.[78]

Such overtly didactic scenes are supported by the omniscient narrator's ability to give us access to Werner's thoughts, which often turn to mankind's place in the historical process and the tension between free will and determinism — again, a tension explored in the introduction to the *Bilder*. Werner states:

> Alles was war und Alles was ist, das lebt über seine Erdentage hinaus fort in jedem neuen Dasein, worein es zu dringen vermag, es wirkt vielleicht in Millionen, durch lange Zeiten, die Einzelnen und die Völker bildend, erhebend, verderbend. So werden die Geister der Vergangenheit, die Gewalten der Natur, auch was man selbst geschaffen und erdacht hat, ein unveräußerlicher, Leben wirkender Bestandtheil der eigenen Seele. Und lächelnd sah der Gelehrte, wie fremde, tausend Jahr alte Erinnerungen ihn selbst hierher unter Landsleute geführt hatten [...]. (XI, 83)

It is important to stress the frequency with which this topic is returned to in the early volumes of the novel. The sentimental love story between Ilse and Werner is repeatedly used as a pretext. Romantic exchanges suddenly develop into intellectual discourses on how the 'Volkskraft [...] hilft wacker und stolz machen' (XI, 158), and Werner's talks with his father-in-law, the local farmer, are similarly instrumentalized. Even seemingly unrelated events lead to discursive musings on the nature of history. When a tree is felled by lightning on the farm, for instance, Werner reflects at length on how 'alles einzelne Leben, eigenes und fremdes, unendlich klein ist gegen das große Ganze' (XI, 118). These moments become increasingly wearisome for the reader, not least because they present the same point in countless iterations. They also detract considerably from the narrative energy of the novel, distracting the reader from both the quest for the Tacitus manuscript and the growing relationship between Ilse and Werner. Fundamentally, *Soll und Haben* was no less didactic than is *Die verlorene Handschrift*. But the earlier novel presented its educational themes through a series of carefully constructed oppositions and conflicts: Anton–Itzig; Anton–Fink; Schröter–Ehrenthal; bourgeoisie–aristocracy; German–Slav. Even Schröter's speeches to Anton — perhaps the most overtly didactic sections of the novel — were motivated by conflict, namely by Anton's desire to leave the firm and work for the von Rothsattels. These conflicts are absent in *Die verlorene Handschrift*. Instead, Werner is the single voice of *Bildung*, which has two unfortunate consequences for the novel: it leaches the story of its drama and renders its hero a pedant.

Of greater interest than Werner's monologues are Freytag's attempts to express the *Volkskraft* in imaginative forms in the novel — most frequently in visual manifestations that border on the fantastical and seem out of place in a work of programmatic realism. As Werner and his father-in-law explore the farm, for instance, the narrator notes that they are accompanied by many miniature figures which fly around their heads:

> [W]ie verschiedenartig [war] das unsichtbare Gefolge kleiner Geister [...], welches beiden um Schläfe und Schultern flatterte, Schwärmen unzählbarer Vögel oder Bienen vergleichbar. Die Geister des Landwirths waren in heimischer Wirthschaftstracht, blaue Kittel oder flatternde Kopftücher [...]. Hingegen um den Professor schwärmte ein unabsehbares Gewühl fremder Gebilde mit Toga und antiken Helmen, in Purpurgewand und griechischer Chlamys, auch nacktes Volk in Athletentracht, und solche mit Rutenbündeln und mit zwei Flederwischen an den Hüten. (XI, 84–85)

Lonner argues that the scene shows how 'superstitions and ancient beliefs [...] all continue to be a part of the rural world', noting the similarity with the scene in *Soll und Haben* in which the Schröter house anthropomorphizes in response to Anton's presence (discussed in Chapter 3).[79] There are, indeed, similarities between the two moments, not least in their unexpected use of fantasy. Significantly, though, the scene in *Soll und Haben* directly deployed characters from folk traditions (*Heinzelmännchen*, house spirits, and so on). The figures in the above passage, however, are not immediately derived from folklore, and are instead miniaturized representatives of past epochs. Constantly advising and influencing the unconscious thoughts and actions of Werner and the farmer, they are a whimsical depiction of Freytag's concept of the *Volkskraft*:

> Während die Männer diese anscheinend gleichgültige Unterhaltung führ-

ten, flog ein bösartig aussehender Genius, wahrscheinlich Kaiser Diocletianus selber, vom Professor hinüber unter die bäuerliche Genossenschaft des Landwirths, stellte sich in seinem Purpurgewand mitten auf den Kopf des Herrn, stampfte mit den Beinchen an die Hirnschale und veranlaßte dem Landwirth die Empfindung, daß der Professor ein verständiger und gediegener Mann sei [...]. (XI, 86)

In another imaginative sequence, Fritz, Werner's colleague, scrutinizes Ilse's home, the Bielstein farm, and gradually perceives its development through time until all its historical incarnations coexist in the present in a form of palimpsest:

Der Doctor sah zurück auf den Stein, der das alte Haus trug [...]. Und alle Vergangenheit und Gegenwart der [...] Stätte waren ihm deutlich. [...]. Damals war der Stein einem Heidengotte heilig, schon damals hatte ein Thurm darauf gestanden [...]. (XI, 179)

Significantly, it is not only the geographic location of the farm which is subject to this palimpsestic effect, but also the individuals that inhabit it. As Fritz's gaze passes through the various layers of history, so different incarnations of Ilse are revealed:

[D]ie Ilse hatte darin gewohnt mit ihren gescheitelten blonden Haaren [...]. Damals war sie Priesterin und Prophetin gewesen für einen Stamm wilden Sachsenvolks. [...] Wieder später hatte ein christlicher Sachsenhäuptling dort sein Balkenhaus gebaut, und wieder hatte dieselbe Ilse darin gesessen [...]. Jahrhunderte später war das gemauerte Haus mit steinumfaßten Fenstern und einem Wartthurm [...], und die Ilse von Bielstein hatte wieder darin gehaust [...]. Und viele hundert Jahre später hatte sie in dem Jagdschloß eines Fürsten gesessen [...]. An ihrem Wesen hing etwas von allem, was die Ilsen seit zwei Jahrtausenden gewesen. (XI, 179–80)

The continuity within Ilse's character described in this passage reminds one of Freytag's comment in the *Bilder* that '[e]s rührt und es stimmt heiter, wenn wir in der Urzeit genau denselben Herzschlag erkennen, der noch uns die wechselnden Gedanken der Stunde regelt' (XVII, x). The ability of people and places to hold their past incarnations within themselves is also, as we will see, a central theme of Freytag's final novel *Die Ahnen*, which reveals the connections that link, both consciously and unconsciously, multiple generations of one family. Ilse is in many ways a precursor of the female heroines of *Die Ahnen*: at once housewife (Freytag makes repeated allusions to Lotte from Goethe's *Die Leiden des jungen Werthers* in his descriptions of Ilse and her siblings) and warrior — Ilse is called Thusnelde by Fritz, a female German warrior whose life was partially described by Tacitus (XI, 72, 80). Critics have hitherto failed to note these significant parallels between *Die Ahnen* and *Die verlorene Handschrift*.

Freytag's instrumentalization of the novel to explain his understanding of history reaches a climax in the second volume, which focuses on Ilse's attempts to come to terms with life in the town after marrying Werner and the radical change in world-view that this entails. Finding herself out of her depth in intellectual circles, she develops the desire to learn, and turns to her husband for help: 'Ich bin dein, lehre mich, bilde mich, mache mich verstehen, was du verstehst' (XI, 250). In contrast to the earlier scenes described above, Freytag at this point attempts to inject some drama into his exposition. Ilse is shown as a willing recipient of Werner's teachings, eagerly reading the ancient historians and dramatists. However, she still struggles with the concept of the *Volkskraft*. Werner repeatedly attempts to explain to his wife the significance of this force:

> Das Meiste, was du hast und bist, verdankst du einer Vergangenheit, die anfängt von dem ersten Menschenleben auf Erden. In diesem Sinne hat das ganze Menschengeschlecht gelebt, damit du leben kannst. [...] Dein Volk und dein Geschlecht haben dir Vieles gegeben, sie verlangen dafür ebenso viel von dir. (XI, 346)

Ilse is, however, horrified at a world-view which, in her eyes, has the weight of history bearing down on each individual's shoulders. Interestingly, Ilse's inability to accept Werner's teachings resides in her religious faith, and her sense that God is essentially rendered pointless if the primacy of the *Volkskraft* is admitted. When Werner triumphantly concludes that the *Volkskraft* is a means of defeating death, Ilse responds with reference to the power of a Christian God:

> Sieh, Geliebte [says Werner], bei solcher Auffassung schwindet der Tod aus der Geschichte. Das Resultat des Lebens wird wichtiger als das Leben selbst, über dem Mann steht das Volk, über dem Volk die Menschheit, Alles, was sich menschlich auf Erden regte, hat nicht nur für sich gelebet, sondern auch für alle anderen, auch für uns, denn es ist ein Gewinn geworden für unser Leben. [...]
> 'Ach,' rief Ilse, '[...] Mich friert dabei. [...] [I]hre Seelen [those of the folk] werden doch behütet von einer Macht, welche größer ist als dein großes Netz, das aus Menschenseelen gewebt ist. [...] Beugt euren Menschenstolz vor einer Gewalt, die ihr nicht versteht.' (XI, 347–48)

The clash between Ilse's faith in God and Werner's trust in the *Volkskraft* is of particular note since religious faith does not play a major role anywhere else in Freytag's writings. In *Soll und Haben*, Anton is a symbol of bourgeois virtue, yet this virtue is entirely socially determined and is never expressed in religious terms. Luther is praised extensively in the *Bilder*, but ultimately he is presented as the father of the German nation, not of the German or any other kind of faith. Marriage plays a central role throughout the *Vormärz* dramas and *Die Ahnen*, yet is primarily a tool of social structuring, rather than a moral or religious requirement. That Freytag distrusted religious institutions and orders is revealed in his critical assessment of monasteries and the Jesuits in the *Bilder* and *Die Ahnen*. It is possible that Freytag realized that there were pagan elements to his notion of the *Volkskraft*, and that this is in part reflected here.

The conflict between the *Volkskraft* and orthodox religion in *Die verlorene Handschrift* is not, however, developed further by Freytag. Ilse collapses and falls seriously ill as a result of her crisis of faith, but, rather than choosing to develop this potentially productive seam of drama, Freytag resolves it in a sentence: 'Es war ein langes Ringen zwischen Leben und Vergehen, aber sie überwand' (XI, 351). In his memoirs, Freytag notes that critics felt that 'die religiösen Conflicte und die geistige Entwickelung' (I, 203) of Ilse were underdeveloped, and one can only concur with this assessment. However, these scenes make clear where Freytag's actual interest in his material lay — in the didactic words of Werner, the dialogues and monologues on history, and not primarily in the narrative, its action and even its moral dilemmas. The lack of critical and aesthetic success of the novel is surely rooted in this imbalance between didacticism and plot.

However, Ilse's collapse marks the introduction of another important theme of *Die verlorene Handschrift*, namely the negative potential of *Bildung*. As the novel progresses, Werner's passion for the past develops into an obsession bordering on madness. In particular, this obsession is shown as detrimental to bourgeois values. Werner becomes blind to Ilse's unhappiness at court, and to the social danger she is in as the object of the Prince's predatory gaze. Nor is he able to see that he and his wife are the mere playthings of the aristocracy, and that the concern of the Prince with the manuscript is merely a ploy by the Prince in order to get closer to Ilse. Werner's realization of his error comes only after Ilse has left him:

> Allzugroß ist der Eifer, das weiß ich, er hat mich hart gemacht gegen die kindliche Angst meines Weibes, auch ich bin nicht stärker geworden, seit ich auf dem unsicheren Pfad eines Wildschützen dahinfahre. Jeder hüte sich, daß ihm seine Träume nicht die Herrenrechte des Geistes verringern [...].[80]

This is, of course, a reworking of a theme from *Soll und Haben*, in which Freytag stressed that: 'Aber ein Jeder achte wohl darauf, welche Träume er im heimlichsten Winkel seiner Seele hegt, denn wenn sie erst groß gewachsen sind, werden sie leicht seine Herren, strenge Herren!' (IV, 9). Whether in business or in *Bildung*, you cannot let your dreams become your master, Freytag argues, for this threatens the fundamental basis of bourgeois society. Dreams can distract from the greater good, and both novels demonstrate the dangers in pursuing individual desires or gain to the detriment of others. Underlying all the talk of history, Tacitus and the *Volkskraft*, therefore, there lies Freytag's traditional concern with the values of the bourgeoisie — a concern that comes more clearly to the fore when the novel turns its attention to the aristocracy in its second half. Indeed, *Die verlorene Handschrift* is a novel of two halves. The opening volumes focus predominantly on the role of the historian in society and the education of Ilse at the hands of her husband, as detailed above. It is educational divides, rather than class divisions, which primarily concern the text at this stage. The local Prince is briefly mentioned, but the novel appears to be rooted primarily in the daily lives of its bourgeois figures. However, as the text progresses, the lives of the aristocracy increasingly intrude upon the bourgeois idyll of the opening volumes. The Crown Prince becomes a student at Werner's university, and Werner himself becomes private historian to the Prince. The latter grows infatuated with Ilse, and the final two volumes detail the clash of the two classes, as Freytag returns to the anti-aristocratic themes of his earlier fiction.

Whereas the aristocratic focus of *Soll und Haben* was on the landed gentry, in *Die verlorene Handschrift* it is the upper echelons of the aristocracy, namely the local absolutist Prince, which attract Freytag's attention. Initially, at least, the Prince is depicted in broadly positive terms, seemingly attracting praise usually reserved for the bourgeoisie (although even here there is a certain negative undertone):

> Er selbst war, wo er mit seinem Volk in Verbindung trat, leutselig und von bester Laune, machte den Bittenden leicht, ihm zu nahen, hörte gefällig alle Klagen [...]. Sein Hof war in vieler Beziehung ein Muster von Ordnung und gefälligem Schein. (VII, 155–56)

Gradually, however, the absolutist court is shown to be in decline. Freytag details the many past glories of the court — the extravagant decoration, the abundance of wine, the parties and dances — but notes that '[a]lles [...] war verschwunden und verweht, über den bunten Farben lag die Schwärze der Nacht und des Todes' (VII, 385). Similarly, the country residence of the Princess is presented as a ruin, its one tower rising up 'in der einsamen Landschaft wie der letzte Pfeiler eines zertrümmerten Riesenbaues' (VII, 332). The glory of the aristocracy is revealed as long gone, and in its place has come gloom and decay. Similar themes were present in *Soll und Haben*, both in Freytag's appropriation of Eichendorffian imagery when describing landscapes, and in his description of the von Rothsattels' estate, which, for all that it impressed Anton, was actually shown to be in a state of steady deterioration.[81]

In *Die verlorene Handschrift*, it is the aristocracy's inability to reject their outmoded customs and privileges which is central to this decline. Freytag targets the many rules and regulations which dictate aristocratic behaviour — particularly the etiquette of dining, greeting, and class interaction. During a dinner at the court, Werner explains:

> Vor hundert Jahren war im Leben des Bürgers derselbe peinliche Eifer um Rang und gesellige Bevorzugung. Bei uns ist das anders geworden, seit unser Leben einen stärkern geistigen Inhalt erhielt. In Zukunft wird man auch bei Hof über dergleichen als veralteten Trödelkram lächeln. (VII, 175)

Werner's stance hardly needs explaining: not only are the aristocracy disastrously outdated in their behaviour, but they also lack the intellectual and spiritual nature of the bourgeoisie — the 'Bildung und neue Ideen' which make the middle classes the 'Herzschlag unserer Nation' (VII, 175). The aristocracy is 'durch die Etikette gebannt', condemned to be 'ein Ueberrest aus vergangener Zeit' (VII, 204–05). While *Soll und Haben* presented trade as the life-blood of the nation, *Die verlorene Handschrift* shows that *Bildung* is its heart.

These themes return with a new force when Ilse's father and Werner are offered *Adelsbriefe* — letters which grant aristocratic privileges to those not born into the aristocracy. Ilse is outraged when she realizes that this offer has been made solely to enable them to interact with the aristocracy without causing the latter any social embarrassment:

> Willst du einen Adelsbrief haben? [...] [E]r wird auf der Stelle für dich ausgefertigt und für den Vater auch, damit wir alle den Vorzug erhalten, volle Menschen zu werden, mit denen die Leute im Schloß verkehren können, ohne sich gedemüthigt zu fühlen. (VII, 202)

Lonner has argued that Ilse's anger stems from her own social insecurity.[82] This reading of the novel overestimates the psychological depth of Freytag's characters and underplays his more evident social aims. Ilse's fierce rejection of the offer is a powerful expression of bourgeois pride and an independent middle-class identity, and her anger is an effective means of condemning the aristocracy, rendering their regulations and privileges ridiculous. This subject clearly concerned Freytag greatly, since it was also noted in the *Bilder* (as discussed earlier in this chapter), and in his essays for *Die Grenzboten*.[83] As Lonner herself notes, Freytag had been offered an *Adelsbrief* by the Duke of Coburg Gotha, which he declined, despite his close friendship with the Duke.[84]

*Die verlorene Handschrift* also argues that the decay of the aristocracy is not only reflected in their buildings and behaviour, but has become a physical ailment. The figure of the Prince, for instance, is revealed to be suffering from a form of mental disorder. He sees ghosts, hears voices, and describes himself as an automaton, with a flaw in his motion:

> [I]ch [bin] selbst nur ein Automat [...], welcher aufgezogen nickt und gedankenlos dieselben gnädigen Worte wiederholt [...]. [I]ch fühle ein Gelüst, meinen eigenen Kopf in den Schraubstock zu stellen und zu bessern, was in mir schadhaft wurde [...]. (VII, 236)

This passage is reminiscent of the climax to Georg Büchner's comedy of the absolutist state, *Leonce und Lena* (1836), in which the two lovers appear as robotic versions of themselves, emphasizing the hollowness of the absolutist regime ('man könnte sie eigentlich zu Mitgliedern der menschlichen Gesellschaft machen', comments Valerio ironically).[85] Freytag could have come across *Leonce und Lena* either in its initial publication in the *Telegraph für Deutschland* (by Hoffmann & Campe) in 1838, or in the edition of J. D. Sauerländer from 1850.[86] Other authors too, such as E. T. A. Hoffmann, played with automaton images in works such as *Der Sandmann* (1816). In *Die verlorene Handschrift*, the mental afflictions of the Prince increase until he suffers a complete breakdown, believing himself to be pursued by a 'schwarze[r] Schatten' (VII, 387) — a not uncommon trope of literary depictions of madness. At the dramatic climax of the novel, the Prince even threatens Werner's life during a psychotic episode, directing a weapon at the latter's chest:

> Der Gelehrte sah den Fürsten an, aus den Augen sprühte tötlicher Haß und der glitzernde Schein des bösen Blickes, er sah die Mündung des Gewehres gegen seine Brust gerichtet und daß der gehobene Fuß des Fürsten um den Drücker fuhr. (VII, 393)

Although critics have noted the similarity between the breakdown of the Prince and that of the Freiherr von Rothsattel in *Soll und Haben*, their processes of mental disintegration are quite distinct.[87] The Freiherr's suicide attempt was the result of his shame at the collapse of his business venture, and his depression was worsened by his blindness, exile in Poland, and the death of his son. The Freiherr ends his life a broken man, but he is broken by his own acts, which trigger a series of disasters for his family. The Prince, on the contrary, appears to be suffering from a psychological disorder, an illness, and in this sense lacks any control over his fate. Freytag diagnoses the Prince's disorder as *Cäsarenwahnsinn* — a term he borrows from Tacitus, who describes in Book Three of his *Historiae* the *furor principum* which befell Roman leaders, including the emperors Caligula and Nero. Interestingly, Freytag's use of Tacitus' concept as a means by which to criticize the aristocracy anticipates the famous case of Ludwig Quidde, the liberal German historian who, in 1894, was accused of defaming Kaiser Wilhelm II in his pamphlet *Caligula — Eine Studie über römischen Cäsarenwahnsinn*. Quidde's study drew critical and satirical parallels between Caligula's mental instability and the policies of the Kaiser, and became one of the most popular political pamphlets of the Wilhelmine era.[88] Thirty years earlier, Freytag had already made the connection. It is possible that Quidde was influenced by Freytag's work.

In *Die verlorene Handschrift*, Freytag first introduces the concept of *Cäsarenwahnsinn* when Werner explains to the Prince how history owes Tacitus 'eine Reihe von psychologischen Schilderungen der Krankheit, welche sich damals auf dem Throne entwickelte' (VII, 276). The Prince is strongly affected by Werner's comments, asking: 'Sie nehmen also eine besondere Krankheit an, welche nur die Regenten befällt?' Werner then begins a lengthy explanation of the malady, its symptoms, longevity, and the extent of its impact, concluding that 'keine andere [Erscheinung] hat auf das Schicksal der Nationen so unermeßlichen Einfluß geübt' (VII, 276). Werner has essentially told 'einem Kranken seine eigene Krankheitsgeschichte' (VII, 394), and the chapter ends with the Prince fleeing, making 'der Schrei eines wilden Thieres' (VII, 281), which further confirms his descent into madness.

In updating Tacitus' concept of *Cäsarenwahnsinn* for the nineteenth century, Freytag is essentially positing the existence of a destructive flaw within the aristocratic character which is inherited from one generation to the next. Although he is unable to express it in such terms, it is essentially a genetic abnormality. This focus on heredity clearly reflects increasing awareness of scientific advances in evolutionary theory, which is also a thematic concern of *Die Ahnen*. Whether Freytag had read Charles Darwin's *On the Origin of Species by Means of Natural Selection* (1859) is unknown, though the German translation, *Über die Entstehung der Arten im Thier- und Pflanzen-Reich durch natürliche Züchtung*, was published in 1860, and the strong reaction to Darwin's theory in the popular press (both in England and Germany) is well documented.[89] What is clear, however, is that from the very outset Freytag had intended *Die verlorene Handschrift* to end with this image of aristocratic downfall. For, in selecting Tacitus as the author of the lost manuscript (in the original anecdote the text was by Livy), Freytag chose a historian whose works could be appropriated in order to support his attack on aristocratic rule and privilege.

Freytag's synthesis of class concerns and historical theory is not always smooth in *Die verlorene Handschrift*. However, the bourgeoisie, their social position, and their values are a constant concern of the text. Werner's quest for the manuscript ultimately results in his discovery of love, and his obsession with the past is broken, to be replaced with a new appreciation of his wife and the values of the bourgeois home. Just as Ilse teaches her husband to value the everyday, so Werner teaches his wife about the past, imparting an understanding of historical development derived directly from the *Bilder* and stressing a progressive vision of history. The central position of the bourgeoisie in German society is also directly revealed through the novel's depiction of an outmoded, and ultimately doomed, aristocracy. Freytag's appropriation of Tacitus' concept of *Cäsarenwahnsinn* is an effective means with which to condemn the hegemony of the aristocracy, suggesting that they are not just morally unfit to rule (essentially the stance of the *Vormärz* dramas), but also mentally incapable. Interestingly, the critique of the aristocracy in *Die verlorene Handschrift* differs in this respect from that voiced elsewhere in Freytag, since in this text they are neither incorporated into the bourgeoisie through marriage, nor made useful as part of the wider German national project, but condemned to physical and mental decline. In this sense, *Die verlorene Handschrift* is ultimately more forthright in its anti-aristocratic polemic, clearly suggesting that there is no place in modern German society for a nobility, and that it is the bourgeoisie alone that is truly fit to rule the German state.

The 1860s were a productive decade for Gustav Freytag, both in terms of volume (it marked his most prolific phase of writing) and in terms of the formal variety of his works (which ranged from national history to biography, from dramatic theory to the novel). Although he did not achieve another commercial success to rival *Soll und Haben*, his memoirs suggest that both the *Bilder aus der deutschen Vergangenheit* and *Die verlorene Handschrift* were reasonably successful, while *Die Technik des Dramas* gathered praise and, unexpectedly perhaps, produced what might be called Freytag's most enduring legacy in the form of the Freytag Pyramid. Despite this generic diversity, a consistent theme of Freytag's writings in the 1860s was history — whether in the form of a cultural history (the *Bilder aus der deutschen Vergangenheit*), a history of drama (*Die Technik des Dramas*), a history of a life (*Karl Mathy*), or the use of a historian as the hero of a novel (*Die verlorene Handschrift*). Although Freytag's memoirs claim that his central act of self-reinvention as a writer took place in the 1850s, when he rejected drama in favour of the novel, the 1860s also witnessed a moment of reinvention: as a historian. The significance of this shift should not be underestimated, since all of Freytag's subsequent writings would be concerned in some respect with German history.

As a cultural historian, Freytag's primary aim in the *Bilder aus der deutschen Vergangenheit* was to produce a subjective account of history which viewed the past from the perspective of the present. Many critics have classed Freytag as a historian of the Prussian School of History, and, to an extent, this designation is correct. As seen throughout this chapter, Freytag believed that German national unification could only come about under the auspices of Prussia. However, as also noted, the *Bilder* themselves are not solely concerned with a Prussian-orientated history, and attempted to posit a truly national identity for Germany — one based on middle-class values. The German folk, from businessmen to colonists, are shown as spreading the civilizing force of these values throughout Europe, while the aristocracy are presented as the enemies of progress, clinging on to outmoded privileges in order to sustain their hegemony over the people. Central to the *Bilder* is, indeed, a programmatic reading of history which sees the liberation and success of the bourgeoisie as the key outcome of the historical process. This is the positive, Hegelian-influenced idea which Freytag termed the *Volkskraft*: a concept central to understanding his entire oeuvre.

Similar themes are encoded in Freytag's other major work of the decade: *Die verlorene Handschrift*. Like its predecessor *Soll und Haben*, the novel is burdened with multiple themes — symptomatic of what Peter Heinz Hubrich has termed Freytag's tendency to want 'zu sehr und zu vieles' from his fiction.[90] In many respects, the two novels are similar. Both warn their reader of the dangers of succumbing to irrational fascinations (the search for the manuscript in *Die verlorene Handschrift*, the allure of the aristocracy in *Soll und Haben*), and both praise bourgeois values and a work ethic which favours the greater good over individual gain, whether in terms of intellectual work or of trade. Both also use the aristocracy as a critical counter-image to reveal the significance of these lessons. The bourgeoisie are shown to be in the ascendancy and the aristocracy in irrevocable decline.

Where *Die verlorene Handschrift* differs from *Soll und Haben* is in its overtly didactic presentation of these themes. Werner the academic acts as a direct mouthpiece for concepts and ideas which were represented dramatically in *Soll und Haben*, and, as a result, *Die verlorene Handschrift* is the aesthetically weaker of the two works. However, the text's depiction of the aristocracy's downfall is more powerful than ever — suggestive of a sharpening in Freytag's own interest in politics during the early 1860s, also revealed by his increased level of political engagement, which towards the end of the decade led to his election to the Reichstag des Norddeutschen Bundes. Returning to fiction after the failure of this political career, Freytag would, in 1872, publish his most grandiose project yet: the fusion of his historical, class, and national ideas in the novel-cycle *Die Ahnen*, as discussed in the following chapter.

## Notes to Chapter 4

1. Gustav Freytag, letter to Duke Ernst von Coburg Gotha, 6 March 1861, in *Gustav Freytag und Herzog Ernst von Coburg im Briefwechsel, 1853 bis 1893*, ed. by Eduard Tempeltey (Leipzig: Hirzel, 1904), p. 151.
2. Limited details of the membership and activities of the Kitzinger Kreis can be found in Friedrich Schulze, 'Der Kitzing — ein politischer Kreis um 1860', *Schriften des Vereins für die Geschichte Leipzigs*, 13 (1921), 16–28.
3. Heinrich von Treitschke, letter to his father, 7 May 1862, in *Heinrich von Treitschkes Briefe*, ed. by Max Cornicelius (Leipzig: Hirzel, 1918), p. 213.
4. On the departure of Mathy, see Freytag's letter to Theodor Molinari, 13 January 1863, in *Gustav Freytag an Theodor Molinari und die Seinen: Bislang unbekannte Briefe aus den Beständen der Universitätsbibliothek Wroclaw*, ed. by Edward Bialek (Frankfurt a.M.: Lang, 1987), p. 43. On the arrival of Treitschke, see Freytag's letter to Treitschke, 4 July 1863, in *Gustav Freytag und Heinrich von Treitschke im Briefwechsel*, ed. by Alfred Dove (Leipzig: Hirzel, 1900), p. 6.
5. Schulze, p. 20.
6. Gustav Freytag, *Gesammelte Werke*, I: *Erinnerungen aus meinem Leben* (Leipzig: Hirzel, 1896), p. 210. Further references to this edition are given after quotations in the text.
7. Freytag, letter to Duke Ernst, 30 January 1867, in Tempeltey (ed.), p. 216.

8. Freytag spoke on the 21 March 1867, during the seventeenth session. See *Stenographische Berichte über die Verhandlungen des Reichstages des Norddeutschen Bundes im Jahre 1867*, 2 vols (Berlin: Norddeutsche Allgemeine Zeitung, 1867), I, 311.
9. Freytag, letter to Duke Ernst, June 1867, in Tempeltey (ed.), p. 225.
10. Ibid.
11. Ibid.
12. See Thomas Nipperdey, 'Zum Problem der Objektivität bei Ranke', and Rudolf Vierhaus, 'Die Idee der Kontinuität im historiographischen Werk Leopold von Rankes', in *Leopold von Ranke und die moderne Geschichtswissenschaft*, ed. by Wolfgang J. Mommsen (Stuttgart: Klett, 1988), pp. 215–22 and pp. 166–75.
13. Gustav Freytag, *Die Grenzboten*, 14.4 (1855), 201–15 (p. 201).
14. The catalogues of the *Flugschriftensammlung Gustav Freytags* were kindly digitized by the staff of Frankfurt University Library for the purposes of this mongraph. Particular thanks must go to Bernhard Wirth for his sustained interest and support. The catalogues are now available online at <http://www.ub.uni-frankfurt.de/wertvoll/Sammlung_Freytag.html>.
15. See Friedrich Sengle, *Biedermeierzeit: Deutsche Literatur im Spannungsfeld zwischen Restauration und Revolution 1815-1848*, 2 vols (Stuttgart: Metzler, 1972), II, 28–30.
16. See Abigail Green, *Fatherlands: State-Building and Nationhood in Nineteenth Century Germany* (Cambridge: Cambridge University Press, 2001), p. 103.
17. See *Gustav Freytags Briefe an die Verlegerfamilie Hirzel*, ed. by Jürgen Matoni and Margret Galler (Berlin: Mann, 1994), pp. 180–82.
18. Alyssa A. Lonner, *Mediating the Past: Gustav Freytag, Progress and German Historical Identity, 1848-1871* (Berne: Lang, 2005), p. 40.
19. Quoted in Hans Lindau, *Gustav Freytag* (Leipzig: Hirzel, 1907), p. 242.
20. Quoted in Lindau, p. 242.
21. Quoted in Lindau, p. 243.
22. See Larry L. Ping, *Gustav Freytag and the Prussian Gospel: Novels, Liberalism, and History* (Berne: Lang, 2006), pp. 262–64 and pp. 304–06.
23. See Celia Applegate, 'The Mediated Nation: Regions, Readers and the German Past', in *Saxony in German History: Culture, Society and Politics, 1830-1833*, ed. by James Retallack (Ann Arbor: Michigan University Press, 2000), pp. 33–50 (p. 46).
24. See Lynne Tatlock, 'Realist Historiography and the Historiography of Realism in Gustav Freytag's *Bilder aus der deutschen Vergangenheit*', *German Quarterly*, 63 (1990), 59–74 (p. 67).
25. See Lonner, p. 82.
26. Gustav Freytag, *Gesammelte Werke*, XVII: *Bilder aus der deutschen Vergangenheit. Erster Band. Aus dem Mittelalter* (Leipzig: Hirzel, 1896), p. 107. Further references to this edition are given after quotations in the text.
27. Gustav Freytag, *Gesammelte Werke*, XVIII: *Bilder aus der deutschen Vergangenheit. Zweiter Band, Erste Abtheilung. Vom Mittelalter zur Neuzeit (1200-1500)* (Leipzig: Hirzel, 1896), pp. 161, 120. Further references to this edition are given after quotations in the text.
28. On early manifestations of German colonialism, its themes and language, see Susanne M. Zantop, *Colonial Fantasies: Conquest, Family, and Nation in Precolonial Germany, 1770-1870* (Durham, NC: Duke University Press, 1997).
29. Gustav Freytag, *Gesammelte Werke*, IV: *Soll und Haben: Erster Band* (Leipzig: Hirzel, 1896), p. 383. Further references to this edition are given after quotations in the text.
30. Lynne Tatlock, 'Regional Histories as National History: Gustav Freytag's *Bilder aus der deutschen Vergangenheit* (1859–1867)', in *Searching for Common Ground: Diskurse zur*

*deutschen Identität 1750–1871*, ed. by Nicholas Vazsonyi (Cologne: Böhlau, 2000), pp. 161–78 (p. 175).
31. Tatlock, 'Regional Histories', p. 176.
32. See Brian Vick, *Defining Germany: The 1848 Frankfurt Parliamentarians and National Identity* (Cambridge, MA: Harvard University Press, 2002), p. 59.
33. Tatlock, 'Regional Histories', p. 175.
34. Gustav Freytag, *Gesammelte Werke*, XX: *Bilder aus der deutschen Vergangenheit. Dritter Band. Aus dem Jahrhundert des großen Krieges (1600–1700)* (Leipzig: Hirzel, 1896), pp. 97, 235. Further references to this edition are given after quotations in the text.
35. See Georg Büchner, letter to Wilhelmine Jaeglé, 9–12 March 1834, in Georg Büchner, *Werke und Briefe, Münchner Ausgabe*, ed. by Karl Pörnbacher (Munich: dtv, 1988), p. 288.
36. Gustav Freytag, *Gesammelte Werke*, XXI: *Bilder aus der deutschen Vergangenheit. Vierter Band. Aus neuer Zeit (1700–1848)* (Leipzig: Hirzel, 1896), p. 491. Further references to this edition are given after quotations in the text.
37. For a discussion on the relationship between Herder's concept of the *Geist des Volkes* and Hegel's term *Volksgeist*, see Andreas Großmann, 'Volksgeist — Grund einer praktischen Welt oder metaphysische Spukgestalt? Anmerkungen zur Problemgeschichte eines nicht nur Hegelschen Theorems', in *Metaphysik der praktischen Welt: Perspektiven im Anschluß an Hegel und Heidegger*, ed. by Andreas Großmann and Christoph Jamme (Amsterdam: Rodopi, 2000), pp. 60–77.
38. See Ping, p. 330.
39. Gustav Freytag, *Gesammelte Werke*, XIX: *Bilder aus der deutschen Vergangenheit. Zweiter Band, Zweite Abtheilung. Aus dem Jahrhundert der Reformation (1500–1600)* (Leipzig: Hirzel, 1896), pp. 71, 70.
40. Tatlock, 'Regional Histories', p. 177.
41. Freytag, letter to Duke Ernst, 20 December 1869, in Tempeltey (ed.), p. 240.
42. Ibid.
43. For Ping's comments on a potential Mathy–Tacitus link, see Ping, p. 325.
44. Ibid.
45. Gustav Freytag, *Gesammelte Werke*, XXII: *Karl Mathy* (Leipzig: Hirzel, 1896), p. 2. Further references to this edition are given after quotations in the text.
46. See Freytag's letters to Duke Ernst from 5 December 1862 and 5 January 1863, in Tempeltey (ed.), pp. 171, 175.
47. See Lindau, p. 185.
48. Ibid.
49. Gustav Freytag, *Gesammelte Werke*, XIV: *Die Technik des Dramas* (Leipzig: Hirzel, 1896), p. vii. Further references to this edition are given after quotations in the text.
50. Key: (a) *Einleitung*; (b) *Steigerung*; (c) *Höhepunkt*; (d) *Umkehr*; (e) *Katastrophe*; (f) *das erregende Moment*; (g) *das tragische Moment*; (h) *das Moment der letzten Spannung*.
51. See also the very brief comment in Lindau, p. 210.
52. Wilhelm Dilthey, review of *Die Technik des Dramas* in the *Berliner Allgemeine Zeitung*, reproduced in: *Shakespeare-Jahrbuch*, 69 (1933), 27–60 (p. 34).
53. Freytag, letter to Duke Ernst, 5 January 1863, in Tempeltey (ed.), p. 175.
54. Gustav Freytag, *Die Technik des Dramas* (Berlin: Autorenhaus, 2003).
55. Freytag, letter to Duke Ernst, 5 January 1863, in Tempeltey (ed.), p. 175.
56. Freytag, letter to Duke Ernst, 5 December 1862, in Tempeltey (ed.), p. 171.
57. Edward McInnes, 'Drama und Theater', in *Hansers Sozialgeschichte der deutschen Literatur*, ed. by Edward McInnes and Gerhard Plumpe, VI: *Bürgerlicher Realismus und Gründerzeit, 1848–1890* (Munich: dtv, 1996), pp. 343–93 (p. 344).

58. Ibid., p. 343.
59. Ibid., p. 348.
60. Ibid., pp. 349–50.
61. Lonner, p. 35.
62. See Ping, pp. 159–61, and Lonner, pp. 34–36.
63. Freytag, letter to Molinari, 13 January 1863, in Bialek (ed.), p. 43.
64. Freytag, letter to Molinari, 2 February 1864, in Bialek (ed.), p. 51.
65. Freytag, letter to Max Jordan, 10 August 1864, in J. Hofmann, *Gustav Freytag als Politiker, Journalist und Mensch. Mit unveröffentlichten Briefen von Freytag und Max Jordan* (Leipzig: J. Weber, 1922), p. 23.
66. Freytag, letter to Molinari, 15 September 1864, in Bialek (ed.), pp. 58–59.
67. Kurt Classe, 'Gustav Freytag als Politischer Dichter' (doctoral thesis, University of Münster, 1914), p. 88.
68. Freytag, letter to Duke Ernst, 29 July 1856, in Tempeltey (ed.), p. 66.
69. Ibid.
70. Ibid.
71. Freytag, letter to Heinrich Hirzel, 9 August 1863, in Matoni and Galler (eds.), p. 264.
72. Freytag, letter to Treitschke, 12 December 1864, in Dove (ed.), p. 35.
73. Ping, p. 160.
74. See, for instance Lindau, p. 213.
75. See Lonner, p. 200.
76. Ping, p. 179.
77. Ibid., p.180.
78. Gustav Freytag, *Gesammelte Werke*, VI: *Die verlorene Handschrift: Erster Band* (Leipzig: Hirzel, 1896), p. 157. Further references to this edition are given after quotations in the text.
79. See Lonner, p. 135.
80. Gustav Freytag, *Gesammelte Werke*, VII: *Die verlorene Handschrift: Zweiter Band* (Leipzig: Hirzel, 1896), p. 331. Further references to this edition are given after quotations in the text.
81. On symbols of decline in *Soll und Haben*, see Lothar Schneider, 'Die Diätetik der Dinge: Dimensionen des Gegenständlichen in Gustav Freytags *Soll und Haben*', in *150 Jahre 'Soll und Haben': Studien zu Gustav Freytags kontroversem Roman*, ed. by Florian Krobb (Würzburg: Königshausen & Neumann, 2005), pp. 103–20.
82. See Lonner, p. 221.
83. Gustav Freytag, *Gesammelte Werke*, XV: *Politische Aufsätze* (Leipzig: Hirzel, 1896), p. 325.
84. See Tempeltey (ed.), esp. p. 180.
85. Büchner, p. 186
86. Ibid., p. 564.
87. On the similarity, see, for instance, Lonner, pp. 194–95.
88. See Utz-Friedebert Taube, *Ludwig Quidde: Ein Beitrag zur Geschichte des demokratischen Gedankens in Deutschland* (Kallmünz: Michael Lassleben, 1963), pp. 4–6.
89. See Pietro Corsi and Paul J. Weindling, 'Darwinism in Germany, France and Italy', in *The Darwinian Heritage*, ed. by David Kohn (Princeton: Princeton University Press, 1985), pp. 683–729 (pp. 685–87).
90. Peter Heinz Hubrich, *Gustav Freytags 'Deutsche Ideologie' in 'Soll und Haben'* (Kronberg: Scriptor, 1974), p. 57.

CHAPTER 5

## Writing Unification: Love as an Exercise in Nation-Building

Although Freytag had been campaigning actively for the unification of Germany under Prussian rule throughout the 1860s, he had not foreseen the speed with which unification would occur in 1871 in the aftermath of the Franco-Prussian War. In his articles on the war in *Die Grenzboten*, he never raises the possibility that German success in the military campaign against France might lead to unification, and when it does, his jubilation at the turn of events is clear:

> Denn den Aelterern unter uns ist das größte Glück zu Theil geworden, welches ein gnadenvolles Geschick den Geschlechtern der Erde gewährt; sie haben erlebt, Allen greifbar und verständlich, wie unsere Nation zu politischer Einheit und Größe heraufwuchs. [...] Als die jung waren, welche jetzt auf der Höhe ihres Lebens stehen, da waren Kaiser und Reich nur ein undeutliches Traumbild in verbotenen Studentenverbindungen [...]. Vieles hat der Deutsche sich selbstthätig auf eigene Hand verschafft, Eines hat er lange entbehrt, den edeln Stolz auf die politische Geltung seines Volkes. Jetzt fühlt er das Glück, so voll, so mächtig![1]

It might appear peculiar that a committed national liberal and Prussian patriot such as Freytag did not see how success in the Franco-Prussian War could lead to a shift in German power politics which would result in national unity. Yet few foresaw at the start of the 1870s that unification would occur when it did. By the end of the 1860s, the Prussian Minister President Otto von Bismarck's unification policy was in tatters. In 1867, his foundation of a Zollparlament, designed to mark the first step in uniting the southern and northern states, had foundered; in 1868, the national liberals had suffered a series of defeats in elections in the south and west; and in 1869, Bavaria and Württemberg had rejected his plans for the revival of the imperial title.[2] At the turn of the decade, anti-Prussian sentiment was higher than ever in the south, and Bismarck did not seem to have a clear policy regarding the future relationship between these states and the Norddeutscher Bund. This failure to implement national unity no doubt underpinned Freytag's extreme dislike of Bismarck — one so great that he voiced it repeatedly in the pages of *Die Grenzboten*, in spite of his support for a Prussian-led solution to the German question:[3] 'Das flackernde Feuer seiner [Bismarck's] Pläne verbreitet keine Wärme, es zündet nicht und wird wie eine Theaterflamme von den Gegnern abgeschüttelt, auf welche es gerade geschleudert wird'.[4] Whether Bismarck had initially planned the war with France in order to bring about unification is a question still debated by historians.[5] Although its starting point was the mutual distrust between the two countries — the legacy of the Wars of Liberation — the spark for war came when it was announced that a member of the House of Hohenzollern-Sigmaringen, Prince Leopold, had been offered the Spanish crown. Publicly, Bismarck claimed to have had no idea that this offer was about to be made. In private, however, he had been involved in negotiations since 1869 and had urged Prince Leopold to accept the crown, fearful that if he did not, the states of Bavaria and Baden might offer candidates, thus strengthening their political position against Prussia.[6] France reacted to the news with anger, arguing that by placing a Hohenzollern on the Spanish throne, Prussia was attempting to suppress France. The French demanded the withdrawal of Leopold's candidature, which subsequently took place, and Bismarck's play for power appeared to have failed.[7]

However, France then demanded confirmation from the Prussian King that Prussia would never again put forward a candidate to such a position. The King, seeing this as a deliberate act of humiliation by France, refused to accede and referred France's envoys to Bismarck. Bismarck sensed an opportunity: the chance to justify a war with France in which she was the aggressor against the national honour of a greater Germany. Such a war would not only allow Prussia to defeat France once and for all, but could unite Germany by allowing the north and south to come together against a common enemy. He released an account of France's demands — the so-called Ems telegram — stressing the humiliating nature of the request. It was a clear attempt to provoke France, and a successful one. France declared war on 19 July 1870.[8]

In Germany, the response to the war was positive, although it is difficult to gauge public opinion accurately since, as Breuilly has noted, the press was dominated by the national liberal faction who supported the war.[9] Nevertheless, patriotic sentiment does seem to have unified the country, with the politicians and the public associations of the southern German states openly supporting not only the military campaign but also a potential unification of Germany under a *kleindeutsch* solution.[10] Freytag himself was actively involved in the Franco-Prussian conflict — not as a combatant, but as an official reporter accompanying the Third Prussian Army into battle.[11] His war reports were published in *Die Grenzboten*.

With the capture of Napoleon III at the Battle of Sedan in September 1870, the Franco-Prussian war essentially came to an end (although Paris was under siege for a further five months). Baden and Hesse immediately declared their wish for unification with Prussia, although Bavaria still resisted, as did Württemberg. Eventually, both were placated with special privileges and the newly created German Empire was formed.[12] On 18 January 1871, Frederick William of Prussia was crowned Kaiser Wilhelm. The German question had been resolved with a *kleindeutsch* solution of the kind Freytag had been advocating consistently during the previous two decades.

### *Im neuen Reich* (1871) and *Die Ahnen* (1872–80)

In 1871, Freytag gave up his editorship of *Die Grenzboten*, although his career as a journalist did not come to an end, and he continued to publish articles — albeit sporadically — in *Im neuen Reich*, a journal edited by Alfred Dove, his friend and, after his death, the editor of much of his correspondence. Freytag's gradual withdrawal from journalism was the result of a sense of frustration he had begun to feel since the mid-1860s that his journalistic work was preventing him from undertaking bigger literary projects. In 1866, he commented to the Prussian general Albrecht von Stosch:

> Denn ich bin so alt u habe mir durch 18jährige Arbeit für die Tagesinteressen meines lieben, einfältigen Volkes wohl auch das Recht erkauft, um die Zeit, welche meine Kraft noch dauert, in größerer Arbeit zu verleben. Ach, ich bin längst nur Journalist, weil ich durch die Pflicht gegen andere gefesselt bin.[13]

After stepping down from *Die Grenzboten* in 1871, Freytag was thus free to begin another literary project. Over the next decade, he would do precisely this, in the form of his mammoth novel cycle *Die Ahnen* — a historical fiction covering over two thousand years of German history, and formed of nine novels, published in six volumes, over eight years, between 1872 and 1880. Dating the works of *Die Ahnen* is a relatively simple process, since they were all reviewed by contemporary critics and Freytag himself commented on their writing in letters to his friends and colleagues. The first two novels, *Ingo* and *Ingraban*, were published in one volume by Hirzel in 1872. The third novel, *Das Nest der Zaunkönige*, appeared in 1873, followed by the fourth volume, *Die Brüder vom deutschen Hause*, in 1874. The yearly publication rate was then broken, with Volume Five, *Marcus König*, first appearing in 1876. It was a further two years before Part Six (*Der Rittmeister von Alt-Rosen*) and Part Seven (*Der Freicorporal bei Markgraf-Albrecht*) were published as one volume under the title *Die Geschwister* in 1878, with the final two works in the cycle, *Aus einer kleinen Stadt* and *Schluß der Ahnen*, appearing as one volume in 1880.

Freytag's memoirs state that *Die Ahnen* was prompted by his experiences of the Franco-Prussian war, during which, so he claims, he found himself repeatedly struck by imaginative comparisons between the present day military campaign and earlier phases of German battle and conquest:

> Aber die mächtigen Eindrücke jener Wochen arbeiteten in der Stille fort; schon während ich auf den Landstraßen Frankreichs im Gedränge der Männer, Rosse und Fuhrwerke einherzog, waren mir immer wieder die Einbrüche unserer germanischen Vorfahren in das römische Gallien eingefallen, ich sah sie auf Flößen und Holzschilden über die Ströme schwimmen, hörte hinter dem Hurrah meiner Landsleute vom fünften und elften Corps das Harageschrei der alten Franken und Alemannen. [...] — Aus solchen Träumen und aus einem gewissen historischen Stil, welcher meiner Erfindung durch die Erlebnisse von 1870 gekommen war, entstand allmählich die Idee zu dem Roman *die Ahnen*. (I, 237)

Read in such a light, *Die Ahnen* was a direct response to the conflict and the subsequent unification of Germany. However, in a letter to Moritz Haupt accompanying the first volume of the cycle, Freytag admits that his idea for the work originated not in 1870, but in 1867, although it reached what he terms maturity during his experience of the military campaigns: 'Ich habe mich seit 67 damit getragen, aber reif ist die Geschichte mir erst unter den Eindrücken des Feldzuges von 70 geworden'.[14] Freytag's comments to Haupt are lent credence by his letter to von Stosch from 1866 (cited above), in which he stated that he wished to end his editorship of *Die Grenzboten* in order to concentrate on a new literary project, as well as by other references to a new work — presumably *Die Ahnen* — that are to be found in his letters throughout the late 1860s: 'Unser Privatleben läuft still, mehr Bücher als Menschen und ich dachte grade an eine größere Arbeit'.[15] In fact, it seems likely that the idea for *Die Ahnen* can be traced back even further, to Freytag's work on the *Bilder aus der deutschen Vergangenheit* (1859–67) during the early to mid-1860s. The notion that *Die Ahnen* is somehow a poeticized version of the *Bilder* is frequently raised in criticism, although few have noted that Freytag himself states this explicitly in his letter to Haupt, noting that it was Haupt who first suggested that the material Freytag had gathered for his cultural history could also serve as the basis for a historical novel: 'Vor Jahren, da ich mich mit den Bildern herumschlug, sagten Sie einmal, daß sie Studien sein sollten für einen historischen Roman. Es ist nun wohl so gekommen'.[16] Such comments are of significance, since they demonstrate that *Die Ahnen* is not solely a reaction to unification, even if that remains the primary impetus for its composition. Clearly, it was also a continuation of the wider engagement with German history and the *Volkskraft* which had dominated Freytag's literary practice for the previous decade, resulting in the *Bilder* and his second novel *Die verlorene Handschrift* (1864), detailed in Chapter 4. Elsewhere in his letters, Freytag even notes the fortuitous timing of his new novel, which suggests that it had not been originally conceived in 1871, but some time earlier: 'Es ist grade noch gute Zeit, der Reichsbürger hat doch ein stärkeres Interesse an seiner Vergangenheit erhalten'.[17] Freytag's assessment of the renewed public curiosity about national history in the 1870s was correct. Fascination with German history, already strong throughout the nineteenth century, had increased rapidly after the *Reichsgründung*, and manifested itself in all areas of society, not least in the proliferation of historical fiction. The period 1850 to 1900 saw the publication of over 750 historical novels in Germany; a high point of production was reached in 1861, but after a drop in the years to 1870, 1871–80 once again saw interest in the form. Critics such as Harro Müller and Brent O. Peterson have read this as an effect of the *Reichsgründung*, a time when public life was increasingly geared towards the creation and consolidation of German national consciousness.[18] The significance of history can also be seen in the new Prussian curricular plans of 1872, which demanded an unprecedented eight hours of historical instruction in schools per week.[19]

Freytag's cycle appears directly to fit such trends, depicting in its nine volumes over two thousand years of German history, with each of the stories set against a key historical development. *Ingo* opens in the year 357 — the time of the *Völkerwanderung* and the last of the Roman wars on German soil. *Ingraban* is set some four centuries later, in 724, during the spread of Christianity. *Das Nest der Zaunkönige* takes place in 1003, as the church and royal powers fight for control over the Germanic peoples, while *Die Brüder vom deutschen Hause* jumps to 1226, during the last of the German crusades. *Marcus König* is set in 1519 during the Reformation, while *Der Rittmeister von Alt-Rosen* is set in the Thirty Years War (in 1647) and *Der Freicorporal bei Markgraf Albrecht* during absolutism (in 1721). The final two volumes of the cycle are closely linked, with only a single generation separating the texts: *Aus einer kleinen Stadt* takes place in 1805, during the French revolutionary wars, while the *Schluß der Ahnen* is set in 1848, the year of the European revolutions.

In terms of content, the novels in the cycle rarely emphasize their historical context, and instead revolve around a series of love stories. Taken as a whole, *Die Ahnen* primarily seems concerned with foregrounding the private tales of individuals over a grand narrative of German nationhood. Critics have universally dismissed these love stories as a distraction from the true interest of the cycle — namely history.[20] It is a key concern of mine in this chapter, however, to explore the ways in which *Die Ahnen* can be read as a successful attempt to embody poetically German history and German identity, and the role that the love stories play in this attempt.

Upon publication, the first volume of *Die Ahnen* created a major stir. In an extensive summary of its reception, Hartmut Eggert has noted how it 'erregte bei seinem Erscheinen [...] Aufsehen, wie es als unmittelbare Resonanz keinem anderen deutschen historischen Roman bis dahin widerfahren war'.[21] The reviews themselves were, admittedly, mixed. Positive accounts of *Ingo* and *Ingraban* frequently expressed amazement at Freytag's ability to recreate a realistic sense of the fourth and seventh centuries, and drew connections to his earlier work as a cultural historian. Other enthusiastic reviews considered the novels firmly from an aesthetic standpoint, praising Freytag's narrative control and his ability to build parallels between *Ingo* and *Ingraban*.[22] Many reviewers, however, were more critical. Paul Lindau (to be distinguished from Freytag's biographer, Hans Lindau) was one of many who felt that, by setting *Ingo* in the fourth century, Freytag had produced a world so different from the present that the readers of the novel would be alienated, despite his narrative craft. Lindau also criticized Freytag's use of archaic forms and dialects in *Ingo* and *Ingraban*, again finding this outmoded language alienating. In perhaps the most scathing attack on the work, Theodor Fontane echoed Lindau's concerns. Fontane's main critique was that Freytag's novel, in its historical detail and pseudo-medieval language, gave the impression of an objective past, but was ultimately a deception, which functioned adequately neither as a work of art nor as a history.[23] Despite such critical responses, the novel was a major success for Freytag and his publisher Hirzel. Eggert has collected publication data on the first four volumes, which reveals that, by the time their copyright expired in 1926, *Ingo* and *Ingraban* and *Das Nest der Zaunkönige* had each reached sixty-two imprints, while *Marcus König* had achieved forty-eight. All three novels had also been released as *Volksausgaben* in addition to the *Standardausgabe* — a sign of their widespread popularity — while *Ingo* and *Ingraban* were also published as *Schulausgaben*. According to Eggert, there was less interest in the final volumes, although he provides no data to support this claim.[24]

There are a limited number of recent studies of Freytag's novel cycle, the majority of which focus on its status as a response to German unification. In a highly critical assessment, Claus Holz has argued that *Die Ahnen* marks Freytag's *Flucht aus der Wirklichkeit* (to quote his title). For Holz, *Die Ahnen* avoids direct engagement with contemporary issues and seeks refuge in the past, thereby registering Freytag's disillusionment with post-unification society. Holz's perspective is intriguing and potentially significant, but he fails to support his argument with textual and historical examples, and tends towards generalizations to sustain his claims. Holz views the love stories as the weakest aspect of *Die Ahnen*, characterizing them as 'unwahrscheinlich, selten und unrealistisch, [...] also genau das, was der programmatische Realismus so vehement abgelehnt hat'.[25] Claus-Michael Ort has noted how *Die Ahnen* does not follow the structures typical of the historical novel of the late nineteenth century, and characterizes the work as 'eine Geschichte des Erinnerns und Vergessens', which places historical events next to each other, but fails to connect them into a coherent historical narrative.[26] The status of the text as a historical novel is also considered in comparative contexts in short studies by Daniel Fulda, Michael Limlei, and Charlotte Woodford.[27] Limlei's argument is of particular interest, since he considers the importance of love and marital unions within *Die Ahnen*. Ultimately, however, he views the repetitive love stories of the work as merely a structural attempt to create a sense of coherence between each of its volumes, rather than as a thematic phenomenon worthy of analysis in its own right.

Recent criticism by Lynne Tatlock and Elystan Griffiths has focused on the apparent tension in *Die Ahnen* between its status as a work of national history, and the regional settings of the individual novels. Tatlock has argued that *Die Ahnen* is not a straightforward attempt to create or impose a sense of German identity within the strict traditions of the Prussian School of historiography, noting how *Die Ahnen* eschews a 'bombastic, grandly militaristic, and spectacular centralizing image of nation' and ultimately presents Germany as 'a nation of provincials'.[28] As with her similarly themed assessment of the *Bilder aus der deutschen Vergangenheit*, Tatlock's article, while of real interest, underestimates the fluid nature of Freytag's concept of nationhood, which could simultaneously encompass regional and national identities (as demonstrated in Chapter 4).[29]

In a convincing analysis of the *Die Ahnen*, Elystan Griffiths also notes how the novels present a provincial image of Germany, but counters Tatlock by demonstrating how Freytag combined provincialism with a nationally orientated awareness 'that particularist loyalties must not be allowed to hold back political and economic progress'.[30] Griffiths's persuasive reading also argues — contrary to Holz — that *Die Ahnen* does not show disillusionment with unification, but rather asks its middle-class readership to maintain their bourgeois values, which had helped bring about the *Reichsgründung*. However, like other critics before him, Griffiths focuses solely on the political and historical context of the novels, ignoring their primary content: the domestic love stories. Griffiths glosses this latter aspect as 'tortuous', and as following 'basic conventions of bourgeois realism, with its mix of sentiment and suspense, and its simple, relatively closed plot structure'.[31] Yet, as I will demonstrate in this chapter, it is precisely through recourse to the world of romance and marriage that Freytag encodes his class and political agenda in accessible and popular ways for his target audience. In general, thus, while critics of *Die Ahnen* have all shown an awareness of the thematic foregrounding of the love stories in the cycle, these stories have been dismissed as irrelevant to, or a distraction from, the primary message of the text — a message about German history and identity in the new empire. While it is easy to agree with Griffiths that the main interest of *Die Ahnen* 'now lies, not in its literary quality, but in the intricate structure which Freytag employs in order to achieve his political-pedagogical purpose', for Freytag, as the following discussion will reveal, the sentimental and domestic were in fact key facets of any foundation myth of German identity and national belonging.[32]

To claim that *Die Ahnen* is primarily a novel focused on domestic issues such as love, rather than overtly national-historical concerns, at first seems counterintuitive, since, as noted in the summary of the novels above, each is clearly set in a specific historical epoch, from the *Völkerwanderung* to the revolutions of 1848. The cycle appears so purposefully designed to chart the relentless progress of German history through these major events: the arrival of Christianity, the Reformation, the Thirty Years War. It is striking, however, that the overall flow of the historical narrative of *Die Ahnen* is highly disjointed. For instance, each volume of the novel is set almost three centuries after its predecessor, and Freytag makes no attempt to bridge these gaps with historical explanations or clarifications. In this sense, *Die Ahnen* is quite distinct from its cultural-historical predecessor, the *Bilder aus der deutschen Vergangenheit*, which went out of its way to explain the interconnectivity of German history, in order to demonstrate the inexorable character of Germany's path to nationhood. When reading *Die Ahnen* it is unclear how the family narrative the reader is supposedly following across each novel is connected to what came before and after, as the breaks of three hundred years between each volume sever the very ancestral line the cycle's title claims is so significant. At no time does Freytag elucidate the nature of the familial relationships he explores, and the text is not accompanied by family trees or other means of determining the blood relations. The sense of triumphal German historical progress, which a reader of the *Bilder* might have expected from *Die Ahnen*, is thus mostly lacking from the work.

In other respects, however, *Die Ahnen* remains closely allied to Freytag's earlier historical writings, specifically in its portrayal of the *Volkskraft* — his vision of history based on the dialectical interaction between individual autonomy and a historical folk-force (discussed in detail in Chapter 4). This dialectic is emphasized from early on in the cycle, as the following passage from the end of the second novel, *Ingraban*, displays:

> Länger wurde die Kette der Ahnen, welche jeden Einzelnen an die Vergangenheit band, größer sein Erbe, das er von der alten Zeit erhielt [...]. Aber wundervoll wuchs dem Enkel zugleich mit dem Zwange, den die alte Zeit auf ihn legte, auch die eigene Freiheit und schöpferische Kraft.[33]

Similar sentiments can be found in the *Schluß der Ahnen*, in which the final generation of the protagonists are shown to be entirely unaware of their history, until they stumble across a record of it in a museum. Although interested, they in no way see themselves as beholden or indebted to their ancestry, and instead stress the importance of their own individuality and independent existence in the present. The novel's hero Victor (a clear autobiographical portrait of Freytag) states:

> Vielleicht bin ich ein Stück von jenem Manne, welcher einst an dieser Stelle von dem Reformator gesegnet wurde, und vielleicht war ich es selbst in

anderer Erscheinung, der schon auf diesem Berge lagerte, lange bevor die ehrwürdige Feste gebaut wurde. Aber [...] [w]as wir uns selbst gewinnen an Freude und Leid durch eigenes Wagen und eigene Werke, das ist doch immer der beste Inhalt unseres Lebens, ihn schafft sich jeder Lebende neu. Und je länger das Leben einer Nation in den Jahrhunderten läuft, um so geringer wird die zwingende Macht, welche durch die Thaten des Ahnen auf das Schicksal des Enkels ausgeübt wird, desto stärker aber die Einwirkung des ganzen Volkes auf den Einzelnen und größer die Freiheit, mit welcher der Mann sich selbst Glück und Unglück zu bereiten vermag. Dies aber ist das Höchste und Hoffnungsreichste in dem geheimnißvollen Wirken der Volkskraft.[34]

The final passage of the entire cycle thus precisely echoes Freytag's view of the *Volkskraft* dialectic. Seen in this light, the cycle as a whole appears less concerned with the specific events of history, and rather with the experiences of the individual within the historical process. This not only links back to the *Bilder*, but also to the historical debates central to Freytag's second novel *Die verlorene Handschrift* (discussed in Chapter 4).

Significantly, Freytag's correspondence also suggests that he was not wholly concerned with historical facts when it came to writing *Die Ahnen*, with a number of letters expressing his irritation at having to include historical detail in his fiction at all. Typical is the following complaint to the Duke of Coburg Gotha from 1874: 'Aber das Eindringen der Geschichte, diesmal leider unvermeidlich, wird für jedes Gedicht, Drama oder Roman im Grunde ein Uebelstand, dessen üble Folgen für das Kunstwerk schwer zu beseitigen sind'.[35] Any study of *Die Ahnen* must thus free itself from a conception of the work as a straightforward exercise in historical posturing and nation-building. Rather, a quite different narrative and ideological strategy is developed in the novel, which rests not on images of historical pride, but rather resides in an exploration of individual Germans and their relationship to history. Freytag's emphasis on the individual experience of history helps explain his focus on the private and domestic in the cycle (including the love stories): they were the obvious means with which to reveal this theme. Interestingly, Freytag in his memoirs likens *Die Ahnen* to a symphony:

> Den Verfasser der *Ahnen* aber wird freuen, wenn der Leser das Werk wie eine Symphonie betrachtet, in deren acht Theilen ein melodischer Satz so gewandelt, fortgeführt und mit anderen verflochten ist, daß sämmtliche Theile zusammen ein Ganzes bilden. (I, 256)

This conceptualization of *Die Ahnen* is especially useful when considering the love stories in the text, for, essentially, there is only one love story in *Die Ahnen*, which is repeated and varied in each novel. The key elements of this story are easily summarized. Two men — one the hero, the other his enemy — fall in love with the same woman. They compete for her affections, and overcome various barriers to their love in the process. The hero and heroine are briefly united, before they are parted by circumstances beyond their control. The hero must then rescue the heroine, usually from the rival lover, upon which they marry and have children. This basic sequence of events is altered slightly in each novel, but the fundamental progression is always similar and predictable.

The use of repetition in *Die Ahnen* also extends to the characterization of its main figures. Each new generation of protagonists is, to a large extent, a reincarnation of the generation that has gone before. The female characters are, for example, predominantly representations of a *Germania* figure: blond-haired, blue-eyed, and 'both martial and motherly'.[36] Irmgard, the love interest in *Ingo*, is described as follows: 'Frei ringelten die gelben Locken um ihre hohe Gestalt, sie umsäumten die kräftigen Formen des jugendlichen Antlitzes und wallten lang herab bis an die Hüften' (VIII, 8). Friderun, the heroine of *Die Brüder vom deutschen Hause*, scarcely differs in external appearance:

> [Sie war] eine hochgewachsene kräftige Gestalt von vollen Formen, in dem runden Gesicht strahlten zwei tiefblaue Augen, ihr blondes Haar war so lang, daß sie die Zöpfe um das Haupt geschlungen trug, und doch hingen sie ihr bis tief über den Gürtel hinab.[37]

The depiction of the female characters in *Die Ahnen* is particularly interesting, since they are represented as strong, intelligent, independent figures. This is a consistent element across Freytag's writing, as evidenced by Marie in *Die Brautfahrt* (1841), Valentine in *Die Valentine* (1846), Leontine in *Der Gelehrte* (1844), Gertrud in *Graf Waldemar* (1846–47), Adelheid in *Die Journalisten* (1852), and Lenore and Sabine in *Soll und Haben* (1855). Freytag's works would benefit from a gender-based analysis, exploring his precise conceptualization of the feminine and how he integrates this into his image of a (predominantly) patriarchal bourgeois society. Christine Achinger has made the first steps towards such an analysis in her recent study of *Soll und Haben*.[38] Freytag's male figures also share key features with one another, although they do not seem to have been developed from quite such a fixed template as their female counterparts. They are generally average citizens, and as soon as it is historically plausible, they assume solid, middle-class professions — generally as businessmen (*Marcus König*) or doctors (*Aus einer kleinen Stadt*). The male figures also share a keen sense of duty and honour, and a desire to undertake work — elements which for Freytag indicated a bourgeois sensibility, and which are personified by figures such as Anton Wohlfart in *Soll und Haben* (see the discussion in Chapter 3).

In addition to these similarities in structure and characterization, the romances of *Die Ahnen* also share key thematic elements. The stories repeatedly emphasize, for example, the connection between true love and an affinity to nature. In the works, feelings of love are always confessed in the open environment, witnessed by nature. In *Ingo*, Freytag writes:

> Ihm hob sich das Herz in Freude und Liebe, ehrfürchtig trat er an sie heran, sie blieb wie festgebannt, regte leise die Hand zur Abwehr und murmelte bittend: 'Die liebe Sonne sieht's.' Er aber küßte sie herzlich und rief der lachenden Sonne zu: 'Sei gegrüßt, milde Herrin des Tages, sei uns gnädig und bewahre vertraulich, was du schaust.' Er küßte sie wieder und fühlte ihren warmen Mund gegen den seinen. (VIII, 47)

This scene is varied and repeated in every novel in the cycle, as, for example, in *Das Nest der Zaunkönige*:

> Die Jungfrau hob sich zu ihm empor und hielt ihre Hand über sein Haupt: 'Du denke mein, wenn du allein bist und zuweilen unter den wilden Helden, und vor Allem im Abendlicht, wenn du die grünen Blätter über dir siehst, wie jetzt und immer — und immer.' Sie warf die Hände um seinen Hals und küßte ihn herzlich. Er aber hielt sie fest; und das Geschwirr der Grillen übertönte leise Worte, Seufzer und Küsse der Liebenden.[39]

These moments reflect other romantic scenes in Freytag's earlier fiction, particularly the confessions of love between Ilse and Werner in *Die verlorene Handschrift*, and Anton's first meeting with Lenore on the estate in *Soll und Haben*. Although there is not enough evidence to suggest that Freytag believed that there was an element of pantheism engrained in the Germans (as Heine did), he certainly seems to associate emotion with the natural environment, and takes great pleasure in evocative, pseudo-Eichendorffian descriptions of nature.

The love stories of *Die Ahnen* — their structures, their characters and even their imagery — thus appear to have stemmed from a form of central model, from which Freytag produced the variations in each volume. This mirrors Freytag's stated aim in his memoirs, that: '[D]er Leser wird zuletzt die Reihe der Helden ähnlich betrachten, wie einen guten Bekannten, der seine Persönlichkeit in verschiedenen Lebenskreisen und in immer neuer Umgebung geltend macht' (I, 241). While this might initially appear to be a peculiar narrative strategy — one that could potentially cause the entire cycle to become repetitive — the variation of a single love story within *Die Ahnen* reflects directly another core concern of Freytag's concept of history: his sense of a continuity between the past and present. Writing in the *Bilder aus der deutschen Vergangenheit*, he argued how: 'Es rührt und es stimmt heiter, wenn wir in der Urzeit genau denselben Herzschlag erkennen, der noch uns die wechselnden Gedanken der Stunde regelt'.[40] Put simply, with love as a constant, the German of the past does not seem so alien any more. The love stories, then, should be seen as a potentially significant aspect of *Die Ahnen*. Their repetitive character creates a sense of continuity that the historical panorama does not provide, and allows Freytag to humanize the past by providing a means of identification for his readers. They also supply him with the opportunity to focus on the individual's experience of history, revealing the power of the *Volkskraft*. The precise manner in which this is achieved, and the complex relationship between the historical and personal-sentimental narratives of *Die Ahnen*, are considered in further detail in the remainder of this chapter.

Although the love stories of *Die Ahnen* can be seen as a thematic representation of Freytag's belief in the continuity of the German character through the ages, they are nevertheless firmly embedded in the historical context of each novel. In *Ingo*, for instance, the love story takes place between Ingo, a displaced Vandal warrior, and Irmgard, the daughter of the king of a settlement in Thüringen. The arrival of the migrant Ingo and his romance with Irmgard clearly reflect the wider historical context of the novel, which is set during the *Völkerwanderung*. Freytag appears to be prompting his reader to view Ingo's and Irmgard's marriage — the union of two different German tribes — as a microcosmic representation of the mixing of tribes characteristic of the fourth century.

Similarly, in *Ingraban*, the historical background of the novel — the arrival of Christianity in Germany — is directly reflected in the love story, which takes place between the pagan Ingraban, and a new convert to Christianity, Walburg, and details Ingraban's (and by extension Germany's) Christian conversion. In a similar manner, the couple in *Marcus König* require the permission of Luther before they can marry, and thus their romance becomes the means through which Freytag can illustrate the historical context of the Reformation. Such parallels are present in every volume of *Die Ahnen*, something hitherto unacknowledged in research into the work. Seen in this light, the love stories are a tool with which Freytag can present the past in an accessible manner: both a privatization and a personalization of the historical context.

Yet this is not their only function. For, on closer inspection, it becomes clear that Freytag also uses the love stories to promote a series of moral and social values he sees as central to the German character and German identity. This process can clearly be seen in *Ingo*. As stated, the love story is on one level a microcosmic representation of the *Völkerwanderung*. Yet by the end of the novel, the historical context has been entirely forgotten, replaced instead with a moral dilemma. Ingo must choose between two futures: one with his wife and child, and another of luxury with a local Queen. Ingo rejects the Queen, arguing that his love for Irmgard provides him with something of greater value than any riches, namely the intimate and domestic bonds of family:

> 'Eine leise Stimme höre ich in meiner Not,' sagte er vor sich hin, 'meinen kleinen Sohn höre ich über mich klagen, und wie ein Mann, der aus dem Traume erwacht, stehe ich vor der Königin. An Eine bin ich gebunden, die mir teurer ist als mein Leben. Alles hat sie [Irmgard] für mich verlassen, im Ringe der Blutgenossen habe ich ihr gelobt, daß ich um sie sorgen will wie ihr Vater, und mit ihr allein das Lager teilen als ihr echter Gemahl. Wie darf ich sie meiden und zur Königsburg ziehen?' (VIII, 181)

As the novel concludes, Freytag depicts Ingo and Irmgard living peacefully in a small house with their child — very much the nuclear family, and an utterly anachronistic depiction of social relations for the early Middle Ages. The focus of the novel has shifted to promoting a series of values: the importance and sanctity of marriage; the significance of family and the home; and the need for trust, duty, and honour. To those versed in Freytag's earlier writings, these are instantly recognizable as his core values of the bourgeoisie, which have — as in the *Bilder* and his early historical play *Die Brautfahrt* — been projected back into the past with a disregard for historical accuracy. As a whole, *Ingo* leaves us with a strong sense of Freytag's moral and social code, but little sense of life during the *Völkerwanderung*.

All of the love stories in *Die Ahnen* can be shown to follow a similar pattern. Starting off as microcosms of the historical context, they transform into manuals for living a good, bourgeois existence — a tendency that only increases in the later volumes of the cycle, in which Freytag could depict middle-class values without fear of overt anachronism. A prime example is *Aus einer kleinen Stadt*. The novel is set in 1805, against the backdrop of the French revolutionary wars. The hero, Doctor König, falls in love with a local village girl, Henriette. All is well until the war threatens peace and stability in Germany. Some years into the fighting, Henriette is rescued from the hands of a band of drunken German soldiers by Desalle, a Frenchman. Desalle forces Henriette into an engagement, which she accepts out of a sense of duty to her rescuer. Although her desire pulls her towards König, her indebtedness to Desalle must first be resolved before König and Henriette can marry.

The standard pattern of the love story is immediately clear, as is its parallelism with the historical context — the German–French rivalry of the war is directly mirrored in the rivalry of König and Desalle. Freytag keeps his two lovers apart until the end of the Wars of Liberation, allowing König's victory over Desalle in the world of love to parallel Germany's defeat of France on the battlefield. In his study of *Die Ahnen*, Holz has argued that the romance of this novel is entirely unbelievable: 'Ohne Henriettens skrupulöses Verhalten gegenüber ihrem Retter [Desalle] wäre die ganze Handlung auf wenige Wochen verkürzt; und hierin, in einer mangelnden logischen und psychologischen Begründung der fiktiven Problematik, liegt wohl die Hauptschwäche des Romans'.[41] For Holz, the duty-versus-desire conflict at the heart of the novel which keeps the lovers apart is overplayed. His criticism is not without some validity, but overlooks one important factor: Henriette's and König's scruples towards Desalle are central to the didactic function of *Aus einer kleinen Stadt*. For it is through their lengthy love story that Freytag again can present his readership with key lessons in bourgeois values. We may be tested, the story tells us, but patience, trust, loyalty, and hard work will all be rewarded in the end. König and Henriette are tried by their situation, but it is precisely their reactions to their trial that reveals the strength of their bourgeois character (and, by extension, the strength of the German character). Henriette affirms: 'Ich würde ihm [Desalle] dasselbe sagen, was ich heut Ihnen [König] sage: seine Frau kann ich nicht werden, und einem Andern darf ich nicht angehören, solange er sein Anrecht behaupten will' (XIII, 136). The romance that Holz sees as hampering the story is actually the means with which that story achieves its didactic aims.

Throughout *Die Ahnen*, it is precisely the reactions and responses of the protagonists to the tensions of their love stories that help reveal the didactic import of the text. The love stories in *Die Ahnen* should thus not be seen solely as an attempt to render historical circumstance more clearly and approachably. Rather, they indirectly mirror the historical context while directly revealing key lessons the reader should learn. This shows *Die Ahnen* in a new light — less as a tale of the German past, and more as a justification and celebration of bourgeois values. In Chapter 4, Freytag's *Bilder* were shown to be ultimately more concerned with the bourgeois path to social dominance than with Germany's path to nationhood. Exactly the same tendency can be seen in *Die Ahnen*.

*Die Ahnen* is dominated by the act of marriage. Marriage is both the end point of the love stories present in each volume, acting as a moment of closure for each narrative, and also a prerequisite for the continuation of the cycle: the marriages lead to the children and grandchildren who will in turn produce the heroes and heroines of the subsequent volumes. Significantly, the conjugal pairings of each volume are in themselves also symbolic, bringing together representative figures of different classes and different regions of Germany. In the cycle, marriage becomes a medium through which Freytag can cross-fertilize class and regional identity — subsuming the aristocracy into the bourgeoisie and transforming regional interests into national ones. Indeed, *Die Ahnen* marks a highly significant return to the patterns of inter-class marriage identified as central to Freytag's poetic practice in this monograph, after the exceptions of *Soll und Haben* and *Die verlorene Handschrift*.

In the early volumes of the cycle (essentially until its half-way point in the Reformation-set *Marcus König*), Freytag presents marriage explicitly as a tool of social structuring. These early narratives draw clear distinctions between socially conventional, politically expedient marriages, and marriages undertaken for love. In *Ingo*, for example, Ingo's and Irmgard's union is opposed by Irmgard's family and tribe, since Ingo has no land and their marriage would not lead to a strategic enlargement of either Irmgard's power or her estate. In addition, Ingo is a Vandal, while Irmgard is from Thüringen, and marrying outside of the tribe is seen as potentially weakening the political position of Irmgard's people. As Irmgard's father, the King, points out to Ingo:

Wie darf der Vater dem erbelosen Fremdling seine Erbtochter in die Hand geben? Unsinnig würde ihn das ganze Volk schelten, unleidlich wäre es, daß ein Landfremder auf dem Herrenstuhl der Waldlauben säße. Ja, wenn der Vater selbst dir die Tochter im Ringe der Zeugen angeloben wollte, ich, der König dürfte das nimmer leiden, und ich müßte meine Knaben reiten lassen und ein Volksheer aufbieten, um euch zu hindern. (VIII, 129–30)

In these early stories, Freytag depicts a conflict between social marriages, which merely shore up wider interests, and marriages for love, which are depicted as a positive, progressive force, and which ultimately emerge triumphant.

To a degree, a social and political concept of marriage is also present in the later volumes of the novel cycle, as it enters the modern era. Thus, in *Der Freicorporal bei Markgraf-Albrecht*, two mothers worry whether the love matches of their children are appropriate to the social standing of their families. The hero August belongs to the bourgeoisie, while his love interest Dorothea is from the petty aristocracy (precisely the inter-class set-up of *Soll und Haben*). Dorothea's mother is convinced that her daughter could do better than August, and should marry into the higher levels of the aristocracy, thus consolidating her family's name, wealth, and status. August's mother believes that Dorothea could do far worse than her son, who is wealthy and part of an economically confident bourgeoisie. In a rare moment of social comedy for *Die Ahnen* (as opposed to the relatively frequent, and mostly overlooked, comedic scenes in *Soll und Haben*), Freytag depicts the intricacies of such social hierarchies: 'Deshalb war der Verkehr beider Mütter gerade so voll von Hintergedanken, wie der zwischen zwei Diplomaten großer Mächte, welche bald vertraulich Arm in Arm gehen und bald einander mit kühler Zurückgezogenheit behandeln'.[42] In general, however, the later volumes of *Die Ahnen* are less concerned with the specific social politics of marriage, and rather with their symbolic value, as marriage becomes a tool with which Freytag constructs his own idealized vision of German society. Nowhere is his strategic use of marriage as means of social construction more apparent than in the *Schluß der Ahnen*. Set against the turbulent events of the European revolutions of 1848, this novel's love story takes place between the bourgeois Victor, and the aristocrat Valerie, and is paralleled in the love between Victor's sister, Käthe, and his old university rival, the aristocrat Henner. These inter-class relationships are precisely in the mould of Freytag's previous couples from his *Vor-* and *Nachmärz* works: Walter–Leontine in *Der Gelehrte*, Georg–Valentine in *Die Valentine*, Gertrud–Waldemar in *Graf Waldemar*, Bolz–Adelheid in *Die Journalisten*, and Anton–Lenore in *Soll und Haben*. The novel thus threatens — like *Soll und Haben* — to end with a romantic resolution that transgresses class divisions and sees the aristocracy subsumed into a more dominant bourgeoisie.

This outcome is hinted at throughout the novel, as Freytag describes how the events of the Wars of Liberation and the revolution of 1848 have led to a new era in which the social divides of the previous centuries are no longer appropriate. In the words of the novel's narrator:

> [I]m Kriege [hatte] gewissermaßen die Verbrüderung aller Stände stattgefunden [...] und seitdem [entsagte] Jedermann alten Vorurtheilen. (XIII, 253)

> Denn diese Familie hatte längst allen Standesvorurtheilen entsagt, außerdem war, wie ein hochverehrter, leider verstorbener Mitbürger und Rathmann zu sagen pflegte, gerade jetzt eine Conjunction gekommen, wo derartige Vorurtheile nicht zeitgemäß waren. (XIII, 306)

Significantly, the potential marriages of Victor with Valerie and Käthe with Henner not only symbolize the breakdown of class structures in Germany and the end of the hegemony of the aristocracy. They also come to represent a geographical unification of the nation. In the course of the novel, it is stressed that Victor and Käthe are originally Vandals, while Valerie and Henner are originally from Thüringen. This is a conscious reference back to the very first volume of the cycle, *Ingo*, where precisely the same geographical scenario is encountered. When Freytag constructs a double wedding in the final chapter of *Die Ahnen*, the partnerships thus represent a progressive vision of a socially and geographically unified Germany — a confident image of a young, bourgeois nation with which to end the cycle: 'An demselben Tage wurden zwei glückliche Paare verbunden, Käthe verfiel unrettbar dem Hause Ingersleben, und Victor hob sein liebes Weib aus der Kutsche der Bellerwitze sich in die Arme' (XIII, 306). Curiously, some critics have disregarded the marriages of this final volume altogether. Elystan Griffiths has argued, for example, that '[Victor] pulls away from love affairs in 1848 [...] in the hope that, as a journalist, he can help influence the nation's future'.[43] This is a one-sided assessment of the conclusion to Freytag's cycle, since, while Victor does become a journalist with a view to fighting for German civil rights, he is clearly still firmly involved in a love story which is central to the triumphant conclusion of the cycle, noting how the marriage of his sister Käthe to Henner will merge the two houses of Ingersleben and Bellerwitz (and thus, the reader is aware, symbolically bring together the classes and provinces of the nation):

> 'Sie wird zuletzt ihren Vetter Henner heiraten', sagte Viktor trotzig.
> 'Woher weißt du das?' fuhr Käthe auf.
> 'Ich denke mir's nur,' versetzte der Bruder. 'Warum sollen die Häuser Bellerwitz und Ingersleben sich nicht mit einander verbinden?' (XIII, 280)

Importantly, Victor's decision to work as a journalist reinforces the same breakdown of social and geographical divisions as the love story, since he founds his newspaper with Henner — his formerly aristocratic brother-in-law from Thüringen. Like the marriages, the newspaper demonstrates that Germany can only move forward by overcoming regional and class difference. When

Griffiths argues that 'Freytag's readers are implicitly encouraged to look beyond the private, sentimental sphere and to engage dynamically and effectively in shaping the fate of the nation', he has correctly identified Freytag's progressive vision for the nation, yet incorrectly excludes the love story and the domestic realm as a means with which this vision can be both presented and achieved.[44] *Die Ahnen* is thus a clear continuation of an ideological project Freytag began some forty years earlier in his *Vormärz* dramas, with their shared emphasis on inter-class marriage as a tool for social change. In the cycle, as elsewhere in his writings, the private realm is appropriated for the representation of a national-liberal agenda. Considering the marriages in *Die Ahnen*, it appears that, for Freytag, the real dynamic of progress resides not in explicitly historical forces, but rather in the ultimate of dialectics: the union of two individuals.

In addition to being narratives of love and marriage, many of the volumes of *Die Ahnen* are also tales of personal development — stories that play with the tropes and themes of the *Bildungsroman*. The first of these explicitly developmental novels is *Das Nest der Zaunkönige*. In the text, the hero, Immo, matures from a state of youthful rebellion to life as a loyal, committed family man. It is a progression that leads him to shed his early vocation to God in favour of glory in battle, only then to reject vassaldom in order to become an independent man whose primary aim is to support his family. This simple summary of Immo's development makes clear the manner in which his maturation espouses key bourgeois values — essentially he goes through a series of experiences (his *Lehrjahre*), before growing into a good middle-class citizen (this, however, in contrast to Goethe's Wilhelm Meister, who attempts to escape the life of a bourgeois businessman).

As Immo develops as an individual, his character is partially determined by a sequence of proverbs passed on to him by two older monks before he leaves the seminary where he has been brought up. Although this passage at first appears whimsical in tone, the proverbs are gradually revealed to be central to the novel's plot, which revolves around a series of events in which Immo must remember the didactic lessons of his youth:

> 'Vielerlei Lehren gibt es, welche den Mann fest machen, wenn seine Gedanken sich unsicher wälzen [...]. [Vier] Lehren sind es [...]. Die erste bedeutet, daß dem Manne nicht geziemt zu dienen, wo er gebieten darf; und sie lautet: Birg niemals in die Hand eines Herrn, was du allein behaupten kannst.' Und als Immo die Worte wiederholt hatte, reichte Bertram den zweiten Halm: 'Dieser Spruch soll dich mahnen, wenn du einem Freunde unwillkommene Kunde ins Haus trägst, daß du sie ihm vertraust, bevor der Staub auf deinen Schuhen verweht ist; und der Spruch lautet: Ueble Botschaft auf der langen Bank, macht dem Boten und dem Wirth das Herz krank.' Zum dritten Halm sprach er: 'Mißachte den Eid, der in Todesnoth geschworen wird. Wer dir Liebes gelobt sich vom Strange zu lösen, der sinnt dir Leid, so oft er des Strickes sich schämt.' Und beim vierten gebot

er: 'Deines Rosses letzter Sprung, deines Athems letzter Hauch sei für den Helfer, der um deinetwillen das Schwert hob.' (IX, 26–27)

These life rules in many respects reflect the central facets of Freytag's bourgeois value system expressed elsewhere in his writings — they are, for instance, the same lessons that Anton Wohlfart learns from Schröter in *Soll und Haben*. They stress the importance of independence (be your own master), honesty (speak the truth instantly), trust and honour (beware false honour), and loyalty and duty (support those who support you). At the end of the novel, an older and wiser Immo stresses the importance these lessons have played in his life: 'Den guten Lehren, die ihr mir übergeben habt, verdanke ich Leben und Glück' (IX, 320). Immo's maturation story can thus be read as illuminating the importance of key middle-class values to the German character.

In *Die Brüder vom deutschen Hause*, another story of personal development, Freytag expands his use of pseudo-*Bildungsroman* elements to emphasize a link between the maturation of the individual and the evolution of a sense of German identity. The novel opens with the hero Ivo as a young man, actively participating in *Minnedienst* and other courtly activities. Ivo lives to serve the demands of the court and his mistress, and falls in love with an exotic Eastern woman, Hedwig. As he ages, however, he becomes increasingly disaffected with life at court, and its obsession with appearance:

> Langweilig wird mir das Reiterspiel unter meinen Gesellen, und wenn ich in der Halle meiner Väter sitze, empfinde ich die kalte Oede des Winters. Im Herzen schelte ich eitel und nichtig, was ich gerade treibe, mir zucken die Glieder, und die Faust ballt sich, als könnte ich etwas Großes thun und mein Leben wagen für ein heilbringendes Werk. (X, 130)

Seeking a vocation, Ivo chances upon a recruiter for the crusades. Significantly, the crusade is depicted as a specifically German action, designed to bring honour to a German nation-state. The call to fight is not based upon Ivo's Christian faith, but rather on his burgeoning sense of German identity, and the crusade is described not in religious, but rather in colonial terms:

> Denn wie ein Herzland liegt es in der Mitte und die größte Kraft ist hier gesammelt, ich darf das zum Lobe meiner Heimat wohl sagen. Wenn wir jetzt in edler Schaar über das Meer ziehen, so thun wir dies auch, um den Namen der Deutschen zu Ehren zu bringen und eine Herrschaft unseres Blutes über die Länder am Südmeere zu begründen. Das zu bewirken ist das hohe Ziel meines Lebens. Darum bin ich vor Euch getreten mit hoher Mahnung, als Thüring und als Meister einer Bruderschaft, welche sich vom deutschen Hause nennt. [...] Gefesselt durch die warme Rede des mächtigen Mannes saß Ivo mit gerötheten Wangen. Zum erstenmal, seit er lebte, wurde er gerufen, weil er ein Deutscher war; und verwundert dachte er nach, welchen Werth solche Aufforderung für ihn haben könne. (X, 137–38)

The novel suggests that, in deciding to fight in the crusades, Ivo is not only reaching physical and intellectual maturity, but also maturity in his identity as a German citizen. The parallels are manifold: Ivo enters into adulthood, rejects the particularist interests of the regional courts, and embraces his future as a German. Importantly, Ivo is the first consciously German citizen of *Die Ahnen*. This German identity is also expressed as a folk identity, in passages which reflect Freytag's concept of the *Volkskraft*, as Ivo realizes how his own honour is intimately connected to the wider honour of his people:

> Aber während er den Grund eines tiefen Quells erschauen wollte, gewahrte er darin plötzlich sein eigenes Bild. Ihm stieg das Blut ins Gesicht, als er fühlte, daß eine Kränkung seines Volkes auch Kränkung seiner eigenen Ehre war [...]. (x, 138)

This German folk identity is significant, for neither Ingo, Ingraban, nor Immo (the heroes of the three previous volumes) directly expressed an affinity to anything but a specific regional identity. Ivo, however, clearly displays a supra-regional sense of Germanness — an anachronistic notion for the period in question (1226).

The expressly national theme of the novel reaches its apogee in the final chapters of the work. Returning from the crusades, Ivo marries a local village girl, Friderun, and migrates to East Prussia, where together they found a new German settlement, the community of Thorn (now Toruń in Poland). As their first act, Ivo and Friderun convert the people of Thorn to Christianity. Freytag depicts this religious conversion as a civilizing experience for the Polish inhabitants — something that directly mirrors the image of German colonization as a process of civilization in *Soll und Haben* (discussed in Chapter 3). Having established their settlement (described as if it were a modern German village), Ivo's house becomes a symbolic home for all Germans — a new *Heimat* in foreign lands. Freytag describes the couple as having sown the seed of a future German nation:

> Hier im Lande säen wir deutsche Saat. Wenn einst die Zeit der Ernte kommt, dann mögen andere zusehen, die nach uns leben. [...] [U]nd mancher von ihnen betrachtete das Haus, in welchem Frau Friderun waltete, als seine Heimat. (x, 327–29)

Ivo thus moves from his Thüringen identity to a national identity — and it is a transformation of his class identity too, since 'aus einem thüringischen Edeln der Ivo, den sie den König nannten', he has become 'ein Burgmann von Thorn', the founder of a German homeland (x, 329). The *König* has become a *Bürger*, and encoded in the story are the class, national, and folk concerns central to all of Freytag's previous writings. After Ivo, the heroes of the cycle expressly see themselves as middle-class German citizens.

In post-unification Germany, writers were potentially influential agents of self-definition for the new state. An author such as Gustav Freytag — a novelist, historian, and national liberal — was well placed to play a significant role in this process of self-definition. His novel cycle *Die Ahnen* is frequently read as a response to 1871, and he himself noted how it was inspired by the events that led to German unification. Yet in many respects the cycle confounds our expectations of a post-1871 literary project about the German nation and the German past. Rather than detailing the glorious historical route Germany had taken from the Middle Ages to the present day, the work's primary focus seems to be on the lives of individual German citizens and their relationship to the wider processes of history — a series of stories grounded in the private and domestic domains.

In this chapter I have examined the various functions that these private and domestic narratives have in *Die Ahnen*, and have argued that the love stories are a central feature of the work. On the one hand, I have demonstrated how the love stories can be read as a microcosm of the historical context of each novel, providing the reader with ready access to a complex and potentially alien past, humanizing and individualizing the processes of history. The love stories create the potential for identification: engaged by the romance, the reader is able to see historical events through the eyes of average protagonists. This function of the love stories should not be underestimated, since, as noted, it was a core aim of Freytag's historical practice to demonstrate the continuity of the German character through the ages and create a sense in his reader that the German of the past and the German of the present share key characteristics and values. The love stories of *Die Ahnen* should be seen as a poetic expression of this idea, first expressed in the *Bilder aus der deutschen Vergangenheit* and further explored in *Die verlorene Handschrift*.

On the other hand, I have also shown how the love stories are more than just a narrative hook with which to reflect or portray German history. Ultimately, it is not historical fact that is of primary interest to Freytag in *Die Ahnen*, but rather the moral and didactic lessons that can be drawn from the lives of everyday individuals caught up in the processes of history. These lessons are mediated through the romances, and the value system cultivated by the cycle has been shown to be a specifically middle-class one, promoting precisely the concepts of honour, duty, and work central to Freytag's *Vormärz* dramas and, most explicitly, *Soll und Haben*. *Die Ahnen* could be read as an apotheosis of bourgeois values; but it is also a practical guide to these values, which encourages its readers to see that such principles are still of significance in the newly formed nation state of 1871.

Of central significance to the novel is Freytag's use of marriage as a tool of social restructuring. Combining regional and class identities through the act of marriage, Freytag closes his cycle with a socially homogenized — and somewhat utopian — vision of German society and identity, in which the bourgeoisie are presented as economically and politically confident. As such, *Die Ahnen* reflects the class positions of Freytag's *Vormärz* dramas, of *Soll und Haben*, and of *Die verlorene Handschrift*, and uses inter-class marriage as a metaphor for social and political change — the dominant motif of his dramas, from *Die Valentine* to *Die Fabier* (1859). At heart, thus, *Die Ahnen* is not a novel of German unification, but of the German people, the bourgeois class, and their rise to dominance. The precise historical path to 1871 is not detailed in the cycle, and instead it is the foundation of a folk, and a communal German mentality, that is told. Focusing on class, nation, history, and the folk, Freytag's final work contains all of the concerns which dominated his previous poetic practice. *Die Ahnen* creates nothing less than a foundation myth of German folk identity, encouraging its readership to see themselves as part of a historical dynamic which intimately connects the Germans of the past to those of the present and the future.

## Notes to Chapter 5

1. Gustav Freytag, *Gesammelte Werke*, xv: *Politische Aufsätze* (Leipzig: Hirzel, 1896), pp. 496–98. Further references to this edition are given after quotations in the text.
2. See Stefan Berger, *Germany: Inventing the Nation* (London: Arnold, 2004) p. 73, and John Breuilly, 'Revolution to Unification', in *19th Century Germany: Politics, Culture and Society, 1780–1918*, ed. by John Breuilly (London: Arnold, 2001), pp. 138–59 (p. 153).
3. For further details on Freytag's attitudes towards Bismarck, see Renate Herrmann, 'Gustav Freytag: Bürgerliches Selbstverständnis und preußisch-deutsches Nationalbewußtsein' (doctoral thesis, University of Würzburg, 1974), pp. 211–13.
4. Gustav Freytag, 'Das preußische Abgeordnetenhaus und die Zukunft', *Die Grenzboten*, 8 (1863), no page.
5. Breuilly, p. 153.
6. See William Carr, *A History of Germany, 1815–1990* (London: Arnold, 1991), p. 112.
7. See Carr, p. 113.
8. Ibid., p. 114.
9. Breuilly, p. 154.
10. See Berger, p. 74.
11. See Hans Lindau, *Gustav Freytag* (Leipzig: Hirzel, 1907), p. 280.
12. See Carr, p. 116.
13. Gustav Freytag, letter to Albrecht von Stosch, 20 November 1866, in *Gustav Freytags Briefe an Albrecht von Stosch*, ed. by Hans Helmot (Berlin: [n.pub.], 1913), p. 159.
14. Freytag, letter to Mortiz Haupt, 20 November 1872, quoted in C. Belger, *Moritz Haupt als academischer Lehrer* (Berlin: [n.pub.], 1879), p. 38.
15. Freytag, letter to Heinrich von Treitschke, 3 February 1868, in *Gustav Freytag und Heinrich von Treitschke im Briefwechsel*, ed. by Alfred Dove (Leipzig: Hirzel, 1900), p. 138.
16. Freytag, letter to Haupt, 20 November 1872, in Belger, pp. 38–39.
17. Freytag, letter to Heinrich von Treitschke, 27 November 1872, in Dove (ed.), p. 164.
18. See Harro Müller, 'Historische Romane', in *Hansers Sozialgeschichte der deutschen Literatur*, ed. by Edward McInnes and Gerhard Plumpe, vi: *Bürgerlicher Realismus und Gründerzeit, 1848–1890* (Munich: dtv, 1996), pp. 690–707 (pp. 964–66); Brent

O. Peterson, *History, Fiction and Germany: Writing the Nineteenth-Century Nation* (Detroit: Wayne State University Press, 2005), pp. 29–31.
19. Alfred Kelly, 'The Franco-Prussian War and Unification in German History Schoolbooks', in *1870/71–1989/90: German Unifications and the Change of Literary Discourse*, ed. by Walter Pape (Cologne: de Gruyter, 1992), pp. 37–60 (p. 38).
20. For examples, see the discussion of critical responses to *Die Ahnen* later in this chapter.
21. See Hartmut Eggert, *Studien zur Wirkungsgeschichte des deutschen historischen Romans, 1850–1875* (Frankfurt a.M.: Klostermann, 1971), p. 176.
22. On the positive reviews, see Eggert, pp. 176–78.
23. On Paul Lindau and Fontane, see Eggert, pp. 180–82.
24. Ibid., pp. 182–83.
25. Claus Holz, 'Flucht aus der Wirklichkeit: *Die Ahnen* von Gustav Freytag' (doctoral thesis, University of Bonn, 1981), p. 205.
26. Claus-Michael Ort, 'Roman des "Nebeneinander" — Roman des "Nacheinander": Kohärenzprobleme im Geschichtsroman des 19. Jahrhunderts und ihr Funktionswandel', in *Zwischen Goethezeit und Realismus: Wandel und Spezifik in der Phase des Bürgerlichen Realismus*, ed. by Michael Titzmann (Tübingen: Niemeyer, 2002), pp. 347–75 (p. 305).
27. Daniel Fulda, 'Telling German History: Forms and Functions of the Historical Narrative against the Background of the National Unifications', in *1870/71–1989/90: German Unifications and the Change of Literary Discourse*, ed. by Walter Pape (Cologne: de Gruyter, 1992), pp. 195–207; Michael Limlei, *Geschichte als Ort der Bewährung: Menschenbild und Gesellschaftsverständnis in den deutschen historischen Romanen* (Frankfurt a.M.: Lang, 1988); Charlotte Woodford, 'Contrasting Discourses of Nationalism in Historical Novels by Freytag and Fontane', in *German Literature, History and the Nation: Papers from the Conference 'The Fragile Tradition'*, ed. by Christian Emden and David Midgley, 2 vols (Berne: Lang, 2002), I, 253–76.
28. Lynne Tatlock, '"In the Heart of the Heart of the Country": Regional Histories as National History in Gustav Freytag's *Die Ahnen* (1872–80)', in *A Companion to German Realism 1848–1900*, ed. by Todd Kontje (Rochester, NY: Camden House, 2002), pp. 85–108 (pp. 104, 87).
29. For Tatlock's assessment of the *Bilder*, see Lynne Tatlock, 'Regional Histories as National History: Gustav Freytag's *Bilder aus der deutschen Vergangenheit* (1859–1867)', in *Searching for Common Ground: Diskurse zur deutschen Identität 1750–1871*, ed. by Nicholas Vazsonyi (Cologne: Böhlau, 2000), pp. 161–68.
30. Elystan Griffiths, 'A Nation of Provincials? German Identity in Gustav Freytag's Novel-Cycle *Die Ahnen* (1872–1880)', *Monatshefte*, 96 (2004), 220–33 (p. 230).
31. Ibid., p. 221.
32. Ibid., pp. 221–22.
33. Gustav Freytag, *Gesammelte Werke*, VIII: *Die Ahnen. Erste Abtheilung: Ingo und Ingraban* (Leipzig: Hirzel, 1896), p. 400. Further references to this edition are given after quotations in the text.
34. Gustav Freytag, *Gesammelte Werke*, XIII: *Die Ahnen. Sechste Abtheilung: Aus einer kleinen Stadt* (Leipzig: Hirzel, 1896), pp. 311–12. Further references to this edition are given after quotations in the text.
35. Freytag, letter to Duke Ernst of Coburg-Gotha, 21 December 1874, in *Gustav Freytag und Herzog Ernst von Coburg im Briefwechsel, 1853 bis 1893*, ed. by Eduard Tempeltey (Leipzig: Hirzel, 1904), p. 267.
36. Tatlock, '"In the Heart of the Heart of the Country"', p. 100.

37. Gustav Freytag, *Gesammelte Werke*, x: *Die Ahnen. Dritte Abtheilung: Die Brüder vom deutschen Hause* (Leipzig: Hirzel, 1896), p. 21. Further references to this edition are given after quotations in the text.
38. Christine Achinger, *Gespaltene Moderne. Gustav Freytags 'Soll und Haben'. Nation, Geschlecht und Judenbild* (Würzburg: Königshausen & Neumann, 2007).
39. Gustav Freytag, *Gesammelte Werke*, ix: *Die Ahnen. Zweite Abtheilung: Das Nest der Zaunkönige*, (Leipzig: Hirzel, 1896), pp. 148–49. Further references to this edition are given after quotations in the text.
40. Gustav Freytag, *Gesammelte Werke*, xvii: *Bilder aus der deutschen Vergangenheit. Erster Band. Aus dem Mittelalter* (Leipzig: Hirzel, 1896), p. x.
41. Holz, p. 151.
42. Gustav Freytag, *Gesammelte Werke*, xii: *Die Ahnen. Fünfte Abtheilung: Die Geschwister* (Leipzig: Hirzel, 1896), p. 204.
43. Griffiths, p. 225.
44. Ibid., p. 226.

# CONCLUSION

In his comprehensive study of so-called *Trivialliteratur*, Peter Nusser notes the largely pejorative connotations of expressions such as *Unterhaltungs-* and *Massenliteratur*, detailing how they have become detached from their literal meanings and are frequently applied to texts merely judged to be aesthetically defective and non-canonical. Arguing for the rehabilitation of popular literature into the German literary canon, Nusser proposes a more nuanced reading of supposedly trivial texts that critically assesses their place in literary and social history: '[Es ist] vernünftig, am Begriff der Trivialliteratur festzuhalten, der sowohl den ästhetischen Aspekt (das Triviale als das leicht Eingängige) als auch den gesellschaftlichen Aspekt (das Triviale als das weit Verbreitete) vereinbart'.[1] Nusser's re-evaluative definition of *Trivialliteratur* is particularly apposite to the works of Gustav Freytag. Aesthetically, Freytag employed a diverse range of popular formats with which to present his social and political views, often embedding a didactic theme within an accessible and palatable story of love and adventure. Socially, his writings appealed to a large and predominantly middle-class readership — precisely the group he wished to influence with his politics. In such a light, Freytag's use of popular and entertaining forms, often taken as a sign of the aesthetic weakness of his writings, can also be seen as part of a deliberate strategy — one which responded or pandered to the tastes of his core audience and thus gave his literary-political project as wide and powerful a dissemination as possible.

In this monograph, I have sought to identify the precise nature and scope of Freytag's literary-political project, specifically by analysing the representation of class and national identity in his writings, providing for the first time a comprehensive account of their changing nature between the early 1840s and the late 1880s. I have argued that Freytag's works presented a systematic attempt to reimagine the structures of German society, positioning the bourgeoisie at the heart of the German nation. In doing so, I have identified a number of significant trends within Freytag's writings. First, I have shown how his concept of class remained largely consistent across his works, with each text revolving around an anti-aristocratic class polemic which saw the bourgeoisie as morally and socially superior to a debauched and outmoded nobility. I have identified a thematic preoccupation in his texts with inter-class relationships, which result in the subsumption of the aristocracy into a dominant bourgeois identity through symbolic acts of marriage — a process of *Klassenvermischung*. This finding marks an important corrective to existing critical works on Freytag, which have universally regarded his vision of the classes as based on their strict division (*Klassenausgrenzung*). As I have shown, Freytag's texts were not intent on upholding the social status quo, but rather presented German society as undergoing a process of gradual bourgeoisification.

Secondly, I have identified the increasing significance of national themes in Freytag's writings after the failure of the revolutions of 1848. I have traced how changes in the socio-political climate of Germany — not least the intensifying quest of the National Liberal party for German unification — found a voice in Freytag's *Nachmärz* texts. I have argued that Freytag's representation of national issues primarily involved the recasting of his class concerns as national ones, and that his typology of a German folk identity was based on a reformulation of bourgeois class characteristics. I have shown how, in contrast to the judgements found in previous research, Freytag's understanding of German national identity was essentially expressed through the depiction of common German values, rather than, say, the explicit portrayal of distinct racial identities.

Thirdly, I have noted the significance of German history in Freytag's post-*Nachmärz* writing. In particular, I have analysed the workings of Freytag's semi-philosophical concept of the *Volkskraft*, which presented the German folk at the centre of a progressive historical dialectic which would lead to national unification. I have argued that the idea of the *Volkskraft* not only influenced Freytag's explicitly historiographical texts, but also his later literary production, which increasingly sought to create a myth of German folk identity that synthesized his social and national concerns. It has been a central contention of this monograph that Freytag's texts not only reflected these issues of class, nation, history, and the folk, but were designed to disseminate his ideas on these topics. Each of Freytag's works has been shown to be an inherently didactic project, designed to influence the political opinion of his bourgeois readership, condition public debate, and thus stimulate social and national change.

## Class

Freytag's focus on class issues can be traced back to his earliest poetry. We have seen how his collection *In Breslau* chronicled bourgeois experience through what I characterized as a form of domestic poetry. I noted the emphasis on a strong folk identity in the more political of Freytag's poems: the sense of the folk as an incipient force for social change, which, I argued, should be seen as a direct precursor to his later progressive concept of the *Volkskraft*. Similarly, we have seen how Freytag's *Vormärz* dramas praised bourgeois values, but how they placed this praise within plots critical of the aristocracy. I argued that these dramas marked the beginning of a systematic class polemic which would become a central element of Freytag's subsequent writing: a polemic that demanded the termination of aristocratic hegemony not through political revolution, but through social change, symbolically represented in the act of inter-class marriage. Only by giving up their social privilege and taking on middle-class values — a process of bourgeoisification — could the aristocracy find salvation. This discussion of the early poems and plays provides substantial evidence that Freytag's understanding of the bourgeois class struggle was a product of the *Vormärz*, and not a response to the failure of the revolutions of 1848 — a hitherto unacknowledged aspect of his writing.

We have seen, too, how the notion of bourgeoisification remained central to Freytag's class project after 1848. In stressing this particular aspect, I have again attempted to counter a central assumption of existing research, which has thus far considered Freytag's vision of class to be based on the firm division of the upper and middle classes (the result of a tendency in criticism to read *Soll und Haben* as paradigmatic of his wider attitudes). Yet, as I have argued, the emphasis in *Soll und Haben* on *Klassenausgrenzung* marks an exception to Freytag's standard model, and was the result of his attempt to prioritize a nationally orientated colonial narrative over the novel's initial tale of bourgeois trade — necessitating a reformulation and moderation of its social polemic. Similar patterns of reformulation were also seen in Freytag's second novel, *Die verlorene Handschrift*. However, aside from these two exceptions, it is clear that Freytag's vision of class repeatedly returned to the principle of *Klassenvermischung*, not least in his final novel cycle, *Die Ahnen*. Overall, I have shown Freytag's concept of class to have been based on an ideal of social evolution, rather than political revolution — the bourgeoisie, his works suggest, will rise to dominance through patterns of social interaction, rather than political uprising. Nevertheless, there remains an undeniable radicalism to Freytag's vision of class relations, calling as it does for the subsumption (and thus dissolution) of aristocratic into bourgeois identity. Even when Freytag does not directly promote inter-class relations, his texts still repudiate all that the aristocracy stands for, consistently arguing for the reconfiguration of German society as a bourgeois society.

## Nation

Although Freytag's preoccupation with national themes is most evident in his later writings, reflections of his national agenda were also to be found in his *Vormärz* texts. Freytag's political poetry engaged with a range of national issues and events — concerns also identifiable in his early plays. These works, I argued, displayed at the very least an incipient sense of national community. As a whole, though, I have argued that Freytag's interest in national themes increased in the post-1848 period. In particular, I have considered Freytag's literary-political reaction to 1848, which he presented in his memoirs as a moment of aesthetic and political reorientation away from drama and towards the novel. As seen, the actual nature of this shift was far from clear cut, and Freytag neither stopped writing dramas, nor did he immediately embark on a novel, but first undertook eight years of dedicated political journalism at *Die Grenzboten*.

We have seen how Freytag's literary works from the post-1848 period also demonstrated his new-found interest in German national politics. His successful *Nachmärz* comedy *Die Journalisten* recast the class polemics of the *Vormärz* dramas into a political battle between conservative (aristocratic) and liberal (bourgeois) forces. We have also observed how *Soll und Haben* — Freytag's most popular work — was marked by an increasing concern with national themes and gradually repositioned bourgeois values as national ones. In particular, I have argued that this process led to a number of structural and thematic anomalies in the novel which went against Freytag's usual practices — not least his preservation of the aristocracy as a form of proto-colonial force in Poland, rather than their subsumption into the bourgeoisie, and the related reformulation of two inter-class marriages into intra-class pairings at the end of the novel. That the conflation of class and national identity became an important factor in Freytag's later texts is one of my central arguments in this monograph, and is evidenced by his final drama, *Die Fabier*, a work that I suggested reflects particularly clearly Freytag's personal hopes for the breakdown of class structures and the rise of a politically strong bourgeois nation-state in the late 1850s.

### Folk

In its classical subject matter, *Die Fabier* also pointed forward to what would become an overriding theme of Freytag's subsequent writing: history. Indeed, it was Freytag's major historical projects, the *Bilder aus der deutschen Vergangenheit*, *Die verlorene Handschrift*, and *Die Ahnen*, which first fully synthesized his class and national concerns, creating in the process a historical myth of German folk identity. In general, critical studies of Freytag's literary writings have ignored his historical works, perhaps because of an assumption that they are generically distinct from his fictional output and thus of little relevance to an interpretation of the latter. Even when studies have considered his historical views, there has been little attempt to explore systematically the links between these and the presentation of history in his fiction. I have attempted to provide precisely such an analysis, presenting substantial evidence that Freytag's understanding of history in the *Bilder* impacted on both his literary writings and his social and political views. Indeed, I have identified a concern with the German past in Freytag's writings from the *Vormärz* onwards — in the historically progressive vision of the poems of *In Breslau*; in the medieval setting of *Die Brautfahrt*; and in the historian hero and incipient presentation of the *Volkskraft* in *Der Gelehrte*. It is often overlooked that, aside from his contemporary comedy *Die Journalisten*, Freytag did not produce a single work that was not in some sense historical — whether that be the setting of *Soll und Haben* and *Die verlorene Handschrift* in the recent past, or the more directly historical fiction of *Die Ahnen*.

Although some critics have seen Freytag's turn to historical subject matter in the *Bilder* as a means of escaping the political realities of his present, I have argued that Freytag's understanding of history was deeply indebted to contemporary German politics and his support of the national-liberal cause. I have shown how the *Bilder* not only read the past through the needs of the present, but also sought to rewrite German history from a folk and bourgeois-national perspective — a significant act of historical and national reimagination. In retelling national history as the story of the folk and middle classes, Freytag was able to suggest that the unification of Germany under bourgeois leadership was not only desirable, but a historical inevitability. I have also stressed the importance of Freytag's concept of the *Volkskraft* in his historical writings. This notion allowed Freytag to argue that contemporary German identity rested on a series of eternal folk values which were also those of the middle class. However, this progressive vision of history was not solely the preserve of the *Bilder*, but also a dominant factor in Freytag's subsequent fiction, not least in *Die verlorene Handschrift* and his final novel cycle, *Die Ahnen*, a sequence of novels that reworked the concept into a more seductive myth of German national community. *Die Ahnen*, I have argued, through its focus on inter-class relations, also marked a return to both the structural principles and the anti-aristocratic class polemics of Freytag's earliest fiction — an element of continuity across his works overlooked in criticism. Significantly, the novel achieves a successful synthesis of class and national concerns, with the inter-class relationships simultaneously being inter-regional pairings, resulting in the subsumption of the aristocracy into a ruling bourgeoisie, and the coexistence of regional identities and a unified national identity. In its tripartite focus on class, nation, and the folk, *Die Ahnen* thus emerges as the most ideologically coherent of Freytag's works — one which systematically reimagines concepts of German history, society, and nationhood.

Gustav Freytag produced an extensive range of texts between the early 1840s and the late 1880s, which ranged across numerous genres: poetry, drama, journalism, the novel, history, dramatic theory, and biography. Despite the superficial diversity of his oeuvre, I have identified in this monograph the core tendencies across his writings — above all his overriding thematic interest in class relations. I have shown how he presented the middle classes as united by a common set of values, and how he gradually recast these values as national characteristics. I have noted how he traced these characteristics back through history, creating a myth of German folk identity. Ultimately, I have argued that Freytag's works conflated concepts of class and nation: the bourgeoisie develop into a nationalized folk, and national and middle-class identities become synonymous. Above all, Freytag's works have been seen to reimagine and reconceptualize political and class relations in Germany in a more consistent, comprehensive, and radical manner than has hitherto been acknowledged. His texts have all been shown to be projections of his ideological views: works that are predominantly concerned with the political, rather than the expressive and the aesthetic. On the basis of this study, it is clear that Heinrich Heine's definition of the politically engaged author as 'zu gleicher Zeit Künstler, Tribune und Apostel', invoked in the introduction to this monograph, is wholly applicable to Gustav Freytag: an author who saw himself not only as a bourgeois poet, but also as a tribune for the German folk and an apostle of historical and national progress.[2]

### Notes to the Conclusion

1. Peter Nusser, *Trivialliteratur* (Stuttgart: Metzler, 1991), p. 3.
2. Heinrich Heine, *Historisch-kritische Gesamtausgabe der Werke, Düsseldorfer Heine-Ausgabe*, ed. by Manfred Windfuhr, VIII.I: *Zur Geschichte der Religion und Philosophie in Deutschland; Die romantische Schule. Text* (Hamburg: Hoffmann & Campe, 1981), p. 218.

# BIBLIOGRAPHY

## Primary Texts

BECKER, NIKLAUS, *Gedichte*, in *Bibliothek der deutschen Literatur. Mikrofiche-Gesamtausgabe nach den Angaben des Taschengoedeke* (Munich: Sauer, 1990), B.1/F. 58
BÜCHNER, GEORG, *Werke und Briefe, Münchner Ausgabe*, ed. by Karl Pörnbacher (Munich: dtv, 1988)
FALLERSLEBEN, AUGUST HEINRICH HOFFMANN VON, *Gedichte* (Berlin: Grote, 1874)
FONTANE, THEODOR, *Sämtliche Werke* (Munich: Nymphenburger, 1964)
FREYTAG, GUSTAV, *Erinnerungen aus meinem Leben* (Leipzig: Hirzel, 1887)
—— *Die Fabier*, in *Bibliothek der deutschen Literatur. Mikrofiche-Gesamtausgabe nach den Angaben des Taschengoedeke* (Munich: Sauer, 1999), B.9/F.3951–3952
—— *In Breslau* (Breslau: Johann Kern, 1845)
—— *Gesammelte Werke*, 22 vols (Leipzig: Hirzel, 1896)
—— *Soll und Haben* (Leipzig: Manuscriptum, 2002)
—— *Die Technik des Dramas* (Berlin: Autorenhaus, 2003)
GRILLPARZER, FRANZ, *Sämtliche Werke, Historisch-kritische Gesamtausgabe Wien*, 6 vols (Vienna: Anton Schroll, 1927)
GUTZKOW, KARL, *Gutzkows Werke und Briefe: Autobiographische Schriften, II: Rückblicke auf mein Leben*, ed. by Peter Hasubek (Münster: Oktober, 2006)
HEINE, HEINRICH, *Historisch-kritische Gesamtausgabe der Werke, Düsseldorfer Heine-Ausgabe*, ed. by Manfred Windfuhr, 16 vols (Hamburg: Hoffmann & Campe, 1973–97)
HERWEGH, GEORG, *Gedichte eines Lebendigen* (Leipzig: Max Helles, [n.d.])
HOFFMANN, E. T. A., *Sämtliche Werke in sechs Bänden* (Frankfurt a.M.: dtv, 2004)
LAUBE, HEINRICH, *Heinrich Laubes Gesammelte Werke*, ed. by H. Houben (Leipzig: Max Helles, 1909)
LIVIUS, TITUS, *The History of Rome: The First Eight Books*, trans. by D. Spillan (London: Bell, 1896)
STIFTER, ADALBERT, *Werke und Briefe, Historisch-kritische Gesamtausgabe*, ed. by Alfred Doppler and Wolfgang Frühwald (Stuttgart: Kohlhammer, 1995)

## Secondary Texts

ACHINGER, CHRISTINE, *Gespaltene Moderne. Gustav Freytags 'Soll und Haben': Nation, Geschlecht und Judenbild* (Würzburg: Königshausen & Neumann, 2007)
—— '"Prosa der Verhältnisse" und Poesie der Ware: Versöhnte Moderne und Realismus in *Soll und Haben*', in *150 Jahre 'Soll und Haben': Studien zu Gustav Freytags kontroversem Roman*, ed. Florian Krobb (Würzburg: Königshausen & Neumann, 2005), pp. 67–86

ALBERTI, CONRAD, *Gustav Freytag: Sein Leben und Schaffen* (Leipzig: Schloemp, 1885)
—— *Gustav Freytag (geb. den 13. Juli 1816): Ein Festblatt zur Feier seines siebzigsten Geburtstags* (Leipzig: [n.pub.], 1886)
—— 'Gustav Freytag', *Die Gartenlaube*, 29 (1886), 514–15
AMÉRY, JEAN, 'Schlecht klingt das Lied vom braven Mann. Anläßlich der Neuauflage von Gustav Freytag's *Soll und Haben*', *Neue Rundschau*, 89 (1978), 84–93
AMORETTI, GIOVANNI VITTORIO, ed., *August Wilhelm Schlegels Vorlesungen über dramatische Kunst und Literatur*, 2 vols (Bonn: [n.pub.], 1923)
ANDERSON, ANTJE S., 'Ein Kaufmann "von sehr englischem Aussehen": Die literarische und soziokulturelle Funktion Englands in *Soll und Haben*', in *150 Jahre 'Soll und Haben'. Studien zu Gustav Freytags kontroversem Roman*, ed. by Florian Krobb (Würzburg: Königshausen & Neumann, 2005), pp. 209–24
ANDERSON, BENEDICT, *Imagined Communities: Reflections on the Origin and Spread of Nationalism* (London: Verso, 1991)
APPLEGATE, CELIA, *A Nation of Provincials: The German Idea of Heimat* (Berkeley: University of California Press, 1990)
—— 'The Mediated Nation: Regions, Readers and the German Past', in *Saxony in German History: Culture, Society and Politics, 1830–1833*, ed. by James Retallack (Ann Arbor: Michigan University Press, 2000), pp. 33–50
AUERBACH, BERTHOLD, 'Besprechung von *Soll und Haben*', *Gustav Freytag-Blätter*, 14 (1969), 2–7
BARTH, CHRISTA, 'Gustav Freytags *Journalisten*: Versuch einer Monographie' (doctoral thesis, University of Munich, 1949)
BEATON, KENNETH BRUCE, 'Gustav Freytag, Julian Schmidt und die Romantheorie nach der Revolution von 1848', *Raabe-Jahrbuch* (1976), 7–32
—— 'Gustav Freytags *Die Journalisten*: eine "politische" Komödie der Revolutionszeit', *Zeitschrift für Deutsche Philologie*, 105 (1986), 516–43
BECKER, SABINA, *Bürgerlicher Realismus: Literatur und Kultur im bürgerlichen Zeitalter 1848–1900* (Tübingen: Francke, 2003)
—— 'Erziehung zur Bürgerlichkeit: Eine kulturgeschichtliche Lektüre von Gustav Freytags *Soll und Haben*', in *150 Jahre 'Soll und Haben'. Studien zu Gustav Freytags kontroversem Roman*, ed. by Florian Krobb (Würzburg: Königshausen & Neumann, 2005), pp. 29–46
BELGER, C., *Moriz Haupt als academischer Lehrer* (Berlin: [n.pub.], 1879)
BENARIO, HERBERT W., 'Tacitus, Gustav Freytag, Mommsen', *Classical and Modern Literature: A Quarterly*, 20 (2000), 71–79
BERGER, STEFAN, *Germany: Inventing the Nation* (London: Arnold, 2004)
BERGHAUS, SABINE, 'Die Rolle der Adelheid in Gustav Freytags Drama *Die Journalisten*', *Gustav Freytag-Blätter*, 49 (1991), 1–11
BHABHA, HOMI, ed., *Nation and Narration* (London: Routledge, 1990)
BIALEK, EDWARD, ed., *Gustav Freytag an Theodor Molinari und die Seinen: Bislang unbekannte Briefe aus den Beständen der Universitätsbibliothek Wroclaw* (Frankfurt a.M.: Lang, 1987)
BLACKBOURN, DAVID, and GEOFF ELEY, *The Peculiarities of German History* (Oxford: Oxford University Press, 1984)
BLACKBOURN, DAVID, *The Long Nineteenth Century: A History of Germany, 1780–1918* (Oxford: Oxford University Press, 1998)

BÖHME, HELMUT, ed., *Die Reichsgründung* (Munich: dtv, 1967)
BRÄUTIGAM, BERND, 'Candide im Comptoir: Zur Bedeutung der Poesie in Gustav Freytags *Soll und Haben*', *Germanisch-Romantische Monatsschrift*, 66 (1985), 395-411
BREUER, DIETER, *Geschichte der literarischen Zensur in Deutschland* (Heidelberg: Quelle, 1982)
BREUILLY, JOHN, ed., *19th Century Germany: Politics, Culture and Society, 1780-1918* (London: Arnold, 2001)
—— 'Revolution to Unification', in *19th Century Germany. Politics, Culture and Society, 1780-1918*, ed. by John Breuilly (London: Arnold, 2001), pp. 138-59
BRUNS, KARIN, ROLF PARR, and WULF WÜLFING, eds, *Handbuch literarisch-kultureller Vereine, Gruppen und Bünde, 1825-1933* (Weimar: Metzler, 1997)
BRUNT, P. A., *Ancient Culture and Society: Social Conflicts in the Roman Republic* (London: Chatto & Windus, 1978)
BUCHER, MAX, ed., *Realismus und Gründerzeit: Manifeste und Dokumente zur deutschen Literatur 1848-1880* (Stuttgart: Metzler, 1975)
BÜCHLER-HAUSCHILD, GABRIELE, *Erzählte Arbeit: Gustav Freytag und die soziale Prosa des Vor- und Nachmärz* (Paderborn: Schöningh, 1987)
—— '"Verbürgerlichung" durch Arbeit: Freytags *Soll und Haben* in neuer Perspektive', in *Gustav Freytag-Blätter*, 47 (1989), 1-16
BUSSMANN, WALTER, 'Gustav Freytag, Maßstäbe seiner Zeitkritik', *Archiv für Kulturgeschichte*, 34 (1952), 261-87
CARR, WILLIAM, *A History of Germany. 1815-1990* (London: Arnold, 1991)
CARTER, T. E., 'Freytag's *Soll und Haben*: A Liberal National Manifesto as a Bestseller', *German Life and Letters*, 21 (1967/68), 320-29
CLARK, CHRISTOPHER, 'Germany 1815-1848: Restoration or Pre-March?', in *19th Century Germany: Politics, Culture and Society, 1780-1918*, ed. by John Breuilly (London: Arnold, 2001), pp. 40-65
CLASSE, KURT, 'Gustav Freytag als politischer Dichter' (doctoral thesis, University of Münster, 1914)
CORNICELIUS, MAX, ed., *Heinrich von Treitschkes Briefe* (Leipzig: Hirzel, 1918)
CORSI, PIETRO, and PAUL J. WEINDLING, 'Darwinism in Germany, France and Italy', in *The Darwinian Heritage*, ed. by David Kohn, (Princeton: Princeton University Press, 1985), pp. 683-729
CRAIG, GORDON, *Germany 1866-1945* (Oxford: Oxford University Press, 1978)
CRANKSHAW, EDWARD, *The Habsburgs* (London: Weidenfeld & Nicolson, 1971)
DAMMANN, OSWALD, 'Gustav Freytag und der Konstitutionalismus' (doctoral thesis, University of Freiburg, 1916)
—— 'Gustav Freytag bei den *Grenzboten*: Zu seinem hundertsten Geburtstag am 13. Juli 1916', *Die Grenzboten*, 75 (1916), 3-11
DENKLER, HORST, ed., *Romane und Erzählungen des bürgerlichen Realismus* (Stuttgart: Reclam, 1980)
DEVRIENT, EMIL, 'Briefwechsel zwischen Gustav Freytag und Eduard Devrient', *Westermanns illustrierte deutsche Monatshefte*, 91 (1901-02), 130-33
DILTHEY, WILHELM, 'Die Technik des Dramas', *Shakespeare-Jahrbuch*, 69 (1933), 27-60
DÖRR, VOLKER, 'Idealistische Wissenschaft: Der (bürgerliche) Realismus und

Gustav Freytags Roman *Die verlorene Handschrift'*, *Zeitschrift für Deutsche Philologie*, 120 (2001), 3–33

DOTZLER, BERNHARD J., 'Litterarum secreta — fraus litteraria. Über Gustav Freytag: *Die verlorene Handschrift'*, in *Literatur und Politik in der Heine-Zeit. Die 48er Revolution in Texten zwischen Vormärz und Nachmärz*, ed. by Harmut Kircher and Maria Klanska (Cologne: Böhlau, 1998), pp. 235–50

DOVE, ALFRED, ed., *Gustav Freytag und Heinrich von Treitschke im Briefwechsel* (Leipzig: Hirzel, 1900)

—— *Gustav Freytag's Briefwechsel mit Emil Devrient* (Brunswick: [n. pub.], 1902)

—— *Gustav Freytag an Salomon Hirzel und die Seinen* (Leipzig: Breitkopf & Härtel, 1902)

DROESCHER, GEORG, 'Gustav Freytags Schriftwechsel mit der Generalintendanz der königlichen Schauspiele zu Berlin', *Deutsche Rundschau*, 45 (1918), 129–46

—— *Gustav Freytag in seinen Lustspielen: Inaugural-Dissertation* (Weida: Thomas & Hubert, 1919)

EGGERT, HARTMUT, *Studien zur Wirkungsgeschichte des deutschen historischen Romans, 1850–1875* (Frankfurt a.M.: Klostermann, 1971)

EICHER, THOMAS, 'Poesie, Poetisierung und Poetizität in Gustav Freytag's *Soll und Haben*', *Wirkendes Wort*, 45 (1995), 64–81

EINHOLZ, SYBILLE, 'Die Große Granitschale im Lustgarten: Zur Bedeutung eines Berliner Solitärs', *Der Bär von Berlin: Jahrbuch des Vereins Geschichte für Berlin*, 46 (1997), 41–59

EKE, NORBERT OTTO, and RENATE WERNER, eds, *Vormärz-Nachmärz: Bruch oder Kontinuität?* (Bielefeld: Aisthesis, 2000)

ELOESSER, A., ed., *Gustav Freytag. Briefe an seine Gattin* (Berlin: W. Borngräber, 1913)

FINNEY, GAIL, 'Revolution, Resignation, Realism (1830–1890)', in *The Cambridge History of German Literature*, ed. by Helen Watanabe O'Kelly (Cambridge: Cambridge University Press, 1997), pp. 272–326

FRENZEL, HERBERT, and ELISABETH FRENZEL, *Daten deutscher Dichtung: Chronologischer Abriß der deutschen Literaturgeschichte*, 2 vols (Munich: dtv, 1970)

FREYMOND, ROLAND, *Der Einfluß von Charles Dickens auf Gustav Freytag* (Prague: Bellmann, 1912)

FRIEDRICH, KARIN, 'Cultural and Intellectual Trends', in *19th Century Germany: Politics, Culture and Society, 1780–1918*, ed. by John Breuilly (London: Arnold, 2001), pp. 96–116

FULDA, DANIEL, 'Telling German History: Forms and Functions of the Historical Narrative against the Background of the National Unifications', in *1870/71– 1989/90: German Unifications and the Change of Literary Discourse*, ed. by Walter Pape (Berlin: de Gruyter, 1993), pp. 195–207

FULDA, LUDWIG, 'Gustav Freytag als Dramatiker', *Deutsche Revue*, 21 (1896), 69–79

GALL, LOTHAR, ed., *Fragen an die deutschen Geschichte. Ideen, Kräfte, Entscheidungen. Von 1800 bis zur Gegenwart. Historische Ausstellung im Reichstagsgebäude in Berlin, Katalog* (Bonn: Deutscher Bundestag, 1980)

GALLER, MARGRET, and JÜRGEN MATONI, eds, *Gustav Freytags Briefe an die Verlegerfamilie Hirzel* (Berlin: Mann, 1994)

GARLAND, HENRY, and MARY GARLAND, *The Oxford Companion to German Literature* (Oxford: Oxford University Press, 1976)

GEBHARDT, BRUNO, *Handbuch der deutschen Geschichte*, 2 vols (Stuttgart: UDV, 1955)
GEBHARDT, WALTHER, 'Die Briefsammlung Gustav Freytags', *Jahrbuch der schlesischen Friedrich-Wilhelms-Universität zu Breslau*, 4 (1959), 152–75
GEFFCKEN, JOHANNES, 'Die Tendenz in Gustav Freytags *Soll und Haben*', *Zeitschrift für vergleichende Literaturgeschichte*, 13 (1899), 88–91
GELBER, MARK, 'Teaching "Literary Anti-Semitism": Dickens' *Oliver Twist* and Freytag's *Soll und Haben*', *Comparative Literature Studies*, 16 (1979), 1–11
—— 'Aspects of Literary Anti-Semitism, Charles Dickens' *Oliver Twist* and Gustav Freytag's *Soll und Haben*' (doctoral thesis, Yale, 1980)
—— 'Die literarische Umwelt zu Gustav Freytags *Soll und Haben* und die Realismustheorie der *Grenzboten*', *Orbis litterarum*, 39 (1984), 38–53
—— 'An Alternative Reading of the Role of the Jewish Scholar in Gustav Freytag's *Soll und Haben*', *Germanic Review*, 58 (1983), 83–88
—— 'Antisemitismus, literarischer Antisemitismus und die Konstellation der bösen Juden in Gustav Freytags *Soll und Haben*', in *150 Jahre 'Soll und Haben'. Studien zu Gustav Freytags kontroversem Roman*, ed. by Florian Krobb (Würzburg: Könighausen & Neumann, 2005), pp. 285–300
GLÜCKSMANN, HEINRICH, '*Die Journalisten* — ein Plagiat', *Jahrbuch deutscher Bibliophilen*, 10/11 (1924), 111–14
GOETZINGER, G., 'Die Situation der Autorinnen und Autoren', in *Hansers Sozialgeschichte der deutschen Literatur vom 16. Jahrhundert bis zur Gegenwart*, ed. by G. Sautermeister and U. Schmid, 12 vols (Munich: dtv, 1998), V: *Zwischen Restauration und Revolution 1815–1848*, pp. 38–59
GOLDMANN, BERND, 'Nachwort', in Gustav Freytag, *Die Journalisten* (Stuttgart: Reclam, 1977), pp. 111–18
GREEN, ABIGAIL, *Fatherlands: State-Building and Nationhood in Nineteenth-Century Germany* (Cambridge: Cambridge University Press, 2001)
GRESKY, WOLFGANG, 'Gustav Freytag als Reichstagsabgeordneter', *Gustav Freytag-Blätter*, 14 (1969), 8–15
GRIFFITHS, ELYSTAN, 'A Nation of Provincials? German Identity in Gustav Freytag's Novel-cycle *Die Ahnen* (1872–1880)', *Monatshefte*, 96 (2004), 220–33
GROSSMANN, ANDREAS, 'Volksgeist — Grund einer praktischen Welt oder metaphysische Spukgestalt? Anmerkungen zur Problemgeschichte eines nicht nur Hegelschen Theorems', in *Metaphysik der praktischen Welt. Perspektiven im Anschluß an Hegel und Heidegger*, ed. by Andreas Großmann and Christoph Jamme (Amsterdam: Rodopi, 2000), pp. 60–77
GRUNERT, MARK, 'Lenore oder die Versuchung des Bürgers: Romantische "Zauber" und realistische Ideologie in Gustav Freytags *Soll und Haben*', *Monatshefte*, 85 (1993), 134–51
GUBSER, MARTIN, *Literarischer Antisemitismus: Untersuchungen zu Gustav Freytag und anderen bürgerlichen Schriftstellern des 19. Jahrhunderts* (Göttingen: Wallstein, 1998)
HABERMAS, JÜRGEN, *Strukturwandel der Öffentlichkeit: Untersuchungen zu einer Kategorie der bürgerlichen Gesellschaft* (Frankfurt a.M.: Suhrkamp, 1990)
HAHN, HANS J., *The 1848 Revolutions in German-Speaking Europe* (London: Longman, 2001)

—— 'Die "Polenwirtschaft" in Gustav Freytags Roman *Soll und Haben*', in *150 Jahre 'Soll und Haben': Studien zu Gustav Freytags kontroversem Roman*, ed. by Florian Krobb (Würzburg: Königshausen & Neumann, 2005), pp. 239–54

HAHN, HERBERT, 'Die Bedeutung der Naturdarstellung in der Komposition von Gustav Freytags "Verlorene Handschrift"' (doctoral thesis, University of Greifswald, 1921)

HAIDA, PETER, *Kritik und Satire im Lustspiel* (Stuttgart: Klett, 1989)

HAMEROW, THEODORE, *Restoration, Revolution, Reaction: Economics and Politics in Germany, 1815–1871* (Princeton: Princeton University Press, 1972)

HAYM, ROBERT, ed., '*Die Fabier*: Trauerspiel in fünf Akten von Gustav Freytag. Leipzig bei Hirzel 1859', *Preußische Jahrbücher*, 3 (1859), 657–88

HEADY, KATY, *Literature and Censorship in Restoration Germany: Repression and Rhetoric* (Rochester, NY: Camden House, 2009)

HEILBORN, E., 'Gustav Freytag, der Dramatiker', *Das Magazin für Literatur*, 64 (1895), 583–87

HELMOT, HANS, ed., *Gustav Freytags Briefe an Albrecht von Stosch* (Berlin: [n.pub.], 1913)

HERMANN, OTTO, 'Die Anfänge Gustav Freytags' (doctoral thesis, University of Hamburg, 1934)

HERRMANN, RENATE, 'Gustav Freytag. Bürgerliches Selbstverständnis und preußisch-deutsches Nationalbewußtsein: Ein Beitrag zur Geschichte des nationalen-liberalen Bürgertums der Reichgründungszeit' (doctoral thesis, University of Würzburg, 1974)

HELMHOLDT, H. F., ed., *Briefe an Albrecht von Stosch* (Stuttgart: Deutscher Verlag, 1913)

HINRICHS, CARL, 'Unveröffentliche Briefe Gustav Freytags an Heinrich Geffecken aus der Zeit der Reichsgründung', *Jahrbuch für die Geschichte Mittel- und Ostdeutschlands*, 3 (1954), 65–117

HOBSBAWM, ERIC, *The Age of Revolution, 1789–1848* (London: Weidenfeld and Nicolson, 1995)

—— 'Introduction: Inventing Traditions', in *The Invention of Tradition*, ed. by Eric Hobsbawm and Terence Ranger (Cambridge: Cambridge University Press, 1983), pp. 1–14

HODENBURG, CHRISTINA VON, *Aufstand der Weber: Die Revolte von 1844 und ihr Aufstieg zum Mythos* (Bonn: Dietz, 1997)

HOFMANN, J., *Gustav Freytag als Politiker, Journalist und Mensch: Mit unveröffentlichten Briefen von Freytag und Max Jordan* (Leipzig: J. Weber, 1922)

HOHENDAHL, PETER UWE, *Building a National Literature: The Case of Germany, 1830–1870* (Ithaca: Cornell University Press, 1989)

—— *Literarische Kultur im Zeitalter des Liberalismus 1830–1870* (Munich: Beck, 1985)

HOHENEMSER, PAUL, *Flugschriftensammlung Gustav Freytags* (Hildesheim: [n. pub.], 1925)

HOLZ, CLAUS, 'Flucht aus der Wirklichkeit. "Die Ahnen" von Gustav Freytag: Untersuchungen zum realistischen historischen Roman der Gründerzeit 1872–1880' (doctoral thesis, University of Bonn, 1981)

HORAWITZ, ADALBERT H., *Gustav Freytag als Dichter und Historiker* (Vienna: Hölder, 1871)

HORCH, HANS OTTO, 'Gustav Freytag und Berthold Auerbach. Eine repräsentative deutsch-jüdische Schriftstellerfreundschaft im 19. Jahrhundert. Mit unveröffentlichen Briefen beider Autoren', *Raabe-Jahrbuch*, (1985), 154–74
—— 'Judenbilder in der realistischen Erzählliteratur: Jüdische Figuren bei Gustav Freytag, Fritz Reuter, Berthold Auerbach und Wilhelm Raabe', in *Juden und Judentum in der Literatur*, ed. by Herbert A. Strauß and Christhard Hoffmann (Munich: dtv, 1985), pp. 140–71
HOROVITZ-BARNAY, ILKA, 'Gustav Freytag über den deutschen Staatspreis und über *Die Fabier*', *Deutsche Revue*, 31 (1906), 40–52
HOUBEN, HEINRICH HUBERT, *Verbotene Literatur von der klassischen Zeit bis zur Gegenwart* (Hildesheim, Georg Olm, 1965)
HUBER, ERNST ROBERT, *Dokumente zur deutschen Verfassungsgeschichte* (Stuttgart: Kohlhammer, 1978)
HUBRICH, PETER HEINZ, *Gustav Freytags 'Deutsche Ideologie' in 'Soll und Haben'* (Kronberg: Scriptor, 1974)
JÄGER, HANS-WOLF, 'Versepik', in *Hansers Sozialgeschichte der deutschen Literatur vom 16. Jahrhundert bis zur Gegenwart*, ed. by G. Sautermeister and U. Schmid (Munich: dtv, 1998), V: *Zwischen Restauration und Revolution 1815–1848*, pp. 434–58
KAFITZ, DIETER, *Figurenkonstellation als Mittel der Wirklichkeitserfassung. Dargestellt an Romanen der zweiten Hälfte des 19. Jahrhunderts: Freytag, Spielhagen, Fontane, Raabe* (Kronberg: Athenäum, 1978)
—— *Gründzüge einer Geschichte des deutschen Dramas von Lessing bis zum Naturalismus*, 2 vols (Königstein: Athenäum, 1982)
KAISER, HERBERT, *Studien zum deutschen Roman nach 1848. Karl Gutzkow: 'Die Ritter vom Geiste', Gustav Freytag: 'Soll und Haben', Adalbert Stifter: 'Der Nachsommer'* (Duisburg: Braun, 1977)
KAISER, NANCY, 'Gustav Freytag (1816–1895)', in *Dictionary of Literary Biography, Nineteenth-Century German Writers 1841–1900*, ed. by James Hardin and Siegfried Mews (Detroit: Gale, 1993), pp. 92–100
—— *Social Integration and Narrative Structure: Patterns of Realism in Auerbach, Freytag, Fontane and Raabe* (New York: Peter Lang, 1986)
KELLY, ALFRED, 'The Franco-Prussian War and Unification in German History Schoolbooks', in *1870/71–1989/90: German Unifications and the Change of Literary Discourse*, ed. Walter Pape (Cologne: de Gruyter, 1992), pp. 37–60
KIENZLE, MICHAEL, *Der Erfolgsroman: Zur Kritik seiner poetischen Ökonomie bei Gustav Freytag und Eugenie Marlitt* (Stuttgart: Metzler, 1975)
*Kleines Brockhaus Konversationslexikon* (Leipzig: Brockhaus, 1906)
KOCH, H. W., *A History of Prussia* (London: Longman, 1978)
KÖHNKE, KLAUS CHRISTIAN, 'Ein antisemitischer Autor wider Willen: Zu Gustav Freytags *Soll und Haben*', in *Conditio Judaica. Judentum, Antisemitismus und deutschsprachige Literatur vom 18. Jahrhundert bis zum Ersten Weltkrieg*, ed. by Hans Otto Horch and Horst Denkler (Tübingen: Niemeyer, 1989), pp. 130–47
KOHUT, ADOLPH, *Gustav Freytag als Patriot und Politiker* (Berlin: Schall, 1916)
KONTJE, TODD, ed., *A Companion to German Realism 1848–1890* (Rochester, NY: Camden House, 2002)

—— *The German Bildungsroman: History of a National Genre* (Rochester, NY: Camden House, 1993)
—— 'Introduction: Reawakening German Realism', in *A Companion to German Realism 1848–1900*, ed. by Todd Kontje (Rochester, NY: Camden House, 2002), pp. 1–28
—— *Private Lives in the Public Sphere: The German Bildungsroman as Metafiction* (University Park, PA: Pennsylvania State University Press, 1994)
—— *Women, the Novel, and the German Nation, 1771–1871: Domestic Fiction in the Fatherland* (Cambridge: Cambridge University Press, 1998)
KOOPMANN, HELMUT, *Das Junge Deutschland: Analyse seines Selbstverständnisses* (Stuttgart: Metzler, 1970)
—— *Das Junge Deutschland: Eine Einführung* (Darmstadt: Wissenschaftliche Buchgesellschaft, 1993)
—— and MICHAEL PERRAUDIN, eds, *Formen der Wirklichkeitserfassung nach 1848: Deutsche Literatur und Kultur vom Nachmärz bis zur Gründerzeit in europäischer Perspektive I* (Bielefeld: Aisthesis, 2001)
KOPP, KRISTIN, '"Ich stehe jetzt hier als einer von den Eroberern": Soll und Haben als Kolonialroman', in *150 Jahre 'Soll und Haben': Studien zu Gustav Freytags kontroversem Roman*, ed. by Florian Krobb (Würzburg: Königshausen & Neumann, 2005), pp. 225–37
KREN, GEORGE M., 'Gustav Freytag and the Assimilation of the German Middle Class', *American Journal of Economics and Sociology*, 22 (1963), 483–94
KRIEGER, KLAUS, 'Die Tscherkessin, ein Opernfragment von Gustav Freytag', *Gustav Freytag-Blätter*, 10 (1965), 3–8
KROBB, FLORIAN, 'Einleitung: Soll und Haben nach 150 Jahren', in *150 Jahre 'Soll und Haben': Studien zu Gustav Freytags kontroversem Roman*, ed. by Florian Krobb (Würzburg: Königshausen & Neumann, 2005), pp. 9–28
—— '"das Gewühl der Häuser und Straßen": Soll und Haben als Großstadtroman', in *150 Jahre 'Soll und Haben': Studien zu Gustav Freytags kontroversem Roman*, ed. by Florian Krobb (Würzburg: Königshausen & Neumann, 2005), pp. 137–52
——, ed., *150 Jahre 'Soll und Haben': Studien zu Gustav Freytags kontroversem Roman* (Würzburg: Königshausen & Neumann, 2005)
LAATHS, ERWIN, 'Der Nationalliberalismus im Werke Gustav Freytags' (doctoral thesis, University of Cologne, 1934)
LANDMANN, KARL, 'Deutsche Liebe und deutsche Treue in Gustav Freytags *Ahnen*', *Zeitschrift für den deutschen Unterricht*, 6 (1892), 81–104
LEE, ROBERT, 'Relative Backwardness and Long-Run Development: Economic, Demographic and Social Changes', in *19th Century Germany: Politics, Culture and Society, 1780–1918*, ed. by John Breuilly (London: Arnold, 2001), pp. 66–95
LEPP, EDWIN, *Die deutsche Art und der protestantische Geist in Gustav Freytags Werken* (Pforzheim: [n.pub.], 1895)
LIMLEI, MICHAEL, *Geschichte als Ort der Bewährung: Menschenbild und Gesellschaftsverständnis in den deutschen historischen Romanen (1820–1890)* (Frankfurt a.M.: Peter Lang, 1988)
LINDAU, HANS, *Gustav Freytag* (Leipzig: Hirzel, 1907)
LINDAU, PAUL, '*Die Ahnen*: Ein Roman von Gustav Freytag', *Nord und Süd*, 16 (1881), 218–84

LOHRMANN, HEINRICH-FRIEDRICH, *Die Entwicklung zur realistischen Seelenhaltung im Zeitdrama von 1840 bis 1850* (Berlin: Jünker & Dünnhaupt, 1931)

LONNER, ALYSSA A., 'History's Attic: Artifacts, Museums, and Historical Rupture in Gustav Freytag's *Die verlorene Handschrift*', *The Germanic Review*, 82 (2007), 321–41

—— *Mediating the Past: Gustav Freytag, Progress and German Historical Identity, 1848-1871* (Berne: Peter Lang, 2005)

LORENZ, OTTOKAR, *Staatsmänner und Geschichtsschreiber des 19 Jahrhunderts* (Berlin: Hetz, 1896)

LÖWENTHAL, LEO, 'Gustav Freytag — der bürgerliche Materialismus', in Leo Löwenthal, *Das bürgerliche Bewußtsein in der Literatur* (Frankfurt a. M: Suhrkamp, 1990), pp. 349–63

LÜER, ERWIN, 'Gustav Freytag als Märchensammler', *Gustav Freytag Blätter*, 51 (1994/95), 1–15

—— 'Lyriktheoretische Betrachtungen zu den Gedichten Gustav Freytags', *Gustav Freytag Blätter*, 50 (1992/93), 8–22

MALTBY, JOSEPHINE, 'Accounting and the Soul of the Middle Class: Gustav Freytag's *Soll und Haben*', *Accounting, Organizations and Society*, 22 (1997), 69–87

MARTINI, FRITZ, *Deutsche Literatur im bürgerlichen Realismus 1848–1898* (Stuttgart: Metzler, 1962)

MATONI, JÜRGEN, and MARGRET GALLER, eds, *Gustav Freytag Bibliographie* (Dülmen: Laumann, 1990)

MAUFF, IRENE, 'Aus Gustav Freytag's Nachlaß. Aus Gustav Freytag's Heimat: Briefe aus und über Oberschlesien, besonders von Gustav Freytag's Mutter an ihren Sohn', *Jahrbuch der Schlesischen Friedrich-Wilhelms-Universität zu Breslau*, 11 (1966), 197–243

MAYRHOFER, OTTO, *Gustav Freytag und das Junge Deutschland* (Marburg: Koch, 1907)

MCINNES, EDWARD, '"Die Poesie des Geschäfts": Social Analysis and Polemic in Freytag's *Soll und Haben*', in *Formen realistischer Erzählkunst*, ed. by Jörg Thunecke and Eda Sagarra (Nottingham: Sherwood Press, 1979), pp. 99–107

—— 'Drama und Theater', in *Hansers Sozialgeschichte der deutschen Literatur vom 16. Jahrhundert bis zur Gegenwart*, ed. by Edward McInnes and Gerhard Plumpe, 12 vols (Munich: dtv, 1996), VI: *Bürgerlicher Realismus und Gründerzeit 1848–1890*, pp. 343–93

—— and GERHARD PLUMPE, eds, *Hansers Sozialgeschichte der deutschen Literatur vom 16. Jahrhundert bis zur Gegenwart*, VI: *Bürgerlicher Realismus und Gründerzeit 1848–1890* (Munich: dtv, 1996)

MEHRING, FRANZ, *Aufsätze zur deutschen Literatur von Hebbel bis Schweichel* (Berlin: Dietz, 1890)

MINDEN, MICHAEL, *The German Bildungsroman: Incest and Inheritance* (Cambridge: Cambridge University Press, 1997)

MÜLLER, HARRO, 'Historische Romane', in *Hansers Sozialgeschichte der deutschen Literatur vom 16. Jahrhundert bis zur Gegenwart*, ed. by Edward McInnes and Gerhard Plumpe (Munich: dtv, 1996), VI: *Bürgerlicher Realismus und Gründerzeit 1848–1890*, pp. 690–707

NAUJOKS, EBERHARD, 'Die Grenzboten (1841–1922)', in *Deutsche Zeitschriften des 17.*

*bis 20. Jahrhunderts*, ed. by Heinz-Dietrich Fischer (Munich: Dokumentation, 1973)

NIPPERDEY, THOMAS, *Deutsche Geschichte 1800–1866* (Munich: Beck, 1983)

—— 'Zum Problem der Objektivität bei Ranke', in *Leopold von Ranke und die moderne Geschichtswissenschaft*, ed. by Wolfgang J. Mommsen (Stuttgart: Klett, 1988), pp. 215–22

NUSSER, PETER, *Trivialliteratur* (Stuttgart: Metzler, 1991)

ORT, CLAUS-MICHAEL, 'Roman des "Nebeneinander" — Roman des "Nacheinander": Kohärenzprobleme im Geschichtsroman des 19. Jahrhunderts und ihr Funktionswandel', in *Zwischen Goethezeit und Realismus: Wandel und Spezifik in der Phase des Bürgerlichen Realismus*, ed. by Michael Titzmann (Tübingen: Niemeyer, 2002), pp. 347–75

OSTERKAMP, BARBARA, *Arbeit und Identität: Studien zur Erzählkunst des bürgerlichen Realismus* (Würzburg: Königshausen & Neumann, 1983)

OSTWALD, PAUL, *Gustav Freytag als Politiker* (Berlin: Staatspolitischer Verlag, 1927)

PAZI, MARGARITA, 'Wie gleicht man auch ethisch *Soll und Haben* aus?', *Zeitschrift für deutsche Philologie*, 106 (1987), 198–218

PERRAUDIN, MICHAEL, 'Einleitung', in *Formen der Wirklichkeitserfassung nach 1848: Deutsche Literatur und Kultur vom Nachmärz bis zur Gründerzeit in europäischer Perspektive I*, ed. by Helmut Koopmann and Michael Perraudin (Bielefeld: Aisthesis, 2003), pp. 1–12

—— *Literature, the Volk and Revolution in Mid-Nineteenth Century Germany* (New York: Berghahn, 2000)

—— 'Sinn und Sinnlichkeit im Deutschland des Vor- und Nachmärz', in *Formen der Wirklichkeitserfassung nach 1848. Deutsche Literatur und Kultur vom Nachmärz bis zur Gründerzeit in europäischer Perspektive I*, ed. by Helmut Koopmann and Michael Perraudin (Bielefeld: Aisthesis, 2003), pp. 13–42

PESCHKEN, BERND, and CLAUS-DIETER KROHN, *Der liberale Roman und der preussische Verfassungskonflikt: Analyseskizzen und Materialien* (Stuttgart: Metzler, 1976)

PETERSON, BRENT O., *History, Fiction and Germany: Writing the Nineteenth-Century Nation* (Detroit: Wayne State University Press, 2005)

PING, LARRY L., *Gustav Freytag and the Prussian Gospel: Novels, Liberalism, and History* (Berne: Peter Lang, 2006)

PLUMPE, GERHARD, 'Einleitung', in Edward McInnes and Gerhard Plumpe, eds, *Hansers Sozialgeschichte der deutschen Literatur vom 16. Jahrhundert bis zur Gegenwart*, 12 vols (Munich: dtv, 1996), VI: *Bürgerlicher Realismus und Gründerzeit 1848–1890*, pp. 1–83

PRUTZ, ROBERT, *Die deutsche Literatur der Gegenwart, 1848–1858*, 2 vols (Leipzig: Voigt & Günther, 1860)

RHÖSE, FRANZ, *Konflikt und Versöhnung: Untersuchungen zur Theorie des Romans von Hegel bis zum Naturalismus* (Stuttgart: Metzler, 1978)

RICHTER, CLAUS, *Leiden an der Gesellschaft: Vom literarischen Liberalismus zum poetischen Realismus* (Königstein: Athenäum, 1978)

RIDLEY, HUGH, 'Zwischen Anstand und Ästhetik: Zu sozialen und literarischen Codes in Gustav Freytags *Soll und Haben*', *Zeitschrift für Germanistik*, 11 (2001), pp 105–16

RINDISBACHER, HANS J., 'From National Task to Individual Pursuit: The Poetics of Work in Freytag, Stifter and Raabe', in *A Companion to German Realism 1848-1890*, ed. by Todd Kontje (Rochester, NY: Camden House, 2002), pp. 183–221

RINSUM, ANNEMARIE, and WOLFGANG VAN RINSUM, *Deutsche Literaturgeschichte*, VI: *Frührealismus*; VII: *Naturalismus* (Munich: dtv, 2001)

RITTER, ALEXANDER, 'Der patriosierte Roman als gesellschaftspolitischer Kassensturz: Gustav Freytags paratextuelle Fesselung von *Soll und Haben* ans ideologische "Leitseil [...] im Reiche der Poesie als Demimonde"', in *150 Jahre 'Soll und Haben'. Studien zu Gustav Freytags kontroversem Roman*, ed. by Florian Krobb (Würzburg: Königshausen & Neumann, 2005), pp. 47–66

RÖSSLER, CONSTANTIN, *Gustav Freytag und die deutsche Dichtung der Gegenwart* (Berlin: Springer, 1860)

ROTHFUCHS, EDUARD, 'Der Selbstbiographische Gehalt in Gustav Freytags Werken (bis 1855)' (doctoral thesis, University of Münster, 1929)

RÜCKHABERLE, HANS JOACHIN, and HELMUTH WIDHAMMER, *Roman und Romantheorie des deutschen Realismus: Darstellung und Dokumente* (Kronberg: Athenäum 1977)

RYCHLIK, OTMAR, 'Gustav Freytag — Schriftsteller und Journalist', *Gustav Freytag-Blätter*, 51 (1994/95), 16–31

SAGARRA, EDA, *Tradition and Revolution: German Literature and Society 1830–1890* (New York: Basic Books, 1971)

—— 'Jewish Emancipation in Nineteenth-Century Germany and the Stereotyping of the Jew in Gustav Freytag's Novel *Soll und Haben* (1855)', in *The Writer as Witness. Literature as Historical Evidence*, ed. by Tom Dunne (Cork: Cork University Press, 1987), pp. 160–76

—— *Germany in the Nineteenth Century: History and Literature* (New York: Peter Lang, 2001)

SAMMONS, JEFFREY L., 'The Evaluation of Freytag's *Soll und Haben*', *German Life and Letters*, 22 (1968–69), 315–24

—— 'Der Amerikaner als Jude: Kontextualisierte Beobachtungen zur Amerika-Episode in Gustav Freytags *Soll und Haben*', in *150 Jahre 'Soll und Haben: Studien zu Gustav Freytags kontroversem Roman*, ed. by Florian Krobb (Würzburg: Königshausen & Neumann, 2005), pp. 255–68

SAUL, NICHOLAS, 'Aesthetic humanism (1790–1830)', in *The Cambridge History of German Literature*, ed. by Helen Watanabe O'Kelly (Cambridge: Cambridge University Press, 1997), pp. 202–72

SAUTERMEISTER, G., and U. SCHMID, eds, *Hansers Sozialgeschichte der deutschen Literatur vom 16. Jahrhundert bis zur Gegenwart*, ed. by G. Sautermeister and U. Schmid, 12 vols, V: *Zwischen Restauration und Revolution 1815–1848* (Munich: dtv, 1998)

—— 'Einleitung', in *Hansers Sozialgeschichte der deutschen Literatur vom 16. Jahrhundert bis zur Gegenwart*, ed. by G. Sautermeister and U. Schmid (Munich: dtv, 1998), 12 vols, V: *Zwischen Restauration und Revolution 1815–1848*, pp. 9–15

—— 'Lyrik und literarisches Leben', in *Hansers Sozialgeschichte der deutschen Literatur vom 16. Jahrhundert bis zur Gegenwart*, ed. by G. Sautermeister and U. Schmid, 12 vols, V: *Zwischen Restauration und Revolution 1815–1848* (Munich: dtv, 1998), pp. 459–84

—— 'Religiöse und soziale Lyrik', in *Hansers Sozialgeschichte der deutschen Literatur vom 16. Jahrhundert bis zur Gegenwart*, ed. by G. Sautermeister and U. Schmid, 12 vols (Munich: dtv, 1998), v: *Zwischen Restauration und Revolution 1815-1848*, pp. 505-25

SCHMID, U., 'Buchmarkt und Literaturvermittlung', in *Hansers Sozialgeschichte der deutschen Literatur vom 16. Jahrhundert bis zur Gegenwart*, ed. by G. Sautermeister and U. Schmid, 12 vols (Munich: dtv, 1998), v: *Zwischen Restauration und Revolution 1815-1848*, pp. 60-93

SCHMIDT, JULIAN, *Geschichte der deutschen Literatur seit Lessings Tod*, III (Leipzig: [n.pub.], 1858)

—— '*Der natürliche Sohn* (Alexandre Dumas)', in *Die Grenzboten*, 1 (1858), 344-46

—— 'Neue deutsche Romane', in Hartmut Steinecke, *Romantheorie und Romankritik in Deutschland: Die Entwicklung des Gattungsverständnisses von der Scott-Rezeption bis zum programmatischen Realismus*, 2 vols (Stuttgart: Metzler, 1975), I, 207

—— 'Der neueste englische Roman und das Princip des Realismus', in *Realismus und Gründerzeit: Manifeste und Dokumente zur deutschen Literatur, 1848-1880*, ed. by M. Bucher and W. Hahl, 2 vols (Stuttgart: Metzler, 1975), II, 94

SCHNEIDER, LOTHAR, ' "Das Gurgeln des Brüllfrosches": Zur Regelung des Begehrens in Gustav Freytags *Soll und Haben*', in *Sentimente, Gefühle, Empfindungen. Zur Geschichte und Literatur des Affektiven von 1770 bis heute. Tagung zum 60. Geburtstag von Hugh Ridley im Juli 2001*, ed. by Anne Fuchs and Sabine Strümper-Krobb (Würzburg: Königshausen & Neumann, 2001), pp. 121-34

—— 'Die Diätetik der Dinge: Dimensionen des Gegenständlichen in Gustav Freytags *Soll und Haben*', in *150 Jahre 'Soll und Haben': Studien zu Gustav Freytags kontroversem Roman*, ed. by Florian Krobb (Würzburg: Königshausen & Neumann, 2005), pp. 103-20

SCHNEIDER, MICHAEL, *Geschichte als Gestalt: Formen der Wirklichkeit und Wirklichkeit der Form in Gustav Freytags Roman 'Soll und Haben'* (Stuttgart: Akademischer Verlag, 1980)

—— 'Apologie des Bürgers: Zur Problematik von Rassismus und Antisemitismus in Gustav Freytags Roman *Soll und Haben*', *Jahrbuch der deutschen Schiller-Gesellschaft*, 25 (1981), 385-413

SCHULTZE, JOHANN, 'Gustav Freytag und die preußische Polizei', *Preußische Jahrbücher*, 183 (1921), 331-40

SCHULZ, GÜNTER, 'Briefe Arnolds Ruges an Gustav Freytag', *Jahrbuch der Schlesischen Friedrich-Wilhelms-Universität zu Breslau*, 11 (1966), 240-52

SCHULZE, FRIEDRICH, 'Der Kitzing — ein politischer Kreis um 1860', *Schriften des Vereins für die Geschichte Leipzigs*, 13 (1921), 16-28

SCHWITZGEBEL, HELMUT, 'Gustav Freytags *Soll und Haben* in der Tradition des deutschen Kaufmannsromans', *Gustav Freytag-Blätter*, 24 (1980), 3-12

SEILER, FRIEDRICH, *Gustav Freytag* (Leipzig: Voigtländer, 1898)

SENGLE, FRIEDRICH, *Biedermeierzeit: Deutsche Literatur im Spannungsfeld zwischen Restauration und Revolution 1815-1848*, 2 vols (Stuttgart: Metzler, 1972)

SHEEHAN, JAMES J., *German History. 1770-1866* (Oxford: Oxford University Press, 1989)

SIEMANN, WOLFRAM, 'Von der offenen zur mittelbaren Kontrolle: Der Wandel in der deutschen Preßgesetzgebung und Zensurpraxis des 19. Jahrhunderts', in

*"Unmoralisch an sich..." Zensur im 18. und 19. Jahrhundert*, ed. by H. Göpfert, H. and E. Weyrauch (Wiesbaden: Harrassowitz, 1988), pp. 293–308
—— 'The Revolutions of 1848–1849 and the Persistence of the Old Regime in Germany (1848–1850)', in *19th Century Germany: Politics, Culture and Society, 1780–1918*, ed. by John Breuilly (London: Arnold, 2001), pp. 117–37
—— 'Zensur im Übergang zur Moderne: Die Bedeutung des "langen 19. Jahrhunderts"', in *Zensur im Jahrhundert der Aufklärung. Geschichte — Theorie — Praxis*, ed. by Wilhelm Haefs and York-Gothart Mix (Göttingen: Wallstein, 2007), pp. 357–88
SMITH, SIDONIE, and JULIA WATSON, *Reading Autobiography: A Guide for Interpreting Life Narratives* (Minnesota: University of Minnesota Press, 2001)
SPRENGEL, PETER, 'Der Liberalismus auf dem Weg ins "Neue Reich": Gustav Freytag und die Seinen 1966–1871', in *Literatur und Nation: Die Gründung des Deutschen Reiches 1871 in der deutschsprachigen Literatur*, ed. by Klaus Amann and Karl Wagner (Vienna: Böhlau, 1996), pp. 153–81
STEIN, PETER, 'Operative Literatur', in *Hansers Sozialgeschichte der deutschen Literatur vom 16. Jahrhundert bis zur Gegenwart*, ed. by G. Sautermeister and U. Schmid, 12 vols (Munich: dtv, 1998), V: *Zwischen Restauration und Revolution 1815–1848*, pp. 485–504
—— 'Sozialgeschichtliche Signatur 1815–1848', in *Hansers Sozialgeschichte der deutschen Literatur vom 16. Jahrhundert bis zur Gegenwart*, ed. by G. Sautermeister and U. Schmid, 12 vols (Munich: dtv, 1998), V: *Zwischen Restauration und Revolution 1815–1848*, pp. 16–37
STEINECKE, HARTMUT, *Romantheorie und Romankritik in Deutschland*, 2 vols (Stuttgart: Metzler, 1975)
—— 'Gustav Freytag's *Soll und Haben* — ein realistischer Roman?' in *Formen realistischer Erzählkunst*, ed. by Jörg Thunecke and Eda Sagarra (Nottingham: Sherwood Press, 1979), pp. 108–17
—— 'Gustav Freytag: *Soll und Haben* (1855): Weltbild und Wirkung eines deutschen Bestsellers', in *Romane und Erzählungen des bürgerlichen Realismus*, ed. by Horst Denkler (Stuttgart: Reclam, 1980), pp. 138–52
*Stenographische Berichte über die Verhandlungen des Reichstages des Norddeutschen Bundes im Jahre 1867*, 2 vols (Berlin: Norddeutsche Allgemeine Zeitung, 1867)
STRAKOSCH-FREYTAG, HERMANCE, and CURT L. WALTER-VAN DER BLEEK, eds, *Gustav Freytag: Briefe an seine Gattin* (Berlin: Lehmann, 1913)
SURYNT, IZABELA, *Das 'ferne', 'unheimliche' Land: Gustav Freytags Polen* (Dresden: Thelem, 2004)
SWALES, MARTIN, *The German Bildungsroman from Wieland to Hesse* (Princeton: Princeton University Press, 1978)
—— *Epochenbruch Realismus: Romane und Erzählungen* (Berlin: Schmidt, 1997)
TATLOCK, LYNNE, 'Realist Historiography and the Historiography of Realism in Gustav Freytag's *Bilder aus der deutschen Vergangenheit*', *German Quarterly*, 63 (1990), 59–74
—— 'Regional Histories as National History: Gustav Freytag's *Bilder aus der deutschen Vergangenheit* (1859–1867)', in *Searching for Common Ground. Diskurse zur deutschen Identität 1750–1871*, ed. by Nicholas Vazsonyi (Cologne: Böhlau, 2000), pp. 161–78

—— '"In the Heart of the Heart of the Country": Regional Histories as National History in Gustav Freytag's *Die Ahnen* (1872–80)', in *A Companion to German Realism 1848–1900*, ed. by Todd Kontje (Rochester, NY: Camden House, 2002), pp. 85–108

TAUBE, UTZ-FRIEDEBERT, *Ludwig Quidde: Ein Beitrag zur Geschichte des demokratischen Gedankens in Deutschland* (Kallmünz: Michael Lassleben, 1963)

TEMPELTEY, EDUARD, ed., *Gustav Freytag und Herzog Ernst von Coburg im Briefwechsel, 1853 bis 1893* (Leipzig: Hirzel, 1904)

THEEL, ROBERT, 'Kommunikationsstörungen: Gustav Freytags Kritik an Parteipresse und Politikgeschäft in seinem Lustspiel *Die Journalisten* (1852)', *Euphorion*, 90 (1996), 185–205

THIELE, ADOLF, 'Gustav Freytag, der Grenzbotenjournalist' (doctoral thesis, University of Münster, 1924)

THOMAS, LIONEL, 'Bourgeois Attitudes: Gustav Freytag's Novels of Life in Nineteenth Century Germany', *Leeds Philosophical and Literary Society*, 15 (1972/74), 59–73

THORMANN, MICHAEL, 'Für die "nationale Hälfte des Bewusstseins": der Beitrag der *Grenzboten* zur kleindeutschen Nationalstaatsgründung 1871', in *Literatur und Nation: die Gründung des Deutschen Reiches 1871 in der deutschsprachigen Literatur*, ed. by Klaus Amann and Karl Wagner (Vienna: Böhlau, 1996), pp. 79–152

VICK, BRIAN, *Defining Germany: The 1848 Frankfurt Parliamentarians and National Identity* (Cambridge, MA: Harvard University Press, 2002)

VIERHAUS, RUDOLF, 'Die Idee der Kontinuität im historiographischen Werk Leopold von Rankes', in *Leopold von Ranke und die moderne Geschichtswissenschaft*, ed. by Wolfgang J. Mommsen (Stuttgart: Klett, 1988), pp. 166–75

WEHLER, HANS-ULRICH, *Deutsche Gesellschaftsgeschichte* (Munich: Beck, 1995)

WEIGEL, S., 'Literarische Gegenöffentlichkeit in der März-Revolution', in *Hansers Sozialgeschichte der deutschen Literatur vom 16. Jahrhundert bis zur Gegenwart*, ed. by G. Sautermeister and U. Schmid, 12 vols (Munich: dtv, 1998), V: *Zwischen Restauration und Revolution 1815–1848*, pp. 94–115

WEISS, JOCHEN, 'Die protestantische Ethik und der Geist der Buchführung: Bürgerliche Lebensbilanz in *Soll und Haben*', in *150 Jahre 'Soll und Haben': Studien zu Gustav Freytags kontroversem Roman*, ed. by Florian Krobb (Würzburg: Könighausen & Neumann, 2005), pp. 87–102

WESER-BISSÉ, PETRA, *Arbeitscredo und Bürgersinn: Das Motiv der Lebensarbeit in Werken von Gustav Freytag, Otto Ludwig, Gottfried Keller und Theodor Storm* (Würzburg: Könighausen & Neumann, 2007)

WICKE, RICHARD, 'Gustav Freytags Romane *Soll und Haben* und *Die verlorene Handschrift*: Ein Beitrag zur Geschichte des Gesellschaftsromans im neunzehnten Jahrhundert' (doctoral thesis, University of Würzburg, 1949)

WILLEMS, EMILIO, *Der preußisch-deutsche Militarismus. Ein Kulturkomplex im sozialen Wandel* (Cologne: Wissenschaft & Politik, 1984)

WIRSCHEM, KARIN, *Die Suche des bürgerlichen Individuums nach einer Bestimmung. Analyse und Begriff des Bildungsromans, erarbeitet am Beispiel von Wilhelm Raabes 'Hungerpastor' und Gustav Freytags 'Soll und Haben'* (Frankfurt a.M: Peter Lang, 1986)

WOODFORD, CHARLOTTE, 'Contrasting Discourses of Nationalism in Historical

Novels by Freytag and Fontane', in *German Literature, History and the Nation: Papers from the Conference 'The Fragile Tradition'*, ed. by Christian Emden and David Midgley, 2 vols (Berne: Peter Lang, 2002), II, 97–117

WORTHMANN, JOACHIM, *Probleme des Zeitromans: Studien zur Geschichte des deutschen Romans im 19. Jahrhundert* (Heidelberg: Winter, 1974)

ZANTOP, SUSANNE M., *Colonial Fantasies. Conquest, Family, and Nation in Precolonial Germany, 1770–1870* (Durham, NC: Duke University Press, 1997)

# INDEX

Achinger, Christine  5, 12 n. 16, 13 n. 19, 100, 122 n. 60, 123 n. 68, 178, 191 n. 38
Aeschylus  146
Agricola, Gnaeus Julius  142
Alberti, Conrad  3-4, 11 nn. 6 & 8, 38 n. 5, 41, 75 n. 2
Anderson, Antje  108, 123 n. 71
Anderson, Benedict  7, 13 n. 26, 132
Applegate, Celia  5, 13 n. 20, 132, 166 n. 23
Aristotle  56, 148-50
Arminius  23
Arnim, Achim von, *Des Knaben Wunderhorn*  19
Auerbach, Berthold  1
Austro-Prussian War (1866)  125, 131
*Autographische Korrespondenz*  84

*Badische Ständeversammlung*  143
Barbarossa, Friedrich  31
Barth, Christa  11 n. 11, 85-86, 121 nn. 27 & 32-35, 122 n. 37
battle of Cremera (477 BC)  114, 118
battle of Sedan (1870)  170
Becker, Niklaus, *Der deutsche Rhein*  24, 38 n. 10, 47, 75 n. 14
Becker, Sabine  5, 12 n. 16, 121 n. 19, 122 n. 48
*Befreiungskriege*  23, 27-28, 170, 181, 183
*Berliner Allgemeine Zeitung*  147, 167 n. 52
*Berliner Hoftheater*  42-45, 51, 53, 74, 76 n. 38, 87
Bethmann-Hollweg, August von  114, 123 n. 94, 124 nn. 95-96
*Bildung*  42, 83-84, 102, 109, 125, 133, 135, 138-39, 154, 156, 159, 161
*Bildungsroman*  96, 110, 119, 185-86
Bismarck, Otto von  90, 126-27, 169-70, 189 n. 2
Blackbourn, David  82, 121 n. 20
Blücher, Gebhardt Leberecht von  27, 33
Boßler, Marie  67
bourgeoisification  93, 106-07, 150, 194-95
Brentano, Clemens  44
  *Des Knaben Wunderhorn*  19
Breuer, Dieter  64, 76 nn. 40-41, 77 nn. 43 & 50
Breuilly, John  38 n. 9, 77 nn. 62 & 65, 170, 189 nn. 2, 5 & 9

Büchler-Hauschild, Gabriele  4, 11 n. 14, 94, 122 nn. 50 & 59
Büchner, Georg  138, 167 n. 35, 168 n. 85
  *Dantons Tod*  73
  *Leonce und Lena*  161-62
  *Woyzeck*  61
Bülow, Friedrich Wilhelm Freiherr von  27
*bürgerlicher Realismus*  82
*bürgerliches Trauerspiel*  149
*Burschenschaft*  32, 42, 58, 62, 66, 72
Busch, Moritz  126

Caligula  162
Canuleius, Gaius  117
Carr, William  75 n. 8, 77 n. 64, 78, 89, 120 n. 3, 121 n. 28, 122 nn. 41 & 46, 189 nn. 6, 7 & 12
Carter, T. E.  4, 11 n. 13, 38 n. 1, 107, 122 n. 56, 123 n. 70
*Cäsarenwahnsinn*  162-63
Censorship  43, 143
  *Bundesversammlung* Decree of 1835:  64-65, 71
  of drama  64-67, 76 n. 41, 87-88
  Karlsbad Decrees  64
  of poetry  28, 64
  of the press  64, 80, 84-85
  of prose  64
  *Selbstzensur*  67
  *Wiener Zensurbehörde für das Habsburgerreich*  64, 80
Chamisso, Adelbert von  26
Charlemagne  23
Charles the Bold  48
Classe, Kurt  11 n. 10, 46-47, 57-58, 72, 75 n. 13, 76 n. 27, 77 n. 61, 89, 121 n. 28, 122 n. 43, 152, 168 n. 67
Coburg Gotha, Duke Ernst of  8, 14 n. 31, 17, 38 n. 4, 84-85, 95, 121 nn. 23, 24-25, 122 nn. 44 & 52, 128, 141, 145, 147, 152, 161, 165 nn. 1 & 7, 166 nn. 9-11, 167 nn. 41, 46, 53, 55-56, 168 nn. 68-70, 177, 190 n. 35
colonialism  98, 101-07, 109-10, 199, 133-35, 137, 140, 166 n. 28, 186, 195-96
*commedia dell'arte*  49
Conscience, Hendrik  80

Cooper, James Fenimore 101–02, 104–05, 110
Crankshaw, Edward 48, 75 n. 11
crusades 109, 173, 186–87

Darwin, Charles 163
Deinhardstein, Johann Ludwig 43
*deutsche Frage* 22, 81, 104, 134, 170–71
  *großdeutsche Lösung* 46, 80–81, 104
  *kleindeutsche Lösung* 3, 46, 81, 104, 125, 127, 132, 134, 170–71
*Deutscher Bund* 23, 80, 103
Devrient, Eduard 86, 111–12, 118, 121 n. 31, 123 nn. 81–85 & 87–93
Devrient, Emil 8, 14 n. 41, 63, 65
Dickens, Charles 82
Dilthey, Wilhelm 147, 167 n. 52
Dove, Alfred 14 nn. 31 & 33, 52–53, 76 nn. 21, 23 & 25, 122 nn. 51 & 55, 165 n. 4, 168 n. 72, 171, 189 nn. 15 & 17
*Dresdner Hoftheater* 65–67, 87, 113
Droescher, Georg 4, 11 n. 10, 14 n. 33, 75 nn. 4, 7, 10 & 17, 76 n. 38, 77 n. 68, 121 nn. 28 & 36, 123 n. 80
Dürer, Albrecht 35

Eggert, Hartmut 173–74, 190 nn. 21–24
Eichendorff, Joseph von 31, 33, 42, 53, 59, 105, 160, 179
  *Dichter und ihre Gesellen* 54
emigration 72–73
Ernst August I (Hannover) 22
Euripides 146

Fallersleben, August Heinrich Hoffmann von 2, 22, 24, 30–31, 38 nn. 8 & 17
  *Bundeslied* 21
  *Das Lied der Deutschen* 47
  *Unpolitische Lieder* 19, 41
  *Der Wein zieht uns zum Himmel hin* 31
Fielding, Henry 82
Flemish Movement 80
Fontane, Theodor 15, 63–64, 76 nn. 35 & 39, 174, 190 n. 23
Franco-Prussian War (1870) 3, 169–71
*Frankfurter Nationalversammlung* 86, 89–90, 93, 123 n. 67, 143
Franz, Agnes 29–30
Frederick William IV 45, 52, 171
Freytag, Gustav:
  life:
    arrest warrant 85, 121 n. 26
    birth 2
  career as *Privatdozent* 2, 18, 40–41
  career as war correspondent 3
  childhood 2, 17–18, 28
  death 3
  doctoral dissertation 4, 40–41
  election to the *Reichstag des Norddeutschen Bundes* 3, 41, 90, 125, 127–28
  *Flugschriften* collection 19, 166 n.14
  *Habilitation* thesis 2, 18, 40–41, 147
  involvement in the *Dresdner Handwerkerverein* 82–84
  involvement in the *Fremdenverein* (Dresden) 83
  membership of the *Breslauer Künstlerverein* 2, 9, 18–19, 28, 31, 37, 40, 83
  membership of the *Central-Verein* 25, 83
  membership of the *Kitzinger Kreis* 126–27, 131, 141, 143, 165 n. 2
  membership of the *Literarisch-politischer Verein* 82, 84–85, 119, 126–27, 131
  military service and illness 2, 18
  move to Dresden 2
  move to Leipzig 2
  study at the University of Berlin 2
  study at the University of Breslau 2, 40
  works:
    biographies:
      *Karl Mathy* 2, 3, 84, 126, 141–44, 164
      *Lebensschilderungen* 142
    collected editions:
      *Gesammelte Werke* 3, 7, 16–18, 23, 25, 33–34, 52, 81, 87, 112, 130, 142
    dramas:
      *Die Brautfahrt* 2, 16, 20, 31, 42–54, 58–62, 74, 87, 136, 178, 181, 197
      *Dornröschen* 41, 55
      *Die Fabier* 2, 3, 9, 57, 80, 95, 111–20, 125, 147, 150–51, 189, 196
      *Der Gelehrte* 2, 16, 52–63, 68, 75, 116, 178, 183, 197
      *Graf Waldemar* 2, 53–54, 57, 62–75, 87, 93, 108, 116, 178, 183
      *Der Hussit* 41–42
      *Die Journalisten* 2, 3, 9, 80, 85–94, 110, 118–20, 135, 127, 143, 147, 178, 183, 196–97
      *Russen und Tscherkessen* 41, 55
      *Die Sühne der Falkensteiner* 41–42
      *Die Valentine* 2, 53, 57, 62–75, 93, 108, 178, 183, 189
    dramatic theory:

*Die Technik des Dramas* 2, 3, 55–56, 80, 95, 145–51, 164
historical studies:
 *Bilder aus der deutschen Vergangenheit* 126, 128–42, 144–47, 150–51, 154–55, 157–59, 161, 163–64
journalism:
 *Die Grenzboten* 2–4, 19, 61, 66, 80–85, 90, 94, 104, 110, 114, 119, 126–27, 129–30, 142–43, 145, 148, 152, 161, 169–72, 196
 *Im neuen Reich* 2, 3, 171
 *Politische Aufsätze* 168 n. 83, 189 n. 1, 120 n. 13
memoirs:
 *Erinnerungen aus meinem Leben* 3–4, 7–9, 16–26, 28, 30, 34, 40–42, 44–45, 49, 52–55, 58, 62–63, 65, 67, 71–72, 74, 78–81, 83–86, 94–95, 101, 103, 109, 111–13, 118, 126–28, 130–31, 141, 145, 147, 151–54, 159, 164, 171, 177, 179, 196
novels:
 *Die Ahnen* 2–3, 5–6, 8, 10, 18–19, 23, 27, 30, 49, 57, 61, 73–74, 79, 136, 140, 154, 157, 159, 163, 165, 171–89, 195–97
 *Aus einer kleinen Stadt* 171, 173, 178, 181
 *Die Brüder vom deutschen Hause* 171, 173, 178, 186
 *Der Freicorporal bei Markgraf-Albrecht* 171, 183
 *Die Geschwister* 171
 *Ingo* 171, 173–74, 178–82, 184, 187
 *Ingraban* 171, 173–74, 176, 180, 187
 *Marcus König* 171, 173–74, 178, 180, 182
 *Das Nest der Zaunkönige* 171, 173–74, 179, 185
 *Der Rittmeister von Alt-Rosen* 171, 173
 *Schluß der Ahnen* 171, 173, 176, 183
 *Soll und Haben* 2–6, 8–10, 15, 34, 60–61, 72–75, 79, 82, 97, 94–111, 116, 118–20, 130, 133–35, 137, 140, 142–44, 147, 151–52, 154, 156, 158–62, 164–65, 178–79, 182–83, 186–89, 195–97
 *Die verlorene Handschrift* 2–3, 6, 10, 19, 60–61, 74, 128–29, 137, 140, 142, 147, 151–65, 172, 177, 179, 182, 188, 189, 195–97
poems:
 *Albrecht Dürer* 35
 *Die Bauern und der Schulmeister* 23–24, 27–28, 47
 *Die Beschwörung* 35
 *Bilder aus dem Volke* 16
 *Die Blume des Weins* 31–32
 *In Breslau* 2, 16–38, 40–41, 51, 101, 194, 197
 *Des Burschen Ende* 32
 *Feste in Breslau* 16
 *Ein Geburtstag von Agnes Franz (März 1842)* 29–30
 *Die Granitschale* 26–28, 33, 37
 *Die Hausfrau* 29
 *Die heilige Elisabeth* 25
 *Junker Gotthelf Habenichts* 32
 *Ein Kindertraum* 32–33, 37
 *Die Krone* 32, 37
 *Kunst und Wissenschaft* 34–35
 *Lebende Bilder* 25–26, 28
 *Der Nachtjäger* 31
 *Dem Oheim, zum funfzigjährigen Amtsjubiläum 1843*: 28–29
 *Die Poesie* 30
 *Der polnische Bettler* 26, 28, 53
 *Prolog zum 13. November 1842*: 29, 33
 *Der Sänger des Waldes* 36–37
 *Scenen aus dem Maskenfest des guten König René* 16
 *Das Schmugglermädchen* 31
 *Die Schöpfung des Künstlers* 35–36
 *An die Studenten* 36–37
 *Das tausendjährige Deutschland* 23
 *Das Theater. Prolog zum 13. Novbr. 1842*: 29, 33
 *An Theodor Molinari* 20–22, 37
 *Ein Trinkgelage* 16
 *Das Trinklied vom kleinen Teufel* 30–31
 *Unser Land* 21, 28
 *Die Wellen* 16, 22–23, 26, 28, 32, 37, 41
 *Winckelmann* 34–35
Fugger, Johann 45
Fulda, Daniel 5, 12 n. 18, 174, 190 n. 27

Gebrüder Grimm 19
Gelber, Mark 5, 12 n. 15, 106, 123 n. 70
Germania 36, 178
Geyder, August 19
Goethe, Johann Wolfgang von 31, 40, 50, 110, 146
 *Kennst du das Land* 25
 *Der König in Thule* 27–28
 *Die Leiden des jungen Werthers* 157
 *West-östlicher Divan* 34–35
 *Wilhelm Meisters Lehrjahre* 185

# Index

Goldsmith, Oliver  82
Görres, Joseph  42
Gotthelf, Jeremias  58–59
*Göttinger Sieben*  22–23, 28, 41
Gottschall, Rudolf  148
Grabbe, Christian Dietrich  43–44
Griffiths, Elystan  5, 12 n. 18, 175, 184–85, 190 n. 30, 191 n. 43
Grillparzer, Franz  26, 79
  *König Ottokars Glück und Ende*  43
  *Ein Bruderzwist in Habsburg*  46
*Gründerzeit*  1, 28
Gubser, Martin  5, 12 n. 15
Gutzkow, Karl  65–67, 71–72, 77 nn. 45–46 & 48–49
  *Wally: Die Zweiflerin*  65

Habsburg dynasty  43, 45–46, 48, 52, 74, 80
Hahn, Hans J.  5, 12 n. 17, 122 n. 40
Haupt, Moritz  151, 172, 189 n. 14
Hegel, Georg Wilhelm Friedrich  7, 129, 138–40, 150, 164, 167 n. 37
*Heiliges Römisches Reich Deutscher Nation*  45, 144
*Heimat*  29, 97–98, 101, 104, 108–09, 187
Heine, Heinrich  1, 18–19, 45, 59, 71, 73, 78–80, 120 n. 11, 179, 198
  *Englische Fragmente*  43, 50, 52
  *Französische Maler*  25
  *Gedichte. 1853 und 1854*:  38 n. 6
  *Ludwig Börne und kleinere politische Schriften*  120 n. 5
  *Neue Gedichte*  38 n. 11, 75 n. 9
  *Reisebilder III/IV*  76 n. 20
  *Die Romantische Schule*  10 n. 2, 76 n. 32, 198 n. 2
  *Romanzero*  38 n. 6
  *Weberlied*  24–25, 78
  *Zur Geschichte der Religion und Philosophie in Deutschland*  76 n. 32, 198 n. 2
Herder, Johann Gottfried  7, 19
  *Auch eine Philosophie der Geschichte zur Bildung der Menschheit*  138
Hermann, Renate  4
Herwegh, Georg  22, 24, 39 n. 19
  *An Ferdinand Freiligrath*  37
Hettner, Hermann  148
Hirzel, Heinrich  168 n. 71
Hirzel, Salomon  7, 52–53, 76 nn. 21, 23 & 25, 84, 95, 122 nn. 51 & 55, 127, 130, 171, 174
Hobsbawm, Eric  78, 120 n. 4
Hodenburg, Christina von  26, 38 n. 12

Hoffmann, E. T. A.:
  *Meister Floh*  33
  *Der Sandmann*  162
Holz, Claus  5, 12 n. 18, 174–75, 181–82, 190 n. 25, 191 n. 41
Horch, Hans Otto  5, 12 n. 15
Houben, Heinrich  65, 67, 76 n. 36, 77 nn. 44, 46–47 & 51
Hrosvith of Gandersheim  2, 40
Hubrich, Peter Heinz  4–5, 11 nn. 5 & 14, 109, 122 nn. 49 & 59, 123 nn. 75–76, 165, 168 n. 90
Hülsen, Botho von  87, 121 n. 36
Humboldt, Wilhelm von  58

Immermann, Carl Leberecht:
  *Friedrich II*  43
  *Tulifäntchen*  33

Jordaan, Max  126
*Junges Deutschland*  9, 64–67, 71–74, 77 n. 60, 80

Kafitz, Dieter  4, 11 n. 14, 42, 75 n. 3, 77 n. 69
Kaiser Wilhelm II  162, 205
Kaiser, Herbert  4, 11 n. 14
Kaiser, Nancy  4, 11 n. 14
Keller, Gottfried  15
Kern, Johann  16
Kienzle, Michael  4, 11 n. 14, 100, 122 nn. 59 & 61
*Klassenausgrenzung*  108–09, 111, 115, 117, 119, 160, 194–95
*Klassenvermischung*  108–09, 111, 118, 183, 193, 195
Kleist, Heinrich von  105, 146
  *Das Erdbeben in Chili*  79
  *Der zerbrochene Krug*  85
Köhnke, Klaus Christian  5, 12 n. 15, 84, 95–96, 106, 121 n. 22, 122 n. 54, 123 n. 69
*Kölnische Zeitung*  84
Kopp, Kristin  5, 12 n. 17, 101–03, 122 n. 62
Körner, Theodor  27
Krobb, Florian  5, 104, 109, 123 nn. 66 & 74
Kuranda, Ignaz  80–81
Küstner, Karl Theodor von  42, 77 n. 68, 87

Laath, Erwin  4, 11 n. 12
Laube, Heinrich  1, 67, 71–72, 80, 87, 113, 122 n. 38
Lenau, Nikolaus  26
Leopold, Prince of Hohenzollern  170
Lessing, Gotthold Ephraim:
  *Emilia Galotti*  149–50
  *Minna von Barnhelm*  85
  *Hamburgische Dramaturgie*  146, 148–49
Limlei, Michael  5, 12 n. 18, 174, 190 n. 27

Lindau, Hans 3–4, 11 n. 8, 57, 77 n. 55, 86, 121 nn. 30 & 32, 124 n. 97, 145, 166 nn. 19–21, 167 nn. 47 & 51, 168 n. 74, 174, 189 n. 11
Lindau, Paul 11 n. 9, 174, 190 n. 23
Livius, Titus (Livy) 117–18, 151, 163
  *Ab Urbe Condita* 114
Lonner, Alyssa A. 6, 13 nn. 21–22, 122 n. 57, 130, 132, 152, 154, 161, 166 nn. 18 & 25, 168 nn. 61–62, 75, 79, 82 & 87
Ludwig, Otto 148
*Lustspiel* 44–45, 47, 85
Luther, Martin 139, 158, 180
Lüttichau, Graf Wolf Adolf von 65–67

Mann, Thomas, *Buddenbrooks: Verfall einer Familie* 15
Mary of Burgundy 43, 45, 48
*Massenliteratur* 193
Maximilian I (Holy Roman Emperor) 43, 46, 49
  *Weißkunig* 45, 49
McInnes, Edward 4, 11 n. 14, 148–50, 167 n. 57
melodrama 62, 69–70, 74, 153
Molinari, Theodor 20–22, 28, 37, 101, 127, 152, 165 n. 4, 168 nn. 63–64 & 66
Moltke, Helmut von 78–79
Mommsen, Theodor 114, 129
*Monumenta Germaniae Historica* 130
Müller, Harro 173, 189 n. 18
Mundt, Theodor 1, 71, 148

*Nachmärz* 1, 3, 9–10, 28, 42, 46, 59–61, 73–75, 78, 80–82, 84–85, 92–93, 118–20, 122, 183, 194, 196
Napoleon III 170
national liberalism 2–3, 10, 28, 73, 78, 85, 120, 127, 129, 141–42, 169–70, 185, 188, 194, 197
*Nationalverein* 82, 110, 127, 143
*Nationalzeitung* 84
Nero 162
Nipperdey, Thomas 72, 76 n. 30, 77 n. 66, 166 n. 12
*Norddeutscher Bund* 3, 41, 90, 125–27, 165, 166 n. 8, 169
Nusser, Peter 193, 198 n. 1

Ort, Claus-Michael 5, 12 n. 18, 174, 190 n. 26
*Ostdeutsche Post*, 81

Peterson, Brent O. 173, 190 n. 18
Ping, Larry L. 6, 13 n. 21, 79, 120 n. 8, 132, 139, 143, 152, 154, 166 n. 22, 167 nn. 38 & 43, 168 nn. 62, 73 & 76

Platen, August Graf von 26
*Preußische Jahrbücher* 131
Prussian School of History 6, 129, 132, 164, 175
Prutz, Robert 71, 77 n. 58, 148
Putlitz, Gustav Heinrich Gans von, *Das Testament des Großen Kurfürsten* 114

Quidde, Ludwig 162

Ranke, Leopold von 129
Raupach, Ernst, *Die Hohenstaufen* 43
reaction 45, 58, 84–85, 87–88, 121 n. 28, 152
realism 4, 5, 15, 98
  *bürgerlicher Realismus* 82, 175
  programmatic realism 81–82, 94, 119, 140, 151, 156, 174
Redern, Friedrich Wilhelm Graf von 42, 45, 75 n. 7
Reformation 139, 173, 176, 180, 182
*Reichsgründung* 6–7, 10, 142, 169–89, 194, 197
revolution 101–03, 119
  1789: 78–79
  1830: 15, 67, 78, 142
  1848: 1–2, 6, 9, 15, 38, 57, 63, 67, 71–72, 78–80, 82, 85–86, 110, 115, 141–43, 173, 176, 183, 194–95
*Rheinbund* 144
*Rheinkrise* 22–23, 28, 46–47, 52
Richter, Claus 4
romanticism 42, 45, 54, 74
Rössler, Constantin 3–4, 11 n. 8, 53, 76 n. 24
Rothfuchs, Eduard 4, 11 n. 12, 57–58, 71, 76 n. 28, 77 n. 57, 121 n. 28
Ruge, Arnold 26–27, 53, 63, 71, 76 n. 37, 77 n. 56, 86

Sammons, Jeffrey 4, 11 n. 13, 123 n. 77
Sautermeister, Gert 26, 38 n. 12
Scharnhorst, Gerhard von 27
*Schauspiel* 44, 54, 62, 74
Scherer, Wilhelm 131
Schiller, Friedrich 40, 50, 146
  *Kabale und Liebe* 63
  *Schillerpreis* 113, 147
Schlegel, August Wilhelm, *Wiener Vorlesungen über neuere Geschichte* 42–43, 75 n. 5
*Schleswig-Holsteinischer Krieg* (1848–51) 22, 125, 152
Schmidt, Julian 2, 81–82, 84, 85, 101, 121 nn. 15–18 & 29
  *Geschichte der deutschen Literatur seit Lessing's Tod* 148
Schneider, Michael 4–5, 12 nn. 14–15

Schopenhauer, Arthur  138
Schulze, Friedrich  126, 165 nn. 2 & 5
Scott, Sir Walter  82
Shakespeare, William  43, 49, 146, 149
   *Romeo and Juliet*  153
Shaw, George Bernard, *Pygmalion*  71
Siemann, Wolfram  67, 77 n. 54
Simon, Heinrich  86
Society of Jesus (Jesuits)  159
Sophocles  146
Steinecke, Hartmut  4, 12 n. 14, 110, 121 nn. 17–18, 123 n. 78
Stephani, Eduard  126
Stifter, Adalbert  79
   *Bunte Steine*  1, 10 n. 3
Stosch, Albrecht von  171–72, 189 n. 13
Surynt, Izabela  5, 12 n. 17
Sybel, Heinrich von  129

Tacitus, Publius Cornelius  133, 153–54, 156–57, 159, 162–63
   *Agricola*  142, 167 n. 43
   *Historiae*  151
Tatlock, Lynne  5, 12 n. 18, 13 n. 20, 132, 133–34, 140, 166 nn. 24 & 30, 167 nn. 31, 33 & 40, 175, 190 nn. 28–29 & 36
*Telegraph für Deutschland*  162
Tendenzliteratur  1, 19, 61, 66, 74, 80–81, 109
Thiele, August  4, 11 n. 12, 81, 120 n. 14
   *Dreißigjähriger Krieg*  136–37, 173, 176

Tieck, Ludwig  31, 42, 44, 86
   *Des Lebens Überfluß*  53–54
tragedy  54–62, 122, 145–51
   *anagnorisis*  55
   *catharsis*  149–50
   *hamartia*  55
   *peripeteia*  55
Treitschke, Heinrich von  153, 165 nn. 3–4, 168 n. 72, 189 nn. 15 & 17
*Trivialliteratur*  193, 198 n. 1

Uhland, Ludwig  24, 26, 80
*Unterhaltungsliteratur*  193

Vischer, Friedrich  148
*Völkerwanderung*  128, 132, 173, 176, 180–81
*Vormärz*  1, 9–10, 15, 19–21, 24, 26, 28, 32, 36, 38, 40–42, 44, 51–52, 56, 61–62, 64–66, 71–75, 78–81, 91–95, 105–06, 108, 110, 115, 118–20, 125, 135, 137, 143, 158, 163, 185, 188–89, 194–98

Weberaufstand  22, 24–26, 28, 78, 83
Weinbarg, Ludolf  71
*Weserzeitung*  84
Wiener Burgtheater  43, 67, 87
Wiener Kongress (1815)  23
Woodford, Charlotte  5, 12 n. 18, 174, 190 n. 27

*Zollparlament*  169

www.ingramcontent.com/pod-product-compliance
Lightning Source LLC
Chambersburg PA
CBHW071436150426
43191CB00008B/1151